Managing Records as Evidence and Information

Managing Records as Evidence and Information

Richard J. Cox

Q

QUORUM BOOKS
Westport, Connecticut • London

Library of Congress Cataloging-in-Publication Data

Cox, Richard J.
    Managing records as evidence and information / Richard J. Cox.
      p.   cm.
    Includes bibliographical references and index.
    ISBN 1–56720–231–4 (alk. paper)
    1. Archives—Administration.   2. Records—Management. I. Title.
CD950.C694   2001
  025.1'97—dc21   00–032812

British Library Cataloguing in Publication Data is available.

Library of Congress Catalog Card Number: 00–032812
ISBN: 1–56720–231–4

First published in 2001

Quorum Books, 88 Post Road West, Westport, CT 06881
An imprint of Greenwood Publishing Group, Inc.
www.quorumbooks.com

Printed in the United States of America

The paper used in this book complies with the
Permanent Paper Standard issued by the National
Information Standards Organization (Z39.48–1984).

10 9 8 7 6 5 4 3 2 1

Contents

Preface   vii

1. Starting Policy: Defining Records   1

2. Driving Policy: Focusing on Records, Not Technology   43

3. The Policy's Spine: Appraising and Maintaining Records   87

4. The Policy's Aim: Reaching the Public   131

5. Supporting Policy: Educating Records Professionals   189

Index   235

Preface

The concept of "policy" has been used so often and so broadly in the modern Information Age as to become *both* commonplace *and* misunderstood. Federal policies seem to be issued weekly. In our global era, international organizations regularly call for and release policies. All organizations seem to desire a policy on every function and activity or, at the least, to be aware of external policies affecting their work. Citizens demand policies protecting them in a vast range of spheres, from privacy to consumer rights to the use of information generated by and for them. Many worry if they might be working unaware of some policy that should be guiding them, or commence a new project by searching for and being aware of relevant policies.

The nature and impact of policies is a prevalent concern but also constitutes a somewhat uncertain business. Not long ago my school hosted a public lecture on information policy and ethics. During the question-and-answer session, one of my students politely but astutely posed a question about the differences between law and policy. Not unexpectedly, the answer was somewhat muddled, not because the speaker didn't know how to respond but because it is difficult to discern where law ends and policy begins or how policy differs from so many other rules, guidelines, or even common sense. Law and policy are intertwined in complex ways, and because the process and effectiveness of making laws regarding cyberspace are both very complicated and uncertain, it can only be said that laws constitute part of policy and that policy often supports the application of laws. All of this, of course, is then subject to the outcomes of court cases and the development of professional best practices.

Some of this is not new, only speeded up and exacerbated by the accelerating use of computers from classrooms to courtrooms. Historian Michael Kammen identifies the "most worrisome threats to our freedom" as coming "from the misuse of electronic data bases, from imprudent government legislation, from environmental degradation, and from those whose business it literally is to manipulate the marketplace."[1] Policies are being proposed to address these and other concerns. Sometimes they help, sometimes they muddle things more.

The idea of policy has been used freely for hundreds of years. The word itself derives from the Greek concepts of citizenship and government and later focused on organized government systems, the conduct of public affairs, political skill, and the most current concept of any "course of action adopted and pursued by a government, party, ruler, statesman, etc." Now private organizations are also wrapped up in deliberations about policy, generally meant to relate to internally uniform or regulated actions. And many of these policies, both private and public, relate to the use of information and records, drawing on another aspect of the origins of policy. Policy has long been associated with particular records "policing" action, such as an insurance policy, vouchers, and warrants.[2] But it has been the Information Age that has added an impetus to policy making, not just for information but the unique kind of information provided by records—evidence.

A useful discussion about the nature of policy is found in a monograph by H. K. Colebatch, a political scientist. Colebatch indicates that in government a policy has "coherence" (all the parts fit together in a single system), emanates from the top of the hierarchy, and possesses "instrumentality" (the policy is written in "pursuit of particular purposes"). Colebatch also indicates that in non-government organizations the term policy is often "simply the standardization and articulation of practice." All policies, regardless of the nature of the organization producing them, generate from authority, implies "expertise," and are "concerned with order" (they build or relate to a system and are consistent).[3]

For the past three decades, policies regarding a variety of information issues have emanated from federal agencies, legislative chambers, and corporate boardrooms. Charles McClure defines information policy as a "term used to describe a set of interrelated principles, laws, guidelines, rules and regulations, directives, procedures, judgments, interpretations, and practices that guide the creation, management, access, and use of information. Information policy can be set at a national level . . . , by state and local governments, and by other agencies and institutions."[4] A quick substitute of "records" for "information," and we have a reasonably good sense of the *purposes* of records policies. The substance of records policies, from international to national to local domains, is an altogether different matter.

Despite the present focus on information policy, it is still a relatively new concept and a concept only now beginning to be studied. Robert Burger argues that the difficulties stem from the challenges of understanding (or agreeing on precise meanings of the terms) for "information" and "policy," while comprehending that "All information policies have a cultural, social, historical, and political context in which they are formulated."[5] Archives and records policies have been identified as part of the various categories of information policies, which also include information resources management, information technology, telecommunications, international communications, privacy and confidentiality, computer regulation and crime, intellectual property, and information systems and dissemination.[6] For some, figuring out what constitutes archives and records management adds to the complexity and confusion of determining and regulating information policy. In essence, this is what this book addresses, although one of its primary premises is that *records* are more precisely defined than *information*, even though records are a major source of information.

Many national and organizational policies have been set and discussed regarding records *and* information. Some of this has happened quite recently as the limitations, dangers, opportunities, and benefits of increasingly using electronic records management have become more obvious or the subject of court cases. This is why some records professionals have labored on an international standard, the International Records Management Standard (ISO15489), under discussion for the past few years.[7] The proposed ISO standard suggests that an organization "should establish, document, maintain and promulgate policies, procedures and practices for records management to ensure that its business need for evidence, accountability and information about its activities is met." The standard also states that "Organizations should define and document a corporate policy for records management. The objective of the policies should be the creation and maintenance of authentic and reliable records capable of supporting business functions and activities, for as long as they are required. Organizations should ensure that the policies are implemented and maintained at all levels in the organization."[8]

This is why other records professionals, including those at the United States National Archives (NARA), continue to search for policies *and* methods ensuring the long-term maintenance of records in electronic form, albeit not very successfully. In January 2000 a story broke about the loss of a portion of NARA's own electronic mail, and as one commentator points out, "NARA comes away from this incident with the wrong lesson. Rather then develop a fool proof way of managing electronic mail, one which saves each Federal e-mail at the time of creation in an off line tamper proof records management system suitable for Archival retention, NARA instead points to the incident to justify its 'you see how unreliable e-mail systems are?' as further justification for their 'print out Federal e-mail Records.' " Despite a decade-long court case and thirty years of experience with electronic records, much of this failure stems from a policy glitch—the "Problem is that NARA had no internal rule as to when to print and file the Official Records."[9] The National Archives problems are compounded through state and local governments, colleges and universities, corporations and community organizations, and cultural institutions. Few other archives and records management programs are doing any better.

Another story, breaking almost at the same time, reveals the need for clear records policy in an even more fundamental fashion. In late January 2000 a lengthy story appeared in the *Toledo Blade* decrying the destruction of forty-six volumes of mostly nineteenth-century prison records by the Ohio Historical Society (serving as the archives for the Ohio state government). There were many dimensions to this story, revealing problems with the public's understanding of archives. The records had been previously microfilmed, but the news story conveyed the strong opinion that no original records should *ever* be destroyed. This was the least of the problems. The story also showed that internal records management procedures had been carelessly followed. More dramatically, the Toledo reporter chronicled severe problems in the relationship between the state government and the private historical society serving as the government's archives that brought into sharp relief the need for a better public records policy and accountability.[10] The newspaper's staunch view that "microfilm should only be a backup" and that records always should be kept in their original format suggests that records professionals need to be engaged in public policy making that educates the public.[11]

Records professionals have been concerned with setting records policies for most of the twentieth century, since the advent of the modern records profession, and there is no reason to think that this will not be a continuing preoccupation with them for most of the twenty-first century. Some of the earliest presidential addresses to the Society of American Archivists concerned the elements of drafting state archives and records legislation.[12] Much of the energy of the National Archives has focused on various federal records acts from 1950 to the present, including the Federal Records Act itself through the various laws relating to presidential records and their ownership. The International Conference of Archives has issued report after report on the elements of national records laws. Records consulting firms or lobbying groups, such as the International Records Management Trust and the National Security Archive, have issued reports arguing for the adoption of public policy that ensures the maintenance of records for purposes such as accountability and evidence. And professional associations, such as the Society of American Archivists and the Association of Records Managers and Administrators, with an orientation both to public and private records, have issued statements with an aim to affecting public and organizational policy.[13]

Despite a long-term discussion and debate about the notion of records management and/or archives policies, the stress has often been on *issuing* policies with little critical analysis of what provides the foundation for or sustains the policies. On more than one occassion I have witnessed the massive replication of records policies across institutions, the policies ranging from practical methods to recover records from natural and man-made disasters to the business of developing acquisition objectives or access regulations to the vastly more complicated technical aspects of the uses of digital technologies for capturing and reformatting records. Such mindless replication cannot produce useful organizational or social policy, since we know that such policies are the result of "top management" formulating "policy in order to enhance organizational effectiveness"; the emergence at "lower levels" "informally from a seemingly consistent

set of senior management decisions on an issue"; or "set by factors in the organization's external environment, such as the enactment of laws, and the guidelines issued by government agencies."[14] Simple copying of policies lessens the
potential success of such policies because it eliminates many of the reasons why
they need to be adopted.

This book is *not* a compendium of policies to be used in this fashion. Rather,
it is the effort to explore in a more detailed fashion the fundamental principles
supporting the setting of records policies. Records policies are critically important for records professionals to develop and use as a means of strategically
managing the information and evidence found in the millions of records created
daily, *provided* that the policies are based on comprehensible principles.

What follows in this book is a series of discourses on the fundamentals of
archives and records management needing to be understood *before* any organization attempts to define and set *any* policy affecting records and information.
The chapters concern defining records, how information technology plays into
policy compiling, the fundamental tasks of identifying and maintaining records
as critical to records and information policy, public outreach and advocacy as a
key objective for such policy, and the role of educating records professionals in
supporting sensible records policies. All of these chapters derive from a series
of articles and technical reports written over the past decade and complement a
companion volume published earlier by Greenwood Press, *Closing an Era:
Historical Perspectives on Modern Archives and Records Professionals*, providing historical background to these and other issues.

Specifically, the sources for this book include the following articles (incorporated completely or in part, and always in a substantially revised fashion).
Chapter 1 considers that the primary foundation of having a suitable records
policy is possessing a good, working definition of a record. This chapter recounts
the recent rediscovery of the concept of the record, recordkeeping functional
requirements and warrant as a strategy for a more precise definition of record,
the presistent terminological problems records professionals face in working in
the Information Age, and the internal tensions about defining records such as
has been evident in the debates between electronic records managers and archivists working with personal papers. The chapter draws on "The Record: Is
It Evolving?" *Records and Retrieval Report* 10 (March 1994): 1–16; "Archives
as a Multi-faceted Term in the Information Professions," *Records and Retrieval
Report* 11 (March 1995): 1–15; "The Record in the Manuscript Collection,"
Archives and Manuscripts 24 (May 1996): 46–61; "Re-Discovering the Archival
Mission: The Recordkeeping Functional Requirements Project at the University
of Pittsburgh; A Progress Report," *Archives and Museum Informatics* 8, no. 4
(1994): 279–300; "The Record in the Information Age: A Progress Report on
Research," *Records and Retrieval Report* 12 (January 1996): 1–16; and "More
Than Diplomatic: Functional Requirements for Evidence in Recordkeeping,"
Records Management Journal 7 (April 1997): 31–57.

Chapter 2 is a discussion about why technology should not be at the heart of records policies. Records need to be the focal point since technology is no more than one means by which records are created. This chapter mostly concentrates on the ideas of computer literacy and critiques the idea of disciplinary convergence caused by electronic information technology. Chapter 2 builds on "The Importance of Records in the Information Age," *Records Management Quarterly* 32 (January 1998): 36–46, 48–49, 52; "Computer Literacy and Records Professionals," *Records and Retrieval Report* 12 (October 1996): 1–16; and "Why Technology Convergence Is Not Enough for the Management of Information and Records," *Records and Retrieval Report* 13 (October 1997): 1–16.

Chapter 3 is an analysis of selection and maintenance as core concepts needed in any records and archives policy. The chapter considers the differences between archival appraisal and records management scheduling, the changing concepts of maintaining records, the impact of electronic records management on selection and maintenance approaches and objectives, and the importance of these ideas being incorporated into records and archives policies. The chapter is based on "Records Management Scheduling and Archival Appraisal: Some Unconventional Thoughts on History, Purpose, and Process," *Records and Information Management Report* 14 (April 1998): 1–16; "Blown to Bits: Electronic Records, Archivy, and the Corporation," in James M. O'Toole, ed., *The Records of American Business* (Chicago: Society of American Archivists, 1997); and "The Documentation Strategy and Archival Appraisal Principles: A Different Perspective," *Archivaria* 38 (Fall 1994): 11–36.

Chapter 4, the longest chapter, grapples with the importance of advocacy in records policy making. It examines, first, the difficulty records professionals have in developing policy with images that are misleading or, in some cases, non-existent. Records professionals need to understand how ubiquitous records are and, more importantly, how to capitalize on their commonness in society and its organizations. The chapter also discusses the importance of a non-technocratic view of policy, one that examines the challenges of dealing with difficult issues like privacy and access, by considering the human characteristics that must be taken into account. This chapter builds on "International Perspectives on the Image of Archivists and Archives: Coverage by *The New York Times*, 1992–93," *International Information and Library Review* 25 (1993): 195–231; "A Sense of the Future: A Child's View of Archives," in *Archivists: The Image and Future of the Profession; 1995 Conference Proceedings*, ed. Michael Piggott and Colleen McEwen (Canberra: Australian Society of Archivists, 1996), pp. 189–209; and "Privacy, Access, and Human Values in the World of the Records Professional," *Records and Information Retrieval Report* 15 (October 1999): 1–16.

Chapter 5 considers the last critical element for developing records policies, the education of records professionals. As happens in so many disciplines, the reasons why there are problems or the solutions for these problems rest with the quality of the education of records professionals. This chapter considers continuing issues facing professional education, the implications of the interdisciplinary quality of the knowledge supporting records work for this education, the degree of change inflicted on this education by emerging electronic record-keeping systems, the role of continuing education, and the nature of professional advocacy and its relationship to professional education. This chapter derives from largely unpublished work, including a talk to a 1996 conference on graduate archival education and a preliminary analysis of the interdisciplinary foundation of research on records and recordkeeping systems. Some of this chapter is also based on previously published essays, including "The Roles of Graduate and Continuing Education in Preparing Archivists for the Information Age," *American Archivist* 56 (Summer 1993): 444–457; "Continuing Education and Special Collections Professionals: The Need for Rethinking," *Rare Books and Manuscripts Librarianship* 10, no. 2 (1995): 78–96; and "Advocacy in the Graduate Archives Curriculum: A North American Perspective," *Janus* no. 1 (1997): 30–41.

Are there summary lessons or principles emanating from these analyses of the foundation of policy for archives and records management? There are some basic issues that every organization must consider *before* launching into archives and records management policy writing. These are, as follows:

- Every organization needs to manage its records to support accountability, the protection of crucial evidence, and the nurturing of corporate memory.
- Records are real things, whether paper or electronic.
- Records and archives programs and professionals administer records first and foremost.
- Personal papers, while not normally part of organizations and governments, are records nevertheless.
- All records are created for a reason, and this reason ought to have the preeminent role in their subsequent management.
- Records are essential, as reflected by their consistent featuring in news stories.
- The selection of records for long-term maintenance is the key responsibility in all archival and records management programs.
- All organizations should hire records professionals.
- All individuals responsible for records should have some rudimentary training about the nature of records and recordkeeping systems.

Many individuals have influenced my thinking about records policies and policy making in general, through discussions with them or by reading their writings or both. They include Kimberly Barata, Jeannatte Bastian, David Bearman, Tom Blanton, Toni Carbo, Terry Cook, Bruce Dearstyne, Luciana Duranti, Wendy Duff, Timothy Ericson, Frank B. Evans, David Gracy, Larry Hackman, Margaret Hedstrom, Sue McKemmish and her colleagues at Monash University, Page Putnam Miller, James M. O'Toole, David Roberts, Helen W. Samuels, Hugh Taylor, Harold Thiele, David Wallace, and Elizabeth Yakel. A few of these individuals are former students. I also include in this group some current

doctoral students—Bernadette Callery, Jennifer Marshall, and Tywanna Whor-
ley—who constantly push me to re-examine my ideas.

NOTES

1. Michael Kammen, "The Futures of American Freedom," *Virginia Quarterly Re-view* 76 (Winter 2000): 19.

2. From the online version of the *Oxford English Dictionary*, 2nd ed., accessed on January 10, 2000 at http://digital.library.pitt.edu/cg . . . d-idx.pl?type=entry$byte= 332473931.

3. H. K. Colebatch, *Policy* (Minneapolis: University of Minnesota Press, 1998), pp. 3–4, 6, 7.

4. Charles R. McClure, "United States Information Policy," *Encyclopedia of Library and Information Science* (New York: Marcel Dekker, 1999), pp. 306–307.

5. Robert H. Burger, *Information Policy: A Framework for Evaluation and Policy Research* (Norwood, NJ: Ablex Publishing Corporation, 1993), p. 66.

6. Burger, *Information Policy*, pp. 87–88.

7. At the final stage of preparing this book, the ISO draft was available for consultation at http://www.archivists.org.au/council/recmandraft.html. Work continues on the efforts by the International Organization for Standardization to set an international standard for records management (ISO15489), based on an Australian records management standard. The present text of the proposed standard describes general records management purposes and principles, the characteristics of a record, the regulatory environment for records, the elements of records management policies, strategies for managing records, and records management operations. The proposed standard "does not include the management of archival records within archival institutions," although it certainly deals with the administration of institutional archives.

8. Sections 6.1 and 6.2 of the proposed ISO standard.

9. Eddie Becker posting to the Archives and Archivists listserv on January 9, 2000 02:11:57–0500. The article was George Lardner, Jr., "Archives Loses 43,000 E-Mails," *Washington Post*, January 6, 2000, p. A17. The article reveals that the National Archives had little trust in its own systems and that it was relying on printing out (selected by the records creators) electronic mail. An internal memorandum by Archivist John Carlin reassured his staff that nothing of value had been lost; "This is of course because, in accordance with standard NARA practice pending the development of dependable electronic recordkeeping systems, we print out on paper and file for safekeeping messages warranting retention as official Federal records"; John Carlin, January 6, 2000, NARA2000–067.

10. James Drew, "Special Report: How Historic Records End Up as History," *Toledo Blade*, January 23, 2000; James Drew, "Historian Decries Loss of Prison Registers," *Toledo Blade*, January 26, 2000.

11. "Editorial: Once Destroyed, Forever Lost," *Toledo Blade*, January 27, 2000.

12. For examples of the many early writings on this topic, refer to Frank B. Evans, comp., *Modern Archives and Manuscripts: A Select Bibliography* (Chicago: Society of American Archivists, 1975), pp. 119–120.

13. These statements are featured on these organizations' Web sites. For an example,

examine the International Records Management Trust site at http://www.irmt.org/in-dex2.html.

   14. Deon Nel, Leyland Pitt, and Richard Watson, "Business Ethics: Defining the Twi-light Zone," *Journal of Business Ethics* 8 (1989): 781.

Managing Records as Evidence and Information

Chapter 1

Starting Policy: Defining Records

INTRODUCTION: DANCING AROUND DEFINITIONS

Most people have a sense about what makes something a record. There is no mystery here. Records have become wrapped up with certain standard and quite recognizable forms. A letter, memorandum, receipt, and check are all typical objects in our personal and professional lives, the result of centuries of organizational and societal activity and evolution. We have been conditioned to these forms by years of personal experience, convention, common sense, and education and training. Even newer electronic versions of records mimic the older forms on our computer screens.

If discerning a record is so obvious, why do we need to devote any attention to its definition? The predictions of the demise of the record by some technologists, describing a paperless office and later offering software promising to manage clumps of data, prompt serious reconsideration of what constitutes a record, similar to what has occurred with the debate about the future of the printed book. Our information era has brought immense changes. The advent of the computer, supporting ever more complex and powerful software applications, seems to have transformed the way in which records are viewed. We risk losing sight of records. Even records professionals, archivists, and records managers engage in protracted debates about what constitutes a record. Definitions with a focus on information, data, structure, origination, or end-user potential are all offered. Commonsense approaches and obvious forms become confused or pushed aside. Even archival theory can be a problem, producing theoretical frameworks that are difficult to place into policy.[1] None of this is very promising for records professionals as they set out to write policy, since policy needs to be concise, clear, and convincing.

Are we really witnessing the evolution to a new record? For many, what they see on the computer screen looks suspiciously like older versions of a record, although the record may be little more than a brief image on a computer screen and certainly not a physical entity to be touched. Yet, there are different concerns. Will this record image always be the same? Is my "record" version the memorandum drafted for initial review, the second version sent to its intended audience, or the third version which has been modified by the recipient as he or she included the memorandum in a report? Or, are all three records? Is my record the spreadsheet of financial figures and sales trends retrieved at 9:31 A.M. or the spreadsheet called up three hours later when the figures have been modified? Or, are both legitimate records? Can we possess a record that is largely composed of text, images, and statistics loaded from online bibliographic systems or transferred from documents created by other organizational staff?

Our modern era has given us the electronic record and troubling questions. When we examine electronic records—how do we know that they are the *original* records? Can electronic records be *authenticated*? *How* should they be *preserved* for any requisite period of time—in paper or electronic form? And how can electronic records be *managed* to ensure that organizational requirements are met? What was once the province of file clerks, now is the domain of systems designers, information policy specialists, and other highly educated technical experts. But do these technocrats understand records and their importance?

Since records are essential to any organization, questions challenging the record's definition are also crucial to the organization. The records management and archival literature portrays a record as relatively fixed, easily ascertained, and conveniently handled. One typical archives textbook defined record as "any type of recorded information, regardless of physical form or characteristics, created, received, or maintained by a person, institution, or organization. . . . Records are extensions of the human memory, purposefully created to record information, document transactions, communicate thoughts, substantiate claims, advance explanations, offer justifications, and provide lasting evidence of events. Their creation results from a fundamental human need to create and store information, to retrieve and transmit it, and to establish tangible connections with the past."[2] This definition (or similar versions of it) has long been used by archivists and records managers. It is a variation of definitions in half-century-old federal records laws, and these laws themselves are based on another half-century of both North American and international custom and definition.[3] While these definitions incorporate and accommodate a wide array of technology, they suggest that a record has only changed in the medium in which it might reside or be retrieved.

The old Renaissance science of diplomatics, undergoing a recent emergence of interest in North American records management and archival practice, posits that documents can be described by representation rules and that these rules "reflect political, legal, administrative, and economic structures, culture, habits, myths, and constitute an integral part of the written document, because they formulate or condition the ideas or facts which we take to be the context of the documents."[4] Over a long period of time, several thousand years, these various structures have significantly changed and, partly spurred on by the dynamic transformation of information technology, so have the basic aspects of a record (or so it seems). It is important to remember that cultural and other societal factors, other than technological utility or advantages, often influence what kinds of information technologies a society or an organization adopts. It is also important to remember that the records creators choose both medium and form for administrative and business conveniences, not the records custodians such as archivists and records managers. A recent history suggests that writing in a particular society is dependent on its need for information: "If all writing is information storage, then all writing is of equal value. . . . There is in fact no essential difference between prehistoric rock paintings, memory aids (mnemonic devices), wintercounts, tallies, knotted cords, pictographic, syllabic and consonantal scripts, or the alphabet. . . . If a form of information storage fulfills its purpose as far as a particular society is concerned then it is (for this particular society) 'proper' writing."[5] But, as it turns out, this kind of definition, readily latched onto by computer and information scientists, may not be so helpful for the definition of a record for use by archivists and records managers, the organizations they serve, administrators and policy makers, and citizens.

Because of the changing information technology and its use within organizations, the record's definition is important. Records professionals have become particularly animated about this within the past decade. Charles Dollar, reporting the initial results of an international collaboration, notes that the "traditional concept of record refers to recorded information that is captured as a physical entity in such a way that it provides 'first-hand evidence' or contemporary proof of a transaction" and argues that electronic information technology stretches considerably this traditional definition.[6] Edwin Southern has more pointedly captured the archivist's angst about such changes, speculating, "we may be seeing the end of [the traditional] document in an entity called the 'virtual document.' . . . The 'virtual document' exists in a kind of electronic subuniverse, able to take on attributes and contexts according to the wishes of the creator or user. The conclusion seems inescapable: The 'virtual document,' or its near relative, the document existing in the infinitely manipulable database, means the obliteration of the document as a tangible, visible link between creator and user, with the archivist as intermediary."[7]

Compounding the confusion is the fact that the nomenclature has not substantially changed, meaning that terms such as "document" and "record" are used but with very different implications. It is easy to get twisted up in internal disciplinary debates without resolving anything of potential use for managing records to benefit and protect society and its organizations.[8] German archival educator Angelika Menne-Haritz notes, "In the language of office information, individual documentation entities are often simply called 'documents.' As opposed to data formed in a definite structure, documents are formed from combination of texts, drawings, tables, calculations, etc., which have no definite structure."[9] Those who advocate the notion of "information resources management" display the tendency to adopt *similar* nomenclature but with very *different* practical implications. Forest Woody Horton describes the convergence between data, documents, and information, and while he has maintained substantial notions of what purpose records serve others, extending the concept has created definitions that seem to have jettisoned fairly substantial portions of traditional views of a record.[10] These views often reveal that some essential dimensions of the record and its purpose have been lost or confused in the maze of computer and high-tech wizardry, and this leaves society and its institutions in a vulnerable position.

THE REDISCOVERY OF THE RECORD AS EVIDENCE RATHER THAN INFORMATION SOURCE

The Information Age has produced a debate for records creators, users, and custodians about the definition of a record. The rapid development in the technological capabilities of computers, and their plunging costs and increasing user-friendliness, has created disciplines concerned with information management. Information is usually defined using data, ideas, and knowledge, and its use, organization, and means of dissemination have been separated from its form of carrier. The modern electronic compound document (text, spreadsheets, images, audio, and video) has focused more concern on the nature of the information. Records must first be defined and then come the technical solutions for maintaining them. Australian archivists have done precisely this, noting that the "pivot of archival science is evidence not information. Archivists do not deal with isolated and free-floating bits of information, but with their documentary expression."[11] This is a valid viewpoint for the records manager as well.

What is problematic for the records professional is the legal definition of a document. The records manager relies on legal guidelines for determining what records are maintained and how they are accessed, but modern information technology has made this far more complicated. Writings on the legal aspects of records have cast doubt about the sufficiency of the legal definitions because the means by which such electronic records are created and maintained are often dependent on factors external to the organization. In the medical world, the increased emphasis on patients' rights as their records are transferred from one health care provider to the next, along with more precise and detailed diagnostic data, have challenged the growing use of medical information technology. Add legal and ethical problems, and we have a scenario in which the concept of the medical record has changed; while older paper records were more difficult to access, they may actually have been richer in diagnostic information. Such problems reflect the difficulties in setting legal parameters in cyberspace, something that has proved to be as difficult as "information" to define.[12]

The decade-long court case on the maintenance of electronic mail files by the Reagan and Bush presidencies reveals both challenges and solutions. The Bush administration was prepared to erase these electronic records, including those documenting the Iran-Contra affair, offering to produce selective paper print-outs. While the matters of legislative definitions and executive privilege are complicated, the U.S. Court of Appeals ruling in the case affirms that such paper print-outs are insufficient because they "may omit fundamental pieces of information which are an integral part of the original electronic records, such as the identity of the sender and/or recipient and the time of the receipt." The ruling further states, "our refusal to agree with the government that electronic records are merely 'extra copies' of the paper versions amounts to far more than judicial nitpicking. Without the missing information the paper print-outs—akin to traditional memoranda with the 'to' and 'from' cut off and even the 'received' stamp pruned away—are dismembered documents indeed."[13] The fact that this ruling concludes that the White House and National Archives *both* had violated the intent of the Federal Records Act of 1950 and the Presidential Records Act of 1974, both with the standard definitions of records cited at the beginning of this chapter, suggests the need for rethinking records concepts. The subsequent decisions and debates only affirm this need.

The irony is that as technology increased in its complexity and potential for processing, using, and storing information, basic archival and records management principles were codified by archivists in France, Prussia, and the Netherlands. By the dawn of the twentieth century, basic notions of record had been more precisely formulated, drawing on tradition and practice. The 1898 Dutch archival manual discusses records' "organic" nature, the matter of their natural accretion and the importance of their context and role as organizational evidence.[14] English archivist Hilary Jenkinson, writing a generation later, made the matter of the "administrative or executive transaction" the keystone of the record concept and one of the fundamental notions of archives.[15] Margaret Cross Norton, spanning the age of the pioneer American archival programs and the emergence of modern records management, also emphasized concern for transactions and evidence, defining the purpose of a state government archives as having the "duty of planning and supervising the preservation of all those records of the business transactions of its government required by law or other legal implication to be preserved indefinitely."[16] A contemporary of Norton, and the foremost American archival theoretician, T. R. Schellenberg provides a similar records definition.[17] Thus, by the mid-twentieth century, there seemed to be a firm sense of a record as evidence of transactions.

Why is there now such a struggle with the record concept? Archivists and records managers serve their organizations in essential ways, by making sure that investments in records and information systems are worthwhile and that the organizations maintain their accountability through the protection of their evidence captured in records. Changing information technologies have challenged the ability of archivists and records managers to provide such services. Form, which often dictated the degree of importance of evidence of a particular document, continues to change. And the physical entity of the document, which in the past dictated aspects of access, security, and maintenance, has so changed as to call all such functions into serious re-evaluation as to their applicability. The fact that the long-standing definitions of record pre-date considerably the computer has caused archivists and records managers to worry about a competition with information technologists within their organizations and across disciplines. And some records professionals tend to gravitate to the idea of records as "recorded information" making them easily distracted by many things which are not records (that is, evidence of transactions or activities).[18]

The rapid and ever more pervasive use of computers may have contributed to records managers and archivists losing sight of records. Australian Frank Upward captures the essence of this problem: "During the last thirty years there has been a steady shift to emphasizing the importance of data, and this has been at the expense of perceptions about the importance of documents, a term which temporarily was considered to be more applicable to paper records. . . . A difference between data and documents is starting to again be observed, which can be broadly equated with ancient meanings of the terms, in which data is described as content, and a document as data in context. This implies that a document is both data and something extra. . . . Rather than dueling concepts, document characteristics and data characteristics are starting to be thought of as a 'duality' present in all records."[19] There are other reasons. In the United States the archival profession has long been influenced by historians and manuscripts curators, and there has been an emphasis on the acquisition of older records primarily for research purposes. This is not a new problem. Jenkinson worried about this many years ago in England when he wrote that "archives are not drawn up in the interest or for the information of posterity."[20] In the United States many individuals working as archivists seem predisposed to acquiring records as historical information to serve specific research clienteles, and this has made them prey to abandoning basic archival principles or losing sight of their primary objectives as archivists. Some of this has carried over to archives located in corporations and other institutions, where the archivist often seems predisposed to acquire interesting historical artifacts to be used by researchers.

Records managers have also faced similar problems, but for different reasons. Many records managers believe that their primary aim is to provide efficiency and economy through the systematic identification of obsolete records for destruction or through the maintenance of record classification systems. Other records managers also latched onto keywords such as "information" or "information resources management" as a means of remaining relevant in organizations stressing an increasing reliance on electronic information systems. The fuzziness of initial definitions only suggests why strong conceptions of records have eroded. An essay on the issue of records *or* information management reveals this dilemma even more. The author argues that where "in the past the transmission of thought to paper was the crucial stage in document production," this is now done electronically "where the entire documentation process becomes an extension of the human brain." While much of the advice in this essay is sound, it is based on a weak conception of what a record is or the responsibilities of *both* archivists and records managers.[21]

Records professionals need new strategies for focusing on evidence not information. The Information Age has been seductive with its stress on managing vast quantities of information created from many and diverse sources and used in new and interesting ways. As more memory becomes available, attention shifts from needing to distinguish records from everything else to the technical ability to save and access everything. Yet, records' evidence provides a means to identify essential information for organizations and society. The archivist and records manager must reassert their commitment to maintain accountability by stressing evidence of the organization's activities and transactions. Archivists and records managers need to re-evaluate their traditional end of life cycle approaches (the point of disposition or destruction) in scheduling and appraising. The nature of the new electronic document requires that office records creators will need to have greater responsibility in maintaining records and that organizational policies, systems designs work, implementation procedures, and the use of new information technology standards will have to be developed to enable this to happen. Records professionals shift from custodians to designers, implementers, and advisors.

TERMINOLOGICAL PROBLEMS: "ARCHIVES" IN THE INFORMATION PROFESSIONS

It may be that the technical issues facing organizations in their maintenance of new records forms is less a problem than the competition and communication between various kinds of information professionals. Recent technical language has been called "technobabble" because it can be "jargon [that] devolves into babble" when it is "used as filler or decoration," "employed intentionally for obfuscatory purpose," "employed gratuitously," "used obsessively," and "used by those unfamiliar with its meanings in an attempt to sound as if they know what they are talking about."[22] Technobabble plagues the information professions, including records and information resources management, where technology has become of central importance. When terms already familiar to one segment of the information professions are appropriated by another, there is not only the possibility of confusion but the danger that vital functions will be minimized or lost altogether. The information technologists have appropriated "archives" to indicate backing up files for security or similar purposes, for storing information no longer needed on a regular basis, and as a product term for backup software programs.

Such use of "archives" has had two other consequences. First, the technologists' usage reflects a lack of understanding of the validity of records of continuing value to an organization and even of the basic concept of a record itself.

Second, the technologists' use of "archives" has also made it difficult for archivists and records managers to communicate effectively to others designing and implementing organizations' information systems. Archivists and records managers seem unable to establish effective linkages with the information technology professionals (or even with each other) in order to ensure that vital and archival records in electronic form are maintained. Another result of "technobabble," therefore, may be the unnecessary erection of barriers undermining the basic goals of various information professionals. Technical jargon cannot only harm a particular discipline's broader mission, but it can mask a real lack of understanding of basic concepts, principles, and practices. "Archives" and its usage is a prime example of such a dilemma.

Archivists struggle to recognize how "archives" is being used in the information technology literature. Data processing articles and reports recognize the problems with preserving older data, utilizing terminology familiar to archivists. One article, for example, refers to "historical data," and offers this opinion: "With today's capability (and need) to access, retrieve, and process this data . . . historical data issues are gaining attention. . . . More difficult still is archiving this data. The data must be archived according to the underlying object's structure at the time of archival."[23] Its authors note, "from a data professional's perspective, history is a significant design issue that must be considered from conceptual architecture, through logical and physical models, to physical implementation, and finally, to access definition and tuning."[24] There are similar ideas throughout the technical literature. One article poses an essential preservation question long faced by archivists and other information professionals: "How long will my storage keep? For managers, this is an agonizing question—the part of the data-archiving equation. . . . [T]here is always a chance that the need for your data will outlast the life of your storage media."[25] Another article states, "archiving is for long-term storage of important files."[26]

While there is some affinity between archivists, records managers, and data processors, the latter's use of the terminology is quite disparate from that employed by professional archivists and records managers. "Archives," or some variant of it, is a term used to describe backing up various files: "an archive system can selectively move unused or rarely accessed files to offline media in an orderly fashion, freeing up disk space and thus improving file-access performance."[27] Another essay describes a system automatically backing up documents, an "archive device," after thirty days.[28] Nearly all forms of the term "archives" are used to describe some sort of backup, and the term is often used as a part of a product name for such software,[29] perhaps confusing the issue (certainly making it difficult to conduct bibliographic searching to identify literature on *real* archives).

The problem of communication between records professionals and managers of information systems or data processors is clearer in an examination of the latter's textbooks. Most of these textbooks include no mention of "archives" or any variant term.[30] One textbook mentions "archival files," but it does not define the concept except to state that they are similar to master files.[31] Another includes a reference to a "historical database," which is "a database that models time by recording the time in which a state correctly models reality. Historical DBMSs cannot rollback; they only store the current knowledge about the past."[32] One textbook includes a reference to historical storage medium in the following manner: "Magnetic tape is best suited for use as a historical storage medium. The firm can store data on tape and retain the tape as a record of business activity."[33] It is necessary to consider how data and record are used in this statement. Data are "facts and figures that are relatively meaningless to the user. Data is transformed into information by an information processor. Data is the raw material of information." Record is a "collection of data elements that relate to a certain subject."[34]

Such statements reflect a gulf between records and information professionals—a precise definition of record. One textbook writer defines a "logical record" as a "collection of related data items" and a "physical record" as "one or more logical records combined to increase input/output speeds and to reduce space required for storage."[35] At the core of this is professional competition. Peter Waegemann, writing from the records management perspective, describes how "data processing professionals" tend "to call themselves 'information managers.' Simply put, their philosophy is that all traditional information carriers will have to disappear as computers and their storage devices take over." Waegemann then describes how data processors have resisted the encroachments of records managers, to the degree that "94 percent of all data stored on magnetic media are not managed in, or by, the records department."[36]

Archives in the information professions suggests that the differences between the disciplines are so immense as to make communication and cooperation extremely difficult. These differences could be closed by how organizational managers, who determine an organization's information policy, view records. It is difficult to determine whether these individuals have an appropriate view of records. While there is a genre of writing about corporate and institutional archives in the mainstream archival literature, a literature that is not known by administrators, there is, at best, a modicum of writing on this topic in the public administration, business, and related literatures. What such essays convey about archives is not likely to make the work of an archivist or records manager any easier.

The primary theme in this literature is that archives may possess some positive public relations value for the corporation or organization. One essay depicts how older images of commercial products, culled from the archives of corporations, can be effectively utilized in current advertising campaigns.[37] Other essays are far more explicit in conveying how archives are viewed. Archival records are seen as corporate treasures for public relations: "As with an authentic Chippendale, the intrinsic public relations value of a yellowed ledger sheet, statement of incorporation, or patent application can be almost incalculable."[38] A brief note in *Management Review* suggests corporate archival records "may be of practical business use as well as historically interesting." The practical aspect is that "archived material is valuable from a promotional standpoint."[39] An essay by an archives consultant notes, "a sensitivity to the significance of corporate archives undergirds legal recordkeeping requirements, and it may be used prospectively as a heuristic device for aiding in the structuring of corporate public relations, as an employee fringe benefit, and even for developing an industrywide sense of the positive impact of the capitalist system."[40] What is most curious about this is the author's suggestion that because institutional archives are too expensive or that institutional leadership will change or dispose of certain records, organizations need to place their records in archival repositories for the benefit of researchers, a viewpoint undermining any sense of archival records as corporate assets.

There are essays in the management literature providing fuller views of the organizational importance of records. One essay discusses archives as a means of improving organizational decision making, saving money and other resources, helping form corporate memory, and, finally, supporting public relations. This essay, written by a freelancer, was the fullest viewpoint on archival records in this literature, and it provides a softening of some of the archives stereotypes: "The term 'archives' suggests some dusty backroom with an ancient corporate retainer surrounded by piles of relics. Some, it is true, are like this. Others are small museums of well-tended memorabilia charting the company's history with old posters, packaging, transport vehicles, photographic albums, oral-history tape recordings, manufacturing equipment, and old policy, sales, and manufacturing manuals. Some of this material is merely sentimental, but much of it can be used as a rich reservoir of strategic information for the whole company."[41] Even this essay suggests the problems existing for understanding an organization's archival records as vital corporate assets. Other essays provide similar mixed evidence of the value of archival records for corporations and similar institutions, with statements such as the "historical artifacts of a financial institution—its photographs, memorabilia, documents—may have great practical value and can be a practical resource for solving many of today's banking problems."[42]

While there are some writings advocating the use of information technology for the preservation and continued use of archival records, these seem to be a rarity and often convey incomplete views of the nature of archival records. One article discusses various new and older technologies (such as microforms and optical disks) that could be utilized to maintain archival records. However, the major issue discussed in this article was the matter of financial resources: "In all, the new technologies and storage devices coming to market, though they promote better access to archival documents, will mean little to the archivists if their agency or firm does not have a budget to implement such devices. Ultimately, it could mean that, while the new approaches are there, the upward trend in archiving may be toward continued frustration of the archivist, as there will be little they can do to apply the new methods to their everyday needs."[43] This essay does not provide any definition of an archival record.

These perspectives reflect organizational managers' general views toward *technology*, rather than records. Technology is seen through the lens of the general administration of corporate records. In the medical institution, for example, such technology is often discussed first from the perspective of easing access to large amounts of medical case files and then issues of accuracy or maintenance are considered as concerns to be resolved as best as possible.[44] Similar perspectives can be detected in publishing firms' use of photographic archives.[45] And it is not difficult to find such views in the financial industry; as one essay suggests, "In order to survive, modern executives and managers have jumped into the middle of the information age. They are becoming computer literate and are bypassing their data processing departments to get the exact information they want in the most responsive manner they know—information right at their fingertips, using their personal computers and a myriad of software tools (i.e., self-designed data bases, spreadsheets and marketing management software)."[46] There is also a body of literature that details the accessibility of online databases for organizational managers and other staff.[47]

The question left either unasked or poorly described in such writings is the impact on the institution's recordkeeping. One writer advised this management view for electronic mail: "Chatting near the water cooler may be replaced by electronic mail in the next decade, but unlike yesterday's idle conversations, everything that's transmitted can and may be held against you if your company ends up in court."[48] The solution presented was the systematic destruction of *all* electronic mail, revealing not only a sense of the driving factors in managing records and information but reflecting that despite progress made in record-keeping the management of such systems has not kept pace. Some writings provide the appropriate perspective. In an essay on the use of digital imaging technology for the maintenance of photographic collections in newspaper and journal publishing, the author describes the lack of standards for the preservation of the images: "photographers and publishers should first think about extending the useful life of media, not simply worry about implementing an archiving system." The term "archival" is simply misunderstood in this context, the author warns.[49] It is a term and concept misunderstood in much of the organizational management literature.

The challenge to maintaining archival records in organizations exists not only because of the manner in which information resources managers, data processors, other technicians, and organizational administrators view such records. Records managers, archivists, public historians, and other related professionals have also failed to develop adequate viewpoints on records with continuing value. Records managers, archivists, and public historians supposedly hold to some common concepts about the value of archival records in organizations. Archivists have participated in the establishment of institutional archives since the 1930s. Corporate archivists hold that archival records are vital to the organization's ongoing business, as well as to related concerns such as the records' public relations values. Records managers have traditionally seen themselves as enabling an institution to use its records economically and efficiently. Records managers have also supposedly utilized the records life cycle as a management device, although they have also been prone to view their organization's records primarily through legal requirements. Finally, public historians see themselves as bringing historical perspective to organizations and the greater public, working to ensure that organizations do not neglect the value of the long-term view on their activities, including the preservation and use of archival records.

The problem with the archival–public history perspective, especially in dealing with an organization's electronic records, is evident in a standard work on the subject, *Corporate Archives and History: Making the Past Work.*[50] Published as a contribution to public history studies, this volume includes the work of both public historians and archivists, with case studies, a series of essays on corporate memory, professional concerns for archivists and public historians, and the value of the historical perspective for corporations. While many of the essays were previously published, a greater problem is the emphasis on scholarly historical research and the public relations value of archival work. The unevenness of the essays also detracts. Complex topics tend to be discussed in a few paragraphs, important issues ignored, archival basics repeated from essay to essay. This makes the volume miss its intended purposes—to reach "managers in corporations who have responsibility for records," to provide a "supplement to the curriculum in archives and public history programs in higher education institutions," and to "create a better understanding of the role of business in American life."[51]

While there is a need for studies on the value of corporate archives from the scholarly historical perspective, these arguments will not convince most corporate and organizational managers they should invest money to preserve corporate records. Historian Roland Marchand's assertion, "we may ultimately find that some of the most perplexing, unanswerable questions in cultural history can best be approached, although never entirely resolved, through the kinds of evidence that corporations, through astute archival practice or passive accumulation, may have preserved,"[52] is compelling but not necessarily so for corporate leaders concerned with competition, financial bottom lines, legal and other regulatory mandates, and effective decision making. Moreover, the kinds of evidence Marchand describes is more in the realm of ephemera whose value many corporate archivists question.

Corporate records need to be seen for what they are—blood flowing through the veins of a living organism. A healthy organization must learn to manage its records, and this means understanding *why* records are created and useful. Poor advice about records management has been exaggerated due to the accelerating challenges posed by new information technologies. Company employees using the Internet and World Wide Web pose additional problems that did not exist before organizations were networked. What is interesting is that such concerns lead to an old solution, one urged by many for the past half-century—the destruction of records as quickly as possible. Such destruction is the first of many ill-advised solutions for a company's management of its records.

Such concerns have supported the creation of a new industry, computer forensics, where lawsuits lead to discovery searches through electronic records and information systems. The problem is the bad advice sometimes emanating from this new occupation, where experts urge the destruction of old computer records, electronic mail, and voice mail on a regular, but rapid, schedule. Such destruction must *only* occur within full knowledge of records management needs, although the question remains as to what constitutes good records management practice. An article in the *Wall Street Journal* quotes one of the new experts on records disposition as saying, "as long as [workers] follow the company's retention policies, management won't hold them accountable for discarded documents."[53] This presupposes, of course, that the retention policies are sound and that the records are being managed for the appropriate reasons. This is not a completely reliable statement, and worse yet, it reduces records management to a game of destruction. What is lost is that records are a valuable asset to a company. Focusing on the destruction of records is *not* the same as managing them for the benefit of the company.

New records and information technologies are not, of course, the only reason for why many advise the destruction of records as quickly and as often as can be done. Nearly a half-century ago, *Fortune* featured an essay on the excessive financial strains being caused by records maintenance in American businesses. Typical of this article's advice was the following statement: "Even more important than such savings [the use of records disposition schedules and records centers] is the fact that management is finally finding out how inefficient paperwork operations really are, and, in a few cases, is beginning to practice what records specialists call 'birth control.' The simplest tool for this is what the military services have called the circular file, or File #13—the wastebasket."[54] Unfortunately, the wastebasket has been the chosen storage device for far too many records possessing continuing value to a business. In this environment, records management is reduced to merely a matter of fiscal economy and records are seen as a financial bogeyman. Records need to be administered, instead, in accordance with their *value* to the company.

Recent court cases, investigations, and allegations of improper conduct provide conflicting advice about whether or how businesses ought to destroy records in an expeditious manner, or at all. In late 1996 a Texaco official faced an obstruction of justice charge for concealing and allegedly destroying records needed in a discovery process prompted by a civil case against the company. A meeting of company's officials to consider this destruction affirmed that the company detected no problem in destroying records to impede a court case, and a tape recording revealed this sentiment: "It is clear from the laughter and banter among the men on that now-famous Texaco tape that it never occurred to them that they could harm themselves and the company by destroying files. In fact, they apparently believed that by eradicating damaging information, they would be protecting themselves and the company."[55] Around the same time, following raids of Prudential Insurance Company branch offices by the New York State Insurance Department to secure records, lawyers asked a judge to order a criminal investigation to determine if Prudential had destroyed records in order to block another investigation into possible fraud by the company's sales agents. Ultimately the judge fined the company $1 million because Prudential consistently failed to prevent unauthorized document destruction.[56] In early 1997 Germany's Commerzbank AG was invaded by 250 tax inspectors who seized records, including floppy disks sitting around on office desktops, in order to ferret out evidence that the bank had assisted its customers to cheat on taxes.[57] Such instances of records mismanagement, deliberate and otherwise, continue to occur because business leaders generally do not understand the importance of records to their organization and, as is now likely, believe the focus should be on information systems and their uses.

Corporations either hear that their records need to be managed only for the short-term benefit to the organization—with an eye on possible litigation, breaches in corporate security, or excessive costs—or are told that their records will be useful to historians and other scholars studying a variety of topics (and mostly valuable to others rather than the corporation). The continuing value of records for a wide range of uses and functions has been lost partly because the administration of these records has been dismembered among different information disciplines and units within a business. Records management, archives administration, and other information sciences need to be better coordinated. Businesses need to adopt a holistic approach to the management of their records enabling them to understand why records are created, why they need to be maintained, and when they can be destroyed. Now, a cacophony of voices confuses organizational leaders about how their records should be managed.

The argument about historical value, for example, has been most prone to lead to poor advice. In 1984, in a review essay about public history and the corporate sector, Candace Floyd started by stating that "businesses are turning to historians for help in preserving corporate records. Today's business managers have discovered that company histories are worth preserving, and, perhaps, are even corporate assets." Floyd argues, "Through the centralization of records into organized archives, businesses have access to past decisions, to public opinion on past advertising campaigns, to the financial and economic trends caused by the introduction of new products. They are now able to use the raw data of history."[58] Such statements are found everywhere. A May 27, 1996 *Washington Post* article describing the work of such firms as the History Factory and History Associates, Inc. confused historians with archivists and writing history with managing records. According to the reporter, "Corporate historians organize papers and artifacts, help find information, write about events and people, and dream up ways to assemble old facts in new packages."[59] This is too limiting a view of the value of business (or any organization's) records.

Arguments like these are common, and they possess several problems. First, they focus on the preservation of "corporate history" instead of the maintenance of corporate records. This is not just a semantic matter, it is at the core of *misplaced* priorities. Businesses need to manage records in order to meet an array of legal, fiscal, and administrative requirements—some internal, but many more external. The stress on corporate history leads to a greater interest in writing and interpreting the past of American businesses than the more important issues of records management and the value of records as an ongoing source of information for companies. While business history is important, archives of such organizations do not exist only for such research and writing.

This latter concern suggests the second problem with such perspectives. The litany of the values of records for activities like discerning past decisions and understanding past events like advertising campaigns ignores the more important concerns for records maintenance for corporate memory, accountability, and evidence. American corporations operate in highly regulated environments and are part of a broad social and economic landscape; records are essential to corporations to understand such roles and responsibilities. American business archives and records management are not just functions tied to esoteric interests or social values of these institutions; these are business activities essential to the well-being of the corporation's competition and survival.

The premier American business serial, *Harvard Business Review*, has fallen into the trap of considering business archives as something akin to old artifacts left along the corporate path. These artifacts are considered interesting but often non-essential. In one of the most cited articles on the value of history to business, authors George David Smith and Laurence E. Steadman started their 1981 *Harvard Business Review* essay with, "what ultimately gives managers confidence in their decisions is their accumulated knowledge of the way things work—their experience." Smith and Steadman then discussed formal business history, writing for purposes of diagnostics, as analogy, as heritage, and as memory. In the latter value, corporate archives were introduced as a necessity, with the caution that corporations do not need records management programs interested only in records destruction. The idea that "correspondence, memoranda, recorded interviews, and even informal notes that might shed light on the decision-making processes of the organization must be available for study and analysis" is a sound concept, but it is also incomplete.[60] Records must be maintained for a variety of regulatory and other requirements, *not* just for historical research. It is possible that the quantity and quality of records maintained for purposes of evidence and accountability will be more than sufficient for purposes of corporate memory and historical research. For this to happen, of course, requires that records managers and archivists work together or that their functions are united in some logical fashion within a business.

The Smith-Steadman essay is a typical contribution to the *Harvard Business Review* (and it is typical of writings about records in *most* business journals). In the early 1960s, in one effort to persuade business leaders to be interested in history, the *Review*'s editors commented on business history's relevance to the "problems of present-day management." Using the better histories, the "businessman can see himself featured as a historical figure fully as important as the politician or the statesman, and can derive insights and understanding to help him to do his job better."[61] In fact, there has been no serious essay in the *HBR* on the nature and importance of corporate records. Business records management needs to be re-invented, with an emphasis on three areas. First, businesses need to understand that records must be managed as often as not because of external requirements and regulations. Full compliance to such external sources will also support the maintenance of records with archival value. Archival value is not merely a value assigned to records with historical or research potential, but it suggests a continuing use to the records-generating organization. Second, businesses need to understand that the maintenance of records is essential for maintaining a genuine corporate memory. Such organizational memory is not for supporting public relations campaigns, issuing commemorative booklets at key anniversaries, or for peppering the annual report with historical data and illustrations. Organizational memory is an essential source of information for current decision making and for planning for the future. Third, and finally, businesses must understand the nature of records. Records are discrete entities, with characteristics separating them from other information sources. They capture evidence because they document transactions. Records have, as a result, differing requirements for their administration than do other information sources.

While it is not surprising for archivists and public historians to hold viewpoints that corporate and organizational managers may find uninteresting or less than compelling, it is surprising to see records managers' perspectives. Records managers, although they have evolved from the archival profession, seem to have lost understanding of or interest in what archival records constitute. One result of this is the propensity for records managers to want to destroy records largely dictated by legal and other such regulatory concerns without considering the archival value of some records. Donald Skupsky's essay on electronic records scheduling starts with the premise that "you first determine which computer information is a 'record' and which is a 'non-record.' " Skupsky concludes, "electronic mail is a non-record unless converted to records by some formal process" such as "moving the records to a special electronic storage area on the computer or producing paper prints."[62] This reveals an extremely low-level definition of *both* records and archives.

Such weaknesses are evident in the many records management textbooks reflecting an extremely shallow knowledge about the nature, theory, and practice of archival administration. In fifteen records management textbooks published between the mid-1960s and the mid-1990s, none provide either a sufficient or accurate portrait of archival work. A publication from the 1960s has a single page on archives, equating it with the need to provide storage for records of long-term value.[63] Another volume includes four pages on archives, mostly a list of records with potential archival value.[64] Another textbook advises: "Local professional librarians are usually knowledgeable about archival procedures, but for special problems, consult the state archivist at the state capitol."[65] Such a viewpoint reveals a complete disregard for the crucial importance of archival records to the records management mission and, more importantly, to the organization that creates and needs such records.

Other records management textbooks have provided more and better information on archives, but such treatment is still a minor aspect of the volumes.[66] *All* records management textbooks treat archives in either stereotypical fashion or in a manner suggesting high professional *boundaries*. In one records management textbook the following statement typifies this larger problem: "Although the role of the archivist has expanded to include other types of records management, the distinction between archives and records centers is still based to a large extent on the type of records stored. In fact, in records management circles, archivists are sometimes unkindly referred to as pack rats, since their primary concern is the permanent preservation of all records that have or may have historical value."[67] When the "pack rat" arrives at the meeting, what chance is there for the organization to take seriously the importance of it's archival records and the maintenance of records with long-term value for evidence, accountability, and administration? After all, records with continuing value to the organization are the organization's archives, since archives are best defined as those records possessing continuing value to the institution and to others (researchers such as historians or political scientists or sociologists). If the organization does a good job in managing its records it will save more than enough records for others to use—in other words, it will serve a broader social role. And since the reason why many records are maintained resides in the political-economic-legal regulations created by society to meet its needs and to protect itself, this social role should not be seen as being something that is an unrealistic or ephemeral objective.

What is the mission of the institutional records manager? Key to this issue must be the concept of the records "life cycle." While the concept seems to neatly tie together the archivist and records manager in the administration of records, some have questioned whether, in fact, it hasn't actually confused the relationship. For one thing, records managers often seem to end the life cycle with a final disposition, either destruction or placement in the archives. Even if an archival function is included, there is still a sense that continuing use has ended, relegating an archives to a kind of cabinet of curiosities.

The life cycle problem may be even more severe than this. Jay Atherton writes that "strict adherence to its principles undermines any trend toward greater cooperation and coordination of archivists and records managers. It ignores the many ways in which the records management and archives operations are interrelated, even intertwined."[68] Atherton argues for a different kind of continuum. The continuum—creation, classification, scheduling, and maintenance and use—would have archivists and records managers involved at every stage. What pulls it together is this: "service—to the creators of the records and all other users, whoever they may be and for whatever reason they may wish to consult the documentation. Records are created to serve an administrative purpose, usually to document a transaction or decision. Their value is directly related to their availability to those requiring them."[69] Atherton argues that "records are not created to serve the interests of some future archivist or historian, or even to document for posterity some significant decision or operation. They are created and managed to serve immediate operational needs."[70] This is very different from many of the standard records management textbooks or basic archival primers that state something like the "primary distinction between a records center and an archives repository is that the archives preserves records for the benefit of the scholar and posterity, whereas the records center preserves records for administrative and operating purposes."[71] It is the kind of clearer mission or purpose that Atherton describes that can resolve the problem of the purpose of records management or archival administration and provide the basis for better communication between organizational manager, information systems manager, records manager, and archivist. The immediate or long-term administrative needs for records should provide the records for cultural and historical purposes, and this provides the keystone for any organizational records policy.

The development of information resources management (IRM), seeing records management as a subset of this broader array of functions and objectives, has for some weakened the concept of archival records. One IRM proponent states, "Archives . . . have very little to do with the business of the corporation nor, for that matter, with its business planning activities. Archives exist for different purposes than, for instance, the enhancing of an organization's profitability. Now I know (and I believe) that archives form the corporate memory of an organization, and that corporations often find it useful to refer to the old files when formulating policy or reviewing current operations. In terms of an organization's total information requirement, however, and in terms of the business processes which information resource management endeavors to support, the archival corporate memory role is, of necessity, a function of lesser significance. Stated another way, the raisons d'être of archives and of information resource management are different, and any attempt to link the two closer than they are now, or to have the former assume an influence over the latter, will flounder because of inherent incompatibility."[72] The logical extension of such notions only seems to portend significant problems for organizations, especially as they increasingly rely upon electronic information technology. The loss of any organism's memory, living or institutional, is bound to bring greater problems to its functioning. In fact, records management, archives administration, and information resources management *cannot* be incompatible if the organization is to meet its obligations. That they may be seen as incompatible is a failure of society to care for its own best interests and a definite failure of the records and information professionals, especially as records move to electronic systems.

Recordkeeping systems are becoming electronically dependent. While this presents challenges to (and opportunities for) records professionals, it has deepened the boundaries between various disciplines. Organizations look to technicians for solutions while the technicians tend to discuss issues in technical jargon and while archivists and records managers have tended to be viewed as only concerned with paper records. C. Peter Waegemann surmises that with the "rise of the information managers came the belief that they personified the computerized future. An unfortunate corollary to this belief then emerged—that many traditional records managers were only concerned with 'old paper.' "[73] While it is certainly the case that paper remains an important form of communication and recordkeeping in most organizations, it is also true, as Monique Attinger explains that "paper-based data remains isolated if it is not managed jointly with an organization's electronic resources."[74]

The image of archivists, archives, records, and records professionals in the *New York Times* reveals more about this problem.[75] Archives and records only appear in newspaper articles when they are curiosities or embroiled in political scandal of one sort or another. While it can be argued that records are seen as valuable for organizations and for public accountability from a reading of such news stories, it is also true that this importance is only identified or rediscovered when a crisis or controversy arises, such as mentioned earlier with Texaco and various financial institutions. Archivists and records managers are not very visible or newsworthy in this newspaper. It is no wonder, then, that other information professionals have such views about archivists and archives as they seem to do.

Some of the problem of the archivists' image compared to other information professionals and society-at-large have to do with the ways in which archivists have viewed themselves and their mission. David Gracy suggests that the use of "non-current" to encompass archival records is a relegation of the archival records to the status of *unimportant*.[76] Archivists who relegate records management to a function that primarily serves the archivist in identifying and preserving those organizational records with continuing value miss the other aspects of records management responsibilities that are also extremely important to an institution's administration.[77] Records managers who see their responsibility as only the cost-efficient cleaning out of obsolete, non-current records, not only confuse their notions of archives, but they may have lost sight of organizational needs for records, no matter what the financial obligations may entail.

SOLUTIONS FOR RE-ESTABLISHING THE CENTRALITY OF THE RECORD AS A BASIC WORKING CONCEPT FOR THE INFORMATION PROFESSIONS AND THEIR POLICIES

Records professionals need to link with other disciplines with a stake in the management and preservation of records within institutions. Professional jargon cannot diminish efforts to administer those records that possess continuing value, nor can it be allowed that unfortunate stereotypes of archivists or records managers act as barriers preventing organizations from establishing policies and procedures to manage their records.

While many have argued for the strengthening of education and the core knowledge for the records professions, these arguments have been made within the context of records professionals' place within its greater information disciplines' and societal ecology. While archivist or records managers must improve their own abilities, skills, and knowledge, they must also enhance professional standing so that there is credibility within the organizations and larger society in which they function. The records professional's mission is dependent on an understanding of that mission by organizational executives and public policy makers and a more cooperative stance with other related professionals. The advice offered by Richard Kesner of utilizing information resources management as a unifying concept for records managers, archivists, organizational librarians, and data processors appears useful but untried and unproved.[78]

A long-term solution is the *education* of archivists and records managers and other information professionals, described briefly here and in more detail latter in this volume. All have taken different routes to educating their own, but this trend has diminished the cooperation and mutual understanding of these related fields. Records management education has been critiqued for holding fast to an educational paradigm that is out of touch with the current realities of information and recordkeeping technology and its use by modern organizations. The continuing emphasis on paper records and on lower levels of technical education has certainly hindered records managers' efforts to contend with the shift to electronic recordkeeping systems. Again as Attinger suggests, the "records manager has not had sufficient status within the organization . . . [but has] been perceived as merely 'custodians' of information"[79] in much the same manner as records managers have viewed archivists as custodians of old records.

There have been efforts in the past to survey records managers to gain an understanding of their perceptions in order to develop meaningful curriculum. One survey from the 1980s reveals the problem with this approach. Archival issues were accorded a low level of importance.[80] A similar survey for IRM-type education some years later does *not* even include archives as an identified component or need.[81] What are the issues raised by such analyses? First, the current perceptions work against integrated approaches enabling records managers and archivists to cooperate in meaningful ways. Second, the last thing the records professions and the organizations they serve need is to construct educational programs that reflect *current* activities, since education is intended to provide tools for careers, changing technologies, and new legal and other administrative needs. Third, such surveys only reflect the prevailing lack of knowledge about certain issues that current professionals possess. It is unwise to develop a records management program lacking an archives component because it skews basic principles such as the life cycle or records continuum concept and harms an organization's ability to administer its most important records—current and historical, active and inactive.

Building bridges between the various records disciplines requires developing a firm *definition of the record.* Many of the definitions appear to be efforts to net anything remotely similar to what a record might be, probably one result of the convergence of technologies and information disciplines (something akin to the reduction of complex, differing creeds to one common, watered down theology). There is a fundamental *difference* between a data processor and a records manager. The larger, continuing problem is that there are many definitions of "information," and a complex interplay of various meanings within the information professions.

Agreeing on the definition of record relates to trying to *emphasize the commonalties* of the missions between the various segments of the information management professions. There have been many articles describing the *differences* between archivists and records managers, and even those striving to propose unification often spend too much printed space emphasizing different cultures and perspectives. Robert Sanders's essay places the common ground in records scheduling, but this undermines the larger and more important reasons why records are essential to an organization.[82] Scheduling records is but one means to an end, and with electronic information systems, it is a means that may have questionable value. What records managers and archivists have to be careful of is confusing professional rivalries with real disciplinary functions and activities. A decade and a half ago, Jake Knoppers described how archivists and records managers sometimes tend to consider each other: "archivists, always being a breed apart, are quietly plotting their moves of how to sight their two big guns, namely, their black box of 'archival appraisal' and the cry of 'corporate memory' on the whole squabbling crowd so that at the appropriate moment they can fire the blast that will ensure them a place and role in the 'electronic' age . . . [Archivists] take a combative attitude towards 'fellow information specialists' either by downgrading the other or by claiming new or expanded territory (read, in order to obtain status, staff, and funding)."[83] What Knoppers failed to grasp is how important it is for any organization to manage their records of continuing value, whether that value is defined as being for legal, administrative, fiscal, or research purposes. What such commentators also fail to see is that archival appraisal and records scheduling are closely related (in fact, one cannot really succeed without the other) and that such functions have some common links in theory and knowledge.

A new attitude to electronic information technology is needed. Some segments of the information professions see technology as *the* solution. A data processor will strive to resolve informational and managerial problems by developing software applications. Often these solutions only perpetuate the problems because the user needs are not considered as carefully as they should be. Archivists and records managers view the technology as a problem or challenge to be overcome, worrying about whether their basic principles are valid. Records managers perspire about shifting from managing paper records to an electronically managed organizational environment. Architectural and social critic Witold Rybczynski argues that the "historical record does not support the dour theory of technological inevitability. All technological activity seems to reflect a human desire to gain a greater control over the immediate environment, and every tool . . . is only an attempt to make life more predictable. . . . [T]he evolution of the design of machines from the tool stage to powered devices and finally to automation is a process that progressively, and specifically, increases human control."[84] Rybczynski's perspective is different from that of the data processor in that he sees the issue of choice, adaptability, and other factors enabling humankind to use technology in safe and effective ways.

Archivists and records managers should consider *how* electronic recordkeeping systems enable them to manage an organization's records *more* effectively. While technologies have converged, the various information disciplines have diverged. While it is perfectly reasonable for professionals like archivists to work to strengthen their own education, knowledge, and related areas, they still have to build bridges to these other disciplines and, most important, to explain—in effective and practical ways—what is the nature and significance of archival records.

ANOTHER PROBLEM: RECORDS AND MANUSCRIPTS

The continuing problem with what records are and how they should be managed within organizations may stem from records managers' angst about other Information Age professionals, unnecessary barriers erected between records professionals, and unresolved issues within various segments of the records disciplines. For example, manuscripts curators and many other archivists who are primarily concerned with the acquisition and maintenance of both non-organizational *and* organizational records (apart from institutional archives programs) think that the work, theorizing, and discussion of electronic records archivists is not relevant to them or even that the new work on electronic records management represents a diversion from the real work and mission of the archivist. Should the archivist really be worried about the technicalities of the systems producing records? Isn't the archivist really concerned with those records possessing broad cultural value to society? Don't archivists, with particular mandates by their organizations to document something or to preserve representative records related to some element of the populace and the past, have more pressing concerns with the voluminous paper-based records still being created? Will electronic records really supplant paper records when it appears we are still drowning in the paper files? Is the attraction to archival work lost when we move from the manuscript realm to that of cyberspace?

There also seems to be some concern that the recent emphasis on electronic records by the archival community has diverted attention from other basic concerns most often represented by archivists in their manuscript curatorial role, such as the symbolic importance of archives, the value of records created outside of organizational settings, and the loss of certain organizational records when the institutions give up on the records or when the organizations go out of business. Can that small computer disk really ever have symbolic value? Is the average person really reliant on electronic recordkeeping systems? How will archivists manage those electronic records alienated from their organizational settings when institutions end or purge records? Some of this kind of questioning may be due to electronic recordkeeping outpacing where the archives profession now works, lengthening the gap between the mechanics of recordkeeping and the responsibility for managing the records with continuing value which we call archives. Or, it may be due to the fact that there always continues to be a gap between most practitioners and the theorists or professional leaders, the old friction between theory and practice. The questions may also be the natural result of discussions within a profession that has always been somewhat fragmented, due to institutional allegiances, educational backgrounds, and program size.

The basic mission and objectives or focus of the archivist is at the root of such concerns. The new focus on recordkeeping stemming from the discussions about electronic records management should be a unifying process. The recent debates and discussions are part of a historic swing back to the real business of the archivist, the management of the record and recordkeeping systems with continuing value for evidence, accountability, and memory. While the concerns generated by the recent emphasis on electronic records management are a new twist, the issues about the place of manuscripts curatorship in the archival profession are part of a historic condition of the twentieth-century archival profession, most evident in the North American professional community with three decades of navel-gazing about the historical manuscripts versus public archives tradition. But these concerns are also visible in other parts of the world.

There are scores of essays and books written by historians and other research-ers expressing the sentiment that the residue of private and organizational and governmental records preserved by chance or purpose provides a rich texture for understanding past times and societies. For archivists, records (in whatever form) possess evidence, and it is from this evidence that most of the value for culture, history, and community stem. The "sacred" records enshrined in the rotunda of the United States National Archives are merely part of the infinites-imal quantity of records of evidence that have become imbued with symbolic value. Aren't these records also a symbol of the various values of records for a democratic society and a representation of the records created by many insti-tutions and entrusted to archivists? In other words, while some archivists fix on these historic documents as the raison d'étre for the profession, others view these records as representations of the mandate to preserve the evidence of government and society.

The best statement of such concerns about the emphasis on electronic records and recordkeeping from the manuscripts curator's perspective has been that put forth by Australian archivist Adrian Cunningham. In his 1994 article Cunning-ham first posits that electronic technology is transforming the creation of records by private individuals, drawing on the notion that the "personal computer is

exactly what it says it is—personal!" He then uses an example of the problems
that this poses for the collecting archives, that of the literary manuscripts created
by authors and long a target of many collecting repositories. Cunningham reflects that most collecting programs have ignored this problem hoping that by
the time personal archives are largely electronic that some solution will have
been worked out. He also takes issue with the suggestions that archives will
become non-custodial, that recordkeeping systems will be the primary focus
rather than the fonds or the series, and that standards (and other macro-level
approaches) will need to be the primary strategy to maintaining such records.
While struggling with these notions, Cunningham does accept the idea that personal records archivists will have to become active in the pre-custodial phase,
building ongoing relationships with eventual donors at early stages in their
work.[85]

The chief value of Cunningham's essay is raising precisely the *right* issues
for archivists and manuscripts curators in the electronic information era. Efforts
to work with electronic recordkeeping systems can provide solutions to the problems faced by manuscripts curators because they point to technical solutions in
electronic information systems. But the openness to these solutions still depends
on the manuscripts curators understanding their business—and their business is
archives and records. These are *not* new concerns.

Cunningham is an Australian archivist, and Australian archivists are particularly sensitive to the fact that a separation between "archival organizational
and cultural roles" has weakened some of the post-custodial arguments found
in the renewed emphasis on recordkeeping. These difficulties exist in other countries as well. In the United States, Richard Berner long ago characterized the
public archives and historical manuscripts traditions, and while arguing that
Schellenberg brought the two traditions together, whatever melding occurred
was more in theory than in practice.[86] In Canada, the "total archives" approach
seems to bring both together, but there is ample evidence that a tension exists
between the government and organizational archivists and those archivists and
manuscript curators in collecting programs.[87] There is really no room for disa-
greement. Archivists are archivists. Archives are archives. Archives are composed of records. Historical manuscripts are composed of records, and they
constitute archives. Manuscript curators are responsible for records *and* archives.

Some of the problem in applying recent discussions about records to historical
manuscripts may be the result of a lack of understanding about the nature of
historical manuscripts. In the United States, for example, archives and historical
manuscripts have often been characterized as separate entities. David Gracy, in
his pioneering American manual on archival arrangement and description, attempts to describe the differences between archives and manuscripts: "Archives
are kept primarily to satisfy the needs of their creating organization. A manuscripts collection is accumulated to foster the study of the subjects about which
the repository collects."[88] This means, according to Gracy, that there are very
basic differences in the manner in which archives and historical manuscripts

should be treated. For example, "arrangement is a characteristic inherent in an archival record group because the records were created in, and maintained by, an office for its documentation and use. Personal papers, on the other hand, may or well may not systematically reflect the activity of their creator."[89]

Gracy's statements stress the *wrong* issue and characteristics. Most often the reason why manuscript curators and other archivists think about personal papers in this fashion is because of the disorganization that often results from the lengthy alienation of the records from the custody of their creators prior to coming into an archives. The vast majority of personal and family papers *are* records with the same organic, orderly nature deriving from functions and activities as institutional records discussed by archivists at least since the late nineteenth century. If they are considered in this fashion because they are artificial accumulations or loose odds and ends, fragmentary remnants of the documentary heritage, then archivists need to reflect more critically about why they would want to become absorbed with some items (can they call them records?). While there may be much to study about the nature of personal recordkeeping, it is not a study about chaos but one about the impulses driving individuals and families to create, maintain, and use their *own* records.

If archivists forget that manuscripts produced by individuals and families are archives, they also forget that they are records. The other implications of Gracy's comments are that personal papers are formed for different reasons than institutional and other records, otherwise why would he argue that organizational records are intended to serve the needs of the records' creators and historical manuscripts are intended to serve the needs of historians and other researchers? This is a flawed idea, although it is an idea probably emanating from the reason why many can only see archives as cultural artifacts to be collected (in the same manner that you acquire bottle caps or baseball cards) and useful for those scholars who study such artifacts for a range of historical research (who often seem capable of finding value in *anything*).

An individual maintains records for generally the same reasons as an organization—to meet the needs of accountability, evidence, and corporate memory. Personal records are created to capture transactions, document activities, serve legal and administrative functions, and provide a basis for memory. We maintain records to create our own evidence of crucial work, to protect ourselves, and to provide a kind of corporate memory of home, work, and family. And in this era when many speculate about the rootlessness that new information technologies are bringing to spatial and physical environments, personal records may become more crucial. That personal papers may be acquired as part of an acquisition scheme of a collecting historical manuscripts repository does not negate the fact of the origins of these records. The classic writings on archival science certainly capture a concern for *both* institutional and personal records creators. Hilary Jenkinson wrote with a firm conviction, "The aim of the Archivist is to hand on to future generations the documents confided to him with no diminution in their evidential value: accordingly he has to guard against the destruction not only of those elements whose value as evidence is obvious to him but also of those whose value he does not perceive."[90] This applies *both* to personal and institutional records.

If historical manuscripts are often not perceived to be the same as organizational records, then what are they seen to be? Terry Cook provides the most convincing argument that they have been defined too often as artifacts.[91] We collect them, hoard them, touch them, and otherwise regard them like museum artifacts, all of which can undermine the significance of these records for evidence, accountability, and even corporate memory. Archivists must consider these things differently. In some rare instances, the characteristics of the original record convey important evidential and even informational characteristics that would be lost if the originals were destroyed. This applies only to a small percentage of all records. In even rarer circumstances the record must be acquired and held in its original state because it possesses symbolic value for an institution, a community, or a society. Here the rarity is so great as to not make this a primary occupation for the archivist. If the archivist moves the symbolic importance of archives to the forefront, the archivist is drifting over to that of the antiquarian collecting records often due to their physical characteristics portraying some ancient past time. Archivists, if doing this, have lost sight of records as evidence.

Another problem in conceptualizing personal papers as archives may be the tendency of some information scientists who, when dealing with the convergence of libraries, museums, and archives through electronic information technology, forget that there is more at stake than just similarities and dissimilarities between such cultural institutions. Boyd Rayward describes this convergence seeing that the newer technologies are breaking down former distinctions based on format and arguing that the distinctions are actually rather recent in any event. Rayward focuses on the needs of users, suggesting "digitization eliminates physical distinctions between types of records and thus, presumably, the need for institutional distinctions in the management of the systems within which these records are handled." He believes that the user will not care whether the record is held in a library, archives, museum, commercial database, or the Internet.[92] What Rayward misses is that the issues here are more than information access or professional turf battles. The mixing of multiple kinds of "records" can minimize their "recordness" by threatening their structure, context, and content—in other words, what makes them distinctly a record. An archival record's "information" includes not just its content but its context and its form. A record takes on meaning because of other matters, such as the authority for its creation, the activity that it supports, and the legal and administrative matters surrounding its origination and maintenance.

Archivists and other records professionals must be careful not to discount technologists. Michael Buckland makes the case that information is not random stuff but that it is the process of becoming informed, or as he argues, "The notion of information is meaningful only in relation to someone becoming informed."[93] Much is valuable in his work, especially his understanding of how people make use of a diverse array of sources for information purposes, but this must be recognized as being very different from the perspective of the archivist, manuscripts curator, or records manager. Buckland's idea that "when a specific document is sought, what is happening is that the name of the document is being used as a surrogate definition of the knowledge actually sought"[94] is far different from archivists' emphasis on the value of records as evidence. Archivists and records managers need to incorporate the best of such insights from the technologists with their own mission, while not abandoning their primary purpose.

Mark Brogan's stimulating essay about the market versus regulatory or laissez-faire approaches to electronic records management reveals some of the dangers in such a posture. If archivists worry too much about whether the electronic recordkeeping systems support archival records without any effort to work with industry and government to develop systems that do, there is bound to be a major failure with either the loss of the electronic documentary heritage or the loss of the records professional's identity and role. Brogan believes that time spent with the emerging markets to produce products is essential.[95] Archivists might have a better chance of being successful in the preservation of private, non-organizational records if they worked with software manufacturers to create commercial products individuals could readily acquire that would enable long-term maintenance of their electronic files and easier transfer of these personal papers to real or virtual repositories.

There may be many lessons here, but consider one. Although records professionals have heard and known this for some time, they must corroborate with electronic information technology designers to ensure that the systems institutions are acquiring to create and maintain records can, in fact, do this. Can it be that this prospect so fundamentally changes the work of the archivist or records manager that they resist adapting their approaches and instead retreat to other venues (like personal papers) where the technology may not have had such an impact? Can it be that some have turned to more traditional concerns represented by personal papers as a safe haven in order to resist the need for continual re-tooling, additional education, and staying current with a rapidly changing body of knowledge? How can records professionals resolve this, except to re-focus on their knowledge about records, recordkeeping systems, and archives?

Many worry that the more precise definition of a record will identify materials that may deserve preservation as non-records and hence reduce the possibilities of maintaining such records. Such reduction is a good thing, since the tendency has usually been by both archivists and manuscript curators to err on the side of trying to save *too* much or of being *too* reactive in accepting records and manuscripts as they become available. The emergence of the documentation strategy and macro-appraisal in North American archival thinking in the past decade has been one effort to be more strategic and selective with a clearer appraisal aim in mind. There is another way of viewing this dilemma, however.

David Roberts hints at this when he writes that archives often still have some responsibility for the maintenance of information systems but that they need to recognize them for what they are, information not recordkeeping systems. As he states, "Applying the transaction/evidence test . . . can be expected to pose a dilemma for many archival institutions, which may accept the logic of the transaction/evidence argument . . . but which have custody of, or legislative or jurisdictional responsibility for, databases and electronic information which do not function as records."[96] The issue still may be appropriate appraisal approaches for identifying what non-records systems might be maintained, as well as the attitude and willingness of archivists and manuscripts curators to make the necessary distinctions.

Appraisal models loom large for what might be done with electronic records produced by individuals. Australians have moved to what they call the continuum management of records, a model asserting that records managers and archivists appraise records when records are still active *rather* than at the end of their traditional life cycle. This shift is also evident in other countries, at least in a theoretical fashion, most notably in Canada and the United States. The kind of continuum model for the appraisal of private electronic records posited by Cunningham, in which individuals with potential to produce significant records or to make significant contributions to society are identified and then worked with by archivists to ensure that their records are preserved, is problematic unless it is done within the context of strategies for the appraisal of records focusing on the macro-issues.

Many of the problems detected by manuscript curators with the new electronic records emphasis can be rectified by making a transition from an emphasis on collecting to appraising. Collecting has often been characterized by the acquisition of interesting and often valuable documentary materials by an examination of the records as they materialize rather than through broader appraisal objectives. There are also other easily identified political and psychological aspects evident in collecting which have not been studied as a part of the archival landscape but which are being well documented by other scholars and cultural commentators.[97] Appraising should be characterized by a focus on what is to be documented, and that means a stress on evidence and, as a result, records. Manuscripts curators who lament the recent focus on electronic records may do so only because they realize they cannot *collect* such records.

For the institutional archivist, the purpose is supporting the organization's mission through the identification and preservation of records with continuing value for matters of evidence, administration, and legal concerns. The maintenance of records for this purpose will also identify many records meeting other informational needs of the research communities wanting access to these records. For the manuscript curator, the purpose is on similar evidential aims, conceptualized through acquisition or documentation policies. While the manuscript curator may identify with particular research communities, the manuscript curator must still recognize that not all potential informational value can be preserved or that personal or family papers are somehow materials to be re-molded according to their usefulness rather than maintained according to their archival or record nature. Moreover, the manuscript curator's broader aim to document something cannot be achieved only through acquisition, but such objectives must take into account the fostering of institutional archives and the nurturing of the public's interest in archives and their value.

By re-focusing on the record, the archivist and manuscript curator provides a valuable service to society with a new understanding of the record's importance. Cultural commentator Conor Cruise O'Brien's discussion of the reliability of government records provides a clue about the value of a new perspective: "Billions and billions of transactions must have occurred in the course of what we . . . call 'recorded history.' But of all those billions of transactions, only a tiny proportion has left any record. And even what does survive is as likely to be intended to deceive as to illuminate." O'Brien suggests historians are looking for documents "that are not intended for posterity, but which are there because they were generally known to, and taken for granted by, contemporaries. And the documents which historians most prize are those written down with no thought of posterity in mind but solely for an immediate and mundane purpose. And such documents have been preserved only spottily and by chance, for the greater part of the millennium now expiring. For the later part, especially for the last hundred and fifty years, the problem is the sheer abundance of the documents."[98] The re-focus of the archivist and records manager on the record deals directly with some of O'Brien's concerns, while the continued scurrying about to collect all sorts of documentary material only compounds the problem.

Archivists and manuscripts curators have conveyed *too* many purposes for the archival mission, from preserving evidence to documenting society to protecting the rights of the under-documented to acquiring lots of stuff for any and everyone to use. Manuscript curators worry that grappling with the electronic records of organizations and governments cuts off consideration of other types of archival documents important for their insights into the lives of private citizens, grassroots movements, or even for their symbolic societal importance. They often fail to see that it is with the organizational records themselves that many of these groups are, in fact, best documented or that no matter how effective they are in acquiring private records, the documentation will be incomplete without adequate maintenance of institutional and government records.

Archivists debate the problems with the diversity of recordkeeping media. This is a substantial challenge, but the bigger problem may be how the archivist is appraising. On the one hand, there are the substantial theoretical and conceptual debates within the archives profession that bring attention to specific matters such as the relative merits of evidential and informational values to the broader concerns of documenting organizations and society. On the other hand, the archivist operates within an increasingly complex, diversified society currently engaged in volatile public and academic debates. In one of the recent books on the so-called culture wars in the United States, James Atlas notes, "one of the main weaknesses of the American federation of states is that it's such an amalgam of diverse interests and identities. The rhetoric of our primary documents affirms a vision of America to which most of us assent; but those documents were framed by a dissenting elite for a nation that consisted of a few thousand souls. How are we to address the vastly different constituency that has emerged since the white, male Founding Fathers sat down with their quill pens to compose their decrees?"[99] Far more daunting than the issue of electronic records preservation is the matter of how appraisal can be carried out in such a contested and ideologically charged environment. But to be able to address this, the archivist and manuscript curator must be able to understand that they are appraising first and foremost records and recordkeeping systems. It is here that the real problem emerges, not with a stress on electronic records or on other professional objectives.

This is not the most nagging or persistent problem facing the archival community. Just how many times will we be able to re-discover the idea that manuscript collections are archives and that archives are records? Forty years ago American archivist and manuscript curator Lester Cappon wrote a brief essay forcefully arguing that what often passed for historical manuscripts were in fact archives—"bodies of organic papers of persons or families, organizations, or institutions, in their original order of arrangement."[100] A decade later T. R. Schellenberg's *The Management of Archives* described the same principle in greater detail and with more examples.[101] Twenty years later, Canadians working on descriptive standards determined that archives and historical manuscripts were one and the same with regards to descriptive needs, recognizing that archives are archives and records are records.[102] Within the last few years metadata, driven by the idea of records fundamentally being evidence, has begun to transform even the most trusted dimension of archival work, arrangement and description.[103] Mixed in with all this has been the new interest in diplomatics characterized best by the writings of Luciana Duranti of the University of British Columbia in *Archivaria* and in many other archival journals, all stressing a return to some basic archival fundamentals—namely, the record.[104] Crucial to all this is the strong endorsement of records and recordkeeping as the *core* business of the archivist and manuscript curator.

Given the inevitability of the transformation of all recordkeeping systems, organizational and private, into electronic systems, the records professional had better determine what his or her business is about. Viewing such systems as valuable for information purposes or for evidence will not only mean substantially different things but it will also determine whether there really is a records mission, whether records that should be maintained are lost, and whether organizations and government can possess accountability, evidence, and memory. Archivists and manuscript curators are important to society, *if* they have the right mission. The more precise descriptions of recordkeeping functional requirements can be utilized in the design of all types of recordkeeping systems (at least that is the intent), but that is hardly the first problem to be resolved. The acquisition of personal papers must be seen only in the light of archivists and records managers working to study, understand, and manage records and recordkeeping systems.

FUNCTIONAL REQUIREMENTS FOR EVIDENCE IN RECORDKEEPING AND THEIR WARRANT

For records to possess credibility in Information Age organizations, they must have specifically defined requirements that can be integrated into software design and adhered to through organizational policy or government legislation. Recordkeeping systems are information systems distinguished by the fact that the information they contain is linked to the transactions they document. Records may be consulted for documentation of those transactions or because they contain information that is useful for another purpose, but recordkeeping systems do not just contain data to be reused. Some information age specialists argue that the key to managing information is "focusing on the quality of the data you receive," but these experts often disagree on how to define quality.[105] Records professionals can argue reasonably that managing records is a primary means to achieve this purpose. Recordkeeping systems capture, maintain and access evidence as required by the jurisdiction in which they are implemented and in accordance with common organizational practices. Recordkeeping systems support organizational functions, and these functions require records of transactions in order to continue daily operations, satisfy administrative and legal requirements, and maintain accountability.

Supported by the National Historical Publications and Records Commission, the University of Pittsburgh School of Information Sciences conducted a research project to examine variables affecting the integration of recordkeeping requirements for evidence in electronic information systems.[106] This project had four main products or outcomes: recordkeeping functional requirements, production rules to support the requirements, metadata specifications for recordkeeping, and the warrant reflecting the professional and societal endorsement of recordkeeping.[107]

There are several important aspects to these functional requirements, now largely incorporated into a proposed new international standard.[108] They are contrary to nebulous notions of information. They define precisely records as a part of information sources. They return the archivist and records managers to their original roles. And the functional requirements provide the source for controlling—through definition, policy, regulation, and technical applications—the flood of electronic and other information captured by records. A study on archives and manuscripts notes that the "key turning point for any society undergoing a transition to literacy was the point at which it seems to rely on writing and written records in its everyday operations."[109] We could revise this statement somewhat. The key turning point for any organization undergoing a transition to computerization is the point at which it seems to rely on electronic records in its everyday operation. Traditional notions of records do not need to be rejected in favor of more anomalous concepts such as information or virtual documents. These requirements, embedded in electronic information systems and policies by organizations, could resolve many of the challenges faced in the management of technologies such as electronic mail.

How this research agenda and project fit into the evolution of ideas about electronic records management can be visualized by considering the shifting concepts held by archivists toward electronic records. Thirty years ago, archivists debated whether machine-readable files should be considered as records. By the next decade, archivists were employing social science data archives approaches to manage such machine-readable systems, while the debate about legislative solutions, policy initiatives, and the use of archival principles with such systems continued. By the mid-1980s, it was widely recognized that the records professions were not doing well with machine-readable records, still endeavoring to manage such records at the end of the life cycle or in a purely custodial fashion. The research agenda recognized such problems, leading a number of archivists and records managers to re-focus on the fundamentals of what constitutes a record. The research project at the University of Pittsburgh was designed to deal with this issue.

Defining a set of functional requirements for records was the necessary starting point, stressing compliance to external regulatory and other authorities. Out of this emerged the notion of an accountable recordkeeping system supporting the capture, maintenance, and continued usability of records. By accountable one means that the system produces records when records are required to be created, stipulated by a transaction in organizational or individual business or mandated by some external requirement or by relevant professional best practices. The project's attention ultimately turned to the latter reason for records' creation and maintenance—the warrant idea, defined as the mandate from law, professional best practices, and other social sources requiring the creation and continued maintenance of records, perhaps the most important outcome of the project.

The project's focus was the development of the recordkeeping functional requirements that could be used in both developing and evaluating software for the support of electronic records management. When the project started it was thought that the requirements were for *archival* recordkeeping. This changed to *recordkeeping* requirements, then to functional requirements for *evidence in* recordkeeping. There is more work to be done on whether all elements of the requirements are always needed or whether there are different requirements for recordkeeping for corporate memory, personal recordkeeping, and other types of recordkeeping. The emphasis on recordkeeping for the purposes of evidence largely derived from subsequent research on the warrant concept.

The warrant suggests records are created because of legal, regulatory, professional best practices, and other reasons generally external to the organization. Many records managers have pointed out that the majority of records are shaped by forms, and that these forms often reflect requirements generated from the organization needing to be compliant. The project identified sources for such warrant, matching up the warrant with particular dimensions of the functional requirements and revising the requirements as necessary from ideas and principles derived from the analysis of the warrant. While there is much work yet to be done in determining the value of the warrant, especially in considering the international aspects and value as well as the value of the warrant for assisting archivists and records managers in gaining support for the management of electronic records, the concept seems valuable for both records professionals and creators of records.

A more specific delineation of record, whether in terms suitable for software development[110] or standards development,[111] was needed. The writings of archivists and records managers have been vague in specifics, except for diplomatics, until recent research and application projects. Diplomatics, despite its value in formulating some precision about records, poses additional problems of superimposing another layer of professional language on already jargon-laden interdisciplinary issues. The problem with the language of diplomatics is that it fits into a traditional concept of records/archives that may or may not be relevant to what is going on in modern organizations. Archivists and records managers need to be concerned with how to ensure that records are maintained that are relevant to the creator, not with confusing them by using a needlessly complicated or arcane language. The recent efforts to use diplomatics adopt it as the defining aspect of archival science, see it as a part of a static or rigid archival theory (theory and knowledge can and must evolve as we learn and apply it to new circumstances), and characterize it as something that systems designers need to take into account as part of their own knowledge (which seems unlikely).

The warrant idea, seeking the endorsement of various professionals' literature and professional best practices for records management, supports the various elements of the functional requirements and relates to the idea of a "compliant" organization—the latter a key component of the recordkeeping functional requirements. Other aspects of the concept of a record emerged from the project. Records as evidence of transactions supported both by historical understanding of traditional archives and records management literature and by the use of the warrant surfaced as an extremely workable notion of what a record is, even in the modern Information Age office. This highlighted the fundamental differences between records and information as viewed in definitions of various information profession literatures. Evidence provides an important, practical means by which to define recordkeeping functional requirements, and it has other possible benefits for other archival functions such as appraisal and descriptive standards. Instead of elaborate and highly subjective schemes to describe content, this emphasis on the record's evidence (that is, the evidence of a transaction that the record captures) provides a means by which to focus on such aspects as the record's origins in compliant regulations and the record's functions and reflection of activities. The idea of evidence and a compliant organization are crucial to the recordkeeping functional requirements use. It also means that the archivist/ records manager is seeking aspects of compliance (helping organizations discover external regulations) and applying them to their own organization rather than merely seeking to save old records for often difficult-to-define historical purposes and values.

Working on developing a precise definition of a record shows how *far* from records both archivists and records managers had wandered. Archivists stressed the cultural or historical role, while records managers shifted to the information side. Both shifts have taken records professionals far from describing meaningfully their mission and activities in modern society. Records need to be the focus, as the source of evidence of the work of organizations and individuals and for purposes of corporate memory and accountability. In other words, records provide both essential information and, in some cases, even a historical/ cultural/symbolic source. Both archivists and records managers need to stop feeling apologetic about their focus on records in the Information Age.

Developing the concept of a warrant for the recordkeeping functional requirements also provides a new mission. The warrant drives records professionals to cite external regulations, legislation, and best practice as the primary mandate for the management of recordkeeping systems, rather than a more vaguely defined argument for the historic value for records. This focus makes archivists shift their attention from looking through closets for old files to becoming the experts on why records should be managed by any institution and for society. This focus also moves records managers away from running records warehouses to advocating throughout their institution (and the society) why records need to be carefully managed by all professionals, technicians, and clerks. Records should not become a symbol for antiquated, bureaucratic organizations, as some tend to suggest, but they need to be viewed as vital to the organization and society. Archivists and records managers need to be experts in records and recordkeeping systems.

CONCLUSION: STEERING, NOT ROWING

The recent research projects are part of the records professions' re-discovery of the record. Australian archival educator Sue McKemmish suggests that this re-discovery is akin to assuming a better steering role for the archival profession.[112] Policy, the subject of this book, is a form of steering. Records professionals can establish recordkeeping regimes with the ability to capture, manage, and deliver evidence through time, nurturing the recordkeeping culture. Archivists can better specify what to capture as evidence and how long to keep it, with appropriate maintenance (preservation) strategies. It provides the substance of what constitutes their guidance.

Such projects also have implications for the new partners that archivists and records managers have long discussed as needed for their ability to maintain records in the modern office. Archivists and records managers need to ally with policy makers, business analysts, information technology standards setters, information technology designers and software engineers, the information brokers establishing themselves in the wild new world of deregulated information resources management, and accountability agents. Records professionals not only have new allies but they need to develop creative strategies to implement new tactics. Again, as McKemmish and her Australian colleagues suggest, archivists and records managers need to influence, educate, negotiate, monitor, and solve problems. This is very different from the more passive archival role suggested by modern interpretations of earlier writings by archival pioneers such as Jenkinson and Schellenberg or their modern followers; neither Jenkinson nor Schellenberg, whose careers spanned from the First World War into the 1960s, foresaw the challenges of new recordkeeping technologies. These pioneers provided a useful orientation to the nature of records and recordkeeping systems, but they did not answer all the troubling questions or resolve all the perplexing problems. Armed with a more precise definition of record, a definition which can serve as the foundation for delineating recordkeeping systems and be expanded and revised as necessary, archivists and records managers can reject their traditional passivity, in both their own institutions and in the larger society. Records professionals can step beyond orthodox or rigid theoretical concepts to deal with the specific challenges of the twenty-first century organization and society. Records professionals have something to say, and it is too important to be lost in old ideas and practices looking backwards.

NOTES

1. For example, Tom Nesmith, reviewing a book on the subject of records, states that the idea that "documents made or received in the course of affairs and preserved" is not adequate. Nesmith argues, "A record is an evolving mediation of understanding about some phenomena—a mediation created by social and technical processes of inscription, transmission, and contextualization." See Tom Nesmith, "Still Fuzzy, but More Accurate: Some Thoughts on the 'Ghosts' of Archival Theory," *Archivaria* 47 (Spring 1999): 136–150 (quotation p. 145).

2. Bruce W. Dearstyne, *The Archival Enterprise: Modern Archival Principles, Practices, and Management Techniques* (Chicago: American Library Association, 1993), p. 1.

3. See a similar definition in Mary F. Robek, Gerald F. Brown, and Wilmer O. Maedke, *Information and Records Management*, 3rd ed. (Encino, CA: Glencoe Publishing Co., 1987), p. 4.

4. Luciana Duranti, "Diplomatics: New Uses for an Old Science," *Archivaria* 28 (Summer 1989): 15.

5. Albertine Gaur, *A History of Writing*, rev. ed. (New York: Cross River Press, 1992), p. 14.

6. Charles M. Dollar, *Archival Theory and Information Technologies: The Impact of Information Technologies on Archival Principles and Methods* (Macerata, Italy: University of Macerata, 1992), pp. 45–49.

7. Edwin Southern, "The Document and the Computer: The Historian's Sources and the Cultural Context of Automation," *Carolina Comments* 41 (March 1993): 56.

8. See Trevor Livelton, *Archival Theory, Records, and the Public* (Lanham, MD: The Society of American Archivists and the Scarecrow Press, 1996). This study is interesting for what it reveals about the nature and limitations of archival knowledge, but it does not intend to be of any particular help in resolving issues of records or archives management. If anything, Livelton's book suggests that much more work needs to be done, such as making technology usage consistent or challenging records professionals to re-examine their assumptions. Where I differ with Livelton is what I deem to be the essential task of re-focusing records creators on the importance of records without confusing them with elaborate, abstract, or highly theoretical definitions.

9. Angelika Menne-Haritz, "The Impact of Convergence on the Life Cycle of Records," in *Management of Recorded Information: Converging Disciplines*, ed. Cynthia J. Durance (New York: K. G. Saur, 1990), pp. 123–124.

10. The Horton definition is in his *Information Resources Management: Harnessing Information Assets for Productivity Gains in the Office, Factory, and Laboratory* (Englewood Cliffs, NJ: Prentice-Hall, 1985), pp. 23–25. While Horton considers all the elements and functions long associated with records and archives management, others have written definitions that are hard to relate to such concerns. Another "IRM" book contains this definition of a record: "A logical and/or physical collection of one or more data elements. A logical record is constructed through a process called 'normalization.' A 'basic grouping' of data elements is used as the selection criteria for building records"; Milt and Tim Bryce, *The IRM Revolution: Blueprint for the 21st Century* (Palm Harbor, FL: MBA Publications, 1988), p. 228. This is a definition perhaps useful for developing an information system, but it is hardly helpful for distinguishing records with research, legal, fiscal, and administrative uses—in other words, it is not helpful for designing a records management system.

11. Glenda Acland, "Managing the Record Rather Than the Relic," *Archives and Manuscripts* 20, no. 1 (1992): 58.

12. See, for example, Jonathan Wallace and Mark Mangan, *Sex, Laws, and Cyberspace: Freedom and Censorship on the Frontiers of the Online Revolution* (New York: Henry Holt and Co., 1997) and Brian Kahin and Charles Nelson, eds., *Borders in Cyberspace: Information Policy and the Global Information Infrastructure* (Cambridge, MA: MIT Press, 1997).

13. U.S. Court of Appeals for the District of Columbia Circuit, *Scott Armstrong, et al., v. Executive Office of the President, Office of Administration, et al.*, August 13, 1993, no. 93–5002, pp. 4 and 19.

14. S. Muller, J. A. Feith, and R. Fruin, *Manual for the Arrangement and Description of Archives*, trans. Arthur H. Leavitt (New York: H. W. Wilson, 1968; orig. 1898).

15. Hilary Jenkinson, *A Manual of Archive Administration* (London: Percy Lund, Humphries and Co., Ltd., 1966; orig. 1922), pp. 2–15.

16. *Norton on Archives: The Writings of Margaret Cross Norton on Archival and Records Management*, ed. Thornton W. Mitchell (Carbondale: Southern Illinois University Press, 1975), p. 13.

17. T. R. Schellenberg, *Modern Archives: Principles and Techniques* (Chicago: University of Chicago Press, 1956), p. 16.

18. Livelton, *Archival Theory*, pp. 60–63, demonstrates the problems, and he moves to the use of the term "document" as more precisely defined in diplomatics. The problem is, of course, that "document" carries many meanings for other information professionals.

19. Frank Upward, "The Significance of Bearman's 'Simple Shared Goal' for Aus-

tralian Records Managers," in *Archival Documents: Providing Accountability Through Recordkeeping*, ed. Sue McKemmish and Frank Upward (Melbourne: Ancora Press, 1993), pp. 237–238.

20. Jenkinson, *A Manual of Archive Administration*, p. 11.

21. Veronica Davies, "Records Management or Information Management?" in *Management Skills for the Information Manager*, ed. Ann Lawes (Aldershot, England: Ashgate, 1993), p. 137.

22. John A. Barry, *Technobabble* (Cambridge, MA: MIT Press, 1991), pp. 4–5.

23. Charles Tupper and Richard Yevich, "Gone but Not Forgotten," *Database Programming and Design* 6 (November 1993): 33.

24. Tupper and Yevich, "Gone but Not Forgotten," p. 33.

25. Mitzi Waltz, "How Long Will Your Data Archives Last?" *Macweek* 6 (April 6, 1992): 32.

26. Eric J. Adams, "Storage Strategies," *Publish* 7 (April 1, 1992): 74.

27. Barry Sobel, "The Art of Archiving," *DEC Professional* 12 (February 1993): 56.

28. Mark Brownstein, "Document Management Software," *Info World* (July 6, 1992), pp. 66–67, 70–71, 74–75, 78–79, 82–84.

29. Such as the Arc program by System Enhancement Associates and UIS-Archive by UIS Inc. Steve Gibson, "Archiving Utilities Provide Valuable Space-Saving Functions," *Info World* 13 (May 8, 1991): 34; Sobel, "The Art of Archiving," pp. 56, 58, 60, 62–63.

30. Examples of such textbooks are Bartow Hodge, Robert A. Fleck, Jr., and C. Brian Honess, *Management Information Systems* (Reston, VA: Reston Publishing Co., 1984); Donald W. Kroeber and Hugh J. Watson, *Computer-Based Information Systems: A Management Approach*, 2nd ed. (New York: Macmillan Publishing Co., 1987); George W. Reynolds, *Information Systems for Managers* (St. Paul, MN: West Publishing Company, 1988); David Kroenke, *Management Information Systems* (Santa Cruz, CA: Mitchell Publishing, 1989); James I. Cash, Jr., F. Warren McFarlan, James L. McKenney, and Lynda M. Applegate, *Corporate Information Systems Management: Text and Cases*, 3rd ed. (Homewood, IL: Irwin, 1992).

31. John Burch and Gary Grudnitski, *Information Systems: Theory and Practice*, 5th ed. (New York: John Wiley and Sons, 1989), p. 869.

32. James F. Courtney, Jr. and David B. Paradice, *Database Systems for Management* (Homewood, IL: Irwin, 1992), p. 535.

33. Raymond McLeod, Jr., *Management Information Systems: A Study of Computer-Based Information Systems*, 5th ed. (New York: Macmillan Publishing Co., 1993), p. 317.

34. McLeod, *Management Information Systems*, pp. 779, 794.

35. Henry C. Lucas, Jr., *Information Systems Concepts for Management*, 4th ed. (New York: McGraw-Hill, 1990), p. 516. See also his *The Analysis, Design, and Implementation of Information Systems*, 4th ed. (New York: McGraw-Hill, 1992) with his definition that a "file is a collection of data. A computer file is organized in some way; there is some well-defined structure to the information in the file. A computer file consists of a collection of records, each of which is made up of fields" (p. 188).

36. "Integrating Information Carriers," *Records and Retrieval Report* 4 (March 1988): 3.

37. Patricia A. Riedman, "Sales from the Crypt," *Advertising Age* 62 (August 5, 1991): 16–17.

38. Robert M. Finehout, "Treasure It, Don't Trash It," *Public Relations Journal* 42 (April 1986): 8.

39. "Uncovering R. J. Reynolds' Past," *Management Review* 72 (August 1983): 44.

40. J. Wesley Miller, "The Wealth of Insurance Archives," *Journal of American Society of CLU and ChFC* 42 (May 1988): 82.

41. John Thackray, "Where Memory Serves," *Across the Board* 28 (July–August 1991): 44.

42. James D. Monteleone, "Your Bank's Archives May Be Valuable," *Banker's Magazine* 166 (January–February 1983): 69.

43. Douglas Finlay, "Archives: Old Records Meet New Technologies," *Administrative Management* 47 (December 1986): 40.

44. Robert Hindel, "Archiving Radiological Images on WORM Optical Storage," *Optical Information Systems* 10 (May–June 1990): 131–139.

45. Robert J. Salgado, "In-house and Dial-up Photo Archives," *Editor and Publisher* 126 (February 20, 1993): 16, 26.

46. Keith Kuns and Thomas Jarrett, "Mortgage Information Retrieval: Sorting Through Archives of Software," *Mortgage Banking* 47 (April 1987): 18.

47. Curtis Simmonds, "Searching Internet Archive Sites with Archie: Why, What, Where, and How," *Online* 17 (March 1993): 50–55; Flavio Bonifacio, "A Comparison of Archives Held by Three Host Computers: DIALOG, ESA-IRS and DATA-STAR," *Online Review* 16 (August 1992): 207–233.

48. Dennis Eskow, "Lawyers Warn: Don't Back Up Your E-Mail," *PC Week* 6 (September 11, 1989): 81.

49. Jim Rosenberg, "Enduring Data—Disappearing Pictures," *Editor and Publisher*, May 4, 1991, p. 86.

50. Arnita A. Jones and Philip L. Cantelon, eds., *Corporate Archives and History: Making the Past Work* (Malabar, FL: Krieger Publishing Co., 1993).

51. From the introduction by Donn Neal in Jones and Cantelon, *Corporate Archives and History*, pp. ix–x.

52. Roland Marchand, "Cultural History from Corporate Archives," *Public Relations Review* 16 (Fall 1990): 105.

53. Alex Markels, "The Messy Business of Culling Company Files," *Wall Street Journal*, May 22, 1997.

54. Perrin Stryker, "Money in the Wastebasket," *Fortune* (January 1953), 144–145, 156, 158, 160, 162, 167.

55. Kurt Eichenwald, "On Tape, Officials of Texaco Discuss Obstruction of Lawsuit," November 4, 1996; the quotation is from Sharon Walsh, "Experts Say Texaco Case Points Up How Shredders Can Come Back to Haunt Companies," *Washington Post*, January 26, 1997, p. HO1.

56. Leslie Scism, "Prudential Tried to Destroy Papers, Lawyer Alleges," *Wall Street Journal*, October 7, 1997, p. B10.

57. Greg Steinmetz, "Financial Fracas; German Tax Collectors Rile Country's Banks with Aggressive Raids They Say the Institutions Help Customers Cheat; Few Charges Are Filed," *Wall Street Journal*, December 4, 1996, p. A1.

58. Candace Floyd, "The Historian in the Gray Flannel Suit," *History News* 39, no. 5 (May 1984): 6–10.

59. Kevin McManus, "A Few Heritage-Minded Companies Turn to Archivists to Preserve and Present Their Past," *Washington Post*, May 27, 1996, p. F5.

60. George David Smith and Laurence E. Steadman, "Present Value of Corporate History," *Harvard Business Review* 57 (November–December 1981): 164–173.

61. "Business History for the Businessman," *Harvard Business Review* 37 (May–June 1961): 33.

62. Donald S. Skupsky, "Establishing Retention Periods for Electronic Records," *Records Management Quarterly* 27 (April 1993): 40ff.

63. Nina M. Johnson and Norman F. Kallaus, *Records Management: A Collegiate Course in Filing Systems and Procedures* (Cincinnati: South-Western Publishing Co., 1967), p. 286.

64. William Benedon, *Records Management* (Los Angeles: Trident Shop, 1969), pp. 120–124.

65. Irene Place and David J. Hyslop, *Records Management: Controlling Business Information* (Reston, VA: Reston Publishing Co., 1982), p. 269.

66. See, for example, Milburn D. Smith III, *Information and Records Management: A Decision-Maker's Guide to Systems Planning and Implementation* (Westport, CT: Quorum Books, 1986) and Patricia E. Wallace, Dexter R. Schubert, Jo Ann Lee, and Violet S. Thomas, *Records Management: Integrated Information Systems*, 2nd ed. (New York: John Wiley and Sons, 1987).

67. Terry D. Lundgren and Carol A. Lundgren, *Records Management in the Computer Age* (Boston: PWS-Kent Publishing Co., 1989), p. 153.

68. Jay Atherton, "From Life Cycle to Continuum: Some Thoughts on the Records Management–Archives Relationship," *Archivaria* 21 (Winter 1985–1986): 47.

69. Atherton, "From Life Cycle to Continuum," p. 48.

70. Atherton, "From Life Cycle to Continuum," p. 49.

71. Robek, Brown, and Maedke, *Information and Records Management*, p. 403.

72. T. M. Campbell, "Archives and Information Management," *Archivaria* 28 (Summer 1989): 148.

73. C. Peter Waegemann, "Records Management Policy," *Records and Retrieval Report* 5 (May 1989): 5.

74. Monique Attinger, "Integrated Information Management," *Records and Retrieval Report* 8 (January 1992): 4.

75. Richard J. Cox, "International Perspectives on the Image of Archivists and Archives: Coverage by *The New York Times*, 1992–1993," *International Information and Library Review* 25 (1993): 195–231. See Chapter 4 for the incorporation of this essay into a larger discourse on records professionals and advocacy.

76. David Gracy, "Archivists, You Are What People Think You Keep," *American Archivist* 52 (Winter 1989): 72–78.

77. See, for example, Marjorie Rabe Barrett, "Adopting and Adapting Records Management in American Colleges and University Archives," *Midwestern Archivist* 14, no. 1 (1988): 5–12; Patricia Bartkowski, "Records Management and the Walking Archivist," in *A Modern Archives Reader: Basic Readings on Archival Theory and Practice*, ed. Maygene F. Daniels and Timothy Walch (Washington, DC: National Archives and Records Service, 1984), pp. 38–45; and John Dojka and Sheila Conneen, "Records Management as an Appraisal Tool in College and University Libraries," in *Archival Choices: Managing the Historical Record in an Age of Abundance*, ed. Nancy Peace (Lexington, MA: Lexington Books, 1984), pp. 19–40.

78. Richard M. Kesner, *Information Systems: A Strategic Approach to Archives and Records Management* (Chicago: American Library Association, 1988).

79. Attinger, "Integrated Information Management," p. 10.

80. James C. Bennett, "Curriculum Priorities for Records Management," *Business Education Forum* 40 (March 1985): 34–37.

81. Janet F. Laribee, "Building a Stronger IRM Curriculum," *Information Systems Management* 9 (Spring 1992): 22–28.

82. Robert Sanders, "Archivists and Records Managers: Another Marriage in Trouble?" *Records Management Quarterly* 23 (April 1989): 12–14, 16–18, 20.

83. Quoted in Frederick J. Stielow, "Continuing Education and Information Management: Or, the Monk's Dilemma," *Provenance* 3 (Spring 1985): 14.

84. Witold Rybczynski, *Taming the Tiger: The Struggle to Control Technology* (New York: Penguin Books, 1983), pp. 164–165.

85. Adrian Cunningham, "The Archival Management of Personal Records in Electronic Form: Some Suggestions," *Archives and Manuscripts* 22 (May 1994): 94–105.

86. Richard C. Berner, *Archival Theory and Practice in the United States: A Historical Analysis* (Seattle: University of Washington Press, 1983).

87. Teresa Thompson, "Ecumenical Records and Documentation Strategy: Applying 'Total Archives,' " *Archivaria* 30 (Summer 1990): 104–109.

88. David Gracy, *Archives and Manuscripts: Arrangement and Description*, Basic Manual Series (Chicago: Society of American Archivists, 1977), p. 3.

89. Gracy, *Archives and Manuscripts*, p. 3.

90. Jenkinson, *Manual of Archive Administration*, p. 68.

91. Terry Cook, "Electronic Records, Paper Minds: The Revolution in Information Management and Archives in the Post-Custodial and Post-Modernist Era," *Archives and Manuscripts* 22 (November 1994): 300–328.

92. W. Boyd Rayward, "Electronic Information and the Functional Integration of Libraries, Museums, and Archives," in *Electronic Information Resources and Historians: European Perspectives*, ed. Seamus Ross and Edward Higgs (St. Katharinen: Scripta Mercaturae Verlag, 1993), pp. 227–243 (quotation p. 233).

93. Michael Buckland, *Information and Information Systems* (New York: Praeger, 1991), p. 93.

94. Buckland, *Information and Information Systems*, p. 57.

95. Mark Brogan, "Regulation and the Market: A Micro-Economic Analysis of Strategies for Electronic Archives Management," *Archives and Manuscripts* 22 (November 1994): 384–394.

96. David Roberts, "Defining Electronic Records, Documents and Data," *Archives and Manuscripts* 22 (May 1994): 18.

97. See, for example, Werner Muensterberger, *Collecting: An Unruly Passion; Psychological Perspectives* (Princeton, NJ: Princeton University Press, 1994); John Elsner and Roger Cardinal, eds., *The Cultures of Collecting* (Cambridge, MA: Harvard University Press, 1994); and Phyllis Mauch Messenger, ed., *The Ethics of Collecting Cultural Property: Whose Culture? Whose Property?* (Albuquerque: University of New Mexico Press, 1989).

98. Conor Cruise O'Brien, *On the Eve of the Millennium: The Future of Democracy Through an Age of Unreason* (New York: Free Press, 1994), pp. 111–112.

99. James Atlas, *Battle of the Books: The Curriculum Debate in America* (New York: W.W. Norton, 1990), p. 119.

100. Lester J. Cappon, "Historical Manuscripts as Archives: Some Definitions and Their Application," *American Archivist* 19 (April 1956): 103.

101. T. R. Schellenberg, *The Management of Archives* (New York: Columbia University Press, 1965).

102. Canadian Working Group on Archival Descriptive Standards, *Toward Descriptive Standards* (Ottawa: Bureau of Canadian Archivists, December 1985), pp. 63–64.

103. For the best debate on the idea of metadata see the three essays in the Spring 1995 issue of *Archivaria* by David Wallace, Heather MacNeil, and Wendy Duff (especially that by Duff).

104. See Duranti's "Diplomatics: New Uses for an Old Science," published in six parts starting in *Archivaria* 28 (Summer 1989) and also in a revised volume published by the Society of American Archivists and Scarecrow Press.

105. Paul Krill, "Overcoming Information Overload," *InfoWorld*, 7, January 2000, http://www.infoworld.com/articles/ca/xml/00/01/10/000110caoverload.xml, provides a typical perspective. Accessed January 15, 2000.

106. The National Historical Publications and Records Commission funded the project as "Variables in the Satisfaction of Archival Requirements for Electronic Records Management," NHPRC Grant No. 93–030. The project was co-directed by James Williams and Richard J. Cox. Other key members of the research team included Ken Sochats, David Bearman, Wendy Duff, and Kimberly Barata.

107. This project emerged from the 1991 NHPRC-sponsored Electronic Records Research Agenda, which originally identified three research projects that would "define the requirements of archival electronic records programs; explore the conceptual, economic, and technological constraints on the long-term retention of electronic records; and establish criteria against which to measure the effectiveness of policies, methods, and programs." The research agenda was published as *Research Issues in Electronic Records* (St. Paul: Published for the National Historical Publications and Records Commission by the Minnesota Historical Society, 1991). In addition to the research agenda, refer to Margaret Hedstrom, "Understanding Electronic Incunabula: A Framework for Research on Electronic Records," *American Archivist* 54 (Summer 1991): 334–355.

108. Work continues on the efforts by the International Organization for Standardization to set an international standard for records management (ISO15489), based on an Australian records management standard. The proposed standard, available in January 2000 at http://www.archivists.org.au/council/recmandraft.html, describes general records management purposes and principles, the characteristics of a record, the regulatory environment for records, the elements of records management policies, strategies for managing records, and records management operations.

109. James M. O'Toole, *Understanding Archives and Manuscripts*, Archival Fundamental Series (Chicago: Society of American Archivists, 1990), p. 9.

110. As the recordkeeping functional requirements were initially developed, production rules, using horn or "if-then" clauses (a process used by artificial intelligence experts), were developed. These make the recordkeeping functional requirements unambiguous, precise, economical, provable, and expandable; the requirements can now be translated into a software algorithm. The recordkeeping functional requirements become observable and measurable to the degree that the requirements can be used by software engineers to develop systems that incorporate the requirements and, hence, enable records as defined by these requirements to be maintained in such systems.

111. This work led to how the notion of the functional requirements could be recast as a useful standard. The Metadata Model for Business Acceptable Communications emerged through the work of consultant David Bearman. A software independent record

or a metadata encapsulated object, potentially eliminating the need for costly and complicated migration strategies, was suggested with layers termed handle, terms and conditions, structure, context, content, and use history. The metadata concept is the best reflection of the essence of a record with its characteristics of structure, content, and context. This notion of a record is a digital envelope with contextual metadata surrounding the information content of an electronic transaction; this has the potential either to encapsulate the content or to provide required linkages to the content of a record. Much work needs to be done with this model or potential standard.

112. This is based on talks presented by McKemmish and her Monash colleague Frank Upward. Some of their earlier thoughts on the nature of records and recordkeeping can be seen in McKemmish and Upward, eds., *Archival Documents* and Sue McKemmish and Michael Piggott, eds., *The Records Continuum: Ian Maclean and Australian Archives First Fifty Years* (Melbourne: Ancora Press, 1994).

Chapter 2

Driving Policy: Focusing on Records, Not Technology

INTRODUCTION

The management of records has always been closely connected with the technologies of records creating and maintaining, from the humble pencil to the mighty personal computer. Every time there has been a major shift in technology, there has been a period of adjusting and the proposing of technical solutions to ensure viable records. The past thirty years of electronic information technology reveals a more pervasive concern about the future of records and their management. This chapter examines the importance of records, how records professionals need to approach computer literacy, and the impact of organizational change wrought by the new technologies. The response by records professionals to these issues has often been inadequate or over-reactive. This chapter strives to right the boat somewhat, demonstrating how these technologies provide opportunities for a new level of records management and for a new significance for archivists and records managers within organizations and society.

WHY RECORDS ARE IMPORTANT IN THE INFORMATION AGE

Robert Wright, in his interesting book about science, information, and metaphysics, comments: "The information age has made human society more comprehensible in principle and more inscrutable in practice, clearer from afar and murkier up close."[1] Likewise, the Information Age has helped records professionals better define themselves conceptually, but it has also caused them to lose sight of some of their responsibilities. Records professionals need to move away from thinking of records as only clerical or historical functions to understanding records as critical assets to both organization and society.

Individuals seeking to design optimum office systems have often resorted to studying how offices work by observing behavior and tracking processes.[2] This is testimony that records are real things, the results of real activities, and not something to be imagined or re-imagined in the modern Information Age. Records exist because of mandates and needs to do things, and they result as the normal products of business and other work—and it has been that way for a *very* long time. Office workers seeking to order their records are not doing it for their amusement, but they are doing it because they are required to do so or for the practical use of their records. While modern technologies provide the opportunity for us to do many interesting things, these same technologies do not mean that records professionals have to start over with what they have long been responsible to do and support. The developments of the late twentieth century only mean that records professionals have new opportunities for success, that they have to be more innovative than they have been, and that they have to work harder to position themselves to accomplish their objectives.

Many have written about the negative and positive aspects of computers in our lives, so diverse in perspective that it would be possible to build extensive personal libraries focused only on one way or another of looking at the various dimensions of the modern Information Age.[3] Records professionals must evaluate just what they are giving up as they work in the modern information environments. Records have a historic and continuing importance to our institutions and us. Meanwhile we need to remember what computers represent, as Fred Moody recently stated: "For all of its apparently miraculous powers, the personal computer is little more than a mathematical jukebox, a Wurlitzer of digits. . . . The computer, then, is a high-speed simpleton. . . . The story of the personal computer revolution is the story of humankind's success in coping with the computer's shortcomings."[4] We need to make computers do what our organizations and society need them to do, and one of those things is create and maintain records because records continue to serve a useful role in society and because their creation and maintenance are mandated. Records professionals need to guide how records systems are designed and how these systems maintain, allow use of, or enable destruction of records at critical points.

The computer has woven itself into every aspect of society. The computer has largely disappeared, for much of society, as an obstacle to overcome or a tool to master. Computers are in our toasters, automobiles, and in nearly every other facet of the average person's daily life. We bank by computer. We socialize by computer. Some might say we think best when in front of the computer. But we have not seen the technology woven into the records professions in quite the same fashion. Any standard textbook in these fields treats electronic recordkeeping as a *special* problem, usually discussed in a *separate* chapter. The records professions represent cultures increasingly diverging from that of our society. There is often little overlap in how records management, archival administration, and electronic records management are now discussed, despite the substantial evidence that there are few differences between these functions.[5] How can that continue, if records professionals mean to be successful in managing records? Records professionals need to accept that, for better or worse, records for every institution or even every person are moving into the electronic realm. Older, retired people, taking up computers even late in life, maintain records in electronic media, surf the Internet, and explore how to digitize older personal and family records.

Have records professionals reached the Promised Land due to the increasing sophistication of computers and electronic recordkeeping systems? Hardly. There are serious problems wrought by the computer. From the business perspective, some are questioning whether computers have made our organizations and us more productive and efficient. Then there are the side effects of computers—threats to privacy, questions of durability, the challenges of linkage, the rolling costs of updates and replacements, and the ever-present debates about the information "haves" and the information "have-nots." Many of these might be resolved in time, just as other earlier technological revolutions' side effects have been resolved. The challenge archivists and records managers most often mention is the seeming continuing reliance on paper (there is still a lot of paper visible in offices), forcing us to recognize that we are in the early stages of the computer revolution. Michael Heim writes, "In the infant stages of the computer revolution . . . very few working writers actually think of their words as residing on magnetic media in digital form. Most still continue to print out their work at all stages of composition, save hard copy drafts, and even do revisions on the hard copy and transcribe them back to the computer."[6] But this was written more than a decade ago, and much has already changed. We are moving to where the real or primary records will be kept in electronic form and paper will be a convenience copy only with minimum requirements for management.

The issue records professionals now face is to ensure that records are protected for the records creators and society. Many archivists and records managers lost sight of the record, seeing either an artifact or information. Archivists became absorbed with historical records as museum objects, and records managers with current records as items to be managed in warehouses. It is a time for rethinking such matters. For a long time archivists and records managers saw the encroaching electronic records as major challenges. The problems with information relate to source reliability, creation context and purpose, and perception. The modern Information Age raises for many technologists and policy makers issues records professionals have been discussing for generations. Records professionals need to communicate to them that this is what they are doing.

Archivists and records managers have waffled all over the place, in many cases taking themselves out of the forum for dealing with the records essential to organizations and society. Archivists have been more oriented to manuscript curatorship, focused on collecting and on the original manuscript as if the manuscript were a museum artifact. In many cases, this led to the preservation of artifacts for what information they contained. Information is what connects the archivist to the records manager. Records managers, at times, seem to have abandoned their responsibility for records in favor of information management and weakened the definition of record. This caused records professionals to lose, of course, the basic substance of a record—its evidence, transaction, structure, content, and context. The growing dependence on the computer—a literal machine—has forced records professionals to determine more precisely the functions or particular aspects that constitute a record, and this provides archivists and records managers many opportunities for influencing what organizations and society need to do in administering records.

Records professionals have long possessed a working definition of records, as Chapter 1 considers, stressing their documentation of a specific activity or transaction with a particular content (information), structure (form), and context (relationship to a creator, function, and other records). A record is a specific entity and is transaction oriented. It is evidence of activity (transaction), and that evidence can only be preserved if the record's content, structure, and context are maintained. Structure is the record form. Context is the linkage of one record to other records and to the originating process. Content is the data or information, but content without structure and context cannot be reliable data or information.

This is not a new definition. Anthropologist Jack Goody sees from the beginning the "written document served as evidence and guarantee of the legitimacy of a transaction."[7] Writing was tied into the very heart of organizations, recordkeeping, and information technologies. Nevertheless writing, communication, and records have become a more crucial concern in recent years, as seen in the PROFS case in which John Poindexter responded to Ollie North's message about his lying to Congress about the Iran-Contra dealings with "well done." "Well done" is the content, the internal structure is the form of the electronic mail message with header and other information, and the context is that the message was sent via the White House PROFS system, from the National Security Council, on a specific date. All three elements are vital to this "thing" being a record and to being a record documenting a transaction and providing evidence. The elimination of any portion of this undermines its "recordness." It would be akin to photocopying in black and white a color-coded map or microfilming in black and white a rare book with no data on binding, paper, or other dimensions of its physical structure. A re-focus on the essence of the record suggests a clearer mission helping records professionals to re-emphasize strong archival functions such as appraisal to support corporate memory, accountability, and evidence.[8]

There are some obvious choices about how a record is defined. Many definitions try to place records managers into the information professions by trying to define record around the concept of information. Information has always been a fuzzy concept, often placed on a continuum from data to information to knowledge to wisdom with definitions ranging from the biological sciences, mathematics, and psychological and behavioral disciplines.[9] Records professionals need to know the peculiar form of information found in records. Electronic records expert Margaret Hedstrom writes, "Our society inherited many of its institutions and practices for documenting human activity from the paper and print era. Records were defined as physical entities on which information is recorded as a logical structure. Although the definition of records has been expanded to encompass new media . . . the physical record and its logical structure were inextricably linked until the advent of electronic recordkeeping."[10] Canadian archivist Terry Cook adds, "For the first time in 3,000 years of records management and archival activity, we have too much rather than too little information." "For the first time," Cook continues, "we have records that do not exist to the human eye." "For the first time, we have business officers and professionals creating and storing their own records rather than relying on an army of secretaries, file clerks, and records managers to do this work for them." And, "most important, for the first time, we are not producing, managing, and saving physical things as artifacts."[11] This is why records professionals need to determine what new approaches they need, to understand the implications of new research and development, and to know what more they need to do. Records professionals need to keep in mind these words written by Langdon Winner in his cautionary tale about our attitudes toward technology: "Scarcely a new invention comes along that someone doesn't proclaim it as the salvation of a free society."[12] Computers will not free records managers and archivists from their assigned tasks, but they will make their work more difficult unless they keep their roots grounded firmly in the records business.

RESEARCHING ELECTRONIC RECORDS MANAGEMENT

During the past decade, research projects helped re-conceptualize the basic parameters of the work of records professionals. These projects assisted records professionals to communicate with the information technology and policy professionals in organizations and society. They also affirm the *importance* of records and the perspective that electronic information technology represents a tool to be harnessed. We need to remember that recordkeeping has long been tied up with technology and that technology is only a tool for supporting records and recordkeeping systems. The modern personal computers and networks are simply the latest in a long line of technologies, descending from tools designed to help manage information most normally found in records.

Most of the research projects derived from (or, at least, were influenced by) a 1991 National Historical Publications and Records Commission-sponsored research agenda on electronic records and archives. There were mistakes and omissions from this original agenda, well documented in the writings of University of Michigan faculty member Margaret Hedstrom, which are cited throughout this book, but as a whole the meeting and resulting agenda enabled records professionals to begin to deal with important topics that had been long ignored. The University of Michigan School of Information held a second research agenda meeting in June 1996 and the individuals gathered there evaluated progress made since the 1991 agenda and composed an updated research agenda.[13] The measure of good research projects in this discipline is the degree to which they focus on records and their management.

The University of Pittsburgh project to develop functional requirements for evidence in records and recordkeeping systems examined several broad issues concerning the management of electronic records, as described in the first chapter.[14]

The most important discovery (perhaps realization or re-affirmation would be the better term, since the notion of an authority for records creation and maintenance is an old idea) by this project is that there is a recordkeeping warrant. A recordkeeping warrant is the justification for a functional requirement for recordkeeping found in professional literature, standards, regulations, and best practices, all the things that control or influence the conduct of records professionals and that of the recordkeeping organizations. These warrants identify the authority on which the functional requirements are based, and they should also increase the likelihood of their acceptance and implementation within organizations. Warrants provide the language that other professionals understand, raising the better possibility of their being supportive of records management because organizations are already committed to meeting many of these standards, laws, and best practices. These sources have an authority enabling records professionals to meet their mission.[15] The University of Pittsburgh project's main accomplishment was developing functional requirements for recordkeeping for *evidence*. After being compliant (supporting the idea of warrant), the project stressed three main components of functional records—their capture, maintenance, and usability. The concept of the functional requirements and their warrant for recordkeeping has resonated in the records community, and a number of other institutions around the world have adopted, adapted, and experimented with these requirements.[16]

Another project aiding records professionals in ensuring the reliability of electronic recordkeeping systems is headquartered at the University of British Columbia School of Library, Archival, and Information Studies. It has similar goals: to establish what a record is in principle, and how it can be recognized in an electronic environment; to determine what kind of electronic systems generate records; to formulate criteria that allow for the appropriate segregation of records from all other types of information in electronic systems; and to define the conceptual requirements for guaranteeing the reliability and authenticity of records in electronic systems.[17] The primary difference between this project and the one at the University of Pittsburgh was the University of British Columbia's reliance on the archival science of diplomatics originally developed in the seventeenth and eighteenth centuries. Reliability, in this sense, refers to a record's authority and trustworthiness, and authenticity stands for a record's reliability over time and is linked to the record's status, mode, and form of transmission and the manner of its preservation and custody. Reliability and authenticity together equate record integrity. The differences are the diplomatics terminology and the emphasis on physical custody versus Pittsburgh's distributed control concept. Those involved with the Pittsburgh project believed that records professionals can control records without having physical custody of them and that the concept of physical custody is becoming obsolete in the electronic Information Age except when recordkeeping systems must be re-evaluated as a last resort. These two projects, starting from very different premises, nevertheless reflect a fairly strong consensus about a record's basic elements.

Other noteworthy projects provided considerable assistance to records professionals about the management of electronic records. The New York State Archives and Records Administration "Building Partnerships" project is probably the most comprehensive analysis of the state of affairs in electronic records management in a state government. This project found a lack of adequate or coordinated information policy, that agencies were focused on information not records systems, and that policies and procedures were inadequate for ensuring reliable records in electronic systems. It remains a useful profile of what is happening in the use of information technology for records and related matters in an organizational setting.[18] From this project evolved another effort, "Models for Action: Developing Practical Approaches to Electronic Records Management and Preservation," utilizing the recordkeeping functional requirements from both the Pittsburgh and British Columbia efforts to "to combine best practices from the domains of business process analysis, system design and development, and electronic recordkeeping and archiving to create practical tools" for electronic records management.[19] The Philadelphia Electronic Records Project was another important project, using the Pittsburgh recordkeeping functional requirements in the development of an electronic human resources recordkeeping system (among other things) and demonstrating just how practical and acceptable recordkeeping functional requirements are in real world scenarios. Its stress was on the development of one electronic recordkeeping system, that of the municipality's human resources information system, and by virtue of this effort much was learned about how well records can be created, used, and maintained in an extremely important and central function for most organizations.[20] The other significant project is the Indiana University effort. This project also tested the Pittsburgh functional requirements, which should reveal much about the practicality of the metadata. It has focused on two systems, one related to student files and the other dealing with fiscal issues, and it helps records professionals to modify the requirements necessary for revising these functional requirements.[21]

Some other efforts are worth mentioning in the context of recent research, although they represent more practical development efforts than research. The Australians formulated a records management standard that incorporates the Pittsburgh records definitions and functional requirements and, as described in the previous chapter, it has become the basis of a proposed international standard for records management.[22] The standard also builds on the Australian notion of the records continuum, suggesting records professionals are concerned with the delivery of frameworks for accountable recordkeeping regimes enabling access to essential evidence found in records for governance, accountability, corporate and collective memory, both personal and collective identity, and value-added information for new uses.[23] All of these research projects are part of a major re-thinking not just about the substance of a record, but why records are important to organizations and society.

RETHINKING WHY RECORDS ARE CREATED AND NEED TO BE MANAGED

These research initiatives lead records professionals to *why* records matter. There are many reasons why records are important, and information is only part of these reasons. Accountability could be defined in a government setting, for example, as providing evidence that government carried out its responsibilities and that its decisions, actions, and transactions are consistent with and supportive of legislation, regulation, policy, procedures, and best practices. This supports the idea of James Madison, that "If men were angels, no government was necessary."[24] Could we not also say that if people were angels, no records were necessary? Accountability systems involve a higher authority vested with power for oversight, measure or criterion used by the authority to assess compliance or performance, and some sort of explicit reporting mechanism for conveying information to the higher authority.[25] The higher authority could be the concept of warrant, the measure or criterion could be the recordkeeping functional requirements, and the reporting mechanism could be the records themselves.

Government information is crucial in a democracy. Anne Wells Branscomb believes there are four different types of government information: information necessary for citizens acting as voters; information needed for residents to comply with law; information for meeting the purpose of a particular agency; and information necessary to support critical functions that cannot be undertaken by the private sector, such as gathering census data.[26] Yet, the world is also changing rapidly in terms of its technological means and perspectives on information, suggested by Howard Rheingold's statement: "If a government is to rule according to the consent of the governed, the effectiveness of that government is heavily influenced by how much the governed know about the issues that affect them. . . . The political significance of computer-mediated communications lies in its capacity to challenge the existing political hierarchy's monopoly on powerful communications media, and perhaps revitalize citizen-based democracy."[27] If records are not factored into this, there is no way of accomplishing such purposes.

Records professionals also need to bear in mind that records are not just the products of technological achievements, but that they are the products of, or at least influenced by, a variety of social, economic, and other factors. Technology is only one factor, although its degree of importance can certainly be greater at times such as ours. Concerns about access to information and privacy about information become more important because of the rapid changes caused by the technology and our adoption of them. The reason that a concept such as re-cordkeeping requirements has become so crucial is that the increasing storage capacity and declining costs of the capacity have enabled organizations to con-sider entirely new means of communicating and documenting their activities. Why have paper records when you can have an electronic version that can be transmitted across the world in a few seconds? Why have electronic records that are only text when you can have a record with sound and image, providing the capacity for more powerful and persuasive records? Copying and transferring electronic records in a networked environment is extremely easy, making the transition to electrostatic photocopying in the 1960s look as primitive as carving messages in rock. Then again, users of the electronic systems need to know that a record is sent when it is supposed to be, that it has been effectively redacted, and that the record was received and read. Continuing misperceptions about records, as are evident in news stories concerning archives and records, make such concerns even more worrisome.

LESSONS FROM RECORDS IN THE NEWS

Archivists and records managers need a clear message and a loud voice be-cause of the many public controversies involving records, perhaps the most direct evidence of the connection of records to policy. Questions of access to records, the ownership of public records, the challenges of copyright, and even personal rights are all discussed in daily newspapers, the evening news on tel-evision, the World Wide Web, and other forums of public opinion. Just before the 1996 presidential election, the *New York Times* ran an article on the ethical issues that the Clinton-Gore administration needed to resolve. Nearly all of the eight issues concerned records.[28] But where were the records professionals? Of-ten they have no voice, nor are they visible. In the print media there are very few instances where records perspectives are *clearly* presented. The only time records professionals are discussed is when they are controversial, such as when former Archivist of the United States Don Wilson was criticized for transferring the Reagan-Bush Iran-Contra electronic records over to Bush as he left the White House. Are records professionals so dusty that they are embarrassed to come out of their stack caves? Are records professionals so preoccupied with running warehouses that they cannot look up and out of their records centers?

Sometimes the publicly aired issues indicate that the problem with the man-agement of records rests more with the problems generated by inadequate en-forcement clauses in laws and policies. On June 2, 1995, a *New York Times* editorial commented that the former governor of New York had taken his re-cords with him as he left office: "ignoring the pleas of state archivists, [the governor's] office declined to provide internal memos and other material from his files, and from the files of his top aides. . . . New Yorkers should not have to rely on the generosity of outgoing governors to know the full history of their state government."[29] The law, like that of many states, does not require the governor to turn his records over to the state government archives. Since no law was being broken here, what's the issue? The issue is that in the 1980s the New York State Archives and Records Administration emerged as the *leading* state archives and records management program in the United States and the *model* for many other archival programs. In 1975 New York finally staffed a state archives and in 1979 it opened its doors to the public—the last state to establish a formal government archives. Over the next twenty years the state archives took a number of innovative actions: undertaking an ambitious study of needs for archives and historical manuscripts management; knitting together the archives and historical manuscripts professional communities for the first time; producing several major studies on electronic records issues and creating a Center for Electronic Records; positioning itself to be a player in state information policy initiatives; taking over the dormant records management program and developing innovative new policies for making the program self-sufficient; building a strong professional staff; leading in the passage of legislation for two systems of advisory programs for local governments and historical records programs; and producing award-winning publications and videos for the management of archives and current records. So what was going on here with the governor's records? With all this success, all this leadership, why did the state archives and records administration program fail to secure the governor's records?

Government records have always challenged records professionals. A study on government and privacy states, "government is not necessarily the worst offender, but it is the single biggest collector and distributor of information about citizens. This itself increases the probability that such data may be acquired and used under questionable, if not illegal, circumstances. History is filled with instances of government taking liberties with its surveillance capability. Because bureaucracies by definition are powerful and seek to enhance their hold at every opportunity, computer technology makes it easier for our worst totalitarian tendencies to go undetected."[30] In recent years we have had to read about everything from the disclosure of records documenting secret radiation experiments in the 1950s to problems in the Clinton White House with its records.

Government is not the only subject in the daily news concerning the management of records. We also see records figure prominently in other powerful organizations and disciplines. A 1995 *New York Times* editorial states, "private medical information is being bought and sold freely by companies that have ignored a patchwork of varying state laws that have made it difficult to transfer those records across state lines."[31] The disclosure of the so-called "Cigarette Papers" and the continuing concern with the way the tobacco industry manufactures and markets cigarettes moved into a daily page one story.[32] The Mormon murders case in the mid-1980s relates even to the involvement of religious organizations in disclosing sensitive records and the forgery of records concerning the origins of this church.[33]

The culture wars and debates generated by and about post-modernist scholarship also have most often revolved about the use of records. The *Enola Gay* exhibit controversy had much to do with how historical records were being interpreted in an exhibit at the Smithsonian about the end of the Second World War and the decision to drop the atomic bomb.[34] There have been continuing debates about whether the Holocaust actually occurred, and reams of writings have emerged presenting vast amounts of evidence about the historicity of this. Ironically, the Germans and Japanese were meticulous recordkeepers producing a massive quantity of incriminating evidence, yet we have increasing evidence about how many in both Germany and Japan would like to put behind them the degree of crimes against humanity committed by their leaders just a half century ago.[35] The debates about exhibits in this country, textbook censorship, and multicultural perspectives that often raise myth and fable to an equal level with reliable historical evidence reveal that Americans are prone to the same kind of activities. Archivists and records managers' tasks are increasingly important in our current social climate, one that sometimes wants to erase the memory represented in our records and to weaken the accountability these records provide.

REMEMBERING WHY RECORDS ARE IMPORTANT TO RECORDS PROFESSIONALS

If records are important to society, then it should be obvious why records are important to the information professionals in the Information Age. Not too many years ago, Luciana Duranti reminded records professionals that the "functions of the keeper of records were regarded as being as vital to society as those of other high functionaries, and that the creation and preservation of useful and meaningful records were considered the essential foundation of a strong society."[36] As this statement suggests, there is something very important in the ancient tradition of records, implying that records professionals have to get back to basics. Records professionals are experts in recordkeeping systems, understanding the principles derived from the nature of records and recordkeeping systems and guiding the management of records.

Records professionals can be optimistic. They have ceased debating about electronic data as records and moved on to a far more invigorating debate about policy, the relevance of archival and records management principles, and, best of all, a return to what their focus should be—the record. All of the debates continue, but the primacy of the record will win out and this will cause a new type of archives and records management discipline to emerge. Just fifteen years ago, former archivist now information manager Richard Kesner wrote that "if we [archivists and records managers] do not change the way we view the purpose and nature of our performance within our parent organization, I expect that before too long we will be relegated to the antiquarian curatorial role that we have heretofore rejected as a misplaced 'popular' notion of what an archivist does for society."[37] This has not happened.

The rationale for recordkeeping requirements is quite simple. In an electronic environment records must be able to be specifically defined because that is how the computer functions. The requirements provide a template for design into electronic recordkeeping systems that enable the integrity of records to be protected as long as is necessary, and they give the archivist or records manager something understandable to say to the systems designers. The designers may not understand the importance of records or archives, but they should be able to understand the definition of a record when it is broken apart into specific requirements. If records professionals try to resist technology they will isolate themselves increasingly from the hub of society. Some say we will never have the paperless office, and there is evidence to suggest they are right; but will these paper records be anything other than convenience copies? If records professionals isolate themselves they will not meet their mission. However, if archivists and records managers see in the technology the opportunity to manage records better, they will become more important players within their organizations and society. We know that the archivist in many ancient societies had an important function, with the appropriate status, to protect the authentic records. We also know that increasingly, in articles in popular journals such as *Scientific American* and the *Atlantic Monthly*, essays are being published asking archival and other records questions.[38]

Records professionals could become Information Age pothunters, where they pillage looking for the record equivalent of treasures. Records can lose the full potential of their value in the Information Age if they are isolated from their creators, dealt with in a piecemeal fashion, and separated by format and system. For three decades archivists and records managers have viewed electronic records as a problem, when they should consider the advantages of these systems. The advantages are the potential for each transaction to capture all the information needed, easier searching and retrieving, and greater auditing capacity for each and every use. The disadvantages are mainly that many of the traditional archival and records management approaches, such as scheduling and appraisal, must be modified. The biggest challenge may be the continuing concern with migration, although paper records also have a similar problem (migrating to a digital format, then needing to migrate from there adds another level of costs).

Electronic recordkeeping transforms the archives and records management disciplines. Records managers shift from costs and reducing risks to the organization to a focus on risk management—weighing the risks in disposal or retention. The obsession with scheduling and paper warehouses shifts to a new role in recordkeeping systems design and implementation. Archives are becoming post-custodial, with more focus on a role in corporate memory and accountability via recordkeeping systems design and locator systems for records. This is a much more strategic and visible role, stressing evidence preservation, accountability, continuing access, and risk management. Recordkeeping functional requirements, both in the records systems and policies, are essential for these roles.

Records professionals need to focus on new policies for records management. They need to stress assisting the design of recordkeeping systems, not trying to deal with the results of poor systems. They need to stress recordkeeping systems monitoring instead of waiting for records to become endangered or for them to be dumped on their doorsteps. And they need to stress the development of technical standards for records in electronic recordkeeping systems that overcome some of the current problems.

These kinds of issues are not new, as historian M. T. Clanchy reminds us when he writes, "When documents produced by the king's government began to proliferate in the twelfth century, they also were accepted because, by and large, they used traditional materials and skills. The changes which were made in the technology of writing . . . went largely unnoticed by contemporaries. . . . Techniques of writing records tended to be conservative because conservation was their main purpose."[39] As this study of medieval recordkeeping and literacy also suggests, "Documents did not immediately inspire trust. . . . A modern literate tends to assume that statements in writing, especially if they are in print, are more reliable than spoken words. This assumption is the result of schooling in reading and writing from an early age and the constant use of documents, such as bills, for even the smallest transactions."[40]

Archivists and records managers have long adhered to a definition of record cutting across the recording format. Recording formats should not be obstacles for archivists and records managers, since they should be experts of recordkeeping and its technology. They should have such a substantial body of knowledge about recordkeeping systems that they can understand how a new system relates to, builds on, rejects, or challenges earlier systems. There should be no shock of the new with archivists and records managers, even if there are challenges to be met about the specifics of managing such systems. Moreover, the emergence of new recordkeeping technologies should represent opportunities for archivists and records managers, in that they can influence the more advanced systems to provide better security for the archival record and for the maintenance of records for reasons such as evidence and accountability.

There are increasing data, predictions, and concerns about social, legal, political, and other problems caused or intensified by the increasing reliance on the computer. Who will have access to the information and records? What about privacy? Are offices of the future destined to be little more than electronic sweatshops? Who owns information? These concerns suggest opportunities for individuals and professions with solutions. Solutions will be welcome, and in the case of archivists and records managers, the solutions may open up the doors for generating support for other archives and records management objectives. Furthermore, an increasingly computer-literate society will bring rising expectations about access to information, and this has the potential to win new allies from the public and policy makers. Think of it in this fashion: archives have often been viewed as convenient trash cans to send old records, while many records management programs are seen as little more than warehouses for paper records. The changing nature in which society and organizations use records will force different roles and different expectations. It also means that every archival function will be up for grabs, and this should provide the opportunity to try new strategies with better chances for success. Records professionals might be able to gain more information about users, or they might be able to try a new appraisal approach with more objective and strategic criteria. Again, this will be for records professionals to decide and to convince others. Archival programs will also have the opportunity to be transformed—from custodial operations to programs with responsibilities for policies, procedures, and gatekeeping. The opportunity will be to cease viewing records as artifacts and to see them as dynamic, vital sources for administration and other purposes.

Records professionals cannot rely on predictions of technological solutions. As Thomas Landauer suggests, "In the 1960s it was predicted that within ten years computers would convert ordinary speech and handwriting to print, comprehend and compose natural language, drive trucks, do housework, and tutor students better than professors could. Thirty years later many proponents see no reason to change these predictions; they still expect them within ten years."[41] Some of these predictions became truly fantastic, as technology critic Mark Slouka writes: "We . . . need to see two things very clearly . . . : first, that the computer—no longer just an information processor—was rapidly developing into a sort of deluxe copying machine, increasingly capable of imitating certain aspects of our lives; and second, that a large number of very smart, very influential people believed that this computer copy should, and eventually would, replace the original it imitated."[42] A focus on the record should help records professionals to eliminate such problems. At the least, it helps records professionals to re-think the notion of what computer literacy means to them.

COMPUTER LITERACY AND RECORDS PROFESSIONALS

Scientist John Shore starts his popular book about computers by writing, "User-friendly is likely to go down as the advertising talisman of the 1980s, and its prevalence may make you wonder why anyone but the technologically curious still needs a book about computers."[43] Later, Shore reassures the reader with a message with which we have become accustomed: "The history of technology abounds with devices that have become progressively easier to use. Cars, radios, and computers are all good examples. As part of the progression, various control functions are automated, less technical knowledge is required of the user, and less technical information is presented to the user."[44] Shore's pronouncement might suggest to some records professionals that the issue of computer literacy will resolve itself. The language will become easier to use, the technology will become more accessible. Actually, all of this is likely true, except for one matter: since computers are increasingly the devices creating and maintaining records and recordkeeping systems, archivists and records managers must learn something about the language that drives these systems in order to be able to understand the continued evolving of recordkeeping.

But *what* is that "something"? Although people like journalist Fred Moody describe the personal computer as a "high-speed simpleton," the way in which computers and software are designed and implemented is not necessarily a simple process to understand or to influence. The difficulty of the design of one software product, as described by Moody, illustrates the challenges of using the computer. That being computer literate may require little more than the ability to know word processing, be able to type, and keeping up with software products, as Thomas Landauer suggests, is still not sufficient for records managers and archivists who must be able to evaluate electronic recordkeeping systems from an array of technical, economic, organizational, and social perspectives.[45]

Computer literacy requires a core understanding of how a particular technology works so that records professionals can approach the system and its designers or managers to ensure that the systems support records. Furthermore, records managers and archivists must learn from their own past experiences, and these suggest that information policy, professional credentials, professional image, and the archival or records management mission and its viability still will not resolve the effective management of electronic records *if* records professionals are not able to work with the designers and other technical people supporting the electronic recordkeeping systems.

What do we mean by computer literacy? Jonathan Kozol's captures the essence of the problem when he writes, "there will at length be no more places for all but the very privileged to hide," referring to those who are illiterate. There now seems to be no place for the archivist or records manager to hide from the computer and the need to understand it. Kozol adds that the illiterates "live in a truncated present tense. The future seems hopeless. The past remains unknown."[46] Might the same also be stated about the archivists and records managers who are computer illiterate? They have no hope of coping with modern information systems. They translate solutions to working with modern information systems into traditional paper-based approaches, such as printing out electronic records—a solution that is certainly a type of "truncated present tense." These archivists and records managers prefer to work with paper records, despite the immense difficulties posed by these records and the increasing reliance on electronic recordkeeping systems that are not designed to produce anything but electronic records. In some instances, these records managers and archivists will invent, often in very creative fashion, ways of ignoring the use of technology; I can't manage my *own* electronic mail so how can I administer the electronic messages of my organization?

There is something mysterious about this. The problems posed by paper recordkeeping systems (their bulk, ease of misfiles, deterioration due to poor paper quality, costs of storage, and easy destruction), discussed by modern archivists and records managers for half a century before the advent of the computer, tend to be conveniently forgotten in discussions about the new electronic record-keeping systems. The challenges of one system are no more horrendous than those posed by the other *except* that there is the need to re-evaluate records approaches and records professions' education and knowledge. In other words, the primary difficulty is in facing the change. Another challenge is in understanding the different problems posed by the transition to electronic record-keeping systems, such as the threats of misinformation and to privacy. Kozol's analysis of another kind of literacy suggests that records managers and archivists need to be able to "read" computers because computers are increasingly the forum for the creation of records and the maintenance of recordkeeping systems. However, what does it mean to be able to understand or use computers? Once again, what does it mean for the records professional to be computer literate?

A topic like computer literacy is risky because it has a soft meaning. There is the literal computer language, usually utilized by technologists in order to empower networks. Vinton Cerf writes that, "one prerequisite to any successful form of communications is the choice of a common language. In computer networking, it is essential that the communicating programs share conventions for representing the information in digital form and procedures for coordinating communication paths. Like their human counterparts, communicating computers must agree on ground rules for interaction."[47] Here is one form of computer literacy.

Another aspect of computer literacy is the public's ability to use computers in a meaningful fashion. Mark Weisner, believing computer technology will become ubiquitous and seamless in society, argues that computers will bring people together: "people holed up in windowless offices before glowing computer screens may not see their fellows for the better part of each day. . . . Ubiquitous computers, in contrast, reside in the human world and pose no barrier to personal interactions. If anything, the transparent connections that they offer between different locations and times may tend to bring communities closer together."[48] This provides a sense of a fundamental shift in the computer culture from technical programming skills to the abilities to use software effectively and imaginatively.

In this latter sense of computer literacy, there is a clearer idea of obstacles to be overcome by archivists, records managers, and others managing electronic recordkeeping systems. Cultural critic Wendell Berry, skewering the demise of education to mere commercial utility, captures some of the issues: "Literacy does not involve knowing the meanings of words, of learning grammar, or reading books." Rather, there is something to be understood. "The sign of exceptionally smart people is that they speak a language that is intelligible only to other people in their 'field' or only to themselves. This is very impressive and is known as 'professionalism.' " It is easy to obscure what the real meaning of literacy is about if it is used as a wall in some sort of medieval trade guild. "Computers make people even better and smarter than they were made by previous thingamabobs. Or if some people prove incorrigibly wicked or stupid or both, computers will at least speed them up."[49] The goal for the records professional to understand computers is not to join a secret club but to be able to manage the record with various kinds of values despite *whatever* form it might assume.

Many see computer literacy as panacea to the world's problems. The notion of computer literacy has become almost an ideological rallying point for many disciplines (every professional must know how to use the computer) and even the general public (a computer in every home and accessible to all age and education groups). Other definitions of computer literacy may be more helpful for guiding the records professional. An entry in the *Encyclopedia of Library and Information Science* defines "information technology literacy" as being the "knowledge which allows an individual to function efficiently and effectively in whatever circumstance one finds him/herself in a technologically oriented society." Specific competencies were defined as to "(1) operate and communicate with technological devices, (2) understand how subsystems fit together to form systems or networks, (3) understand documentation and how to utilize applications software, (4) understand the basic jargon or terminology of information technology, (5) solve problems through the use of technology, (6) identify and use alternate sources of information about IT issues, (7) discuss the history and the future of information technology at the level of an intelligent layperson, and (8) have some insight into the ethical and human impact issues of information technology."[50] This is more specific, and it certainly avoids the ideological aspects of some definitions.

Distinguishing computer literacy from information literacy, as defined by Jerry Kanter, is critical. Kanter argues that computer literacy is a reference to a "familiarity with the use of personal computers including the employment of word processing, spreadsheets, data bases, and the other popular software tools." Added to these activities, the computer literate are "regular users" of electronic mail and navigate in commercial and other databases. "Information literacy," on the other hand, "implies an understanding of the general concepts of information processing, how information systems shape and support a person's job function, a department or operating unit, or an enterprisewide application that may be linked with the company's customers as well as its suppliers. It is an awareness of the growing role of the technological enablers that allow a company to reengineer entire business processes."[51] Here is the dilemma for the archivist and records manager. Just where on this spectrum do records professionals need to reside? Is it the matter of technical knowledge that is most crucial or other concerns such as administrative placement and authority, how the archival or records management mission is defined, the records professionals' image and resources, or records professionals seeing themselves as a "fit" in their organization?

Computer literacy is not an easily defined term. There have been many models for computer literacy, as well as many debates about the models and the term. There are hierarchical models arranging "computer proficiency into taxonomies of literacies at different levels of expertise." There are approaches looking at various components such as "awareness, skills, and knowledge." Some suggest it means the "ability to read and write computer programs." Finally, some argue, "different disciplines should educate their students about computers in ways that are relevant to that discipline."[52] The computer literacy relevant to the records professional can only be determined by wrestling with what the archivist or records manager does or should be doing in the modern organization.

It is easy to lose perspective about the importance of computer literacy. George Marsh, an education specialist, suggests that "our *greatest* challenge as a society is to recognize the importance of computers and other electronic technologies as the dominant factors in the new global economy."[53] Marsh argues that this is society's *greatest* challenge, beyond poverty, racism, war, injustice, immorality, hunger, and crime. Records professionals should not fall into this trap. Computer literacy is not the *greatest* problem for archivists or records managers. There are other more important issues that should engage their attention, namely the need to return to redefining and redesigning the fundamental mission that should be the focal point for records professionals.

The computer poses many moral and ethical issues that have a tremendous impact on how we approach the issue of computer literacy. Dutch philosopher and engineer Egbert Schuurman argues, "what becomes apparent is that human beings gradually recede into the background and that tools more and more take over what used to be human tasks." The computer, in this sense, may be the most significant tool. Schuurman believes that we have tried to stay current with technology by becoming more specialized. Specialization often makes people less aware of the context of their work, requiring new forms of teamwork.[54]

Why should archivists and records managers be able to use computers intelligently? They need to become conversant with the computer to participate in the standards world. Standards for information technology have a tremendous impact on the ways in which computers are used in the workplace and at home, also influencing the means by which computers might be used in the future. In order to participate in the standards arena, individuals must have some basic understanding of the technology itself as well as how information technology standards are created, refined, and adopted or rejected.

Computer literacy is not very helpful for participating in the standards world or that of information policy or some other related concern unless records professionals have worked out their mission and have something intelligible and precise to say. Management guru Peter Drucker has built a case that institutions must learn to be information literate, including knowing where the organization gets its information. For example, Drucker suggests that for CEOs, the "most important information is not about customers but about noncustomers." Why? "This is the group in which change will occur." And it is for this type of purpose that Drucker sees an understanding of computers being so important. "We are moving from minimal computer literacy—knowing little more than the ABCs and multiplication tables of computing—to the point where we can really do something with computers."[55] Archivists and records managers need to think of computers not merely as tools for description and management or as obstacles to electronic records management and start to think about how they can use them to help organizations use the information in records in ways to benefit the organization.

Organizations *do* need help with their management of computers, and not just from the software engineers or other technical people. Thomas K. Landauer's lengthy chronicle about the "trouble with computers" stresses that because computers offer "enormous power at our fingertips," are "just plain fun," and are "addictive," does not mean that they have been used in the ways and to the benefits that have often been touted. Examining many functions of computers in the modern organization (including records generation and recordkeeping), Landauer concludes, "we need to make computers into much better tools for work, both for the work of individuals and for the work of organizations." For example, while Landauer wonders whether the move to the paperless office has actually created more paper, he also stresses that the need and quest for the elimination of paper is a real issue.[56]

The real need of archival and records management computer literacy is for records professionals to understand new electronic *recordkeeping* systems. George Nichols, head of Australia's National Archives, nicely described this by recognizing that the computer was initially used to manage data *and* records, while in the later stages records are created directly on and to be used only on the computer.[57] This is very different from earlier descriptions in which archivists and records managers were urged to learn basic computer principles, the use of databases, storage technologies, telecommunications, and related technical concerns.[58] This focus is also very different from that advocated by some archivists and records managers who believe they should adopt information management approaches because this is what the organizations creating records are stressing. This view emerges even in an otherwise fine essay on modern records management in health care.[59] It can also be seen in records management approaches to the management of electronic records that often provide much good advice but that opt to stress information *over* records.

Records professionals must make sure they never lose sight of their mission. Terry Eastwood states that the "proper education of archivists must be rooted in inquiry into the nature of archives as records and as institutions and of the archivist's role and function as preserver and communicator of archives and manager of institutions."[60] His message could be modified slightly to include records managers. The role of archivists and records managers must be devoted to knowing records and recordkeeping systems, and whatever archivists or records managers need to know about computers must be connected to enabling them to understand the records. This sets the stage for being able to define better computer literacy for records professionals.

The curriculum guidelines offered by the Society of American Archivists Committee on Automated Records and Techniques build on the concept that *first* the archivist must know about archives and then the technology issues, a point worth remembering.[61] All this is akin to Edward Tenner's argument that "for both technophiles and technophobes, the best, and perhaps the only way to avoid the revenge effects of computing is to maintain skills and resources that are independent of the computer."[62] While for Tenner this means maintaining mathematical skills, personal communications strengths, and related knowledge, for the archivist or records manager this means being an expert on records and recordkeeping. Records professionals understand that *their* information emanates from the evidence found in records.[63]

Archivists and records managers are experts on records and recordkeeping systems. Their function is to understand the purpose, nature, evolution, and continuing utility of records and the systems for the creators and users of records, a mission nicely summarized in the work of the Australian archivists with their statement that archivists are there to help in the "identification of recordkeeping requirements," the "specification, building, and in some cases, the operation of electronic recordkeeping systems," the "development of recordkeeping standards," and the "establishment of improved recordkeeping practices."[64] Unfortunately, much of the archival and records management professions are still debating their missions in the labyrinth of complaints, accusations, navel-gazing, and soul-searching associated with professionalism and the relationship of records professionals with other disciplines like history and information science. Vernon Smith's arguments about the need for archivists to possess a "thorough understanding of scholarly activities" and to bear in mind that their mission is to "keep records in order that people may augment the understanding of their present experiences with those of generations past"[65] sound compelling, but they still only represent *part* of the story. Archivist Mark Greene's arguments that manuscripts curators are becoming disenfranchised by the emphasis on electronic records, what he thinks is the responsibility of "institutional—mostly government—archivists," echoes similar concerns being expressed in Australia, discussed in the first chapter. Yet, Greene and others like him miss the point that the manuscript curator is also responsible for records, that history and symbolic value are only a part of the characteristics of the records preserved in archives and are not necessarily values limited to traditional paper records, and that an increasing portion of personal records will be created in electronic form anyway.[66]

More pertinent is David Bearman's argument to revitalize archival description by re-focusing on the nature of records and the process of the records creation, namely the "functions and information systems giving rise to the records," "attributes of the records-generating context," and the "underlying evidence or record."[67] The same needs to happen with records managers. Records manager Jim Coulson writes, for example, that records managers will only be able to focus on their mission and possess a future if they "take the responsibility for educating themselves about computer and imaging systems and how they affect the work of their organizations. Combined with their detailed knowledge of the records, people, and processes of the organization, this will put records managers in a unique position."[68]

There is an urgency for focusing on records and recordkeeping systems. Physician John Burnum suggests that the increasing reliance on electronic information systems seemed prone only to weaken an already flawed medical record.[69] Linguists, such as Keith Devlin and Duska Rosenberg, are studying the design and use of computerized systems harkening back to the records professional's supposed knowledge of document forms and functions.[70] Any abandonment by archivists and records managers of a focus on the management of records is bound only to make these professionals obsolete in a world increasingly struggling to determine how to use electronic information and recordkeeping systems. Why? Because nearly every modern professional is asking questions about electronic recordkeeping and information systems, and many of these questions concern records.

Archivists and records managers forget that the earliest history of the computer was tied up with the search for better means of managing records, best typified by the career of Herman Hollerith. Hollerith, the developer of the punch card machine in the late nineteenth century, first demonstrated the utility of his machine in the organization of health records and statistics in municipal and state governments. Hollerith's successes led to his more acclaimed work with the U.S. Census Bureau and railroads. This early automation is similar in intent to modern systems even if by today's standards it seems primitive.

There is more to ponder. Despite whatever records professionals might think about computers and their use in recordkeeping, what they need to keep in mind are the lessons they can see in the past generation of the computer revolution. The corporate giant IBM really did not believe that smaller microcomputers would replace the mainframe, and it ignored what was happening for a long time. The result was that IBM lost hundreds of millions of dollars, its place in the personal computer market, and thousands of employees laid off for the first time in its otherwise long and successful history.[71]

Lessons can be learned from other disciplines. Frederick Crews, in his critique of psychoanalysis and the recent movement for recovered memory, writes, "contemporary psychoanalysis possesses neither a core of accepted doctrine, nor an agreement over Freud's hits and misses, nor a common goal of treatment, nor a cogent account of why the therapy sometimes 'works' but sometimes doesn't."[72] We might worry about the records professions in a similar fashion. While there has been a small group of archivists gaining practical experience with the management of electronic records, much of this knowledge has not been widely received nor accepted by the records community. Many records professionals go about their business, ignoring most things challenging their practices and neglecting to build a case literature providing a foundation for knowledge about recordkeeping systems. Unless they build a knowledge about recordkeeping systems, the matter of computer literacy will be irrelevant except for developing internal management systems that could perhaps be better built by professionals other than archivists and records managers anyway. In other words, records professionals develop an understanding of computer literacy only within that larger context of mission.

The relationship of understanding records to records professionals' knowledge about computers has been described beautifully by archivist Joan Schwartz in her article on photographs and diplomatics. Establishing that photographs are records, Schwartz then uses diplomatics to analyze the nature of such records. While wrestling with the technical aspects of the photograph, she also argues that the "meaning of a photographic document lies not in the content or the form but in the context of document creation." One needs to understand such things as visual communication and photographic practice and be able to see that the values of these records "resides in the interrelationships between photographs and the creating structures, animating functions, programs, and information technology that created them."[73] This is important. The technology is part of a many faceted process relating to the life of records, not the only issue.

There is no easy way to define computer literacy *except* in the broader professional mission. Ticking off a list of specific technical knowledge can be useful, as was evident from the effort by the SAA CART Curriculum Project, but it is also easy to get lost in a maze of technical gadgets and tools. Records and recordkeeping systems need to be understood in order to assist organizations and society to be able to manage records for evidence, accountability, corporate memory, and supporting the ongoing, essential work of the organization employing the archivist or records manager. Systems people and technocrats are often not building recordkeeping but information systems, opening up for records professionals the possibility for communicating the importance and necessity of records. The definition of computer literacy flows, indeed, from knowing and agreeing to the mission of maintaining records with continuing value to the particular creators, the organization, and, in some cases, various elements of society.

Knowing their business frees the records professional to exploit information technology for the management of records and understand how information and recordkeeping systems are developed in general so that studies of particular systems can be done, whether this necessitates looking at a legacy system from two decades before or a system put online last week. Archivists and records managers are also liberated to participate in the organization's systems development so that recordkeeping systems can be maintained and the electronic records managed. The National Archives of Canada issued a model for the position of a "Record Keeping Specialist." Four main job functions for this position were identified—systems designer, policy driver, retrieval expert, and advisor/coach. The knowledge areas are interesting, including business functions and activities, recordkeeping practices, awareness of emerging technologies, and "current information management and information technology concepts and practices." Technology, while a knowledge area, is an expert domain amid these other aspects of understanding the organization and its records and recordkeeping systems. This suggests what archivists and records managers need to know, what educators need to teach, and how they need to proceed as a profession in the future.[74]

Clifford Stoll describes computer literacy as a "fuzzy term without fixed meaning."[75] It *is* fuzzy for records professionals, but it is a lot less nebulous if they set the boundaries of their knowledge in records and recordkeeping systems. Conducting research about records, building partnerships for teaching about records, and becoming public advocates for the management of modern recordkeeping systems relate to this. Futurist William Knoke has the best manner in which to view computer literacy, when he writes that becoming prepared to function in the next century "will start by becoming computer literate—to be familiar with a computer keyboard and mouse, to be able to dance through one or more computer applications in all their complexities. Although we have seen that computer interfaces will become increasingly user friendly, it is computer literate persons who will be the least intimidated about experimenting with yet newer capabilities, and they will be able to push their limits to solve real workplace problems."[76] This seems a relevant message for modern records professionals.

WHY TECHNOLOGY WILL NOT RESOLVE ALL PROBLEMS

The amazing development of the computer, especially in the last two decades, prompts many to make dramatic predictions about how organizations and society will create, manage, and use information. Elias Safdie, in an essay about technology convergence, argues that ever increasing technology power, if used in the right manner, improves offices and institutional performance. Safdie starts by stating, "Technology convergence is at once opening huge doors of opportunity and creating incredible chasms into which IT managers can plunge." He then proceeds to describe the progress from the initial mainframes of fifty years ago, through the minicomputers of the 1960s and 1970s, then using personal computers to enable the establishment of local area networks to create departmental office systems, and leading finally to far reaching technological innovations such as integrated information systems, desktop publishing, and the management of more sophisticated documents in a fully networked world. Safdie concludes his essay by postulating that the question before every organization and information professional, given the escalating technical capabilities, is "How can we integrate any given technology into our infrastructure so that the resultant combination is better aligned with our mission objectives than the previous configuration?" He asserts that the question should be answered in this way: "If the answer to any given technology is negative, that technology is wrong; if the resultant combination furthers the goals of the organization, then we have a winner."[77]

Answering a question about technology through technology is not always a good idea. Nor is wrapping the organizational mission or goals with technology always the best means to an end. While our own belief in progress has declined considerably in this century of world wars and atrocities, it is interesting that so many commentators on the use of information technology remain convinced of technology's pervasive influence and good fortune—its ever moving progress. Even critics of technology suggest the continuing domination of a technocratic perspective by issuing dire warnings built on the inevitability of technological progress and domination.

We need a considerable re-wording of Safdie's question and answer. The issue is not always a technology and its use; rather it is first the organizational mission and responsibility and then, and only then, the technology use. This is especially true for information professionals concerned with records management. We can dissect the arguments about technology convergence in three ways. First, and admittedly a more academic exercise, it is necessary to consider how technology convergence relates to the collaboration of various information professionals in particular institutional settings. Most organizations have an array of professionals responsible for information management—archivists, information scientists, librarians, records managers, and others—bringing different educational backgrounds, perspectives, and objectives to an organization. These differences may work both for and against technology convergence. Then, it is also necessary to consider the macro-view, the social, regulatory, and economic context that influences the way an institution uses or does not use information technologies. There is mounting evidence, in fact, that this may be the most important factor determining what an organization does with its information sources such as its records. Finally, we must keep in mind the micro-view, the potential impact of technology on individuals in their workplaces and even in their homes. A growing body of research suggests the importance of this factor. When all is said and done, it might be increasing concerns about individual health, mental health, privacy, and general well-being that determine how and why organizations select and use technology in the manner they do.

Ideas of technology convergence are often *incomplete*. The problems or challenges facing information professionals at crucial spots are even more challenging issues concerning how technology convergence can help, or hinder, the modern organization. We can start by acknowledging that convergence, due to the supposed improvement of technology, is both a frequent and important topic in the information professions. Within academic discourse, there is no secret that certain topics become fads and benchmarks for academic careers, controversies, and publishing. Within industries, the same fads can become the acceptable jargon by which to market new products or to promise new solutions to practical problems. Within the information professions, roughly grouped from librarians and information scientists to archivists and records managers, convergence has taken the lead in writing, research, and discussion.

Convergence in the information professions is fairly easy to characterize. It is the unifying of the professions and professional objectives or functions as opposed to the continuing schismatic nature of specialization, or divergence. It is also, through such unification, the harnessing of technology in particular settings to improve or to create new activities. Such discussion about the information professions is quite important because these professions have become distinguishing characteristics of our Information Age. Information management is essential to government, business, and private individual alike.

These debates also reveal the dynamic nature of the information professions and the education of such professionals. Thomas J. Galvin, a professor of information science and policy at the University at SUNY-Albany, has gotten to the heart of the debate. Professor Galvin's essay is a balanced view of the issues related to the convergence–divergence discussions. He first describes the continuing separation of the various disciplines making up the information professions, and the resulting growth in and diversity of educational programs supporting the disciplines. In his argument for divergence, Galvin notes the practitioners' need for identity, status, and the need to overcome negative connotations of words like library and librarian (we could add, of course, records and records professional). He also muses on the long-standing debate about theory versus practice, and the concern about vocations as opposed to matters of theory and research. In his argument for convergence, Galvin brings up the need to consolidate resources by merging previously distinct academic programs, the genuine need for knowledge building through theorizing and research, and the need for resource-richer programs with better technology. It is in the realm of the relationship of technology to the information professions' debates about convergence and divergence that the most serious problems reside. The information professions are increasingly absorbed by the use, design, and evaluation of information technology. The information professions have always been concerned with utilizing technology in the most productive and effective means possible. The problem arises, however, in trying to ascertain what drives what, a matter Galvin deals with when he states that the "same forces that are rapidly obliterating traditional distinctions between different jobs in professional practice are perhaps the strongest drivers towards the unification of educational programs—the convergence of formerly separate information technologies and the continuing migration of data and information to exclusively electronic formats."[78]

Such comments are echoed in similar essays found in a wide array of journals, collected papers, and conference proceedings having to do with the information professions. Announcements about the impact of technology on this or that element of the information professions are posted to the Internet, listed in newsletters, and described in separate brochures. Books about the impact of the technology on the book, writing, and literacy appear daily and engage us intellectually. Although I am comfortable with computers I like printed books and paper records. Am I converging or diverging? Or am I just confused?

Is convergence, as so often described, the real issue? Convergence sounds suspiciously like a new, more polite or academically acceptable way of being technological determinists. Arnold Pacey's book on technology and culture is a fine primer demonstrating how any technology is greatly influenced by social, cultural, economic, political, and other factors.[79] Apologists for technology forget the more complex societal forces at play at any given time. It is likely that the advent of the paperless office will never happen because there is a socially convenient aspect to reading certain things in traditional paper formats. It is unlikely that organizations will embrace exclusively electronic recordkeeping systems until the legal system supports it or until records can be technically maintained in a reliable fashion, a problem one report asserts is far greater than the much discussed Y2K bug.[80] It is just as possible that the paperless office will emerge not because of electronic information technology but because of an environmentalism forcing the cessation of forest clearing to produce paper. Convergence apologists or advocates also overlook other matters requiring attention or that are far more important in their impact on information professionals, their work, and their education, the latter the source of the images of the new information technologies. What are these matters?

Collaboration among different professions is one aspect for academics and university administrators to confront. David Damrosch contends specialization has taken over most academic departments as well as the administration of the university, likening the university to the tower of Babel.[81] Specialists are everywhere, speaking and writing in their own specialized language and often only to other like-minded specialists. Research is highly specialized. The concept of a technology-driven convergence flies against a deeply balkanized academic culture. Focusing on convergence may be interesting and may even be necessary in our Information Age, but it is not a necessarily very well directed or realistic enterprise.

The way in which we reflect on convergence in the information professions also directs attention away from the extant bodies of knowledge of the various information professions. Library science, information science, or archival science possesses some definition for a basic knowledge foundation that is interdisciplinary in nature. Interdisciplinarity is a process used to "answer complex questions," "address broad issues," "solve problems that are beyond the scope of any one discipline," and, most energetically, "achieve unity of knowledge."[82] Whether the various information disciplines are truly interdisciplinary or not is a matter for debate, but their defined bodies of knowledge at least reflect an interest in this (although some like Landauer worry that the use of computer technology brings with it overspecialization and a corresponding loss of the bigger picture).

Convergence can also ignore practical realities. This can be seen in two ways. There is, first, the reality of the external ecology that sometimes defies description, except in its most concise and clear (or obvious?) problems. Andrew Abbott, in his fine study on the sociology of professions, describes the professional ecology, and he perceives those professions with information as their business as having a leg up in the modern Information Age.[83] While he ably paints in the general contours of the landscape, he misses some of the details and nuances of the particular disciplines, such as the contested relationship between archivists and records managers.

Records management, broadly conceived to be the management of current records for economy and efficiency purposes in an organization and to enable organizations to comply with external legal, fiscal, and administrative regulations, was nurtured by federal government and corporate archivists a half century ago. These professionals needed to develop approaches or strategies for coping with the massive expansion of records caused by the growth in government, increase in regulations, and by the changes in the technology for creating and managing records and information. Similar to the trends characterized by Damrosch, the records managers split from their parent and, ultimately, with the advent of information resources management, also underwent schisms. The Society of American Archivists and the Association of Records Managers and Administrators, despite very similar aims, now meet separately. In 1995, just as one example, the annual programs of these two associations revealed not *one* individual on *both* programs.[84] This problem has much to do with the weaknesses in the management by organizations of their records, electronic and paper.

Convergence within the information professions is a mythology, but it may be a needed mythology. The danger of the current form of convergence is its heavy flavor of technological determinism. Convergence within the information professions should be defined by the social mandates of our age, the need for equitable access to information, protection against invasions of privacy and other unethical intrusions on the individual, and an imperative to maintain records and information of continuing or symbolic value as long as necessary. Herbert Schiller, the astute and controversial social commentator, argues that the center of a "new librarianship curriculum" should be "how to guarantee social use and application of the new information technologies."[85] Landauer argues simply that computers need to become better tools for work. These kinds of concerns can be seen by understanding the social context of records and records administration.

Machines should not dictate to society. If that is the premise of the current arguments for convergence, these arguments should be ignored. The information disciplines must identify the broader social mandate and draw on their own disciplines in developing a curriculum, professional missions, and other approaches for supporting convergence. Convergence can also ignore the manner in which technology fits into social, economic, cultural, and other aspects of both organizations and the larger society. Some case studies related to records issues of the past several years illustrate this point. Records, as anyone working in an institution knows, are an extremely important source of information for the organization, although it seems that paper, especially as records, has become the bogeyman of the Information Age.[86]

The matters concerning how documents are managed have been seen in important cases discussed in the media. The Swiss Banks and Nazi Gold and the

Internal Revenue Service's records mismanagement are examples worth considering. We could also examine the inquiries into the Clinton-Gore campaign
finance contributions and the relevance of records for what they suggest about
actual events, the ongoing litigation about the Reagan-Bush administrations'
efforts to destroy electronic mail messages about the Iran-Contra arms deal, the
theft and release of documents from Brown and Williamson (subsequently
known as the "Cigarette Papers") revealing the tobacco industry's knowledge
about the addictive effects of nicotine and its marketing practices, and, in Australia, the case known as "Shreddergate," the deliberate and apparently unlawful
destruction of records in Queensland in order to impede an investigation.

Records relating to the involvement of major Swiss banks in the laundering
of gold taken from Holocaust victims by Nazi Germany sat untouched for several generations. The United States National Archives holds over fifteen million
documents from the Treasury Department, Federal Reserve Board, and other
agencies related to this wartime activity. Although the majority of these records
have been declassified since 1976, it has only been recently, due to the efforts
of Senator Alfonse D'Amato and others, that these records and the case they
document became important. British journalist Tom Bower's book, the first of
the secondary accounts about these allegations, and a barrage of other works, is
testimony to the importance of records in shedding evidence on past and important events.[87] Based on the continuing revelations in 1996 about the possible
involvement of the Swiss government and Swiss banking institutions, Switzerland enacted a law in December 1996 prohibiting the destruction of any records
held by the government or other organizations relating to Nazi Germany and
the Second World War. In mid-January 1997 a story became public about an
employee of one of Switzerland's largest banks discovering World War II–era
records about to be destroyed. This lent credence to the allegations of the previous year concerning the laundering of Nazi gold looted from Holocaust victims
and, for half a year, daily stories in American, European, and Israeli newspapers
about the Nazi gold. Early in the developing story a confidential strategy paper
from the Swiss Ambassador Carlo Jagmetti was leaked to the press, detailing a
plan about "waging war" against Jewish groups. Jagmetti resigned, as did the
archivist from the bank that destroyed the records. The Swiss government and
banks moved to create a fund for compensation of Holocaust victims, and lawyers began the process of pressing both the banks and the government for res-
titution of funds and property seized over a half century ago.

What this developing story suggests is the *power* of records for providing
evidence for societal memory. Bower, in his book on the case, notes that eleven
American government agencies had been involved in the case since 1944, and
"their accumulated records between 1940 and 1962 . . . amounted to incalculable
millions of sheets of paper."[88] As an industry of scholarship has developed in
the past generation about public memory, it is not hard to suggest why records
are so important and, furthermore, why the technology that supports these records must take into account the technology's capability to maintain such re-

cords. We know that many Americans prefer a sanitized past, what historian Mike Wallace has called "Mickey Mouse history," with all the bumps smoothed out and the unattractive or difficult spots deleted or softened.[89] It has been well documented how both the Germans and Japanese have struggled to try to put their pasts behind them, in particular their responsibilities for the atrocities of World War II.[90] And we have seen how those who deny the Holocaust have gained new positions of authority, if not complete respectability, by using the power of the World Wide Web. The evidence of the past, best represented in records that can appear to be very routine (such as those old financial accounts in Swiss banks) must be protected with renewed vigor as we rely more and more on technology.

Lest anyone in the United States assume a sanctimonious attitude about the activities of Switzerland's banks and government, an examination of the records of one of the most prominent and high profile federal agencies provides a good lesson. The Internal Revenue Service, a federal agency hosting an increasingly automated operation with a long track record of difficulties in this process, has been the target of numerous criticisms about what it does with its information technology. In late 1995, IRS Historian Shelley Davis was fired amidst her allegations of the organization's illegal destruction of records, and the National Archives and Records Administration issued a report on the "serious shortcomings" of the service's records management practices. The negative publicity about this federal agency's records management has continued as Davis has been an outspoken critic, culminating in the publication of her expose, and a group known as Tax Analysts, allied with three historical associations, filing in early 1997 a lawsuit against the IRS and the National Archives.[91]

Despite how the technology may be converging within the IRS, it is clear that this pales in comparison with concerns such as organizational culture, accountability, and management. Davis states that the "gist of my beef with the IRS [is] that it negligently and deliberately destroyed its paper trail, shredded its records, and trashed any chance for accountability, out of some ill-founded and irrational fear of exposure to public scrutiny."[92] Apparently the IRS has repeatedly thwarted any efforts to manage its archives based on its interpretation of section 6103 of the tax code, which ensures the confidentiality of taxpayer records. As the IRS critics argue, the records in question are not the tax returns of individuals or organizations, but the administrative and policy records of the service itself. Still, IRS Commissioner Margaret Milner Richardson responded to the charges of Davis and others that the law justified its records management procedures. Richardson's claim that the IRS does, in fact, release policy documents, manuals, and similar information rings a bit hollow in light of other revelations about the service, including a General Accounting Office report documenting IRS employee firings and disciplinary actions because its computers were being used by its employees to browse through the tax records of friends, relatives, and celebrities.[93] Despite remarkably detailed and useful IRS guidelines on how tax accountants should manage their recordkeeping for tax filings and related activities, the IRS itself seems to have lost control of its own records and information systems.

Finally, Davis's book provides insight into the agency's problems with its use of computers. While functioning as IRS historian, Davis uncovered records concerning that agency's efforts to automate its operations; in her expose, Davis examines the IRS battle with computers as a window into that agency's troubles. Commencing her discussion by relating the Treasury Department's early 1996 confession that over $4 billion dollars of expenditures on computers in five years had failed to modernize the agency's activities, Davis comments on its history as a computer pioneer in the 1960s to continuing failures in the three subsequent decades. Davis blames this on the agency's continuing legacy of mismanagement and inability to admit mistakes. She writes, "I'd as soon compare the IRS effort to tango into the Information Age to Sisyphus pushing that stone up the hill, only to see it roll back down, again and again, into an absurd eternity."[94] The best equipment money could buy was not enough in an agency that had lost sight of its purpose and sense of responsibility.

The challenges posed by the IRS, records management, and the use of technology to manage records should not be surprising given the decade-old court case involving the management of electronic mail systems within the White House. Tom Blanton's 1995 book, *White House E-Mail*,[95] reads like fiction. Blanton, head of the National Security Archive—a non-profit research institute located at George Washington University and dedicated to creating a "collection of contemporary declassified national security information outside of the U. S. government"—describes a case in which e-mail is contested as an electronic messaging system that can transmit records and hence that is subject to management as provided by various records legislation. White House officials labeled the e-mail system as little more than "furniture" needing to be disposed of in order to make way for the next administration. This particular messaging system was established in 1985, after an initial effort to experiment with e-mail capability started in 1982, and the majority of records reproduced in Blanton's book are from the 1985–1987 period.

As Blanton recounts in his introduction to the edition of some five hundred messages (about half as part of the book proper and the remainder in ASCII on an enclosed 3.5 inch disk) culled from a total of 4,000 the NSA managed to obtain, the system was discovered to be in use because of the Iran-Contra scandal in 1986 and the efforts by National Security Council's Oliver North and his boss John Poindexter to delete numerous incriminating messages about illegal covert operations, gun deals, foreign policy dealings with dictators, manipulating the media, working Congress and Capitol Hill, internal squabbles, and efforts to censor and prevent any public scrutiny of the records and other information being created by the White House. The result was a court case starting in early 1989 with the aim of having the e-mail messages declared to be records instead of routine junk intended to be house cleaned by one presidential administration before the next came in.

A major theme of the book relates to the importance of records, with a story of the federal government trying to destroy records in order to cover up illicit or perceived secret activities in which the National Archives and one particular archivist of the United States look very bad. While some may think of the National Archives as little more than an attic in which to place inactive records where they might be used by a few historians, the National Archives needs to be an agency working to ensure that records protecting citizens' rights and the accountability of government are preserved. For the moment, the National Security Archive seems to be serving this purpose.

For the average citizen, *White House E-Mail* should be chilling. Over a decade ago, Richard Neustadt and Ernest May, in their book *Thinking in Time*, demonstrated the acute problems caused by our leaders' misuse or misunderstanding of history.[96] Their book appeared at about the same time that the first report appeared warning about the loss of federal records because of the increasing reliance on electronic information systems. More such warnings have followed. The danger before us is that the increasing dependence on electronic record-keeping by public officials will present opportunities by these officials to engage in questionable activities. *White House E-Mail* is a blunt reminder of this, as well as a wake-up call that we need strong laws and other means to protect government records. None of this is the matter of technology convergence, nor would the successful convergence of electronic information and records technologies make much difference in how these records were maintained or threatened with destruction. The larger, more important issues are the matters of government accountability and openness of government operations.

The importance of such issues can be seen in another government report. In early March 1997 the Report of the Commission on Protecting and Reducing Government Secrecy, chaired by Senator Daniel Patrick Moynihan and charged to conduct "an investigation into all matters in any way related to any legislation, executive order, regulation, practice, or procedure relating to classified information or granting security clearances," was presented to the president. The report, entitled *Secrecy*, was a refreshing view regarding access to government information. Senator Moynihan, in his introduction to the report, suggests that while secrecy was "at times legitimate and necessary," we do not need a "culture of secrecy" but a "culture of openness."[97] The report is a product of the emerging post–Cold War mentality. In other ways the report seemed to be business as usual, with some disturbing aspects weakening any chance for its recommendations to be taken seriously or enacted.

This report argues that the opportunity for secrecy in the federal government should be limited, recommending a new federal statute be drafted, proposed, and adopted allowing information to be classified only in case of national security. Records and other information sources should be closed for no longer than ten years unless a particular case is made for their being classified (and then the information would only be closed for thirty years), and all this would be accomplished through a "National Declassification Center," a body centrally

coordinating all classification through the federal government. The report is can-
did in the numerous problems about classification and declassification of federal
records. The costs of government secrecy are extraordinary. In 1993, Freedom
of Information Act requests cost $108 million, despite the fact that such requests
led to very little information being released. The Commission estimates that
over one and a half billion pages of government records over twenty-five years
old are still classified, at an annual bill of nearly $3 billion. And in 1995 the
government was involved with 3.6 million new classification actions.

Secrecy is also very open in its assessment of why a new approach to government classification is needed, arguing for "broad access." The commission
lamented the failure of standard records management approaches to resolve such
issues as overly zealous classification and problems with access. The more recent
challenges of information technology are also described in *Secrecy*, suggesting
a leadership vacuum in accountability in buying and using information technology. The report also fails to account for the trend of information technology
to transform organizations from traditional hierarchies, the hallmark of government bureaucracy, to encourage individual responsibility.

While the report is a refreshing federal government self-review of this issue,
the first one in forty years, it comes across as business as usual in two ways.
First, there is some troubling evidence about the administrative aspects for handling declassification. Second, there are some larger issues absent in its descriptions and recommendations. The internal problems are fairly obvious. The report
includes Vice Chairman Larry Combest's introductory essay, which reads like
a minority report arguing that we should not be too open, jeopardizing national
interests. There are other more serious problems with the report's recommendations indicating no real change in declassification. The commission takes the
stand that the president should still retain the authority to determine the categories of information that can be classified. Any student of the classification
problems and issues can point out that it has been the changing views of the
presidents along with their commitment to force or, the opposite, to be lax with
federal agencies in declassification that have often created the climate nurturing
the most unfortunate problems.

The most perplexing aspect of *Secrecy* may be its main recommendation about
how to administer the classification process, establishing a "National Declassification Center" in the National Archives because of the logical connection to
records management. There are two problems with the idea of establishing such
a center. The center suggests the typical federal government approach to solutions: establish a new agency or unit, adding another level of bureaucratic control that can impede timely solutions to important problems, especially for a
function such as classification and declassification that requires speed and time-
liness. The primary concern here is what lawyer Philip K. Howard chronicles
in his *The Death of Common Sense*, the strangle hold of rules and regulations,
all with the best of purposes, that impede government carrying out its functions,
serving the citizenry, and protecting us as well. In the millions of words sup-

porting such government procedures, Howard sees the greater quantity of rules providing more loopholes and problems with meeting the intended objectives. In a tract written for records managers, Howard describes a "paper trail of . . . endless procedures" that "accomplishes nothing." In one of the best descriptions of such problems, Howard notes that the "circulating of forms and scratching of initials is sort of like a rosary."[98] While it may be unfair to jump to conclusions that the proposed center is doomed to be just another bureaucratic quagmire, given its sketchy description in *Secrecy*, one must still wonder how such a new administrative unit will be given the authority it needs.

The potential impotency of this recommended new body is the suggestion that it be housed at the National Archives. This is *the* logical choice, since declassification is a process generally related to the information found in records and the National Archives is the premiere federal agency concerned with records. Yet, here are the problems, aptly hinted at in *Secrecy* when this report complains about the failure of records management, linking this to the National Archives and the need for this agency to "exert a strong leadership role within the Government," a need even the report suggests has not often been heeded by the Archives. Whether it is because of poor leadership or the lack of clear statutory authority, the National Archives has mostly compiled a list of failures and lost opportunities in the past decade that would not portend well for this agency to be responsible for the new declassification center. Every records professional wishes this would change.

The recent history of the National Archives includes the following cases that would not seem to support its ability or resolve to take on a responsibility as important as declassification. The National Archives did not exert forceful leadership in dealing with the legal entanglements of the opening of the Nixon White House tapes, accumulating a track record that caused Seymour Hersh to characterize the agency as a "nondescript federal agency whose primary function is to serve as a depository for federal records."[99] The National Archives has been criticized for its lack of creativity in dealing with electronic records issues, resulting in at least one recent congressional report on the subject, and it has been a litigant for the past decade in defending its position that the electronic mail system used by the National Security Council—in less than scrupulous dealings in the Iran-Contra arms deal—could be purged of records by individuals before anyone could review the nature of the records and their importance. The Archives has clung to what many other records professionals see as outmoded ideas.

Admittedly, there are recent bright spots in the National Archives administration, suggesting that the placement of a declassification center could strengthen its mission and authority. The placement of the declassification center in the Archives could jolt that agency from thinking its primary constituency should be scholarly historians on one hand and non-academics like genealogists on the other to seeing that it has an important role in protecting records for use by lawyers, political scientists, journalists, community action groups, and citizens. In reviewing all of these concerns, the miracles caused by the convergence of information technology are minor or even meaningless.

It is in the importance of records and the increasing use of electronic record-keeping systems that we can see the weaknesses of reports like *Secrecy*. The report does not account for why records should be broadly and radically de-classified. The report also does not take into consideration the implications of electronic records systems other than the fact that there are concerns with how these systems can be compromised. It is a moral imperative that seems missing from *Secrecy*. There are the usual platitudes about the importance of an informed citizenry in a democratic society, but no compelling message that government records are far too important to the average American to be left in the hands of government officials and to be prey to the political whimse of presidential administrations and Congress. If a declassification center is to be put into the National Archives, then first the National Archives needs to be given the authority necessary to carry out its responsibilities. Tom Blanton describes how the court case about the Iran-Contra e-mail might never been a court case "if the National Archives & Records Administration had simply done its job under the law, holding even the White House accountable."[100]

Because such dangers are even more pronounced in our increasingly technocratic age, a report on government secrecy should be stronger and more dramatic than this one. It is ironic that there is not a contrast between growing government secrecy and the increasing threats to personal privacy. There is a strong connection between the two. A government intent on maintaining close control of information is not likely to value personal privacy, nor can we as individual citizens keep that government accountable in its actions toward us. At the risk of being paranoid, this may be why government wants to keep information about its activities from us; it does not want us to know what it knows about our personal lives. Ellen Alderman and Caroline Kennedy, in *The Right to Privacy*, provide a litany of cases impacting individual privacy. Alderman and Kennedy suggest that when the Fourth Amendment was written, the amendment protecting our "persons, houses, papers, and effects, against unreasonable searches and seizures," that the drafters did not foresee a time when we would have a "paper trail that leads right out of the door and into a multitude of offices and institutions." These lawyer-authors note that the "device that has outstripped all other threats to privacy is the computer" because it has more accessible information about us. This has been more problematic because "while the digital society is coming of age, laws designed to deal with it are still in their infancy."[101]

Secrecy's problems may be the result of the rapidly changing nature of society, information technology, and the slowly evolving legal–administrative approaches to management and governance. Convergence or computer literacy may have little to do with the issues being addressed by this report. The report's positive aspect is that it brings attention to an important matter long overdue for a more critical discussion and surgery. But the surgery may not be radical enough. If placing the declassification center in the National Archives would change that institution into a vigilant "watchdog," as many urge it to become, then citizens, government, other archivists, records managers, and users of archival records would benefit. If the center sinks into the Archives, lacking resources and teeth, then nothing will change in terms of the shifting to a more secretive government and a less democratic society. What these high-profile cases, reports, and books suggest is that whatever power technology has for the management of information, the technical capability must be used to support the management of records to support uses such as corporate memory, accountability, evidence, and other values. Technology, without an eye to these broader values, is no panacea.

CONCLUSION: RECORDS, TECHNOLOGY, AND POLICY

It is easy to see computer literacy or technology convergence as the solution for the management of work, offices, and the records generated. Professionals can handle more tasks, activities and functions brought together in convenient forms, workers can instantly communicate with other colleagues at distant locations any time, and employees can cope with massive amounts of information. That is the theory, anyway. Yet, there must be caution. As Soshana Zuboff writes, "computer-based technologies are not neutral," altering the "nature of work within our factories and offices, and among workers, professionals, and managers."[102]

Mounting evidence suggests that technology can be a burden. Workers spend more of their time checking messages, creating constant interruptions and making them feel "overwhelmed."[103] Productivity is threatened, the distinction between work and home has blurred, and the general health and attitudes of employees are all affected. Some critics argue that we need to understand that the "normal state of anyone's computer is off" and the "normal state of anyone's relationship to computer networks is unconnected."[104] Such advice begins to make us question the promises of the converged, networked workplace in which we can be monitored, always connected to wherever we happen to be, and constantly interrupted with new commands and advice. Records professionals need to be critical as well.

It is easy to lose sight of such issues. Sherry Turkle argues that being part of the "computer culture" only requires the ability to acquire and use software.[105] Information professionals responsible for records and other vital information must be more critical of software than just taking it out of the box. The market society wants us to do otherwise. Anthony Smith argues that one of the forces in society is to bring together "all forms of communication and information into a kind of latter-day Alexandrian Library."[106] Still, this technology threatens (or promises) a fundamental re-ordering of the *meaning* of work. Many researchers studying the workplace see a transformation because of the new dynamics of technologies represented by the kinds of uses of computers information professionals are concerned to implement.[107] Additional concerns include the ethical dimensions of computer reliance, the loss of the objectives of professionals to contribute to the public good rather than to sell their expertise to the highest bidder, the blurring of work and social responsibilities, and the artificial isolation of humans working against their natural social needs. This seems different from the feeling by some that the computer revolution is "in full steam": "Computing had become totally decentralized. Everyone had the power on his or her desk or at home. The priesthood of the mainframe's information managers was dead. The people had won."[108]

Policy, in organizations and society, is critical to keep the ship righted. Not everyone is part of the computer revolution or is reaping its many supposed benefits. There are many troubling aspects brought to society by the computer. And we need to protect the many benefits to society and the people brought by the computer, including transforming some aspects of work, making many activities more convenient for a large portion of society, and enabling the management of great quantities of information in ways never imagined. The computer is a tool, and a tool can be both beneficial and a weapon. Policies help regulate its use.

Computers are also touted as the solution to the management of records and other information generated and needed by the modern organization. Records can be stored compactly, and paper files can be scanned into convenient digital forms. Individuals can work together, in simultaneous fashion, creating records, reports, and other organizational products. Businesses can harness the power of the computer in order to respond quickly to customers. And the computer can virtually eliminate the paper cluttering and strangling the office. But these solutions, as has been discussed in this book, can bring with them mind-boggling problems. What is the official record? How can records be preserved for long periods of time in such volatile electronic systems? What about the legal requirements for the management of records? Such issues have thrown some organizations into near states of despair about how to resolve them. In some cases, organizations have lost their corporate memory, public officials have flouted the notion of any accountability to their constituents, and society has lost a substantial means of understanding what is going on.

Such claims for computerized recordkeeping are similar to other promises for the computer in our society. Computers are being emphasized as the key to the education of our youth and all age groups in our society. Every student should have access to the computer and to the information available on the Internet, be able to learn from educational software, and mastered the basics of the computer. Computer literacy is as fundamental as reading, or so it is claimed. Is something missing? An educated individual in our modern world does need to have some ability to work at a terminal, but that education requires an understanding of just what this tool represents.

Cybernauts are trumpeting the possibility of using networked computers as the key to a democratic society. Information is seen as the substance of an informed citizenry and an informed citizenry is viewed as crucial to a democratic society. The advent of the Internet and the creation of a community via networking has become the new model of a modern democracy. If the old model was the New England town meeting, the new version is a society linked electronically that will allow new deliberations, decision making, and constituencies to be heard. Networking is a way of overcoming the increasing control of print and other media information in the hands of an ever shrinking number of corporate giants and powerful business moguls. Can the computer really enable a new form of democratic society to emerge? All of this really depends on how good or trustworthy the information is to begin with. Anyone can put a homepage on the World Wide Web with falsehoods, half-truths, or shoddy research. Only the reasonably well informed have any hope of being able to navigate through the dangerous potholes of the Information Highway.

In the computer revolution the people will have won only if we are ever vigilant in our public policy, laws, and social conscience regulating the computer. Where are the archivists and records managers in all this? Where are the Society of American Archivists or the Association of Records Managers and Administrators as advocates in promoting the integrity of the *record* in the modern Information Age? Is there a voice for the records professional in the war about the impact of the computer in society and on the individual? How do we sort out the completely contrary opinions, one optimistic and the other a portrait of doomsday, expressed about the Information Age in many recent books.

The records professions need to recognize that the increasing concerns voiced by individuals about the impact of the computer on literacy, jobs, information access, the general quality of life, economic stability, privacy, and politics provide wonderful opportunities for them to speak up about why records are not only important but essential for our modern society. After all, Hollerith started it all a century ago, almost exactly the same time as the modern archival profession was developing with the establishment of its first associations and the publication of its first textbooks. Surely, archivists and records managers have long since learned that they have something to contribute to the maintenance of the information held in the records generated by the computer.

NOTES

1. Robert Wright, *Three Scientists and Their Gods: Looking for Meaning in an Age of Information* (New York: Harper and Row, 1988), p. 173.

2. Lucy A. Suchman, "Office Procedure as Practical Action: Models of Work and System Design," *ACM Transactions on Office Information Systems* 6 (1983): 326–327.

3. For a sampling of recent writings critical of the Information Age, refer to Sven Bierkerts, *The Gutenberg Elegies: The Fate of Reading in an Electronic Age* (Boston: Faber and Faber, 1995); Barry Sanders, *A Is for Ox: Violence, Electronic Media, and the Silencing of the Written Word* (New York: Pantheon Books, 1994); Clifford Stoll,

Silicon Snake Oil: Second Thoughts on the Information Highway (New York: Anchor Books, 1995); Edward Tenner, *Why Things Bite Back: Technology and the Revenge of Unintended Consequences* (New York: Alfred A. Knopf, 1996); Herbert Schiller, *Information Inequality: The Deepening Social Crisis in America* (New York: Routledge, 1996). For a sampling of writings with a positive view of the Information Age, refer to Richard A. Lanham, *The Electronic Word: Democracy, Technology, and the Arts* (Chicago: University of Chicago Press, 1993); Nicholas Negroponte, *Being Digital* (New York: Alfred A. Knopf, 1995); Arno Penzias, *Digital Harmony: Business, Technology and Life After Paperwork* (New York: HarperBusiness, 1996); and Lawrence K. Grossman, *The Electronic Republic: Reshaping Democracy in the Information Age* (New York: Viking, 1995).

4. Fred Moody, *I Sing the Body Electronic: A Year with Microsoft on the Multimedia Frontier* (New York: Penguin, 1995), p. 51.

5. The relationship between archivists and records managers has been a topic of discussion in both groups since the 1950s. That this is a topic that is still relevant is evident in Dan Zelenyj, "Archivy *Ad Portas*: The Archives–Records Management Paradigm Re-visited in the Electronic Information Age," *Archivaria* 47 (Spring 1999): 66–84. Zelenyj argues: "In a nutshell, archival functions and records management functions are one and the same" (p. 67).

6. Michael Heim, *Electric Language: A Philosophical Study of Word Processing* (New Haven, CT: Yale University Press, 1987), p. 129.

7. Jack Goody, *The Logic of Writing and the Organization of Society* (London: Cambridge University Press, 1986), pp. 77–78.

8. At least it should in principle. Kenneth Thibodeau, of the U. S. National Archives, argues that this same court case holds up the definition as used in the Federal Records Act. See his "Managing Archival Records in the Electronic Age: Fundamental Challenges," in Peter Hernon, Charles R. McClure, and Harold C. Relyea, eds., *Federal Information Policies in the 1990s: Views and Perspectives* (Norwood, NJ: Ablex Publishing Corporation, 1996), pp. 279–295.

9. Examples of such definitions of information include Richard Derr, "The Concept of Information in Ordinary Discourse," *Information Processing and Management* 21, no. 6 (1985): 489–499; Christopher John Fox, *Information and Misinformation: An Investigation of the Notions of Information, Misinformation, Informing, and Misinforming* (Westport, CT: Greenwood Press, 1983); Noriko Kando, "Information Concepts Reexamined," *International Forum on Information and Documentation* 19, no. 2 (1994): 20–24; Clifford Lynch, "The Transformation of Scholarly Communication and the Role of the Library in the Age of Networked Information," *Serials Librarian* 23, nos. 3–4 (1993): 5–20; Joseph Nitecki, "The Concept of Information–Knowledge Continuum: Implications for Librarianship," *Journal of Library History, Philosophy and Comparative Librarianship* 20 (Fall 1985): 387–407; Erhard Oeser, "Information Superhighways for Knowledge Transfer and the Need for a Fundamental Theory of Information," *International Forum on Information and Documentation* 20, no. 1 (1995): 16–21; Norman D. Stevens, "The History of Information," in *Advances in Librarianship*, ed. Wesley Simonton (New York: Academic Press, 1986), 14:1–48; Paul Young, *The Nature of Information* (New York: Praeger, 1987); and Zhang Yuexiao, "Definitions and Sciences of Information," *Information Processing and Management* 24, no. 4 (1988): 479–491.

10. Hedstrom stated this in a paper presented at the 1994 Society of American Ar-

chivists annual meeting about the research conducted to this point in the realm of electronic records management research.

11. Terry Cook, "Electronic Records, Paper Minds: The Revolution in Information Management and Archives in the Post-Custodial and Post-Modernist Era," *Archives and Manuscripts* 22 (November 1994): 300–328.

12. Langdon Winner, *The Whale and the Reactor: A Search for Limits in an Age of High Technology* (Chicago: University of Chicago Press, 1986), p. 20.

13. There is a Web site with links to the majority of important ongoing and recently completed electronic records research and application projects and with full citations to the earlier research agenda. A visit to this site can be useful because there is a summary of the results of this conference, summaries of current projects, and the musings of Hedstrom and several others about the nature of research going on or that needs to be done. See http://www.si.umich.edu/e-recs/. There was also a meeting evaluating research on electronic records held in May 1997 and published as a special issue of *Archives and Museum Informatics* 11, nos. 3–4 (1997).

14. Full information about this project can be seen at the project homepage on the World Wide Web; visit http://www.sis.pitt.edu/~nhprc.

15. See Wendy Duff, "Harnessing the Power of Warrant," *American Archivist* 61 (Spring 1998): 88–105.

16. In addition to the projects described in this essay, the recordkeeping functional requirements have been used by the World Bank, Vermont State Archives, New South Wales (Australia) Archives, Australian Archives (this country's national archives), the International Council on Archives Committee on Electronic Records, and the Victoria (Australia) government. Links to these projects are available at the University of Pittsburgh Web site.

17. Full information on the project, including a bibliography of publications about it, can be found at http://www.slais.ubc.ca/users/duranti. The current phase of this project, now named INTERPARES (International Research on Permanent Authentic Records in Electronic Systems), is documented at http://www.interpares.org/.

18. See http://unix6.nysed.gov/pubs/report for complete information on the results of this project.

19. This project was administered by the Center for Technology in Government located at the State University New York at Albany and is available at http://www.ctg.albany.edu/projects/er/ermn.html.

20. Full information on this project is available at http://www.phila.gov/city/departments/erms/erg.html.

21. Full information on this project is available at http://www.indiana.edu/~libarche.

22. For a description of this standard, refer to David O. Stephens and David Roberts, "From Australia: The World's First National Standard for Records Management," *Records Management Quarterly* 30 (October 1996): 3–7, 62.

23. For more information about the records continuum concept see the work of the Records Continuum Research Group at Monash University at http://www.sims.monash.edu.au/rcrg/.

24. James Madison, *The Federalist*, no. 51 [1788].

25. Kevin P. Kearns, *Managing for Accountability: Preserving the Public Trust in Public and Nonprofit Organizations* (San Francisco: Jossey-Bass Publishers, 1996).

26. Anne Wells Branscomb, *Who Owns Information? From Privacy to Public Access* (New York: Basic Books, 1994). For some excellent recent studies of the problems with

access to government records, refer to Angus MacKenzie, *Secrets: The CIA's War at Home* (Berkeley: University of California Press, 1997) and David Rudenstine, *The Day the Presses Stopped: A History of the Pentagon Papers Case* (Berkeley: University of California Press, 1996).

27. Howard Rheingold, *The Virtual Community: Homesteading on the Electronic Frontier* (New York: HarperPerennial, 1993), p. 13.

28. The ethical issues enumerated were political fund-raising, independent counsels, Whitewater, Whitewater pardons, missing billing records, FBI files, the Travel Office, and withholding documents; "Ethical Issues Facing the White House," *New York Times*, November 3, 1996, p. 20.

29. *New York Times*, June 2, 1995.

30. Richard F. Hixson, *Privacy in a Public Society: Human Rights in Conflict* (New York: Oxford University Press, 1987), p. 209.

31. *New York Times*, November 15, 1995.

32. See http://www.gateway-va.com/pages/news/tobac/tobacco.htm with current information on the so-called "Tobacco Papers" litigation, with ramifications for access to information found in records. See especially Stanton A. Glantz, John Slade, Lisa A. Bero, Peter Hanauer, and Deborah E. Barnes, *The Cigarette Papers* (Berkeley: University of California Press, 1996).

33. See Steven Naifeh and Gregory White Smith, *The Mormon Murders* (New York: New American Library, 1988).

34. See, for a variety of views, Todd Gitlin, *The Twilight of Common Dreams: Why America Is Wracked by Culture Wars* (New York: Metropolitan Books, 1995); Mary Lefkowitz, *Not Out of Africa: How Afrocentrism Became An Excuse to Teach Myth as History* (New York: HarperCollins, 1996); Edward T. Linenthal and Tom Engelhardt, eds., *History Wars: The Enola Gay and Other Battles for the American Past* (New York: Metropolitan Books, 1996); Philip Nobile, ed., *Judgment at the Smithsonian* (New York: Marlowe and Co., 1995); and Arthur M. Schlesinger, Jr., *The Disuniting of America: Reflections on a Multicultural Society* (New York: W. W. Norton and Co., 1992).

35. See, for example, Timothy W. Ryback, "Evidence of Evil," *New Yorker* 69 (November 15, 1993): 68–81; Deborah Lipstadt, *Denying the Holocaust: The Growing Assault on Truth and Memory* (New York: Free Press, 1993); James E. Young, *The Texture of Memory: Holocaust Memorials and Meaning* (New Haven, CT: Yale University Press, 1993); Geoffrey H. Hartman, ed., *Holocaust Remembrance: The Shapes of Memory* (Cambridge, MA: Blackwell, 1994); and Ian Buruma, *The Wages of Guilt: Memories of War in Germany and Japan* (New York: Meridan, 1994).

36. Luciana Duranti, "The Odyssey of Records Managers," *Records Management Quarterly* 23 (July 1989): 5.

37. Richard Kesner, "Automated Information Management: Is There a Role for the Archivist in the Office of the Future?" *Archivaria* 19 (Winter 1984–1985): 163.

38. See Richard J. Cox, "Accountability, Public Scholarship, and Library, Information, and Archival Science Educators," *Journal of Education for Library and Information Science* 41 (Spring 2000): 19–31.

39. M. T. Clanchy, *From Memory to Written Record: England, 1066–1307* (Cambridge MA: Harvard University Press, 1979), p. 144.

40. Clanchy, *From Memory to Written Record*, p. 294.

41. Thomas K. Landauer, *The Trouble with Computers: Usefulness, Usability, and Productivity* (Cambridge, MA: MIT Press, 1995), p. 152.

42. Mark Slouka, *War of the Worlds: Cyberspace and the High-Tech Assault on Reality* (New York: Basic Books, 1995), p. 27.

43. John Shore, *The Sachertorte Algorithm and Other Antidotes to Computer Anxiety* (New York: Penguin Books, 1985), p. xiii.

44. Shore, *The Sachertorte Algorithm*, p. 72.

45. Landauer, *The Trouble with Computers*, pp. 121–122, 144.

46. Jonathan Kozol, *Illiterate America* (Garden City, NY: Anchor Books, 1985), pp. 19, 35.

47. Vinton G. Cerf, "Networks," *Scientific American* 265 (September 1991): 72–73.

48. Mark Weisner, "The Computer for the 21st Century," *Scientific American* 265 (September 1991): 104.

49. Wendell Berry, *Sex, Economy, Freedom and Community: Eight Essays* (New York: Pantheon Books, 1993), pp. xiii–xiv.

50. James I. Penrod and Judith V. Douglas, "Information Technology Literacy: A Definition," in *Encyclopedia of Library and Information Science*, ed. Allen Kent, vol. 40, supplement 5 (New York: Marcel Dekker, 1986), pp. 76, 100–101.

51. Jerry Kanter, "Computer-Information Literacy for Senior Management," *Information Strategy: The Executive's Journal* 11 (Spring 1995): 6–7.

52. Michael Dobberstein, "Computer Literacy for the Rest of Us," *Computers and the Humanities* 27, nos. 5–6 (1993–1994): 430, 431.

53. George E. Marsh, II, *Computers: Literacy and Learning; A Primer for Administrators* (Newbury Park, CA: Corwin Press, 1993), p. 5.

54. Egbert Schuurman, *Perspectives on Technology and Culture*, trans. John H. Kok (Sioux Center, IA: Dordt College Press, 1995), pp. 13, 57.

55. Peter Drucker, "Infoliteracy," *Forbes ASAP*, August, 29 1994, p. 109.

56. Landauer, *The Trouble with Computers*, pp. 136, 183, 191, 354–356.

57. George Nichols, "Evidence in the Machine," unpublished paper, October, 29, 1993.

58. Michael Cook, *Guidelines on Curriculum Development in Information Technology for Librarians, Documentalists and Archivists*, PGI-96/WS/26 (Paris: UNESCO, 1986).

59. Nancy McCall and Lisa A. Mix, with John Dojka and Gerald Shorb, "Making Provisions for the Management of Contemporary Records," in Nancy McCall and Lisa A. Mix, eds., *Designing Archival Programs to Advance Knowledge in the Health Fields* (Baltimore: Johns Hopkins University Press, 1995), pp. 165–183, especially p. 169.

60. Terry Eastwood, "Nurturing Archival Education in the University," *American Archivist* 51 (Summer 1988): 237.

61. Victoria Irons Walch, comp., "Automated Records and Techniques Curriculum Development Project," *American Archivist* 56 (Summer 1993): 468–505.

62. Edward Tenner, *Why Things Bite Back: Technology and the Revenge of Unintended Consequences* (New York: Alfred A. Knopf, 1996), p. 209.

63. J. Michael Pemberton and Christine R. Nugent, "Information Studies: Emergent Field, Convergent Curriculum," *Journal of Education for Library and Information Science* 36 (Spring 1995): 126–138.

64. Australian Council of Archives, "Corporate Memory in the Electronic Age: Statement of a Common Position on Electronic Recordkeeping," October 23, 1995.

65. Vernon R. Smith, "Pedagogy and Professionalism: An Evaluation of Trends and

Choices Confronting Educators in the Archival Community," *Public Historian* 16 (Summer 1994): 35, 38.

66. Mark Greene, "From the Chair: An Editorial," *SAA Manuscript Repositories Section Newsletter*, February 1996, [1–2].

67. David Bearman, "Documenting Documentation," *Archivaria* 34 (Summer 1992): 41.

68. Jim Coulson, "Our Professional Responsibility," *Records Management Quarterly* 27 (April 1993): 25.

69. John F. Burnum, "The Misinformation Era: The Fall of the Medical Record," *Annals of Internal Medicine* 110 (March 15, 1989): 482–484.

70. Keith Devlin and Duska Rosenberg, *Networked Information Flow via Stylized Documents*, Report no. CSLI–94–187 (Menlo Park, CA: Center for the Study of Language and Information, March 1994).

71. Joel Shurkin, *Engines of the Mind: The Evolution of the Computer from Mainframes to Microprocessors* (New York: W. W. Norton and Co., 1996), chap. 11.

72. Frederick Crews, *The Memory Wars: Freud's Legacy in Dispute* (New York: New York Review Book, 1995), p. 13.

73. Joan Schwartz, "We Make Our Tools and Our Tools Make Us: Lessons from Photographs for the Practice, Politics, and Poetics of Diplomatics," *Archivaria* 40 (Fall 1995): 46, 50.

74. Information Management Standards and Practices Division, *Preliminary Study on the Core Competencies of the Future Records Specialist* (Ottawa: National Archives of Canada, May 1996).

75. Clifford Stoll, *Silicon Snake Oil: Second Thoughts on the Information Highway* (New York: Anchor Books, 1995), p. 131.

76. William Knoke, *Bold New World: The Essential Road Map to the Twenty-First Century* (New York: Kodansha International, 1996), p. 52.

77. Elias Safdie, "Caution: Technology Convergence Ahead," *IW (Imaging World)*, April 7, 1997, pp. 33, 36, 39–45.

78. Thomas J. Galvin, "Convergence or Divergence in Education for the Information Professions: An Opinion Paper," *Bulletin* of the American Society for Information Science 21 (August–September 1995): 7–12.

79. Arnold Pacey, *The Culture of Technology* (Cambridge, MA: MIT Press, 1983).

80. CENSA, the Collaborative Electronic Notebook Systems Association, issued a report at the end of December 1999 entitled "Titanic 2020." The report argues that current information technology is not taking into account the need to maintain records over the long term. The authors of the report suggest that within ten years the number of records produced may be doubling every sixty minutes. The report worries about the short-term mentality in designing new systems and suggests that there needs to be a change in this attitude. The report argues that this problem is far greater, more expensive, and laden with serious implications that the Y2K bug. The report is available at http://www.censa.org/html/publications/Titanic-2020-Final-Report-01–05–2000.pdf.

81. David Damrosch, *We Scholars: Changing the Culture of the University* (Cambridge, MA: Harvard University Press, 1995).

82. These are the themes developed by Julie Thompson Klein, *Interdisciplinarity: History, Theory, and Practice* (Detroit: Wayne State University Press, 1990).

83. Andrew Abbott, *The System of Professions: An Essay on the Division of Expert Labor* (Chicago: University of Chicago Press, 1988).

84. These two associations are now working to offer joint sessions at each of their annual meetings, reflecting a recognition of mutual interests. It is too early to determine just what impact this might have on records professionals crossing over to attend each others' meetings.

85. Herbert Schiller, *Information Inequality: The Deepening Social Crisis in America* (New York: Routledge, 1996), p. 36.

86. Consider, for example, the title of Arno Penzias's *Digital Harmony: Business, Technology and Life After Paperwork* (New York: HarperBusiness, 1996).

87. Tom Bower, *Nazi Gold: The Full Story of the Fifty-Year Swiss–Nazi Conspiracy to Steal Billions from Europe's Jews and Holocaust Survivors* (New York: HarperCollins, 1997); Isabel Vincent's *Hitler's Silent Partners: Swiss Banks, Nazi Gold, and the Pursuit of Justice* (New York: William Morrow and Co., 1997) is the most balanced of the accounts. Half a dozen other books have subsequently appeared concerning this case, and more are likely to be written and published.

88. For the extensiveness of records available in American federal agencies, refer to Greg Bradsher, *A Finding Aid to Records at the National Archives at College Park . . . for the Interagency Group on Nazi Assets . . . Department of Commerce* [1997] and William Z. Slany, *U.S. and Allied Efforts to Recover and Restore Gold and Other Assets Stolen or Hidden by Germany During World War II* [May 1997], both available through the World Wide Web, the former and most important listing of records is at www.ushmm.org/assets/nazigold.htm.

89. Mike Wallace, *Mickey Mouse History and Other Essays on American Memory* (Philadelphia: Temple University Press, 1996).

90. Ian Buruma, *The Wages of Guilt: Memories of War in Germany and Japan* (New York: Meridian, 1994).

91. Shelley Davis, *Unbridled Power: Inside the Secret Culture of the IRS* (New York: HarperBusiness, 1997).

92. Davis, *Unbridled Power*, p. 3.

93. Lynda D. Willis, *Tax Administration: IRS Inspection Service and Taxpayer Advocate Roles for Ensuring That Taxpayers Are Treated Properly*, GAO Report T-GGD-98–63, February 5, 1998.

94. Davis, *Unbridled Power*, p. 75.

95. Tom Blanton, *White House E-Mail: The Top Secret Computer Messages the Reagan/Bush White House Tried to Destroy* (New York: New Press, 1995).

96. Richard Neustadt and Ernest May, *Thinking in Time: The Uses of History for Decision Makers* (New York: The Free Press, 1986).

97. U.S. Congress Commission on Protecting and Reducing Government Secrecy, *Secrecy* (Washington, DC.: Government Printing Office, 1997).

98. Philip K. Howard, *The Death of Common Sense: How Law is Suffocating America* (New York: Warner Books, 1994), p. 70.

99. Seymour M. Hersh, "Nixon's Last Cover-up: The Tapes He Wants the Archives to Suppress," *New Yorker* (December 14, 1992): 76–82, 84–88, 90–95.

100. Blanton, *White House E-Mail*, p. 11.

101. Ellen Alderman and Caroline Kennedy, *The Right to Privacy* (New York: Alfred A. Knopf, 1995), pp. 27, 331.

102. Shoshana Zuboff, *In the Age of the Smart Machine: The Future of Work and Power* (New York: Basic Books, 1988), p. 7.

103. Alex Markels, "FYI: Messages Inundate Offices," *Wall Street Journal*, April 8, 1997.

104. Stephen Doheny-Farina, *The Wired Neighborhood* (New Haven, CT: Yale University Press, 1996), pp. 100–101.

105. Sherry Turkle, *Life on the Screen: Identity in the Age of the Internet* (New York: Simon and Schuster, 1995).

106. Anthony Smith, *Software for the Self: Culture and Technology* (New York: Oxford University Press, 1996), p. 77.

107. Stanley Aronowitz and William DiFazio, *The Jobless Future: Sci-Tech and the Dogma of Work* (Minneapolis: University of Minnesota Press, 1994).

108. Joel Shurkin, *Engines of the Mind: The Evolution of the Computer from Mainframes to Microprocessors* (New York: W. W. Norton, 1996), p. 322.

Chapter 3

The Policy's Spine: Appraising and Maintaining Records

INTRODUCTION: THE SEPARATE ROADS OF RECORDS MANAGERS AND ARCHIVISTS

If an extraterrestrial visited a records management program and archives, our visitor from another world might be extremely confused about how to describe their differences. This would be particularly troublesome in the records manager's disposition scheduling and the archivist's appraising. Scott Adams, creator of "Dilbert" and perhaps as close to an alien as we can get, describes records retention as one of his favorite business tasks. Adams argues that once records are sent to a warehouse no one will ever look at them again. For his records retention program, Adams "would move a Dumpster into the office that said, PLACE DOCUMENTS FOR STORAGE INSIDE." The humorist states that "most jobs in corporate life have no value to the economy, but there are scant few that so aggressively ignore any attempt at even appearing useful."[1]

It is easy to dismiss Adams's satire, but we should be cautious about this. His cartoons and books are often based on communications *from* the workplace, so some office workers have commented on their sense of corporate records management. Have records managers and archivists simply confused matters by developing different approaches to records disposition, retention, and maintenance? A decade ago, in one of the many essays exploring the relationship between archivists and records managers, Robert Sanders wondered whether retention or disposition scheduling was the core of the framework for a continuing partnership. There are some mutual interests: "The records manager looks to the archivist to sanction the destruction of obsolete records, and the archivist relies upon the records manager to safeguard what merits preservation."[2] In the same function, there are some fundamental differences: "While the records managers justify their work in part by the cubic feet of records they destroy, the archivists take pride in the pages they preserve forever."[3] Archivists and records managers, despite what differences may exist, are "bound together in a symbiotic relationship for scheduling records retention and disposition."[4] However, as Sanders speculates, the new information technologies may have shifted records managers away from "records scheduling towards identifying it with new image-capturing and automated-retrieval technologies."[5]

Why the relationship, or partnership, between archivists and records managers is troubled should be a surprise to all records professionals, especially when reflecting on the appraisal–disposition functions. The importance of records, even in the midst of the technocratic modern Information Age, suggests a convergence of all records professionals. Yet, there are countless references to the fact that this is *not* the case. The authors of the standard Australian records management text recommend that records managers working on records scheduling should consult with archivists about records of potential historical value or seek to establish effective archival programs within their organizations. But, as they write, "this is not always easy as many organizations are more interested in retaining as little as possible than in meeting the possible needs of future researchers. The records manager has more chance of success if the idea of retaining documents of historical significance can be couched in terms of potential value to the organization in its future planning."[6] A tension between archivists and records managers, both serving organizations and the creators of records, is evident. This tension creates problems in the development and use of records and information policies from the organizational to the national level.

The reason for such problems is that the very heart of what constitutes records management scheduling or archival appraising dramatically overlaps, although there seem to be very different professional missions or cultures involved. Archivists generally consider *values* when considering appraisal. Bruce Dearstyne summarizes this perspective: "Records possess two kinds of values. The first is called 'primary value'—the administrative, fiscal, legal, and operational value for which the record was originally created or received. They also have 'secondary' values—importance for others beyond the current users. Secondary values—key for archivists—are of two types: 'evidential' and 'informational.' Appraisal archivists invest their time, talent, and mental energies to determining the degree to which records fit those abstract concepts."[7] In this brief description, accurately capturing the manner in which most practicing archivists think of appraisal, one can detect *both* the reason for the convergence and divergence of records management and archival approaches to records selection. The records manager certainly identifies with the primary value, given his or her responsibility to a particular organization. The archivist, however, often working in cultural or academic environments, tends to stress the secondary value.

This discontinuity can be seen in various records management textbooks. One such textbook stresses the same kind of values approach, defining "a *records appraisal* [as] an examination of the data gathered through the records inventory to determine the value of each records series to the organization" and describing the values as administrative, fiscal, legal, and historical.[8] This textbook also puts the chapter on archives as an appendix and suggests that the primary value of archives is for use by researchers *external* to the organization. It sees a records retention program possessing three goals: "(1) cost reduction, (2) retrieval efficiency, and (3) retention consistency."[9] These kinds of values have led to odd ideas about records appraisal. Another records management text argues that "records have historical (or archival) value if they have to do with the origin and history of the organization," followed by a list of records forms that should be saved for this purpose.[10] While certainly such records should be maintained, this is not the essence of an archival record.

One might be inclined to assign the blame for such problems to the *authors* of these volumes, reflecting their *own* biases and prejudices. However, the most recent professional glossary, published in 1992, suggests otherwise. Appraisal is defined as the "process of determining the value and thus the disposition of records based upon their current administrative, legal, and fiscal use; their evidential and informational value; their arrangement and condition; their intrinsic value; and their relationship to other records." Scheduling is defined as the "process of determining and recording in a records schedule the appropriate retention period and ultimate disposition of series." Disposition is considered to be the "actions taken with regard to non-current records as determined by their appraisal pursuant to legislation, regulation, or administrative procedure."[11] This is a confusing mix of values and archival appraisal and records management approaches. It makes one want to help Scott Adams move that dumpster into the office in order to be done with it. If anything can be concluded from this, it is that the half-century professional schism between archivists and records managers has not been beneficial for *either* discipline *or* for the management of records for organizations and society.

The ideas of records values float uncomfortably between the records manager and the archivist. The records manager is often prone to want to dispose of "routine" records. For the records manager the purpose of records scheduling is to destroy unnecessary records, ensure that essential records are maintained, enable vital records to be identified and managed, clear out equipment and space, and preserve historical records. The archivist can sometimes argue that the routine records are the most valuable, because of their sensitivity to what historians and other researchers need or may desire. Historians studying scientific experimentation have determined that a "combination of experimental records and notes, diaries or private journals, and correspondence," is often most desired, this combination providing "thick traces of the scientist's ongoing thought and action." These are, in fact, the routine records because they are "intrinsic to the standard routine of *being* an experimental scientist" as they "preserve the accumulating results of one's investigative activity."[12] Unless these records were essential for patent, legal, or another similar purpose, the records manager would not maintain them.

The records manager might see an interest in such records as irresponsible. Social commentator Cullen Murphy wonders "whether as a nation we are compiling archives at a rate that will exceed anyone's ability ever to make sense of them."[13] Similar sentiments are expressed by management gurus who argue about the dangers of bureaucracy and the impact of ever increasing quantities of forms and regulations producing more and more records. Peter Drucker laments, "in the traditional organization, most of the people called 'managers' do not actually manage; they relay orders downward and information upward. When information becomes available, they become redundant."[14] Records managers might see themselves as threatened because they are middle managers with rules and regulations, or they might see themselves as providing a service whereby they can aid in the destruction of the paper mounds and information gluts impeding others' work. Drucker makes it more complicated by noting that a "government agency must of necessity act like a bureaucracy. It must (indeed it should) subordinate productivity to rules and regulations. It must be wrapped in 'red tape.' It must focus on proper paperwork rather than on results. Otherwise it soon becomes a gang of thieves."[15] Here, the records manager and the archivist, armed with records retention schedules, are the guardians of institutional accountability *if* accountability rather than economy or efficiency or historical research is elevated as the purpose of records professionals' work. That archivists and records managers have struggled with their purpose, whether viewed from the institutional or societal perspective, is another legacy of their professional separation, the rise of new recordkeeping technologies, and the appearance of others with a stake in administering records as information.

Determining the appropriate relationship between archival appraisal and records management scheduling is difficult because of the complexities in deciding which records ought to be maintained, *rather* than fundamental professional differences between archivists and records managers. The schism between archivists and records managers has mainly hurt the appraisal/scheduling function because it has eliminated creative dialogue about it. Archivists, for the past two decades, have been arguing about appraisal because of the difficulties with their values approach, the increasing variety of recordkeeping media, and the rapid growth in the quantity of records. The 1991 Association of Canadian Archivists meeting focused on appraisal and revealed disharmony among archivists about being the " 'documenter' of society" or the "mediator between social forces and the people, between the records creators and those for whom the records are created in the first place" or the "societal officer responsible for maintaining the essential values of his or her society by preserving the evidence of its actions and transactions."[16] Such debate continues.

Is scheduling a crucial aspect of archival appraisal, or is archival appraisal a part of records management scheduling and disposition work? While many organizations have either vested these responsibilities in the same professional or administrative unit or have created processes whereby the archivist and records manager must approve jointly the disposition of records, there is more to ap-

praising and maintaining records than simple methods and administrative guidelines. Too many records managers rely on legal and administrative officers to
determine what records should be maintained. Too many archivists fall prey to
broad, open-ended research values to determine what records should be assigned
to the archives. Records professionals must have a substantial intellectual foundation for records disposition, especially as electronic recordkeeping systems
have both speeded up and complicated the appraisal/disposition responsibility.

STARTING OVER: THE ADVENT OF ELECTRONIC
RECORDS AND THE IDEA OF PRESERVATION

The maintenance of records is closely related to their selection, and it has
been just as troubled in recent years. When the Society of American Archivists'
first major preservation manual appeared in 1984, the personal computer was
revolutionizing the workplace and society. It was ironic that at just the time
when a consensus about the preservation of traditional records appeared that
these records seemed to be changing. An entire new spectrum of challenges
emerged. Records professionals have fallen short of preservation approaches for
electronic records, but the substance of the issues wrought by the technology
now are so different as to defy simple characterizations. As the technology
proceeded through five generations of computers in quick order, there have been
two generations of electronic records professionals. The solutions developed by
the first generation for managing flat-file, largely numerical electronic files were
unworkable for the latter technologies. Records could not be carried off on tapes
to be deposited in centralized archives, and new policies, legislation, and technical solutions were needed. The changes caused some archivists to question
whether the record as generally defined still existed, others to wonder whether
the profession itself would even exist a generation from now.

Fissures in the preservation paradigm became more obvious with electronic
records. Electronic records are not protected until they are brought into the
centralized, environmentally secure archival repository, the same mechanism by
which other archival records are "preserved." Problems with the preservation of
electronic media are referred to the preservation specialists once the electronic
records have been received by the repository and processed for use. In return,
priorities for actions are determined by availability of resources, anticipated use,
and importance of the records—all based on the internal repository universe of
records. Permanence is paramount. Most archivists and preservation administrators are working to ensure the permanent preservation of the records under their
control. The continuing anguish about environmental and other storage conditions, resources for reformatting and conservation treatment, and disaster-
preparedness plans emanate from this monumental commitment to preserve for
eternity. This is a preservation paradigm which has worked well enough for
most recording media but which is faulty when considering the preservation of
electronic records. It is a paradigm that records managers must also re-think as

more and more of their responsibilities are focused on electronic recordkeeping systems. Whereas records professionals were writing and conversing about electronic records as "special media" a decade ago, it is likely that the future special media will be *paper* records.

The advent of electronic information technology has generated new interest in the design and standards approach to preservation, and perhaps an entire new notion of preservation—building *into* the recordkeeping systems their preservation. There is both a paper and electronic analogue to this approach. In the 1980s, following the lead of library preservationists, archivists lobbied for the legislative solution for the adoption of non-alkaline paper. The concept was simple, but it had problems. It ignored that the creation of records often involved the intermingling of records produced externally without these controls, undermining the integrity of the records preservation. The technological solution seemed a bit overblown given that there would be a very small portion of the records created with archival value.

It is different in the electronic realm. It is nearly impossible, for one thing, to move these recordkeeping systems over to the archives. With modern electronic recordkeeping systems too much would be lost in such a transfer. Moreover, how would the archives service such a system? What would result would be little more than transitory (and meaningless) information without its provenance, context, and other features that make it a record. It is impossible to survey and scan all the records produced by such a system. Some systems would enable you to see a record on your computer screen, but that record might appear to be different at a second glance seconds later. How do you even begin to determine what should be maintained? In other systems, the records are so voluminous as to defy any manageable means to consider them. There is simply no way for the records professional to manage these transactions traditionally. Yet, the deletion of these records (those that are records) represents a significant and growing preservation problem. Many of these kinds of issues must reside at the heart of records and information policies.

Information and recordkeeping systems can be distinguished by a strict adherence to a definition of record, as the first two chapters have explored, built around a formal business transaction. While many records professionals are dazzled by electronics, a growing number see in the systems not only solutions to their practical management but the possibilities of managing records more effectively than in paper-based systems. Recent efforts to develop recordkeeping functional requirements, discussed in the first two chapters, provide a new possibility for ensuring both that electronic systems which produce records will maintain those records as long as needed *and* will help to make organizational administrators more aware of records issues. Some research suggests that the biggest problem may rest with records professionals, who are either unsure of how to define a record in the electronic realm or define it in such a manner as to avoid grappling with some of the more difficult technological issues.[17]

International discussions about recordkeeping's functional requirements have produced an important preservation principle: *No preservation principle should be adopted which will impede the daily and ongoing work of the records creator.* It is a principle capturing the preservation function within the modern organization. Most preservation approaches were expended after records had moved from an active to an inactive document, meaning that preservation would not impede any one's daily work. In fact, this was exactly the problem. For most organizational administrators, policy makers, and resource allocators, archives or inactive records were nothing more than old stuff being removed to a facility. Previously, records professionals moved freely into public offices and private homes carting off records no longer needed or thought to be useless. Now, these same records are often in electronic systems. The manner in which this "old" stuff must be saved redefines preservation. The only really effective manner in which to preserve such records is to build the archival and recordkeeping requirements into the system before the records are even created and in a fashion that will not obstruct the functioning of the organization.

Continuing education programs have been quite important in strengthening preservation work, but there are problems. Philosophically and practically, continuing education works best when it relates to graduate education, or it is little more than short-term training—good for dealing with immediate concerns but not so good for being applied to the often more essential long-term issues and problems. Graduate education has only existed for two decades, since 1981 when Columbia University's library school opened its preservation education program. With the closure of this school in 1992 the program was shifted to the University of Texas at Austin library school. There has always been concern whether the program has been relevant to the archival community's needs or the even more diverse realm of the records manager. Moreover, do records managers and other records professionals even know about the educational opportunities for preservation administrators? As a result, archivists and records managers both face a real shortage of trained and educated preservation personnel, relying on apprenticeship programs or single courses as part of library science education programs. Funding is the most-cited problem in preservation circles. But what would records professionals do *with* the funding if they suddenly got what they thought they needed? How could they staff the preservation programs? Where would they recruit such professionals? On what criteria would they select records for preservation? What would they emphasize—facilities for storage, reformatting for easier access by our changing research clientele, or conservation treatment or preservation management? What part does any of these issues play in a records or information policy?

All of this is a moot point at present. The immense preservation needs are not well known by the public or policy makers. Records professionals need to develop and to start to implement steady, long-term solutions to these problems, instead of stressing short-term and crisis situations. The means for educating individuals about information technology standards, systems design, information policy, and legal and ethical issues must be improved. There are a modest number of courses on electronic records management in North America, and there is an inadequate context of archival and records management knowledge, theory, and practice to make those courses work. There is the need for an adequate educational foundation, then advanced courses to create the required specialists, and then doctoral programs which foster research on relevant topics. The true measure of the effectiveness of educational programs is in the development of both stronger and new forms of archival operations. Archives and records management programs need individuals equipped to function as preservation administrators. There are few such professionals at the moment, and certainly few preservation administrators who can deal with the full range of preservation issues, from the fading parchment to the deteriorating computer disk. This kind of necessary direction in specialization to staff new kinds of archival and records management programs requires new partnerships.

How can archivists and records managers build the necessary partnerships? It will not happen by continuing to accession paper records while ignoring electronic records, nor will it come as they wait for researchers to arrive at their doorsteps while ignoring information policy issues. At the least, doing this can lead to public attention that makes records professionals look antiquated alongside the growing use of and dependence on electronic recordkeeping technologies.[18] Archivists and records managers need to develop new regulatory and advisory roles in decentralized environments. Archivists and records managers might want to stop thinking of constructing new buildings, when increasingly users want to access records electronically. Records professionals had better stop worrying about how and where archivists and records managers are trained and see that their knowledge base is interdisciplinary. Archivists and records managers cannot see themselves as merely custodians of objects. They are protectors of essential evidence and information. New partnerships are needed. Archivists and records managers must get out into the institution or the field and develop innovative new approaches to basic records work. They must be willing to examine the state of their operations and take more risks to position themselves more meaningfully in institutions and society. They cannot rely, without significant lobbying, pressure, and education, on the information technology industry to understand the preservation implications of their media.[19]

There is a distinction between information found in electronic systems and the media's physical nature. Hardware and software have long been used for this distinction. Elevated to a preservation concern, there is some similarity with the age-old discussion between reformatting and maintaining originals. Electronic records can be copied onto paper or microform, although these actions are more appropriate when dealing with statistical databases in organizations from the 1960s and 1970s rather than the immense variety of modern interactive systems. Regular migration of the records' information is also necessary for their continued protection. Electronic records such as magnetic media should be stored in environmentally stable facilities, not that different from the proper storage areas for paper-based records formats. Stable temperatures and humidity, freedom from dust and dirt, and protection from electrical and magnetic fields are all necessary conditions for the storage of electronic records. Sudden changes in these environments also cause similar problems with salvaging damaged electronic records, and the salvage procedures are often not very different from those used with traditional library and archival materials. Backing up electronic files, regulating "hostile elements" in the environment, and developing cooperative approaches for dealing with natural and man-made disasters are all themes from the recent generation of preservation management writing.

Electronic media challenge the preservation community to develop innovative definitions, methods, and research. Some of the preservation mentality permeating the records community must be jettisoned, including a new notion of records maintenance. Four elements constitute a new preservation paradigm for electronic records. These elements include accepting the decentralization of electronic records to the care of the originators and users of the information systems, developing adequate information policy and technology solutions for the maintenance of electronic records, influencing information technology standards, and, finally, emphasizing the strategic appraisal of electronic information systems.

Archivists and records managers have long seen centralization or custody of records as crucial to their work. Records are centralized for their protection and to facilitate their use. But many electronic records make this type of task virtually impossible because they represent active databases undergoing constant change and transformation and because the users want to take advantage of rapid searching in the electronic environment. The collecting of magnetic tapes and the transference of electronic records to archival repositories and other records facilities may undermine their very long-term use. The practicality of a decentralized records program is dependent on the creation of effective policies for the maintenance of electronic records systems. The archivist or records manager must be able to identify a system as possessing continuing values and to then set guidelines stipulating its maintenance and use. Such policies had not worked well in the era prior to the advent of the computer and, especially, the advent of the microcomputer. This is troublesome. Many archivists view their institutions as cultural organizations rather than institutions with a stake in wider information policy deliberations. Many records managers view their programs as clerical, housekeeping operations rather than as programs with a stake in wider information policy deliberations. A decentralized records program depends on records professionals becoming more involved in the development and regulation of information technology standards. The work by archivists with electronic information standards has only begun, even though many solutions to managing electronic records from an archival perspective rest with the standards-setting process. It is impossible to conceive that traditional appraisal approaches will work with electronic records such as electronic mail without significant reliance on standards and policies.

Strategic appraisal should have transformed this basic records function years ago, but it continues to stimulate heated discussion. Appraisal or records scheduling rests on an assumption of the review of every record and records series, even though the rapid proliferation of modern records has made such an approach impractical. Archivists and records managers need to re-orient themselves to focus on broad appraisal strategies such as the identification of essential or significant programmatic functions or a strategy of identifying and preserving a broad representative record of society rather than examining every nook and cranny in the universe of documentation. Archivists also need to focus on evidential value rather than the softer and less well defined informational value, the latter encouraging archivists to want to preserve everything just in case it might be used. Records professionals considering the preservation of their repository's holdings need to understand how their institutional records relate to the broader records universe, especially the impact of new electronic recordkeeping and information systems on their world.

BLOWN TO BITS: ELECTRONIC RECORDS, ARCHIVY, AND THE CORPORATION

Records professionals have not been very successful in convincing American capitalists and other business leaders why records are important. The roots of the problems in appraising and managing business electronic records extend back long before electronic recordkeeping and information systems. Christopher Hives suggests that it was in the late 1930s when archivists discovered that the collecting of business records was not a satisfactory solution.[20] The American archival profession has stressed the collecting of business records for historical research purposes rather than the nurturing of institutional archives in American corporations for administrative and other purposes more immediately relevant to the businesses. Records managers, as already noted, have been inclined to help rid these organizations of their "old stuff." While the number of corporate archives may have grown, the quantity of business records accessioned into archives has probably increased at a much higher rate. Is this due to the focus of the archivist and records manager, or to the predilection of American businesses not to value archives? Is it easier to persuade businesses to dump their older records onto repositories rather than to communicate with them why archival records are valuable? Collecting may have worked when the size of American businesses was generally smaller and the quantity of their records substantially less. This strategy may be necessary for companies going out of business and inclined to destroy their records, although here the question of the significance of the records and their potential use has often been swept aside by the rush to make sure that the records would not be destroyed, adopting, as Tim Ericson says, the role of "Horatius-at-the-Bridge: the last line of defense between preservation and oblivion."[21] This strategy may have been useful when there was no need for the archivist to justify to the records creator the rationale for expending money on supporting an institutional archives.

Electronic recordkeeping systems end the *practical* collecting of modern business records (unless one engages in highly selective collecting). Such collecting often has risked the integrity of the records because of the desire to acquire information for researchers' uses rather than evidence needed to support the corporation or for documenting its evolution and work. Records professionals need to understand that new and rapidly changing electronic information and recordkeeping systems provide the incentive for them to return to the appropriate mission, helping and encouraging businesses to develop their own institutional archives serving their own needs first and foremost.

Society and its institutions, including its businesses, are moving away from dependence on paper-based record systems to electronic-based systems. While the transformation is not without major organizational and societal problems, it is nonetheless true that the computer is firmly ensconced in the corporate world and that many of the institutional resources will be used to improve and refine (not reject) computer-run tools. Records professionals will become problem solvers in electronic records management rather than apologists for paper, filing cabinets, and records cartons. They will create virtual repositories through the development of policies, standards, and other gatekeeper (the assumption of broader responsibilities than custody) functions. They also will need to stop thinking of custodianship and develop different approaches as appropriate. Records professionals will need to cease thinking of older corporate records as grist for the historian's mill and make, instead, new arguments in favor of evidence for the support of the corporation's ongoing work.

Where is the modern corporation heading in the currents of the Information Age? William J. Mitchell, a professor of architecture and dean of the School of Architecture and Planning at the Massachusetts Institute of Technology, provides an engaging prediction about technology, culture, and institutions in his *City of Bits*. He writes, the "new virtual city becomes a kind of electronic shadow of the existing physical one. In many (though not all) cases, a citizen can choose between going to an actual public building or to the corresponding virtual one."[22] Mitchell is optimistic about technology, but he has written the most balanced of texts predicting future society. Commerce is changing. Record and book stores are moving to virtual operations through central servers producing books and records on demand or even transporting them over the network. Banking is already largely electronic: "Money is no longer bullion in a strongbox, but bits in an online database."[23] Stock trading is already being planned as a nearly complete virtual process. Businesses have already been deeply affected by bar codes, credit cards, and cash cards: "Salesperson, customer, and product supplier no longer have to be brought together in the same spot; they just have to establish electronic contact."[24] Offices, a centerpiece of the corporation, are "sites of information work—specialized places where numbers, words, and sometimes pictures are collected, stored, transformed, and disseminated. So their issue is mostly composed of desks equipped with information-handling devices (telephones, computers, fax machines, printers, file cabinets, inboxes and outboxes, and the like), meeting and conference rooms, copying centers and mailrooms, and receptions and circulation spaces."[25] As corporations grew larger, and as various technologies and accompanying social changes made it possible for them to expand, the familiar corporate headquarters of the central skyscraper area and then the industrial park became a part of our cityscape and landscape. Mitchell sees this changing as well: "We are entering the era of the temporary, recombinant, virtual organization—of business arrangements that demand good computing and telecommunications environments rather than large, permanent home offices."[26] The corporation and smaller businesses will be considerably changed in Mitchell's future world: "So cyberspace communities . . . are stops on the infobahn. The world's apparently insatiable greed for bits will fuel their growth, as demand for manufactured goods drove developments of earlier industrial cities and transportation centers. They will flourish as places to make bucks from bits by producing them, skimming them, stealing them, and inventing new ways to add value to them."[27] Records professionals will have different issues to contend with as they work with such "stops on the infobahn."

While they must be cautious not to believe every prediction, records professionals must be careful not to dismiss all. Another recent book on cities, in this case "as they are, not as they might be," suggests that contending with the challenges of the city emanated at least partly from "our inability to anticipate the new technological and social forces that came to bear on our urban condition: the automobile, air travel, electronic communications."[28] Is there a lesson here for records professionals and records users? Some of the problems with the rise of modern cities came about because of the lack of adequate planning systems to regulate growth and to make cities beneficial to all aspects of society. Likewise, unless records professionals understand how to develop effective records policies, the value of records will be lost to technological and other forces shaping the information aspects of recordkeeping.

The historical view provides the best glimpse of the impact of the computer on the modern corporation. The business computer has gone from a preoccupation with the most basic data crunching and the rawest of information (an objective of technologists for centuries before the electronic computer) to the creation of all sorts of electronic systems to control both information and records. The change has taken us from primitive punch cards to electronic calculating machines to electronic devices with large memories and broad computing capacities. There was a remarkably rapid change from using these machines to solve mathematical problems to serving a wide array of business functions, even though in the 1950s many still argued that computers would not be useful to American business interests. Labor, production, accounting, labor subdivision for control and order, measurements, and paperwork have become dependent on the computer. By 1990 over 50 million Americans were using computers in their work, when only twenty years before that there had been 75,000 computers in all of the United States and twenty years before that only ten computers in the country. The dependence on software rather than hardware and the growth of networked organizations made it possible to conduct business using less paper. The development of the personal computer has made every employee a records-generating dynamo within their organizations, as well as in their personal lives and homes, posing in the process significant problems about the nature of work, individual self-worth and identity, and society.

The rapidly changing nature of information technology in the corporation is evident in the changes in data processing textbooks. Thirty years ago computers had had an impact on organizational management in purchasing, inventory control, accounting, and payroll—focusing on routine and repetitive work. Even in 1967, however, it was determined that "perhaps the most important characteristic in the present corporate environment is the primacy of information and communication."[29] Textbooks described the traditional office equipment, such as typewriters and calculators, and the mainframe computers for large-scale number use in accounting, marketing, and other related functions. Thirty years ago, these volumes were predicting the transition from data processing to information services.[30]

Current computer magazines are mirrors for the possible and real uses of electronic information technology in the American corporation. Issues of *Wired*, written by computer enthusiasts bordering on religious fanatics, provide advertisements for powerful notebooks, new workstations, computer display monitors, software promising to change the world and business, and a variety of online services. The promises are dazzling, heralding direct connections to customers, video conferencing, and instant worldwide communications. While this can be dismissed as advertising hype, it is obvious that the possibilities for electronic information applications and electronic records are immense.

A sense of the modern business can be gained by considering the paperless office, first predicted more than twenty years ago. Current wisdom suggests that the future office will not be paperless. While the simplest view is to state that the paperless office is a myth, that paper continues to increase as a presence in the modern office,[31] the implications of the use of office electronic information technology need to be constantly evaluated. Some note that the key to developing nearly paperless offices is "document retrieval—how each document would be coded for searches."[32] Archivists and records managers, while recognizing the importance of retrieving information from records, also stress the integrity of the record. The emergence of a substantial legal literature on electronic recordkeeping is but one indication of the concern for the electronic record.[33] Another commentator believes "technology has created a paper paradox: As an explosion of information flows in bits across electronic networks, the Internet and on-line services, the ability to create low-cost, high quality, personalized paper-based documents on demand ramps up paper usage to unprecedented levels."[34] This observation does not address the matter of what is the official record—the paper or electronic version?

A nearly paperless office suggests that powerful document servers instead of file cabinets will store electronically all documents (records and other data entities). Office workers will access these document servers through keyword searches, natural language processing, or some other information retrieval technique. Technology will be managed by the development of a variety of search devices. These will focus on *any* information rather than information defined by evidence, legal, administrative, fiscal or other concerns generally most pertinent to archivists and records managers. The present fixation is document management systems, defined as "automated systems for scanning, storing, retrieving and managing paper documents." Paper records are inputted into the systems, indexed, stored electronically, retrieved through the keywords and indexes, and outputted by reading on the computer screen, printed, or faxed. Advantages enumerated include that paper filing cabinets are eliminated, many people can access documents immediately and simultaneously, and individual documents can be made secure by the addition of passwords.[35]

Whether corporations achieve the paperless office is *not* the kind of issue archivists or records managers should focus on. Paper may only be a side issue and not the real concern for these organizations. Archivists and records managers need to understand that the growing dependence on electronic information technology will bring many questions about the reliability and nature of the new recordkeeping systems. In these questions there are opportunities for archivists and records managers. For most of the past thirty years in which records professionals have been mulling over the challenge of electronic information technology, they have viewed the technology and its uses and problems as the primary issue. This concern needs to be forgotten. Corporations are but a window into all modern organizations in this regard, from the small community association to the largest government entity.

It seems as if the entire corporate milieu has been unkind to recordkeeping. Robert Jackall's study of ethics in business paints a portrait of a corporate fealty structure where personal loyalties and ambitions often override all other concerns. Long-term goals, rational objectives, and even legal and administrative common sense are pushed aside in favor of getting ahead. Personal and corporate success are all that matter. While Jackall does not discuss much about the nature of corporate recordkeeping, he does make a passing reference to it, suggesting that recordkeeping is not favored because it implies a regularity and strictures standing in the way of getting ahead: "Even where one can follow a paper trail, most written documents in the corporate world constitute simply official versions of reality that often bear little resemblance to the tangled, ambiguous, and verbally negotiated transactions that they purportedly represent. As a result, whatever meaningful tracking does take place occurs within managers' cognitive maps of their world, which, of course, are constantly changing and subject to retrospective interpretation and reinterpretation."[36] Seen in this light, corporate politics are more important than most other issues that the archivist or records manager might be interested in. As records professionals should also be concerned with evidence and the orderly nature of records and recordkeeping systems, it is no wonder that they weary at the thought of working in the corporation's political culture.

This seems pessimistic, but there is a bright spot. The American model for the administration of electronic records is that "any business entity may, if it desires, utilize electronic recordkeeping as long as its practices and records meet certain prescribed conditions. . . . All that is required is that a taxpayer be able to demonstrate that its system satisfies certain requirements geared towards assuring the integrity of the system and the reliability of the stored data."[37] These "certain prescribed conditions" are where archivists and records managers meet the real world. The final report of the United States Advisory Council on the National Information Infrastructure (NII) suggests principles for electronic commerce. It notes that since "workplaces will be transformed," there will be a continuing need for new "worker training, education, and adaptation to mechanisms." Issues of "protection of intellectual property, transaction security, integrity of data, consumer protection, and privacy" will be needs in all organizations and society, and government will have to ensure that these matters are worked on, via legislation, enabling competition, and research and other funding incentives.[38] Such issues are familiar to records professionals, many relating to basic control of information needed for the successful management of any organization, especially businesses, where such concerns have been endemic in corporate management for generations.

Many of these issues have been made more crucial because of the shift to electronic recordkeeping and information systems. H. Jeff Smith's study of privacy in American business, while documenting the less than satisfactory response by corporate leaders to this issue, demonstrates that the new concern has been driven by the increasing use of information technology.[39] Reliability and control have been (or should have been) the hallmark of the mission of both archivists and records managers. These professionals are in the evidence business, and it is this latter concern that returns records professionals to manage electronic records with archival (or continuing) value produced by American businesses. Electronic recordkeeping and information systems have blown apart the old ways of doing things. While it is technically feasible to acquire electronic records, there are many costs and other barriers to doing this. Archivists and records managers must learn that their role is to serve business interests first and foremost. Archivists and their colleagues do not need to jettison broader social objectives, ethical or moral values, or even their knowledge of the value of business records to scholarly disciplines and various segments of the public. Records professionals must demonstrate that the older records support the ongoing activity and mission of the corporation to justify the considerable costs in managing these records. Otherwise, whatever policies they develop and monitor will be missing vital aspects of records management.

The increasing dependence on electronic recordkeeping systems should provide ample opportunities for the archivist and records managers to develop and convey a more coherent message. Electronic recordkeeping systems need to be maintained by their creators because of the technological considerations and because many of these records and supporting systems will have ongoing value to the immediate work of the organization (better hardware and software, declining costs, increased memory storage and other aspects will make it desirable to maintain many more records in a much more accessible fashion). Records professionals need to make the new recordkeeping systems viable through more aggressive participation in their design and in the articulation of why corporations need to manage records. All organizations are subject to a variety of external regulations and laws requiring many records to be managed in particular ways. Archivists are not antiquarians wandering the halls, probing into closets, or looking in waste cans for the miscellaneous valuable record. Records managers are not scurrying about looking for records to destroy to save costs or to increase efficiency. Records professionals should be part of a team of systems designers working with corporate legal counsel and other administrators to facilitate the management of records with continuing value to the organization. Policy is an essential part of this approach.

Many records professionals believe that the value of their role is for the assurance of accountability, corporate memory, and evidence. To accomplish this, they must be able to influence the design of recordkeeping systems to support these purposes as well as transform or refine their traditional functions of appraisal, description, and reference. Records professionals might need to reconsider informational value as a subset of evidence and embrace such approaches as macro-appraisal in order to support issues of compliance as well as to support the corporation's own work. Records professionals have become gatekeepers to records for users, shifting attention from destroying or collecting to appraisal, description and access, and public advocacy. Records professionals have not been, unfortunately, the most effective advocates in national policy issues or in industry and technical standards. Just as importantly, they need to achieve greater public and government awareness of the importance of records. Opportunity for this abounds everywhere, from scandals about government recordkeeping to controversy about interpretative exhibits in history museums to genuine concern about the impact of the networked information society on political structures, work, and leisure. Being policy advocates requires them to have a clear, understandable message that they understand as well. Archivists and records managers need to focus on records and recordkeeping systems. They need to assume that increasingly the recordkeeping systems will be electronic. They need to move from paper-based approaches to electronic ones. And archivists and records managers need to return to their traditional role as experts on records and recordkeeping systems in order to fulfill their long-standing and important mission. Many of the challenges, then, are not represented by the technology but by records professionals themselves.

ELECTRONIC RECORDS AND THE DEMISE OF RECORDS MANAGEMENT SCHEDULING

The manner in which records managers have tended to consider appraisal, through the mechanism of scheduling records, has put the organization's interests first for records administration, emphasizing concerns such as legal and fiscal interests. This is the strength of the approach, especially as the sophistication of knowledge of external requirements (what is now being called the recordkeeping warrant) has re-emerged in recent years.[40]

The importance of the warrant for recordkeeping can be seen in many ways. It can be understood by considering the history of different forms of recordkeeping. For example, the failure in nineteenth century American hospital recordkeeping can be seen as resulting because "There was little pressure to do so from professional organizations, the law, or the prodding of scholars. . . . The medical record, generally, was considered a personal affair that each doctor handled as he saw fit."[41] Scholars who use rhetorical theory and structuration for studying communication also can see the notion of warrant. Scholars such as these have discovered what they term genres of communication, whereby genres are marked by "structural, linguistic, and substantive conventions."[42] According to them, "when organizational members write business letters or engage in meetings, they implicitly or explicitly draw on the genre rules of the business letter or meeting to generate the substance and form of their documents or interactions."[43] The records professional knows that many of these genre values come from external requirements. The greatest value of using warrant is because it returns records professionals to the need to consider the creators of records, much as the macro-appraisal approaches have done for archivists.

There is a danger in this warrant approach, one that exists as well in the heavily structured, forms-driven records management retention and disposition scheduling. This is the problem lawyer Philip Howard described in his recognition that we have created a "legal colossus unprecedented in the history of civilization, with legal dictates numbering in the millions of words and growing larger every day."[44] Howard thinks that government and modern organizations have lost sight of their purpose in the midst of endless process. In terms of records management scheduling two worries emerge. Is scheduling the real solution to the administration of modern records, or is it simply *another* complicated process that has long since helped records managers lose a vision for their primary responsibilities? Is there anything salvageable in such scheduling, including even the seemingly practical idea of a warrant focus, for records management to be taken seriously *within* the organization?

For archivists, the issue of what organizational records represent is another concern as they consider their appraisal responsibility. It is a mixed bag of what the purpose of appraisal (and archives) is, along with what saving a record accomplishes. Historians have also described such "declining qualitative value" of modern documentation for their research purposes.[45] While the records manager may be satisfied that records are being kept as long as they need to be, the archivist is searching for a deeper level in capturing corporate memory.

The need to re-evaluate the continuing use of records management disposition and retention schedules is especially acute in this modern information era and its increasing reliance on electronic information technology. One ruling in the continuing court cases extending back more than a decade in the federal government's efforts to destroy electronic mail related to the Iran-Contra affair demonstrates how imperative it is that the concept and practice of records scheduling be reconsidered. This ruling initially concluded that the archivist of the United States had exceeded his authority in issuing General Records Schedule 20 for the disposal of electronic records. While such general schedules had been used for decades for the purpose of enabling federal agencies to destroy routine records related to housekeeping and other administrative functions, the court ruled that the new schedule could allow the destruction of *other*, more important records: "The general schedules were designed to handle records that document housekeeping functions, procedures and transactions, such as personnel, maintenance or procurement, not unique aspects of a given agency. . . . Thus, there is a relationship between the commonality of records covered by a general schedule and their diminished value. The common feature of the records scheduled under GRS 20—the fact that they have been generated by electronic technology—has no relation to each record's value. No one would argue, for example, that a cable from the Secretary of State to an Ambassador at a U.S. Embassy abroad about an impending crisis or an electronic mail message written by the Secretary of State regarding the President's decision to declare war on another country has the same value as a GSA word processing file regarding procurement of desks, simply because both records were created by electronic technology. Unlike the GSA record, the Secretary of State's cable or electronic mail message documents unique and important operations of government that may have historic value. The Archivist should not use the same disposal criteria applied to the GSA procurement document on the Secretary's message just because both records are found in computers."[46] By April 1998 the archivist of the United States had been found in contempt by this court due to his continuing advice to federal agencies to continue to use the general schedule for electronic records while the case continued, a finding that produced news coverage and made the National Archives look unable to deal with federal records. The eventual overturning of this ruling still has not given this leading archival program the mechanism to *manage* electronic mail and related records.

Shortly before the court ruling, the National Archives issued a strategic plan with a new promise for electronic records management.[47] The plan's encouraging aspect was its new emphasis on "essential evidence," suggesting a different commitment from the cultural mission. As long as the National Archives is *most* closely allied to the historical profession, it will have little chance of adopting a mission as radical as the plan may suggest. In one sense, it shows that the tensions evident in the early 1940s, when the concept of the records schedule was being developed, is *still* present. Page Putnam Miller, the director of the National Coordinating Committee for the Promotion of History, demonstrates this with her response to the plan, noting that the "plan's title 'Ready Access to Essential Evidence' is troubling for some historians. . . . [S]cholars who wish to understand the activities and policies of the federal government will continue to have to visit research rooms and to confront the immensity of the National

Archives' holdings. . . . Serious archival research is by its very nature labor intensive and anything but easy. . . . The term 'essential evidence' is also discom-
forting. Much of the richness of the current holdings is in records that have
informational value and do not provide 'essential evidence.' Many scholars fear
that beneath the phrase 'essential evidence' will be a tendency to use a more
limiting approach to the task of deciding which records will be retained and
which will be destroyed."[48] Miller is correct that appraisal will have to be more
limited than before, although she fails to understand, as do many, that the values
approach to appraisal has failed.

It is typical of the historical profession to see the National Archives as a
"research" institution only, and it is also unfortunate that many archivists accept
this limited view. As long as archivists adopt this kind of thinking, the institution
(and profession) will face the prospect of dismal failures and appraisal via litigation (as with the PROFS case). Other archivists educated as historians see
new purposes for archives and records management. H. G. Jones, in his 1980
book on local government records management, surmised that the "day is over
for the nineteenth-century antiquarian who assumed that public servants held
office for the convenience of the researcher, saving every scrap of paper and
producing it upon demand. Modern historians must recognize that records are
tools of government, intended initially for administrative or legal purposes, and
that the enormous increase in the volume of records at all levels of government
demands new solutions to old problems."[49] J. Franklin Jameson, another historian and the leading advocate for the establishment of the National Archives,
writing shortly before passage in 1934 of the congressional act founding this
institution, worried about who would be selected to be the first archivist of the
United States. Jameson struggled with the many pressing responsibilities which
would fall on this person: "Whom the President would think of, I have no idea,
but he is enough of a historical scholar to make me think that, in canvassing
qualifications, he will not leave historical-mindedness out of account. Another
prime qualification would be ability to get along with the departments, with
some of whom it would be easy to have a succession of rows; yet the archivist
must have a stiff backbone and power enough to fight well for his own views."[50]
We have not had archivists who use *authority*, including scheduling records, to
chart a strong and high profile mission on behalf of the right issues in the
government and for the American people. There seems to be a reliance on the
old nineteenth century view that records that become archives are those that
become available for preservation because of their "uselessness" to the current
organization.[51] Despite the many policies the National Archives and other archival organizations seem to generate and support, they may be flawed because
of lacks of authority *and* a clear sense of practical purpose in government and
society.

A problem may be many records professionals' dogged determination to rely
on scheduling as a still relevant solution, a process that has become an excuse
for not taking stronger leadership. This stubbornness is evident in a report issued

near the beginning of the PROFS case, suggesting that scheduling electronic records was *not* a workable solution because of the administrative placement of federal records managers and the nature of the electronic recordkeeping systems.[52] NARA's strategic plan report reveals, for example, that only 35 to 40 percent of government records are inventoried and scheduled within two years of their creation and, moreover, that over the past fourteen years NARA had been able to act only on "approximately 23% of the items on records schedules submitted . . . for approval." The response is to re-commit to improving, *while* doing many other things including the incorporation of "NARA recordkeeping requirements in the design, development, and implementation of 50% of the automated recordkeeping systems through which they manage essential evidence." Just how effective can scheduling be today? It returns one to David Stephen's telling comment that *if* scheduling is to work it must be embedded *in* the systems themselves.

Archival appraisal practice needs to be re-evaluated in terms of electronic records management and the reliance by organizations on the scheduling process. Alf Erlandsson, analyzing the recent literature on electronic records, states, "Appraisal and disposition practice in North America will not work in the electronic records world. The method of appraising records by examining them after they have been accessioned by the archives is not suitable for electronic records."[53] He considers alternative methods, using business functions and processes, macro-appraisal, and other approaches. His comment on the U.S. National Archives is interesting: "A somewhat more traditional approach to appraisal of electronic records seems to be taken by the U.S. National Archives (NARA), which may be explained by the fact that NARA has the world's largest collection of first generation 'informational' databases in its custody." This makes it appear as if this institution is appraising in its traditional fashion because it is responsible for these informational databases. In fact, it is the *other* way around. NARA has stayed committed to a custodial approach and an appraisal scheme focused on informational value primarily for scholarly researchers rather than appraisal of recordkeeping systems for continuing value to the government and its citizens. That it is the wrong model seems evident from the court rulings regarding the use of the general schedule and the efforts of the Electronic Records Work Group established to develop approaches to resolve the problems associated with GRS 20.[54]

Writers of basic records management textbooks have questioned the utility of many records management practices such as scheduling in the new electronic organization. The problems of electronic recordkeeping systems—easily manipulated, greater chance for the loss of records in migration and system obsolescence, and operation within a technologically dependent environment—tend to negate the primacy of records inventorying and scheduling.[55] Electronic records systems are sufficiently different from paper systems that disposition and retention schedules need to be modified. These systems not only produce machine-dependent records but they batch together different kinds of records, documents, and data. Decisions need to be made about whether the records will be kept online or stored in backup systems and, for records with long-term value, what the best storage and format means. More fundamental is the need to move from specific record or series scheduling to developing "retention periods for all records related to a program function (such as fiscal management) to which they relate regardless of form, media, format, or document type."[56] Records inventorying and scheduling are useful only if they are part of a broader policy for administering records within an organization and for benefit of both the organization and society (as that organization has ties to the public).

The problems of scheduling as both a records management and archival function are evident even with paper-based recordkeeping systems, suggesting a need for re-evaluation. The 1997 destruction of Naval Research Laboratory records with continuing research use by the National Archives brings this problem into the light. These records—4,200 volumes of laboratory notebooks and 600 boxes of correspondence and memoranda about pioneering work in radar, sonar, oceanographic research, and satellites—apparently had been scheduled "many years ago" *and* the National Archives had given notice (without a response) to the navy of its intent to destroy these records.[57] That important records can be destroyed suggests that scheduling is not always suitable for archival appraisal and is a weak system for records management. The loss of electronic mail messages within the National Archives and the public outcry about the destruction of old Ohio prison records, cases described in the preface of this book, are additional examples of the failures of policy and procedures.

There are other reasons for bringing together the appraising and scheduling functions and archivists and records managers *before* final decisions about the ultimate fate of records. There are times when the merit of records goes beyond accountability and evidence or even research values, and they possess a symbolic importance that suggests continued maintenance. An analysis of a 1993 exhibition at the Imperial War Museum in London of love and familial letters written during the Second World War suggests such a value. While these are certainly *routine* letters, it is possible to see other values. A review of the exhibition explains, "Letters are not just the means of communication but a physical token of the absent other, that gives them a fetishistic quality, easily recognizable by the importance of their physical aspects: the handwriting; the envelope; the way they are hoarded or tied in ribbons."[58] These "letters, both as fetish and as a form of memory, work in ways that exceed their definition as a simple technology of communication, in ways that we can call aesthetic."[59] Some argue that the analysis of personal manuscripts must be accorded different approaches than institutional records, until one realizes that organizations can produce letters with as much emotion and energy as these. Now we realize that such records are being created electronically, and although the process of letter writing may have shifted to electronic mail, the power of emotions may still be there.

In reviewing the matters relating to the connection of archival appraisal and records management scheduling, another issue emerges—the role or primary responsibility of the records professionals in the organization and society. It is not just technical concerns governing how records professionals need to approach recordkeeping systems. The use of computers brings new ethical and legal concerns, as would any major shift in recordkeeping media. As two commentators on computer ethics state, "what is new is that the widespread use of information systems has placed great temptation in the hands of ordinary programmers and systems developers, who are often, among other things, the only people who know how a particular system works."[60] Records professionals must develop appraisal approaches protecting society and its citizens, as well as providing records to support organizational and research functions. Re-examining archival appraisal principles as part of more comprehensive records policies provides a start.

ARCHIVAL APPRAISAL PRINCIPLES

Since the mid-1980s, there has been a steady stream of writings on archival appraisal theory, much of it in reaction to or encompassing the archival documentation strategy.[61] The theoretical concepts range from immutable laws to a view that theory is no more than a codification of practice and principles; some argue that there is no theory at all. These views have swirled about basic archival concepts of evidence and information.[62] Some may have taken too seriously Schellenberg's idea that "ascertaining values in records cannot be reduced to exact standards" but can be "little more than general principles."[63] Archivists have used the terms "art" and "science" too loosely, while most records managers have tended not to address such concerns at all. Some of the debate has bogged down on different conceptions of the archival mission, ranging from the preservation of evidence, through the creation of a representative documentation, to the quest to document all of society. Archivists can learn from records managers in stressing the utilitarian uses of records by the records-creating organization, allowing the other records uses to occur naturally. Records managers can learn from archivists and the kinds of questions they ask.

Analyzing practice as reflected in the substantial professional literature provides a foundation for archival theory. The archival documentation strategy can be viewed as a conceptually simple mechanism to be added to the archivist's arsenal of appraisal approaches. The documentation strategy was developed in response to the nature of modern documentation and perceived weaknesses in archival appraisal approaches. As a result, it must be considered as a part of archival appraisal theory, even though some have simply preferred to describe it as a *new* discussion about *old* concerns.[64] A solid conception of archival appraisal moves beyond a mere catalogue of values to workable process, aiding all records professionals who face the challenges of records selection.

Appraisal has been defined through values, such as evidential and informational, and techniques, such as sampling and institutional collection analysis. The scope of archival appraisal has been transformed from a process that is institutionally bound to one that is multi-institutional. Archival appraisal was originally seen as the process of ascertaining whether a specific document, records series, or even record group or manuscript collection possessed sufficient informational and evidential content. The traditional view focused on archives as evidence; Americans added the informational dimension. Many archivists now view their role to be a selector of recorded information leading to a documentation of society. This view is a result of the archivist's recognition of the immense volume of records, the interrelatedness of records, and the increasing diversity of recorded information forms. Records managers face the same challenges.

There are a number of routes for formulating archival appraisal theory, including evaluating statements made by archivists through the past century. The approach is in line with the notion of theory: *"Theories* are logically interconnected statements about the world that describe, explain, and predict the occurrence of phenomena. They are based on *empirical generalizations* about the world, which are in turn based upon analysis of our direct observations."[65] Michael Buckland emphasizes that theory is a body of generalizations and principles formed in association with practice and leading to the intellectual content of a discipline. Theory requires that there be the possibility of a coherent set of hypothetical, conceptual, and pragmatic principles forming a general frame of reference for a field of inquiry. This allows for defining principles, formulating hypotheses, and considering actions.[66]

Archival appraisal theory starts with the premise that all recorded information has some continuing value, if not to the creator of that information, then to society. The quantity of information is so great that it must be reduced in order to be useful. This reduction requires careful and tested criteria, built upon the notion of evidential and informational values. These criteria are not determined solely by the institutional creators of this information, as there are some generic characteristics of recorded information suggesting some common or universal appraisal criteria and processes. The selection of this information is not for some undetermined future research but for the present needs of the records creators and based upon the present knowledge of the record-generating institutions and society. Archivists must also be cognizant of other, non-textual information sources either complementing or completing gaps in their textual records. In order to ensure that the proper records are preserved, the archivist must be involved with the records creator as far up the life cycle of records (or at the early stages of the records continuum) as is possible. This requires that archivists have as an appraisal mission the documentation of society and that they participate in a team-oriented, multi-disciplinary appraisal process. Archivists must also acknowledge that certain records must be automatically kept because of their age or form. Archivists can also use some methods for reducing the volume of records already determined to have archival value.

All recorded information has some continuing value to the records creators and to society, making archival appraisal difficult but important. It is also difficult because archivists, having largely come from the humanities (history primarily), are prone to find value in virtually anything. Allan Pratt notes, for example, that while the scientist sees nothing wrong in discarding old scientific papers because these papers can be obsolete, the humanist is reluctant to destroy anything.[67] Archivist Maynard Brichford supports this humanistic perspective, indicating, "all records have some research value,"[68] as have other archivists such as Luciana Duranti.[69] This may explain why many archivists have determined that appraisal is a subjective process, and they are critical of the process and results of archival appraisal. F. Gerald Ham states, "archivists waste time and space preserving random bits and pieces, as well as large accessions, of the most dubious value."[70] If so, it is probably because archivists give in to their sense that all recorded information has some continuing value to the records creators and to society, although this is not shared by organizational records creators. Judging by the writings of records managers and information resources managers, institutions are more likely to define the length of time they maintain records through legal and fiscal obligations. This point of view is counter to traditional views of archivists working in the Jenkinsonian tradition, where the records creator determines the archival value and the archivist maintains the records.

The immense quantity of recorded information is an impediment to the information's continuing value, making reduction crucial. Six decades ago, Hilary Jenkinson stated that the bulk of records, caused by easier duplication and other uses of modern technology, is a "new and serious matter" requiring the archivist's attention.[71] Margaret Cross Norton, writing at about the same time from the United States, also thought that the growing quantity of government records meant that the "emphasis of archives work has shifted from preservation of records to selection of records for preservation." She advocated a process whereby the archivist worked also as a records manager, so that the quantity of records could be reduced by selection *and* through the application of photographic processes and the prevention of creation of unnecessary accumulation at the point of records origination.[72] Schellenberg continued this theme: the first sentence of his seminal writing on the appraisal of public records was "Modern public records are very voluminous."[73] The concern with volume has continued to the present as the volume of information continues to increase through the growing sophistication and pervasiveness of information technology.[74]

The reduction of documentary sources may occur accidentally, resulting in a random or partial aggregation of documentation harming the records creators and society. Is this accidental accumulation better or worse than planned archival selection? In a perceptive essay related to this matter, Daniel Boorstin wrote about the durable and the least used as the key to survival, with a "natural and perhaps inevitable tendency toward the destruction and disappearance of the documents most widely used."[75] Individuals from other disciplines have echoed this concern. Kenneth Dowlin, an advocate of the modern high-tech library, writes that "information has reached the stage where a significant proportion of what is produced is throw-away."[76] Historian and material culture specialist Thomas Schlereth supports this: "Evidence comes to us . . . often seriously flawed by the fecklessness of historical survival and the penchant of most collectors to save only those objects . . . that once had the highest monetary value and now do likewise as antiques. Frequently only the best or the most expensive of past craftwork has survived to be enshrined in museums and ensconced in private antique collections."[77] This opens up archivists to think and act more creatively in their documentation efforts.

The accidental or natural survival of records poses some very fundamental questions for the archivist engaged in appraisal. Following Boorstin's lead, if the most important records tend to be those that were the most often referred to while still in the hands of their creator, there is the greater likelihood of their loss, weakening, or misplacement in the files, thus minimizing the contextual knowledge that is so important to the archivist understanding and evaluating the record. This conclusion argues against the more traditional view of the archivist waiting for relatively long periods of time *before* receiving the records from the creator. It also poses some interesting questions about allowing the creator to determine what should be preserved, as the neo-Jenkinsonians contend. There needs to be a more activist stance of archivist interacting with records creator. Hugh Taylor, in his study of diplomatics, said as much: "If the record is to be of maximum value to the administrator and where appropriate, to the general public as user, then archivists must be far closer to the point of creation and original use."[78]

One can make a strong case for the development of solid criteria and planned selection. What should be the desired end of archival appraisal? Should it be what the records creator determines is important, as the Jenkinsonians want? Is it what Ham calls for when he states that our "most important and intellectually demanding task as archivists is to make an informed selection of information that will provide the future with a representative record of human experience in our time?"[79] Or, is it some other paradigm, such as the notion of adequacy of documentation?[80] And, fitting into the theme of this book, can one write records policies without a clear sense of appraisal objectives?

Some contend that a truly random process of survival is an alternative method of identifying what records should be saved.[81] Relying on a true random process instead of a deliberative appraisal process seems dangerous. Even a faulty archival appraisal decision or decision process may be better than records surviving haphazardly or not surviving at all. Because all recorded information has some continuing value to the records creators and to society, each decision must be, by necessity, a borderline decision, as Margaret Cross Norton argued. This has led to somewhat circular statements by pioneer archival theorists. Schellenberg's statement that "in the long run the effectiveness of a record reduction program must be judged according to the correctness of its determination" suggests far more questions than it answers.[82] There is considerable evidence that the researcher, at least the scholarly historians among the users of archival records, will make use of what they can find. Again, Boorstin poses the matter well when he notes, "the historian-creator refuses to be defeated by the biases of survival. For he chooses, defines, and shapes his subject to provide a reasonably truthful account from miscellaneous remains."[83] This is why records professionals, using policies and other approaches, must document their appraisal decisions along with the policies and selection mechanisms.

Archivists should feel freer to experiment, evaluate, develop, and refine their appraisal theory, principles, and practices, since mistakes made may tell records professionals something about the needed criteria and not seriously harm the final documentary record left from a particular period. Archivists should work with their researchers and colleagues in developing better criteria and understanding of their use. The user's perspective is extremely important, since a satisfactory set of output measures for any archives ought to be its ability to meet users' needs. As Brichford comments, "the surest proof of sound records appraisal lies in the quality of use of the archives and the growth of its reputation among the administrators and scholars it serves."[84] This use must be placed alongside of the policies and procedures records professionals use to reduce the records volume.

Archivists have also been loath to admit appraisal mistakes. Archivists seem reluctant to consider such issues, although Jenkinson did state that archivists should not criticize past archival selection decisions if they were made according to the standards of their time.[85] Luciana Duranti, from a different vantage, states that she does not have knowledge of one situation in which "appraisal decisions have destroyed documents that we needed to have for our protection, development, and intellectual growth. When serious losses have occurred, they may have been caused by accidental circumstances in more recent times, by the voluntary destruction by records creators of compromising documents, abducted while they were still active, and sometimes in the initial phase of creation."[86] But archivists need to confer with the user, maintain adequate records, and conduct sufficient research about such concerns. There are some rare instances when the researcher speaks directly to the archivist about this, as did historian JoAnn Yates when she questioned the adequacy of archival appraisal approaches for documenting businesses.[87] Without clear policies and appraisal objectives, there may be little to discuss.

Because of the immensity and importance of recorded information, a well-developed set of common criteria is one of the most important elements for appraisal. Maynard Brichford declares that the "most significant archival function is the appraisal or evaluation of the mass of source material and the selection of that portion that will be kept."[88] What should be the basis for this? It should rest on how organizations, people, and society function. Part of any representative record should be the preservation of records serving as vital evidence for the organization, such as records in a social welfare archives determined by that discipline's self-conscious professional activity.[89] Now we understand this as the warrant for recordkeeping.

The criteria should enable effective decision making about the documentation possessing archival value. N.R.F. Maier, in the management field, developed a formula characterizing an effective decision as equaling quality times acceptance. Quality is the feasibility of a decision arrived at by the use of data, facts, and analysis; it is the result of the cognitive or intellectual process. Acceptance is more subjective, suggesting the personal aspects of a problem that has been determined by those affected by the decision; it is the emotional and non-intellectual aspect of the human decision-making process.[90] This notion suggests that the archivist, in conducting appraisal, must seek to know what he or she is after in the appraisal process and to determine the reactions of the records creators and users to the selection. Some archivists suggest that this is at the heart of the archival appraisal dilemma.[91] Notions of decision making affirm this. Charles McClure, a leading student of library and information professional effectiveness, states that "if one defines decision-making as that process whereby information is converted into action, then decision-making has largely to do with the process of acquiring, controlling, and utilizing information to accomplish some objective."[92] In this sense, the archivist conducting appraisal must do everything necessary in order to determine the desired ends of appraisal, consider the universe of documentation, and reflect on the users' and creators' interest in the appraisal decision. It is then easy to move to drafting policy.

The reason for the significance of selection criteria is that the appraisal process is fundamental to the mission of archival institutions and profession. Peter Drucker notes, "profit is not a cause but a result—the result of the performance of the business in marketing, innovation, and productivity."[93] Archivists must ask what the equivalent of "profit" is for their organizations. Most would state that it is the successful use of their archival holdings by researchers. This successful use is dependent on appropriate and wise appraisal decisions. Akin to what Drucker states about business organizations, use—if equal to profit—is dependent on appraisal that is likewise dependent on knowledge of researchers' needs, specified aims for appraisal, and the appropriate ability to perform these.

Is there a framework or other basis for such criteria? Or, even without a framework, are there suitable criteria for guiding appraisal? As I noted earlier, most archivists (and records managers for that matter) think of the classic formulations of evidential and informational values as the criteria to be followed. The concepts of evidential and informational values, as other specific criteria, have not been well defined.[94] Archivists have tried to refine these criteria. Brichford describes uniqueness, credibility, understandability, time span, accessibility, frequency for use, type and quality of use as more specific criteria for selection for preservation.[95] Many archivists fall back upon these criteria as if they are *precisely* defined and use them as the explanation for most of their decisions. In many cases, the terms lack any methodological rigor.

A classic case is intrinsic value. This value is very specific, possessing a lengthy set of terms used to define its parameters. A close reading of the terms indicates a lack of precision itself. Terms as value laden as "aesthetic or artistic" are used. Ironically, the only publication defining this concept states clearly that its use is relative, "opinions concerning whether records have intrinsic value may vary from archivist to archivist and from one generation of archivists to another." The same publication states that the "archivist is responsible for determining which records have intrinsic value," refuting the notion that archivists probably seek outside assistance in this.[96] Still, intrinsic value is seen by some as one of the major recent contributions to archival theory.[97] Some of this may be the fact that, as lexicographers have found, the precise or ultimate meaning of any word is impossible. Archivists need interaction with individuals at either end of the spectrum of institutional records creator or records (and policy writing is one means for achieving this).

The need to understand how records originate in their environmental setting is important. Schellenberg notes, the "archivist must know how records came into being if he is to judge their value for any purpose."[98] This is clearly seen in Yates's study of internal communication systems in business organizations.[99] It can also be seen in an analysis of individual documents. Maps, for example, are "unique systems of signs. . . . Through both their content and their modes of representation, the making and using of maps has been pervaded by ideology. Yet these mechanisms can only be understood in specific historical situations."[100] The nature of modern documentation poses a number of interesting problems. Helen Samuels concludes, the "analysis of single institutions . . . is insufficient to support the [appraisal] decisions archivists face." "Institutions do not stand alone," Samuels contends, "nor do their archives."[101] Michael Lutzker believes "all working archivists recognize . . . that the records we receive, no matter how voluminous, contain something less than the full administrative history of our institutions."[102] Policies governing or directing how we appraise records must incorporate this larger view. Indeed, without such policies it is easy to react to individual groups of records without seeing their greater context and produce poor appraisal results.

Consensus among archival practitioners seems to run counter to this, seeing experience and knowledge as defined by their institutional setting.[103] While this represents a very practical approach to appraisal, it ignores the need to understand recordkeeping and information systems and the nature of modern documentation. The archivist must make a choice—the dependence on a single institutional perspective or expansion to multi-institutional approaches. The most fundamental aspect of appraisal is the consideration of records as part of an organic whole related to institutional purpose and function. Muller, Feith, and Fruin, in their famous late nineteenth century manual, stated, "an archival collection is an organic whole, a living organism, which grows, takes shape, and undergoes changes in accordance with fixed rules."[104] They also noted the fundamental archival truth that documents are often difficult to understand if removed from their context, since "the various documents of an archival collection throw light upon one another."[105]

This contextual aspect is reflected in many other documentary (and even nondocumentary) fields—including historic preservation,[106] archaeology,[107] material culture studies,[108] and paleontology.[109] This principle requires the archivist to look at records in their institutional context rather than piecemeal,[110] a practice even records managers have fallen prey to in their scheduling process. In general, archivists interpret this solely within an institutional environment, when in fact the changing nature of modern documentation demands a multi-institutional approach and a plan.

Recorded information should be reduced in a planned manner, based upon carefully determined and tested selection criteria. Planning has become a fundamental aspect of archival practice, and it is crucial to the preparation of useful policy. Faye Phillips, in the best statement of archival acquisition policies, sees that "policies must precede active collecting rather than be developed as an afterthought." Why? "Sporadic, unplanned, competitive, and overlapping manuscript collecting has led to the growth of poor collections of marginal value."[111] Judith Endelman also has shown how planning in reverse, using the notion of institutional collection analysis, is essential to the refinement of acquisitions policies.[112] Careful planning is also important because appraisal dictates much of what records professionals do in *all* their activities, the use of their resources, the service to society, and whether they have been successful at all.

Planned archival appraisal is especially important since a decision to save records is also a decision to destroy some. Planned selection is often the result of both the peeling away of documentation that does not have value and a focus on the most critical documentation. It cannot rest on unpredictable *future* research trends but must be based upon the more predictable sense of determining what are the salient and important features of contemporary institutions and society. There have been numerous comments made by archivists through the years that their selection and preservation of archival records is for *future* researchers. Technically, this is true, as records brought into the archives will not be used until *some* point in the future. While encouraging use is a legitimate role for the archivist, any kind of prediction is an unreliable and inadequate basis for appraisal decisions. Andrea Hinding speculates that "outguessing the future by more than a few years is a game that no one, by definition, can win."[113] Jenkinson commented that archives acquired from the past should not be destroyed because it was impossible to predict their future use or unwise to superimpose the values of the present on past decisions that led to the formation of those archives.[114] Jenkinson's concept is contrary to more recent notions such as reappraisal and sampling, but he had a weakened concept of appraisal and his views must be abandoned in light of the vast bulk of modern archives *and* the increasing complexity of modern documentation and information systems. Other information specialists also struggle with this concern.[115] Archivists need to rethink the basis for their appraisal decisions, fixing such decisions to a more concrete foundation than something as indeterminate as future use.

Characterizing the archival appraisal process in this manner brings up the old bugaboo of "objectivity." Trying to conduct planned appraisal suggests questions of *who* decides *what* is important, and the notion of objectivity becomes the prime concern. Records professionals know that they are inadequate in this. David Loewenthal, in an impressive analysis of our knowledge of the past, remarks, the "past as we know it is partly a product of the present; we continually reshape memory, rewrite history, refashion relics."[116] Thomas Schlereth, characterizing the work of history museums and historical societies, believes that "there is bias in every method of collecting" and that the major method of dealing with this bias is to be aware of it.[117] Archivists could say the same.

How does objectivity relate to archivists' concerns? For the American archivist, at least, it derived from their origins as a profession from the old framework constructed by the scientific historians of the late nineteenth and early twentieth centuries. And, as presented by historian Peter Novick, we learn that the concept of objectivity was a *misreading* of the intentions of the German historical school of Leopold von Ranke. As Novick states, von Ranke and his followers did not intend to be in a nomothetic (law-generating) activity but rather in an ideographic (particular-describing) activity; Americans grabbed it as the former. Even if this were not the problem, the American archivist would still be required to re-consider objectivity. Archivists continually argue about the centrality of historical study for the archivist in his or her education and the need to understand their researchers' research methods and trends, but the history profession is in disarray over such concerns as objectivity.[118] Objectivity in archival appraisal led archivists to worry about the under-documented elements of society in the 1960s and 1970s. What are the options? Should the archivist allow the records creator to decide? Should the element of random survival dictate? Should the researcher, not considering objectivity but certainly deciding relevant information from his or her own specific perspective, make the appraisal decision? Or should the archivist, in tandem with and cognizant of researchers' needs and the records creators desires, be the guiding force in determining what records will be selected and re-selected for preservation and other special treatment in order to ensure long-term use?

Appraisal planning requires the archivist to be involved actively in the selection process, operating with the assistance of selection criteria and theory. This activism includes being as close to the beginning of records creation as is possible, likewise not a new concept. Margaret Cross Norton stated that the "archivist as the ultimate custodian is also interested in the creation of records. After the records have been transferred to the archives it is difficult to weed the files and too late to supply gaps where necessary records have not been properly made."[119] Norton, in considering the archivist's relationship to the records manager, probed more into the archivist's connection to the creation process: "The archivist's training in research methods, his intimate knowledge of the history of his government, and his experience with the various ways in which records are used for purposes other than administration qualify him to take an active part in the creation of government records."[120] It is *more* important for this kind of activity to be followed in working with modern electronic records in which the systems are fragile and quickly replaced. Without intervention, documentation in electronic form will be lost long before the archivist ever has a chance to identify and save the record. For some archivists, this concern has been expanded to include the need to assist selectively in the creation of documentation.

An interesting idea to consider is extending the records life cycle to include the kinds of documentation outside of institutions with regularized archival and records management operations. Study is needed about whether the papers of individuals and families and small organizations such as civic associations and family-owned businesses may have specific times when they fall prey to destruction. Could one discover, for example, regular patterns in the cycles of existence of small businesses indicating to archivists when they should be most concerned with the safeguarding of their records (provided the organization has been determined to possess sufficient value to the greater objective of documenting society)?

The main purposes of planned archival appraisal are to document institutions, people, and society. Part of this planned documentation is to be sensitive to the under-documented and often powerless elements of society. Archivists have been especially concerned about the documentation of certain aspects of society, influenced by the work of social historians. This led to a number of efforts to develop special subject archives that collect with the intention of filling in gaps. Danielle Laberge thinks archivists must be cognizant of all elements of society and that these elements may not be well represented in or protected by the kinds of archival documentation most often preserved. This led her to articulate a specific principle that "archivists . . . must remember in designing selection and sampling criteria to protect as far as possible representative slices and samples of case file information in order to document the basic rights of groups and individuals in society."[121] Others have observed a similar trait in a society's collective memory being connected to that society's nature of power.[122] Representative documentation is again an important postulate of archival appraisal. And who is to say that this should not be viewed as an aspect of every institutional archival program's work, since most institutions are responsible for or accountable to society?

There is some legitimate question, however, about consensus among archivists about this issue of representativeness. David Bearman suggests, the "profession does not agree whether this record is intended to be 'representative' of all of recorded memory, or 'representative' of the activities of members of the society, or 'representative' of those aspects of social activity perceived by members of the society at the time as important to the understanding of the culture. Most archivists apply appraisal criteria to records, not to activities or social policy processes, and therefore assume that the goal is not to skew the record as received."[123] These are good points. Terry Cook articulates an appraisal theory encompassing the notion of public interest, suggesting that any other approaches to appraisal must be open to modification by greater interests by the public.[124]

Leonard Rapport, considering archival reappraisal, notes, "appraising is at best an inexact science, perhaps more an art; and a conscientious appraiser, particularly an imaginative one with an awareness of research interests and trends, is apt to know nights of troubled soul searching."[125] One way of improving the nights of all archivists is to see appraisal, as Terry Cook states, as a "work of careful analysis and of archival scholarship, not a mere procedure,"[126] a concern leading archivists to wrestle with some of the complex ideas related to the recent notions of macro-appraisal.

Prior to the archival documentation strategy, American archivists had become deeply aware of the chaotic manner in which appraisal was carried out and the confused set of purposes served by appraisal. Discussions of cooperation, coordination, and assessment began to appear in the literature reminding archivists of the challenges they faced in bringing a sufficient order to a vast universe of documentation.[127] This time may have represented a paradigm shift from the public archives emphasis to a more complex array of documentary goals, concerns with users and the under-documented and powerless elements of society, and recognition of the inadequacies of accepted appraisal approaches. F. Gerald Ham, in his 1974 presidential address to the Society of American Archivists, made a stirring call for archival self-reflection about how well they were determining what records should be saved, whether they possessed sufficient criteria and models for appraisal, and if they extend beyond a mere reflex to the latest fads of research.[128]

The archival documentation strategy, functional analysis, and appraisal strategy all share a similar origin in the need for new strategies to grapple with the significant challenges represented by the rapidly evolving modern recordkeeping systems and their products. They also possess a solid foundation in other areas of archival and records management theory and practice.[129] While there are those who contend that the archivist has always utilized an appraisal approach similar to the documentation strategy or who demean anything resembling theory, these views fall by the wayside in any consideration of what appraisal needs to be in both practice and conception.[130] Records professionals can hardly begin to approach the documentary universe without some strategic or methodological frameworks for cutting that universe down to a manageable size. In my 1989 essay on the Western New York documentation effort, I concluded with a series of questions, including whether the archival documentation strategy was the best means to analyze archival documentation, the practical consideration of how such efforts can be supported, and the validity of the archival documentation strategy itself. The most important question was this: "Even if the documentation strategy model as now proposed is flawed, don't we need some kind of method that enables us to look at the broader issues of identification and selection of historical records?" How would I, some years removed, now answer this question? The archival documentation strategy has helped the North American archivist to re-think archival appraisal as well as the societal mission of the archivist. The archivist must return to a basic emphasis on the record, the stress on continuing evidence as the linchpin of the definition of the archival record, and the value of archives for accountability and corporate memory.

CONCLUSION: APPRAISAL, SCHEDULING, AND THE MANAGING OF RECORDS

In a records management text, Ira Penn and his co-authors provide a useful chapter on records scheduling. They accept the notion of appraisal as the "basis" for scheduling, and by appraising they mean the "process of documenting a record's value in terms of the length of time it is to be retained." Penn also describes the importance of a schedule for an organization: "By establishing a records schedule, an organization ensures that recordkeeping laws are adhered to and that management needs are met, and demonstrates that a systematic program is in place to determine records values prior to destruction of the information."[131] The authors include a concise list of the objectives of records scheduling—disposal, storage of records with temporary value, and the preservation of records with long-term value—as well as a series of four steps to complete an inventory process, starting with the identification of state and federal legislative requirements for an organization's records.[132] While their concept of values is traditional (administrative, fiscal, legal, and other research values) and the process of determining values is likewise standard, flowing from the records inventory work, Penn and his co-authors start from the premise of understanding records functions. Their emphasis on considering what they term "regulatory impact" enhances comprehension of why records are created and their continuing value to the organization creating these records.

Drawing on the previous discussion about the nature of archival appraisal, however, it should be apparent that a scheduling process relying *only* on inventory and legislative and legal mandates is not enough for acceptable records management. What is needed? Records managers and archivists (*all* records professionals) should have as their primary responsibility the compilation and use of the record warrant. This warrant should go far beyond legislation and law to include any mandate (disciplinary, best practice, or contractual) requiring the creation and maintenance of records. A comprehensive knowledge of the record warrant can be used to target the organization's crucial or essential records, whether in paper or electronic media. The difference in use of the warrant may be only the differences in using the warrant to administer paper records along their life cycle or continuum versus the use of the warrant integrated into the design of an electronic recordkeeping system. Records schedules might be necessary only for the records series required by the warrant to be maintained over time and for the purpose of keeping key institutional personnel aware of the records maintenance requirements.

The focus on records warrant has a number of implications for the records professional. It helps shift attention to what ought to be the major knowledge area for such a professional—an understanding of records and recordkeeping systems. The warrant also should help records managers and archivists shift their priorities in a positive manner. The records manager shifts from administering records warehouses to assisting the organization to understand the significance of its records and its records responsibility. The archivist shifts attention from potential external researcher interests to the organization's ongoing needs for information in its own records. Finally, the stress on the record warrant provides a more relevant role for the records professional within his or her own institution because the warrant stresses the importance of accountability and evidence for the organization. Any organization conducting itself appropriately will be very interested in the assistance that can be provided by the archivist and records manager. The record warrant provides a much more concrete identity and responsibility for the records professional than any stress on concepts such as information or knowledge can provide.

Archival macro-appraisal approaches add another element to the records scheduling procedures. Building on the idea of the research aspect brought to appraisal by these approaches, records managers could work within their institutional settings to identify crucial organizational activities and projects deserving comprehensive documentation, ascertain records of continuing value to the organization because of their research value for insights into institutional activities, and formulate case studies guiding records maintenance. Given that any record *can* have value, whether historical or legal, at any time, it is important for organizational records professionals to provide strong guidance about a highly selective process of records appraisal. It is possible, even probable, that providing a mechanism whereby records of strong continuing value for purposes of corporate memory and accountability may provide more than adequate documentation for other research purposes and by external researchers.

It is also important for records professionals to follow the breaking news stories about records. The cases of our federal government and the Iran-Contra electronic mail, the tobacco industry and the efforts by that industry's legal counsel to control the research process and records management functions, and the management of financial records by Switzerland's banks of accounts of Holocaust victims all demonstrate a new, more socially conscious role for records professionals. The statement released by a group of leading cigarette manufacturers that "Those who believe that 20- or 40-year-old documents merit continuation of legal and regulatory hostilities in lieu of a national legislative solution fail to see what is at stake" and that "We must learn from, but not be obsessed by, events past" fails to reflect why records benefit and protect society.[133] Fortunately, the archival appraisal methods and philosophy provide a gateway to this kind of sensitivity not reflected in the more methodical or by-the-book records management scheduling. A melding of archival appraisal's documentary aims for societal purposes with the records manager's scheduling process for organizational benefits seems the best road to take. And it needs to be incorporated into basic records policies from the organizational to societal level.

NOTES

1. Scott Adams, *The Dilbert Future: Thriving on Stupidity in the 21st Century* (New York: HarperBusiness, 1997), p. 188.

2. Robert L. Sanders, "Archivists and Records Managers: Another Marriage in Trouble?" *Records Management Quarterly* 23 (April 1989): 12.

3. Sanders, "Archivists and Records Managers," p. 13.

4. Sanders, "Archivists and Records Managers," p. 14.

5. Sanders, "Archivists and Records Managers," p. 16.

6. Jay Kennedy and Cherryl Schaudar, *Records Management: A Guide for Students and Practitioners of Records and Information Management with Exercises and Case Studies* (Melbourne, Australia: Longman Cheshire, 1994), p. 59.

7. Bruce W. Dearstyne, *The Archival Enterprise: Modern Archival Principles, Practices, and Management Techniques* (Chicago: American Library Association, 1993), p. 115.

8. Betty R. Ricks and Kay F. Gow, *Information Resource Management* (Cincinnati: South-Western Publishing Co., 1984), p. 48.

9. Ricks and Gow, *Information Resource Management*, p. 39.

10. Candy Schwartz and Peter Hernon, *Records Management and the Library: Issues and Practices* (Norwood, NJ: Ablex Publishing Corporation, 1993), p. 80.

11. Lewis J. and Lynn Lady Bellardo, *A Glossary for Archivists, Manuscript Curators, and Records Managers*, Archival Fundamental Series (Chicago: Society of American Archivists, 1992), pp. 2, 11, 31.

12. Frederic L. Holmes, "Laboratory Notebooks: Can the Daily Record Illuminate the Broader Picture?" *Proceedings of the American Philosophical Society* 134, no. 4 (1990): 352.

13. Cullen Murphy, "Backlogs of History," *Atlantic Monthly* 277 (May 1996): 20.

14. Peter F. Drucker, *Post-Capitalist Society* (New York: HarperBusiness, 1993), p. 107.

15. Drucker, *Post-Capitalist Society*, p. 170.

16. Luciana Duranti, "ACA 1991 Conference Overview," *ACA Bulletin* 15 (July 1991): 25.

17. See Charles R. McClure and J. Timothy Sprehe, *Analysis and Development of Model Quality Guidelines for Electronic Records Management on State and Federal Websites; Final Report January 1998* at http://istweb.syr.edu/mcclure/nhprc. The principal investigators demonstrate that most government archivists and records managers are not considering the records implications of Web sites because of inadequate definitions of records or the lack of interest in trying to work with the proliferating use of the World Wide Web.

18. This is evident in the continuing problems of the U.S. National Archives in working with electronic mail and the decade-old series of lawsuits about how it manages such records. However one may feel about the stance of this organization, the media coverage has not been flattering. In an April 8, 1998 article in the *New York Times*, the headline read "Federal Government Clings to Paper Records" and featured a photograph of U.S. Archivist John W. Carlin in front of a sea of boxes full of paper records. The caption read "John W. Carlin, the Archivist of the United States, stands by a policy that encourages agencies to turn electronic documents into paper ones. He is a defendant in

a lawsuit filed by researchers, librarians, historians and journalists" (p. D8). This and other related news stories essentially convey the message—we cannot do our job. An Associated Press story by Mike Feinsilber, released on March 24, 1998, carried the title "Government 'Overwhelmed,' Its Recordkeeper Says."

19. See, for example, *Guidelines on Best Practices for Using Electronic Information: How to Deal with Machine-Readable Data and Electronic Documents*, rev. ed. (Luxembourg: Office for Official Publications of the European Communities, 1997), available at http://www2.echo.lu/dlm/en/gdlines.html.

20. Christopher L. Hives, "History, Business Records, and Corporate Archives in North America," *Archivaria* 22 (Summer 1986): 40–57. See also JoAnne Yates, "Internal Communication Systems in American Business Structures: A Framework to Aid Appraisal," *American Archivist* 48 (Spring 1985): 141–148.

21. Timothy L. Ericson, "At the 'Rim of Creative Dissatisfaction': Archivists and Acquisition Development," *Archivaria* 33 (Winter 1991–1992): 68.

22. William J. Mitchell, *City of Bits: Space, Place, and the Infobahn* (Cambridge, MA: MIT Press, 1995), p. 126.

23. Mitchell, *City of Bits*, p. 81.

24. Mitchell, *City of Bits*, p. 89.

25. Mitchell, *City of Bits*, p. 92.

26. Mitchell, *City of Bits*, p. 97.

27. Mitchell, *City of Bits*, pp. 138–139.

28. Witold Rybczynski, *City Life: Urban Expectations in a New World* (New York: HarperCollins, 1995), p. 12.

29. Charles A. Myers, ed., *The Impact of Computers on Management* (Cambridge, MA: MIT Press, 1967). The quotation is from Charles R. DeCarlo, "Changes in Management Environment and Their Effect Upon Values," p. 245.

30. Carl Heyel, *Computers, Office Machines, and the New Information Technology* (New York: Macmillan Co., 1969).

31. See, for example, Nancy Dunn Cosgrove, "The Paperless Office: Still a Myth in the Nineties," *Office* 117 (April 1993): 25–28. The estimates of paper being produced is staggering, extending to a trillion pages a year; Thomas F. Connolly and Brian H. Kleiner, "The Paperless Office of the Future," *Logistics Information Management* 6, no. 5 (1993): 40–43.

32. James E. Hunton, "Setting Up a Paperless Office," *Journal of Accountancy* 178 (November 1994): 78.

33. For example, in 1994 a new journal, *The EDI Law Review: Legal Aspects of Paperless Communication*, commenced publication.

34. Glenn Rifkin, "The Future of the Document," *Forbes ASAP* (October 9, 1995): 46–47.

35. Mitchell Jay Weiss, "The Paperless Office," *Journal of Accountancy* 178 (November 1994): 73–76 (quotation p. 74).

36. Robert Jackall, *Moral Mazes: The World of Corporate Managers* (New York: Oxford University Press, 1988), p. 88.

37. Amelia H. Boss and Mario A. Decastro, "The Impact of Fiscal Recordkeeping Requirements on the Migration Towards Electronic Technologies: The United States Experience," *EDI Law Review* 1 (1994): 178.

38. United States Advisory Council on the National Information Infrastructure, *A*

Nation of Opportunity: Realizing the Promise of the Information Superhighway ([Washington, DC: The Council], January 1996), pp. 17–19.

39. H. Jeff Smith, *Managing Privacy: Information Technology and Corporate America* (Chapel Hill: University of North Carolina Press, 1994).

40. Wendy Duff, "Harnessing the Power of Warrant," *American Archivist* 61 (Spring 1998): 88–105.

41. Stanley Joel Reiser, "Creating Form Out of Mass: The Development of the Medical Record," in Everett Mendelsohn, ed., *Transformation and Tradition in the Sciences: Essays in Honor of I. Bernard Cohen* (Cambridge: Cambridge University Press, 1984), p. 303.

42. JoAnne Yates and Wanda J. Orlikowski, "Genres of Organizational Communication: A Structurational Approach to Studying Communication and Media," *Academy of Management Review* 17, no. 2 (1992): 300.

43. Yates and Orlikowski, "Genres of Organizational Communication," p. 302.

44. Philip K. Howard, *The Death of Common Sense: How Law Is Suffocating America* (New York: Random House, 1994), p. 10.

45. Donald A. Ritchie, *Doing Oral History* (New York: Twayne Publishers, 1995), p. 132.

46. U.S. District Court for the District of Columbia, Civil Action no. 96–2480 (PLF), *Public Citizen, et al., v. John Carlin, Archivist of the U.S.*, October 22, 1997.

47. NARA, *Ready Access to Essential Evidence: The Strategic Plan of the National Archives and Records Administration 1997–2007 September 30, 1997*, at http://www.nara.gov/nara/vision/naraplan.html.

48. Page Putnam Miller, "National Archives Releases Strategic Plan," *NCC Washington Update* 3 (October 21, 1997), item 1, at http://h-net.msu.edu/~ncc/.

49. H. G. Jones, *Local Government Records: An Introduction to Their Management, Preservation, and Use* (Nashville: American Association for State and Local History, 1980), pp. 20–21.

50. Quoted in Fred Shelley, "The Interest of J. Franklin Jameson in the National Archives: 1908–1934," *American Archivist*, 12 (April 1949): 129.

51. Henry D. Shapiro, in considering the concept of preservation as used in historical societies, museums, and libraries, notes that "All were directed at the collection and preservation of items that were by definition 'useless,' and the very uselessness of which made them available to systematic preservation in most cases. All involved an active work of intervention, not to alter or redirect a normal process of disposal but to remove selected items from its operation and thereby preserve what would otherwise have passed out of currency because it had already ceased to have use. And all manifest a commitment to preservation based not on some sense of the 'higher' usefulness of the apparently useless, much less on a sense of those items' potential for reuse or alternative use, but on the fact of uselessness itself. It was *uselessness*, that is, that made these objects available for preservation in the first place; and it was uselessness that made it possible to endow these objects with 'meaning' of a sort that they could not have possessed during the period of their original use and usefulness." "Putting the Past under Glass: Preservation and the Idea of History in the Mid-Nineteenth Century," *Prospects* 10 (1985): 245.

52. Committee on Government Operations, *Taking a Byte Out of History: The Archival Preservation of Federal Computer Records* (Washington, DC: U.S. Government Printing Office, 1990), p. 28.

53. Alf Erlandsson, *Electronic Records Management: A Literature Review*, ICA Studies CIA 10 (Paris: International Council on Archives, April 1996), chap. 6.

54. The first description of options for replacing or revising the schedule for electronic records reflects the lack of imagination applied to the scheduling process. Two of the proposals, establishing a "uniform minimum retention period for electronic records" and developing "retention standards for electronic records . . . based on an individual's position in the agency hierarchy," reflected a lack of knowledge about the nature of archival appraisal. See http://www.nara.gov/records/grs20/opt312.html.

55. Kennedy and Schaudar, *Records Management*, pp. 72–73.

56. New York State Archives and Records Administration, *Managing Records in Automated Office Systems* (Albany: NYSARA, 1995, revised), p. 14.

57. Page Putnam Miller, "Archivist Orders an Investigation of Recent Destruction of Naval Laboratory Records," *NCC Washington Update* 3 (November 19, 1997), item 2, at http://h-net.msu.edu/~ncc/.

58. Margaretta Jolly, "Love Letters versus Letters Carved in Stone: Gender, Memory and the 'Forces Sweethearts' Exhibition," *War and Memory in the Twentieth Century*, ed. Martin Evans and Ken Lunn (Oxford: Berg, 1997), p. 115.

59. Jolly, "Love Letters," p. 117.

60. Tom Forester and Perry Morrison, *Computer Ethics: Cautionary Tales and Ethical Dilemmas in Computing* (Cambridge, MA: MIT Press, 1990), p. 11.

61. See, for example, the following essays: Helen W. Samuels, "Who Controls the Past," *American Archivist* 49 (Spring 1986): 109–124; Larry J. Hackman and Joan Warnow-Blewett, "The Documentation Strategy Process: A Model and a Case Study," *American Archivist* 50 (Winter 1987): 12–47; Hans Booms, "Society and the Formation of a Documentary Heritage," *Archivaria* 24 (Summer 1987): 69–107; Judith E. Endelman, "Looking Backward to Plan for the Future: Collection Analysis for Manuscript Repositories," *American Archivist* 50 (Summer 1987): 340–355; Philip Alexander and Helen W. Samuels, "The Roots of 128: A Hypothetical Documentation Strategy," *American Archivist* 50 (Fall 1987): 518–531; Richard J. Cox and Helen W. Samuels, "The Archivists' First Responsibility: A Research Agenda for the Identification and Retention of Records of Enduring Value," *American Archivist* 51 (Winter–Spring 1988): 28–42; Margaret Hedstrom, "New Appraisal Techniques: The Effect of Theory on Practice," *Provenance* 7 (Fall 1989): 1–21; Terry Abraham, "Collection Policy or Documentation Strategy: Theory and Practice," *American Archivist* 54 (Winter 1991): 44–52; Terry Cook, "Many Are Called but Few Are Chosen: Appraisal Guidelines for Sampling and Selecting Case Files," *Archivaria* 32 (Summer 1991): 25–50; Hans Booms, "Uberlieferungsbildung: Keeping Archives as a Social and Political Activity," *Archivaria* 33 (Winter 1991–1992): 25–33; Helen W. Samuels, "Improving Our Disposition: Documentation Strategy," *Archivaria* 33 (Winter 1991–1992): 125–140; Richard Brown, "Records Acquisition Strategy and Its Theoretical Foundation: The Case for a Concept of Archival Hermeneutics," *Archivaria* 33 (Winter 1991–1992): 34–56; Terry Cook, "Documentation Strategy," *Archivaria* 34 (Summer 1992): 181–191; Thomas J. Ruller, "Dissimilar Appraisal Documentations as an Impediment to Sharing Appraisal Data: A Survey of Appraisal Documentation in Government Archival Repositories," *Archival Issues* 17, no. 1 (1992): 65–73; and Terry Eastwood, "How Goes It with Appraisal?" *Archivaria* 36 (Autumn 1993): 111–121.

62. The professional debate on archival knowledge and theory that I refer to is typified by the discussion that started with Frank Burke's 1981 essay, "The Future Course

of Archival Theory in the United States," *American Archivist* 44 (Winter 1981): 40–46, and this debate is worth a side trip in this consideration of archival appraisal theory and the documentation strategy. Burke, in his essay, argued that archivists must define their theory, separate it from and then relate it to practice, and that this theory will not be developed until there are archivists working full-time as educators who have the time to enunciate and test this theory. Burke was immediately rejoined by Lester Cappon, who questioned his definition of theory and the practicality of developing such theory in his article "What, Then, Is There to Theorize About?" *American Archivist* 45 (Winter 1982): 19–25 and Michael Lutzker, who turned to look at other disciplines (in this case, sociology and Max Weber) that "offer constructs that can deepen our understanding of how institutions function" (and hence their records) in his "Max Weber and the Analysis of Modern Bureaucratic Organization: Notes Toward a Theory of Appraisal," *American Archivist* 45 (Spring 1982): 119. Gregg D. Kimball, a Burke student, contributed to the debate in 1985 and also urged the empirical process of developing archival theory instead of "law-like theorizing" that Burke seemed disposed to in his original contribution; see his "The Burke-Cappon Debate: Some Further Criticisms and Considerations for Archival Theory," *American Archivist* 48 (Fall 1985): 371. While Kimball summarized and criticized earlier contributions to the debate, John W. Roberts, in 1987 and 1990, presented the most extreme views when he defined the concern with archival theory as merely evidence of the archivist's "emotional need for greater professional acceptance." Roberts saw little that is unique to archival work, arguing that a "knowledge of historical scholarship and of the content of particular collections become the essential components in making informed, professional decisions about appraisal, description, and reference." Archives, states Roberts, is a "fairly straight-forward, down to earth service occupation" in his "Archival Theory: Much Ado about Shelving," *American Archivist* 50 (Winter 1987): 67, 69, 74 and his latter treatment, "Archival Theory: Myth or Banality," *American Archivist* 53 (Winter 1990): 110–120.

63. T. R. Schellenberg, "The Appraisal of Modern Public Records," *National Archives Bulletin* 8 (Washington, DC: National Archives and Records Service, 1956), p. 44.

64. See, for example, Terry Abraham, "Collection Policy or Documentation Strategy."

65. Judith A. Perrolle, *Computers and Social Change: Information, Property, and Power* (Belmont, CA: Wadsworth Publishing Co., 1987), p. 30. Another approach, which is beyond the scope of my book, is to study the manner in which records are created, used by their creators, and re-used by their creators and others. The reason why this is beyond this study is because archivists and others have not analyzed this issue as effectively as they probably should have done. Hugh Taylor stated that "it is very curious and perhaps significant that, despite all the massive corpus of writing about management and administration, so little attention has been given to the impact of the various records" (" 'My Very Act and Deed': Some Reflections on the Role of Textual Records in the Conduct of Affairs," *American Archivist* 51 [Fall 1988]: 461). Clark Elliott has stated the same matter more bluntly: "Documents are at the center of the concern of historians and archivists, and yet neither profession has directed very great attention to a consideration of writing as social communication and to the functional relationship of documents to historical events" ("Communication and Events in History: Toward a Theory for Documenting the Past," *American Archivist* 48 [Fall 1985]: 358). All this extends back to the fundamental conception of theories.

66. *Library Services in Theory and Context*, 2nd ed. (New York: Pergamon Press, 1988), chap. 5.

67. Allan Pratt, *The Information of the Image* (Norwood, NJ: Ablex Publishing Corporation, 1982), p. 48.

68. Maynard J. Brichford, *Archives and Manuscripts: Appraisal and Accessioning* (Chicago: Society of American Archivists, 1977), p. 7.

69. Luciana Duranti, "So? What Else Is New? The Ideology of Appraisal Yesterday and Today," in *Archival Appraisal: Theory and Practice*, ed. Christopher Hives (Vancouver: Archives Association of British Columbia, 1990), p. 2.

70. F. Gerald Ham, "The Archival Edge," *American Archivist* 38 (January 1975): 6.

71. Hilary Jenkinson, *A Manual of Archive Administration*, rev. 2nd ed. (London: Percy Lund, Humphries and Co., 1966), pp. 137–138, 148–149.

72. Thornton W. Mitchell, ed., *Norton on Archives: The Writings of Margaret Cross Norton on Archival and Records Management* (Carbondale: Southern Illinois University Press, 1975), pp. 232–233, 239.

73. Schellenberg, "The Appraisal of Modern Public Records," p. 5.

74. One commentator on the use of online information systems and hypermedia suggests that the premise underlying the use of such systems is to provide as much information as possible, but that this "can simply offer someone, who is already under stress, more information to process, whether or not that information relates directly to the tasks at hand." Philip Rubens, "Online Information, Hypermedia, and the Idea of Literacy," in Edward Barrett, ed., *The Society of Text: Hypertext, Hypermedia, and the Social Construction of Information* (Cambridge, MA: MIT Press, 1989), p. 17.

75. Daniel Boorstin, "A Wrestler with the Angel," in Boorstin, *Hidden History* (New York: Vintage Books, 1988), p. 5.

76. Kenneth Dowlin, *The Electronic Library: The Promise and the Process* (New York: Neal-Schuman Publishers, 1984), p. 14.

77. Thomas J. Schlereth, *Cultural History and Material Culture: Everyday Life, Landscapes, Museums* (Ann Arbor: UMI Research Press, 1990), pp. 121–122.

78. Hugh Taylor, " 'My Very Act and Deed,' " p. 467.

79. Ham, "The Archival Edge," p. 5.

80. Edward F. Barrese, "Adequacy of Documentation in the Federal Government," *Information Management Review* 5 (Spring 1990): 53–58.

81. David Bearman, *Archival Methods, Archives and Museum Informatics Technical Report* 3 (Spring 1989), p. 2.

82. Schellenberg, "Appraisal of Modern Public Records," p. 5.

83. Boorstin, "Wrestler," p. 23.

84. Brichford, *Appraisal and Accessioning*, p. 1.

85. Jenkinson, *Manual of Archive Administration*, pp. 139–140.

86. Duranti, "So? What Else Is New?" p. 12.

87. Yates, "Internal Communication Systems in American Business Structures,"141–148.

88. Brichford, *Appraisal and Accessioning*, p. 1.

89. David Klassen, "The Provenance of Social Work Case Records: Implications for Archival Appraisal and Access," *Provenance* 1 (Spring 1983): 5–26.

90. The work of N.R.F. Maier is discussed in John R. Rizzo, *Management for Librarians: Fundamentals and Issues* (Westport, CT: Greenwood Press, 1980), pp. 202–203.

91. Bearman, *Archival Methods*, pp. 14–15.

92. Charles McClure, "Planning for Library Effectiveness: The Role of Information Resources Management," *Journal of Library Administration* 1 (Fall 1980): 4.

93. Peter Drucker, *Management: Tasks, Responsibilities, Practices* (New York: Harper and Row, 1974), p. 71.

94. Schellenberg, "Appraisal of Modern Public Records," p. 7.

95. Brichford, *Appraisal and Accessioning*. Such criteria have also been extended to museum artifacts, another factor suggesting connections between the archivists and museum curators; see *20th Century Collecting: Guidelines and Case Studies*, Special Report, *History News* 47 (May–June 1991).

96. *Intrinsic Value in Archival Material*, NARS Staff Information Paper 21 (Washington, DC: National Archives and Records Service, 1982), pp. 1, 3.

97. Trudy Huskamp Peterson, "The National Archives and the Archival Theorist Revisited, 1954–1984," *American Archivist* 49 (Spring 1986): 129–130.

98. Schellenberg, "Appraisal of Modern Public Records," p. 8.

99. Yates, "Internal Communication."

100. J. B. Harley, "Maps, Knowledge, and Power," in *The Iconography of Landscape: Essays on the Symbolic Representation, Design and Use of Past Environments*, ed. Denis Cosgrove and Stephen Daniels (Cambridge: Cambridge University Press, 1988), p. 300.

101. Samuels, "Who Controls the Past," pp. 111, 112.

102. Michael J. Lutzker, "Max Weber and the Analysis of Modern Bureaucratic Organizations: Notes Toward a Theory of Appraisal," *American Archivist* 45 (Spring 1982): 129.

103. Frank Boles and Julia Marks Young, "Exploring the Black Box: The Appraisal of University Administrative Records," *American Archivist* 48 (Spring 1985): 129, 131. See also Boles, "Mix Two Parts Interest to One Part Information and Appraise Until Done: Understanding Contemporary Record Selection Processes," *American Archivist* 50 (Summer 1987): 358–359.

104. S. Muller, J. A. Feith, and R. Fruin. *Manual for the Arrangement and Description of Archives* (New York: H. W. Wilson, 1968), p. 19.

105. Muller, Feith, and Fruin, *Manual*, p. 36.

106. Kevin Lynch, *What Time Is This Place?* (Cambridge, MA: MIT Press, 1972), p. 37.

107. Colin Renfrew and Paul Bahn, *Archaelogy: Theories, Methods and Practice* (New York: Thames and Hudson, 1991), p. 42; Leonard Woolley, *Digging Up the Past* (Baltimore: Penguin Books, 1960; orig. pub., 1930), p. 18.

108. Thomas Schlereth, *Cultural History and Material Culture: Everyday Life, Landscapes, Museums* (Ann Arbor, MI: UMI Research Press, 1990), p. 382; Peter Gathercole, "The Fetishism of Artefacts," in *Museum Studies in Material Culture*, ed. Susan M. Pearce (Washington, DC: Smithsonian Institution Press, 1989), p. 76.

109. Stephen Jay Gould, *Wonderful Life: The Burgess Shale and the Nature of History* (New York: W. W. Norton and Co., 1989), p. 97.

110. Jenkinson, *Manual of Archive Administration*, pp. 141–143; Schellenberg, "Appraisal of Modern Public Records," p. 11; Booms, "Society and the Formation of a Documentary Heritage," p. 82.

111. Faye Phillips, "Developing Collecting Policies for Manuscript Collections," *American Archivist* 47 (Winter 1984): 31, 36.

112. Judy Endelman, "Looking Backward to Plan for the Future: Collection Analysis for Manuscript Repositories," *American Archivist* 50 (Summer 1987): 342.

113. Andrea Hinding, "Toward Documentation: New Collecting Strategies in the 1980s," in *Options for the 80s: Proceedings of the Second National Conference of the Association of College and Research Libraries* (Greenwich, CT: JAI Press, 1981), p. 535.

114. Muller, Feith, and Fruin, *Manual of Archive Administration*, pp. 144–145.

115. Benjamin Bates, "Information as an Economic Good: Sources of Individual and Social Value," in *The Political Economy of Information*, ed. Vincent Mosco and Janet Wasko (Madison: University of Wisconsin Press, 1988), pp. 77–78.

116. David Lowenthal, *The Past Is a Foreign Country* (Cambridge: Cambridge University Press, 1985), p. 26.

117. Thomas J. Schlereth, "Contemporary Collecting for Future Recollecting," *Museum Studies Journal* 113 (Spring 1984): 26.

118. Peter Novick, *That Noble Dream: The "Objectivity Question" and the American Historical Profession* (Cambridge: Cambridge University Press, 1988), pp. 593, 628.

119. Mitchell, ed., *Norton on Archives*, p. 234.

120. Mitchell, ed., *Norton on Archives*, p. 248.

121. Danielle Laberge, "Information, Knowledge, and Rights: The Preservation of Archives as a Political and Social Issue," *Archivaria* 25 (Winter 1987–1988): 49.

122. Paul Connerton, *How Societies Remember* (Cambridge: Cambridge University Press, 1989). See also David Thelen, ed., *Memory and American History* (Bloomington: Indiana University Press, 1989).

123. Bearman, *Archival Methods*, pp. 12–13.

124. Terry Cook, "Many Are Called but Few Are Chosen" and "Mind over Matter: Towards a New Theory of Archival Appraisal," in *The Archival Imagination: Essays in Honour of Hugh A. Taylor*, ed. Barbara L. Craig (Ottawa: Association of Canadian Archivists, 1992), pp. 38–70.

125. Leonard Rapport, "No Grandfather Clause: Reappraising Accessioned Records," *American Archivist* 44 (Spring 1981): 149.

126. Cook, "Mind over Matter," p. 47.

127. See, for example, Fredric Miller, "Documenting Modern Cities: The Philadelphia Model," *Public Historian* 5 (Spring 1983): 75–86 and Gloria Thompson, "From Profile to Policy: A Minnesota Historical Society Case Study in Collection Development," *Midwestern Archivist* 8, no. 2 (1983): 29–39. The Miller article describes the advantages of an urban area with private historical society, local government archives, and university focusing on twentieth-century records, while the Thompson essay is a description of an effort to evaluate what a repository's holdings represent from a documentary perspective. Institutional collection analysis, as the method described by Thompson has come to be called, was used for a brief time in several large repositories, but it has not been discussed much since; see Judith E. Endelman, "Looking Backward to Plan for the Future." Endelman's essay is the last published description of the approach.

128. F. Gerald Ham, "The Archival Edge." His other later essays are worth reading as well: "Archival Strategies for the Post-Custodial Era," *American Archivist* 44 (Summer 1981): 207–216 and "Archival Choices: Managing the Historical Record in an Age of Abundance," *American Archivist* 47 (Winter 1984): 11–22. Unfortunately, the power of these previous critiques are lost in his basic manual on appraisal—*Selecting and Appraising Archives and Manuscripts* (Chicago: Society of American Archivists, 1992), which seems to reject his earlier ideas as impractical and resorts instead to a description

of institutional practice rather than conceptual and engaging models or more universal principles. I believe that the problems with Ham's more recent contribution has more to do with the process of preparing basic textbooks seeking to define a consensus orientation to such elements of professional practice; such texts serve a valuable function, but only if used in conjunction with other professional literature and published research.

129. For example, the concept of functions has also developed both as a scheme for more efficient and reliable archival description and as a means of relating to electronic recordkeeping systems. Bearman and Lytle in their effort to consider descriptive approaches noted that "functions are independent of organizational structures, more closely related to the significance of documentation than organizational structures, and both finite in number and linguistically simple. Because archival records are the consequences of activities defined by organizational functions, such a vocabulary can be a powerful indexing language to point to the content of archival holdings, without need for actual examination of the materials themselves or for detailed subject indexing"; David Bearman and Richard Lytle, "The Power of the Principle of Provenance," *Archivaria* 21 (Winter 1985–1986), p. 22. For an effort to consider functions in this context and in relation to modern recordkeeping systems, see also Chris Hurley, "What, If Anything, Is a Function?" *Archives and Manuscripts* 21, no. 2 (1993): 208–220.

130. For the view that the documentation strategy is simply new wine in old wineskins, see Terry Abraham, "Collection Policy or Documentation Strategy." In my view Abraham fails to move past practical issues to realize that collection policies utilized by particular repositories are often not seriously applied and miss the larger issues. The issue of archival theory and appraisal (among other things) has been attacked in John W. Roberts, "Archival Theory: Much Ado about Shelving" and "Archival Theory: Myth or Banality"; see also John W. Roberts, "Practice Makes Perfect, Theory Makes Theorists," *Archivaria* 37 (Spring 1994): 111–121 and Terry Eastwood, "What Is Archival Theory and Why Is It Important?" *Archivaria* 37 (Spring 1994): 122–130.

131. Ira A. Penn, Gail Pennix, and Jim Coulson, *Records Management Handbook*, 2nd ed. (Brookfield, VT: Gower, 1994), p. 107.

132. Penn, Pennix, and Coulson, *Records Management Handbook*, pp. 116, 120–125.

133. Barry Meier, "Release of Tobacco Memos Brings Lawmakers' Demand for More," *New York Times*, December 19, 1997. See for confirmation of such records management problems, Stanton A. Glantz, John Slade, Lisa A. Bero, Peter Hanauer, and Deborah E. Barnes, *The Cigarette Papers* (Berkeley: University of California Press, 1996).

Chapter 4

The Policy's Aim:
Reaching the Public

INTRODUCTION: NO MAGIC BULLETS

Records professionals believe that because records are important, they will be deemed important as well. Archivists and records managers, like many other information professionals, need to work hard to gain support for their mission. There are many reasons for this. For archivists, the changing interest by the public in its memory explains why they and their repositories can slip in and out of fashion. Records managers also have a barrier to overcome because of lingering perceptions that they are interested in the clerical administration of paper records.

Advocating the management of records as an organizational and societal benefit is not an activity to be taken for granted. Records professionals have to know *how* to communicate their mission. Comprehending public and professional perceptions of records professionals is important. Records managers and archivists also need to understand their organizations and their legal, political, and cultural contexts. The importance of records work is not self-evident. Records professionals need to re-think their traditional arguments for why records ought to be maintained and re-invent themselves in their own changing organizations. New professional and organizational alliances, different strategies, reformulated missions, and a variety of new or improved skills and knowledge all may be in order in the twenty-first century. Articles in major news journals and media outlets about dangers to the continuing maintenance of and access to data, information, and records[1] provide opportunities for records professionals *if* they have the right message and are organized to make public responses.

THE IMAGE OF RECORDS AND RECORDS
PROFESSIONALS

For the past two decades, North American records professionals have been vitally concerned about their societal image, and these images suggest something about how archivists and records managers should do public programming. Records professionals are convinced that writing press releases or contacting the media will translate into better newspaper, television, and radio coverage. What they convey about their work and institutions begins with their understanding about what the media has generally been interested in. In one sense, records professionals must see the media as another public. The print and electronic media influence how people view records and records professionals. And this influence is not always what records professionals would like it to be. While archivists and records managers need to convince institutions and policy makers about the significance of records for memory, evidence, and accountability, they are also repeatedly portrayed as caring for records that are little more than delightful tidbits served up for antiquarians and scholars,[2] and such views carry over into the organizations where records professionals work. A 1984 report commissioned to consider how employers viewed archivists, prepared by Social Research, Inc. and sponsored by the Society of American Archivists, interviewed 44 individuals who allocate funds for archival programs in Atlanta, Chicago, Kansas City, Los Angeles, and New York. The study discovered that archivists are valued as employees but not necessarily seen as essential to the organization.[3] How many records managers also could relate to this? Despite two decades of growing interest in public programming and advocacy, there has been only a single effort to consider how well records professionals are doing.[4] There is hardly any public profile of archivists or records managers, their mission, and the valuable materials they administer. It is no wonder that records professionals have had difficulty influencing public and organizational policy.

An analysis of the *New York Times* reveals the societal profile of records professionals. The *New York Times* is one of the most influential newspapers in the United States. Founded in the mid-nineteenth century, its history is well known.[5] As a source for studying potential public images, it is unrivalled. Carlin Romano writes, "on a day-to-day basis, the *Times*'s fact gathering surpasses that of all rivals."[6] The *New York Times* has been identified as one of four national dailies, the others being the *Christian Science Monitor*, the *Wall Street Journal*, and *USA Today*.[7] The *Times* is also a source for other newspapers and news magazines, as Herbert J. Gans reports: "*The New York Times* is a primary peer source inasmuch as the size and quality of its editorial and reporting staff are taken as guarantors of the best professional news judgment."[8] It is also "*the* professional setter of standards. . . . When editors and producers are uncertain about a selection decision, they will check whether, where, and how the *Times* has covered the story; and story selectors see to it that many of the *Times*' front-page stories find their way into television programs and magazines."[9] What is read in the *Times* has an important implication for government officials' view of records and their managers. As Gans suggests, the *Times*, along with several other papers, "are among other things, intragovernmental organs of communication—professional newsletters for public officials."[10]

Thinking about how news is reported provides a sense of what one might expect to see in the *Times* about records. Herbert J. Gans shows how there are certain standard sources and content types that will be regularly reported, some with obvious implications for records professionals. Gans notes, " 'Waste' is always an evil, whatever the amount; the mass of paperwork entailed by bureaucracy is a frequent story, and the additional paperwork generated by attempts to reduce the amount of paperwork is a humorous item that has appeared in the news with regularity over the years."[11] One of the articles in the *New York Times* itself conveys this opinion. Journalist Terry Anderson's quest to obtain U.S. government documents about his Middle East hostage ordeal prompted this comment: "Now I'm at work on a book about my experience. As part of that effort, I have been trying to obtain whatever Government files I can under the Federal Freedom of Information Act. I have never had occasion to use the act before, despite some 25 years in journalism. I've worked mostly in the field, where facts are what jump up in front of you, or behind you, not something you winnow out of a pile of dusty Government documents."[12] The *New York Times*, reviewed from October 1992 through May 1993, reveals patterns of coverage on archives, records, and related topics. Stories featuring archives and records grouped into three major categories: arts, literature, history (or cultural); international events and stories; and national events and stories.

Cultural reporting steadily focused on archives and historical manuscripts. Reporting on exhibitions featuring archival materials was undoubtedly the result of cultural institutions sending out press releases and reporters, such as Herbert Mitgang and John Noble Wilford, with regular beats to cover museums, libraries, and other cultural organizations. Articles appeared on a series of exhibitions commemorating Columbus and the New World, the opening of the Birmingham Civil Rights Institute (a museum and archives), a New York Public Library exhibition on the manuscripts of novels depicting the creative act of writing, an exhibition of the original of the Emancipation Proclamation on its 130th anniversary, a Library of Congress exhibition featuring manuscripts and other rare items from the Vatican Library and the Dead Sea Scrolls, and an exhibition of the early development of the Piermont Morgan Library collections.[13]

Records also appear as an authority in reporting about literary and historical publications and cinematic ventures. Reviews of the Ridley Scott movie on Columbus, "1492: Conquest of Paradise," and a biography of Winston Churchill prompted questions about the use of records as sources.[14] The publication of a John F. Kennedy biography merited coverage when several prominent members of the Kennedy family criticized the work, leading the author to assert that the family had tried to restrict his use of records. Other stories appeared on a biography of Walt Disney using FBI files and suggesting that Disney was an informant for Hoover, the decipherment of a stone monument found in Vera Cruz with new knowledge about pre-Mayan language and civilization, and a movie by Michael Palin based on manuscripts and diaries from a nineteenth-century ancestor of his.[15] In a twist of sorts, a front-page article appeared about the lawsuit filed by psychoanalyst Jeffrey M. Masson against Janet Malcolm for a series of articles about his supervision of the Freud papers at the Library of Congress. The lawsuit focused on the issue of whether Malcolm misquoted Masson in her interviews (and although the coverage focused on the issues of editing and the personalities involved, there were numerous allusions to the Freud papers at the Library of Congress).[16] A review of a George Shultz memoir contained a sidebar describing how the former secretary of state had an executive assistant who maintained meticulous notes and how Shultz copied (at his own expense) his records for Stanford University.[17]

Contemporary records are repeatedly featured in this newspaper, most frequently connected to political events. Records are discussed in instances where they are withheld purposefully from investigators.[18] Articles appeared about apparent efforts by the Bush White House to search and make available State Department records about Bill Clinton's foreign activities in the 1960s, a story unfolding just before the November 1992 presidential election and moving to the front and editorial pages just after the election.[19] The series of articles on the Clinton passport files led to a lengthy essay on the possibility that Bush's aides would destroy many records in the transition between administrations, culminating in an editorial lamenting this possibility and front page stories on the eve of Bush's departure.[20] The stories about the possible destruction of Bush White House electronic records referred to archivists and the Federal Records Act but made few allusions to the role of the National Archives.[21] One article discussed the implications of the growing use of electronic mail in business and other organizations.[22] Shortly after the transition to the Clinton administration an article described how this administration planned to make extensive use of electronic information systems, with an ironic reference to the difficult Prof-Notes case and the definition of electronic records as records.[23] Records are seen as having influence when misplaced, as in one instance when a federal investigator lost a briefcase of records.[24] Notes kept by Caspar Weinberger were found suggesting a different version of events regarding the effort to trade weapons for the hostages held by Iran than that told by President Bush, resulting in a series of articles.[25] Federal financial disclosure records were examined to test allegations against the United States treasurer about "influence peddling."[26] A brief newswire announcement also indicated that a federal appeals court decided that former President Richard Nixon must be compensated for the seizure of his records in 1974, although the next day's paper featured a rare editorial on records, lambasting the decision.[27] Another article described a 1968 memorandum from secretary of state nominee Warren M. Christopher, threatening to make this individual's confirmation hearings more difficult than anticipated.[28]

In one of the most important stories for records professionals, a report appeared about the decision of Judge Charles R. Richey to rule in favor of the National Security Archive against the White House and the National Archives that electronic mail messages used in a White House information system were indeed federal records and must be protected. Reported as the "first case to apply the 50-year-old Federal Records Act to computer records," the article described the details of the lawsuit, especially the aspects related to the Iran-Contra affair. The article also was critical of then Archivist of the United States Don Wilson, stating that the judicial decision "accused the archivist of violating his duty of preventing [the records'] destruction." As the article notes, "administration lawyers took the position that electronic messages and other computer records prepared by officials of the Bush and Reagan administrations fell outside the requirements of the Federal Records Act."[29] Subsequent articles appeared about the problem of the National Archives complying with the judge's ruling, casting aspersions on the role of the National Archives and Archivist of the United States.[30] Judge Richey's issuing of a contempt ruling against the White House and the archivist of the United States for failing to comply with his order to protect the computer records of the Bush administration revealed that the Clinton administration was in agreement with Bush.[31] Similar to such issues was the article describing the possible release of audiotapes made during the Kennedy administration, their declassification delayed because of poor sound quality. In this report, researchers complained that the "library's staff is much more cautious than the staffs at other Presidential libraries, and that it has shown favoritism to scholars friendly with the Kennedy family and denied access to some documents that should be made available."[32]

Closely related to the political uses of records has been the declassification of federal records. In October 1992 a conference was held on the 1962 Cuban missile crisis and its impact, the occasion of this meeting the release of 112 "newly declassified" records from the Central Intelligence Agency.[33] The newspaper featured stories in which classified documents, such as a memorandum tying then Vice President George Bush to secret deals to gain the release of Americans held in Lebanon or the declassification of documents and their publication on the topic of cryptography,[34] were the main focus. The newspaper described an article by Seymour Hersh in the *New Yorker* on secret White House tapes revealing some of President Nixon's efforts to discredit his presidential opponent, George McGovern, and accusing Hersh of having inappropriate access to the unreleased tapes in the National Archives. One of Nixon's lawyers was quoted as stating, "Hersh has obviously written this article based on what he heard from one or more disgruntled archivists."[35] Some months later a brief story appeared about the content of some cleared Nixon tapes, although there was no reference to the earlier controversy about access to these records.[36] Typical of such articles was one written about the release of a report by the United Nations on human rights violations by the Salvadoran military, also commenting on declassified federal records.[37] More compelling was Terry Anderson's description of his efforts to gain information about his own hostage ordeal, using the Freedom of Information Act: "The Air Force sent me 61 pages of documents they deemed relevant to my request. Twenty-six were totally blank, 20 showed only addresses with all text redacted, 3 were newspaper reports and 3 were reports on terrorism in countries outside the Middle East."[38] Many years after these articles, Anderson has been unable to gain access to records about his release.

Discussions of declassified documents often throw new light on other national and international activities, such as stories about what declassified diplomatic and intelligence documents reveal about military and right-wing death squads in El Salvador[39] and efforts by "Jewish groups" to get the Argentine government to release files on former Nazis who migrated there at the end of the Second World War. Argentina's National Archives stated that it had few files and that the government "had lost all files on Adolf Eichmann."[40] Another story revealed how Chinese documents smuggled out of this country suggested vicious human rights violations by Red Guards and Communist officials in the 1980s.[41]

Articles on President Clinton's efforts to reform the declassification process brought considerable news coverage. A letter from Clinton to Senator Howard M. Metzenbaum was quoted, with the president stating, "It is time to re-evaluate the onerous and costly system of security which has led to the overclassification of documents." The essay notes that the National Archives had 325 million pages of classified documents and that the National Archives wanted reform of the process: "The acting National Archivist, Trudy Peterson, said she is drowning under reams of Top Secret paper. For example, under current procedures, it will take 19 years for the National Archives to review recently delivered State Department papers from the early 1960s."[42] These events led to a *Times* editorial moralizing, "The cold war secrecy system has distorted American democracy and sound decision making. Mr. Clinton needs to let in some sunlight."[43] However, the next day a contradictory article appeared, describing efforts by the Clinton administration to make access to federal computer records extremely difficult.[44] So much for sending mixed signals about the nature of federal records policy.

There were reports of the leaking of classified documents, such as in a cable John Poindexter made available to the *Times*[45] and an article on a CBS documentary on Malcolm X, reporting the network's efforts, with mixed results, to review FBI case files and suggesting that the government was hiding details about its role in the assassination of this African-American leader.[46] Continuing interest in declassification prompted an essay about the problems historians have in conducting research on the Cold War, characterizing "those who seek the history of the cold war are like medieval map-makers trying to chart an unknown world." The article was filled with statements by experts about the unevenness of the federal classification system, and it ended with another quotation of a presidential promise to open up records, made by Richard M. Nixon in 1972.[47]

Secrecy is not limited to governments. An article on the ownership of ideas and documents dealt with the increasing concern high-tech companies have about employees who leave to work for a competitor.[48] However, there were few references to such matters beyond those associated with government activities, although this interest produced discussions of records functions like filing and information systems. An announcement from the Central Intelligence Agency spelled out the need for a new organization-wide information system because of difficulties in speedy access to its files.[49] An earlier story on another matter noted that a failure to find a relevant CIA document was due to the "agency's poor filing system and its culture of secrecy," a charge also made against the Justice Department.[50] Given such problems, another article suggested that individual taxpayers should maintain all their tax records permanently instead of the three years normally recommended.[51] In the business section there was an article about how Louis V. Gerstner, the then new head of IBM, was using electronic mail as a way of managing the organization and communicating with staff. Ironically, the e-mail system described was the same one used by Oliver North in the Iran-Contra affair and seen by the White House and the National Archives as not producing official records.[52] Another essay revealed how financial institutions were making less use of paper-based information and employing fewer workers but more computers.[53] Another long article described the shift to electronic medical records, describing advantages and problems.[54] Sometimes, the inadequacy of filing systems was obvious. One article reported on a Philippine native applying to be a United States citizen. Although this individual had reputedly served with the U.S. Army during the Second World War, his appeal was denied "because his name could not be found in the Department of the Army's records in St. Louis."[55] And there is continuing interest in the notion of the "paperless office," a concept attracting public and professional attention for two generations.[56]

The rapidly transforming international scene also made records a central issue. In October 1992 a front page article featured the release of records from the Soviet archives to Polish authorities about Soviet executions of Polish soldiers and citizens in 1940. The article included a photograph of Rudolf Pikhoya, identified as the "chairman of Russia's Archives Commission," holding and pointing to a Stalin executive order for the executions.[57] Shortly thereafter, in the arts section, an article appeared on the agreement to release to American, European, and Asian recording companies more than a million audio and video recordings of prominent former Soviet Union musicians. In a dispute about political changes in transferring Hong Kong from Britain to China, both national governments released formerly secret diplomatic documents. Another article chronicled how the "collapse of Communism in Eastern Europe" will provide microfilm copies of many archival documents to the United States Holocaust Museum. Despite the lessening of the Cold War, and its impact on access to government records, there were occasional stories about the arrest of individuals involved in stealing secret documents.[58]

Some of the international stories had interesting perspectives on archives and records. In October 1992 the Vietnam government released 5,000 photographs of dead American servicemen, prompted by an American doing research about the Vietnamese Army in archives of that country.[59] The next day it was announced that archivists would be dispatched to Vietnam to examine that government's records for additional clues about American soldiers.[60] Subsequent articles tied the events of the records' discovery to the possibilities of the normalization of American relations with Vietnam, perhaps one of the most prominent recent examples of the powerful influences of documents.[61] As the story unfolded, articles appeared on the personal reactions of family members viewing the photographs of their dead husbands and fathers.[62] A month later, detailed accounts of the search in Vietnam led to descriptions of "meticulous . . . record-keeping" and an elaborate system of museums scattered throughout the country to commemorate the war.[63] Interest in this topic re-emerged in April when a newly discovered 1972 document in the Soviet Communist Party archives suggested that North Vietnam held American prisoners of war.[64] This discovery also revealed to the public the problems with authenticity of older records. A *Times* editorial noted that there are "sound reasons to investigate the new document carefully before jumping to . . . conclusions. Communist archives are notorious for disinformation and forgeries,"[65] although a subsequent book revealed that the North Vietnamese were scrupulous recordkeepers.[66] Other related stories followed, such as when a member of the Senate Committee on P.O.W.-M.I.A. Affairs stated that Americans involved in the Korean War could still be alive in Russia. As this brief article relates, "the full story will not be known until Russia grants further access to its archives."[67] From time to time, as well, leaks of foreign documents provided new insights into recent past political events, such as "an official Iraqi memorandum" "circulated by a Kurdish group" revealing the possession by the Iraqis of biological weapons.[68]

Revision of historical interpretations is a possibility as formerly closed government records are opened and new document discoveries made. An example of this was the disclosure by a "high-ranking Russian official" that "newly opened archives clears Alger Hiss of accusations that he ever spied for the Soviet Union," the article describing various interpretations of the statement's reliability and including an interview with Hiss.[69] Early in 1993 a rare full-page article described numerous new insights made possible by the opening of previously closed Soviet archives. Another article discussed a book revealing a 1960 meeting held by "leaders of American Protestantism" to prevent the election of a Catholic, John F. Kennedy, discovered in the "private papers of Dr. [Norman Vincent] Peale." The interest in the opened Communist archives was evident by a lengthy article in a December 1992 issue of the *New York Times Magazine* describing new insights being provided by the records.[70] On a very different note was the story about the opening of the Dead Sea Scrolls to more Biblical scholars[71] and the re-discovery of some late, previously unpublished, Henry Thoreau manuscripts on natural history.[72] An essay on the search for the letters between Adolf Hitler and Eva Braun, long thought destroyed but then suspected to be in the possession of a former member of the U. S. Army Counter Intelligence Corps, revealed the typical curiosity in such discoveries.[73] Another front-page article showed how the tenacity of one individual led to the release of previously sealed French records revealing how France had worked with Nazi Germany to deport French Jewish citizens to concentration camps.[74] Old records tied to famous historical incidents were also sometimes portrayed as the subject of battle between different types of cultural institutions, such as files related to the Lindbergh kidnapping case.[75]

Manuscript discoveries are extraordinarily interesting to journalists, probably because they appeal both to sensationalist revelations and to the average person's interest in collecting. One article reported the discovery of a previously unpublished James Joyce manuscript and the surrounding academic debate.[76] A filler article reported the discovery in Soviet Communist Party records of the "original version of a secret 1939 pact between Nazi Germany and the Soviet Union."[77] A story broke about the auctioning of Ku Klux Klan "memorabilia" in Michigan, including a framed charter of a Klan chapter and "aging documents and letters."[78] Another article chronicled the discovery of Cole Porter notebooks in a house in Kennebunk, Maine.[79] The recovery of a Hector Berlioz score in a Belgium church was featured.[80] A lengthy article described the Lincoln Legal Papers project in which Illinois courthouses were searched for additional information about Lincoln's legal career. This article revealed not only the value of such records but also the stereotypes of how such records are usually maintained, with references to "musty courthouse records." This article also featured the first reference to new means of making such documents available, mentioning "a facsimile edition with some 100,000 documents . . . in an electronic format."[81]

The most important articles on manuscript discoveries concerned the opening by the Library of Congress of the Thurgood Marshall papers. The initial article focused on the insights provided by the Marshall papers on the inner workings of the Supreme Court, but the story soon became the controversy about the opening of the collection. An article reported on Chief Justice William Rehnquist's complaint about the Library "misinterpretation" of the Marshall desire to release his papers to qualified researchers or the wider public, including journalists.[82] These articles dramatically revealed the struggle archivists and other records professionals often face in opening their holdings and the secrecy that public officials desire, with complaints about the Court's "obsessive concern for secrecy," "driven in part by the natural desire, of many organizations to shield their internal workings from public view" and by a "belief among judges that to strip any court of its mystique is also inevitably to strip it of some of its authority and legitimacy."[83] Additional articles by former Marshall law clerks questioned whether his intentions were to release the papers[84] and, in an interesting aside, about terminology employed by archivists in their dealing with donors—the first making the records "available to the public at the library's discretion" and the other limiting the papers to "researchers or scholars engaged in serious research."[85] These were unusual public statements about archival principles and practices. The coverage by the *Times* of this story led to an editorial arguing for open access to public records and the personal papers of public officials, with the Librarian of Congress "clearly" acting "in the best interests of the public, which has a right to information that will help it determine how well its institutions, the Court included, are functioning."[86] In this regard, the story was also a rare discussion of basic archival principles in a publicly controversial case.

Preservation issues occasionally appeared in the newspaper. Buried deep inside the Sunday edition's business section was a brief essay on the use of a diethyl zinc (DEZ) process for deacidifying paper. Another Sunday edition featured an article about the search by British film archivists for important and lost feature films and their efforts in preserving them when they were discovered.[87] The donation of the New York Shakespeare Festival archives and the personal papers of its founder, Joseph Papp, to the New York Public Library for the Performing Arts received considerable treatment in the newspaper's "The Living Arts" section. Rare comments were made in this essay on the potential competition for such records and papers, with Mrs. Papp indicating that her late husband wanted the papers in New York because " 'the library has given us remarkable assurances' about its financial commitment to maintaining the collection."[88] A book review section essay analyzed the changes in literary manuscripts to floppy computer disks, providing a personal lament about the impact of modern information technology on modern recordkeeping and historical and literary research. Jodi Daynard, a Harvard University writing instructor, considered the preservation challenges of the shift from paper to electronic as well as the losses from the "telltale handwriting" and the "process of revision" to the "true beauty of a manuscript" and its "powerful core of mystery."[89] In stories such as these, we can see sensitivity to the larger issues of the long-term maintenance of records, but a far less clear understanding of just how records professionals approach such matters.

Rare was reporting about records repositories or programs. In November 1992 a story appeared about New York Public Library plans to assist the financially troubled New-York Historical Society, the second oldest of such institutions and one of the premier historical manuscripts repositories in the United States (although the focus of the story was more on the museum collections).[90] In early 1993 the story shifted after the society announced the closing of its research library, leading to articles detailing the richness of the society's manuscript and other holdings and an editorial about the loss of the city's memory.[91] Most disconcerting was the constant reference to the society as New York's "attic."[92] A few other archival repositories made the news. The resignation of the archivist of the United States produced several articles discussing the controversy surrounding his tenure, mostly focused on leadership and management and the issue of control of former President Bush's records.[93] A suit by Coretta Scott King against Boston University for the return of King's early papers to the Martin Luther King Jr. Center for Nonviolent Social Change in Atlanta brought two repositories into the national media.[94] The *Times'* interest in archival repositories increases with controversy, with only occasional exceptions. The travel section of the newspaper had two long articles on the Nixon and Carter presidential libraries as tourist destinations.[95] While such stories reveled in the public's stereotypes of archivists as attic dwellers and other records professionals as file clerks, the media coverage suggests topics for investigation by other professionals in ways that may have long-term positive impact on the respective missions of archivists and records managers.[96]

The *New York Times* steadily covered records, archives, and historical manuscripts, carrying about eighteen stories a month on records, an article every few days.[97] The cumulative reporting on archives and records topics reveals that national and international connections were essential for reporting. While stories on the arts and history were important, these stories only accounted for about a third of the stories. Archives-and records-related stories important enough to be treated over a period of time through multiple articles were about national and international events. Michael Schudson states, "stories that matter are stories that persist and take different turns over days or weeks or longer."[98] One-time articles accounted for nearly all of the *Times* reporting on archives and records and with the exception of three stories (the Dead Sea Scrolls, the archivist of the United States, and the New-York Historical Society) all of these articles were on cultural matters. A number of the stories on archives and records were important enough to be reported on the front page of the *Times*. During the eight months, there were twenty-four front-page stories, nearly all related to national and international events. While the patterns reveal continuing interest in records concerns, an effort to summarize the contents of the stories provides some different conclusions with implications about policy making and records.

There are serious omissions in reporting about records and archives. Records professionals are absent, and when they do appear it is as part of larger political investigations or scandals. Leon V. Sigal suggests, "ordinary people appear in the news relatively infrequently, though the frequency rises as they are caught up in official proceedings—arrests, trials, congressional hearings, even unemployment lines."[99] The release of a report on National Archives mismanagement stimulated no coverage (despite the fact that one of the issues was the shredding of documents by National Archives officials) except after the archivist emerged as an accomplice in the administration of Bush's presidential papers; and even then the coverage was spotty.[100] This is surprising, since the lengthy series of articles on the search in Clinton's passport records also implicated the National Archives.[101] This absence may have to do with the nature of journalists' use of sources. James W. Carey believes the deadlines imposed on daily newspapers force journalists to rely on telephone interviews rather than other sources.[102] The absence may also be attributable to the fact that many public records are treated as personal property, have been for a long time, and, as a consequence, do not constitute news.[103] It is possible that a lack of experience with archives and records limits the interest of reporters in their general welfare.

Sometimes stories that may have had substantial viewpoints on the nature of archives and records ignored such matters. The major coverage of the *New Yorker* libel case did not delve into the substance of Janet Malcolm's book, *In the Freud Archives*, which had to do with access to and administration of the personal papers of Sigmund Freud. And the lack of coverage of the Martin Luther King papers case was curious because these papers were related to a figure of national importance. Was the lack of coverage the result of an interpretation that the case concerned only deeds of gift of archives and manuscripts? The Marshall case, which seems similar, may have been more fully reported because of the debate in this case of whether reporters were considered to be qualified researchers.

The only consistent reporting on an archival institution concerned the New-York Historical Society, although this reporting was part of the newspaper's aim to provide news of its *local* cultural institutions. The historical society had been the subject of previous critical stories about its management by the newspaper[104] *and* an example of ethical problems in its administration by the professional museum community.[105] The press treats archives and records as curiosities, generally associated with prominent historical figures or events or when they are directly embroiled in political disputes. It is no wonder that the majority of records professionals, caring for records of regions, individuals and families, and institutions that lack a high profile or the possibility for tantalizing stories, feel neglected. How can they step forward and argue for national policy that protects records? How can records professionals argue for organizational policies within their institutions when they know their bosses read or hear little about such matters? The Levy study considered the image of archivists by employers, but it did not consider the image's source. Did these employers develop their image as a result of work with archivists, or was their perception partly molded by reading such sources as the *Times*? Records professionals lack any data on the perceptions of their work by the general public. In the intense discussions about the impact of the media *on* the public, it is easy to forget that the "interconnection of public and private worlds is often unscheduled, incidental, and haphazard."[106] Even much more publicly known professions, such as librarianship, have suffered in their public image—with stereotypes and low profile, some caused by themselves and some foisted upon them.[107]

THE BEGINNING OF THE IMAGE: A CHILD'S VIEW OF ARCHIVES AND RECORDS

Examining the image of archives and records in children's literature provides a way of determining what *future* generations are learning about archives and records, perhaps explaining why newspapers and other media cover these issues as they do. In 1948 Jacob Bronowski in a BBC broadcast commented that society feared the future in general and science and its contributions in particular. Bronowski speculated, "we no longer have faith in our ability . . . to control our own future" and we fail to understand the "place of science in our world."

He concluded, the "ideas of science are not special ideas." They are readily understandable. "What we need is to stop shutting our minds to these ideas; to stop being afraid of them. We stand on the threshold of a great age of science; we are already over the threshold; it is for us to make that future our own."[108]

Records professionals are at a similar threshold. For thirty-plus years they have struggled with electronic information technology in the office, the home, and the world of children. Records professionals' writings on the impact of electronic information technology have been directed *inward*, only to *other* records professionals. Even those in the records community who draw on the rich scholarship of other fields are largely writing for *other* records professionals. Records professionals have fabricated the foundation for a new "great age," to echo Bronowski's words, but they have failed to convey it to the wider public. Some of the views of archives and records may stem from records professionals being so preoccupied with their own private gardens rather than their public or societal roles. When they turn to making or influencing policy, records professionals suffer as a result.

What does society really think of archivists and records managers? It is easy to find references everywhere about *boring* records. Records professionals have to bring an excitement to the public about the significance of records. Records professionals need to identify and seize opportunities to stir people's interest in what it is they do, placing public programming as a core records function.[109] Records professionals must realize that the images and stereotypes about archives and records in fiction and non-fiction, the popular press, and other media are indicative of deeper social problems they must face, challenge, and resolve.

That records professionals have not achieved a public profile is readily evident in a voluminous body of children's literature concerning itself with archives and records. Where better to find what future records creators, public officials, public opinion makers, and societal leaders might think of records professionals and their mission, and why? Charlie Farrugia's discussion of Australian print media coverage of recordkeeping revealed a remarkable *lack* of understanding by the media of archives and records, a trend with similarities in other nations.[110] This, and what Bob Sharman notes about the public lack of understanding of what an archivist does,[111] may start with the lack of opportunity of young people to learn about archives and records. Individuals continue to discover the records profession by accident, not having been introduced to the profession or its mission at any time before the university and often rarely there.

From basic reference books to genealogy guides to juvenile fantasy and non-fiction, children will not learn much about archives and records. Records professionals are invisible in the child's world. Well-known subject guides to children's books include ample entries under libraries, museums, and history, but not a *single* reference to archives, documents, manuscripts, records, or the National Archives.[112] Records professionals do not do much better in children's encyclopedias and other reference works. In the *Children's Britannica*, archives and records are not treated with a separate essay, although there is a brief definition in the index.[113] Most children's reference works ignore the subject altogether.[114]

There is information on records in some specialized references. A reference on Native North Americans includes a directory of archives and special collections, although an occupation index excludes archivist or records manager.[115] Similarly, a reference on African Americans includes illustrations of archival records with the compelling explanation that they "offer eloquent testimony to the impact of the black on American history—as slave, as freedman, and, ultimately, as full-fledged American citizen."[116] The child will find little that is very illuminating about archives or records in such basic references.

Children's history books are not much better. The introductory volume of Oxford's history of the United States for children includes a few references to a manuscript and its meaning, historical documents, and some consideration of how historical evidence is weighed (in a discussion of the Vineland Map and the Kensington Stone), but there is no sense of records or records professionals.[117] The controversies surrounding the 500th anniversary of Columbus and his voyage to the New World also has affected children's history writing. One interesting book discusses how historians have written about Columbus, the challenge of a paucity of records, the splintering of the family archives by the grandson of Columbus, and how you use archives in historical research.[118]

Children's historical fiction contains a limited sense of the role of records. Alice and Martin Provensen's *Shaker Lane* traces a small community over several generations. At one of the pivotal points in the story, when the county seizes land for the construction of a reservoir, a document declaring the right of eminent domain is pictured,[119] and the significance of records in change or as a symbol of power and transformation is conveyed. It is not explained, but the importance of records is implied, although this is a rare occurrence. Juvenile historical fiction is flourishing, as Lynda Adamson's 1987 reference describes how such writing increased since the Second World War. She also relates its value in a manner that is reminiscence of those who advocate document packets for use in schools.[120] For the sake of a valid education, it is important that the authors of such works are careful historians. For the sake of the records mission, it is important that the value of basic historical sources is reflected in such publications. They usually are not.

Whether all juvenile historical fiction is beneficial to the cause of archivists and records managers is another issue. Gary Crew's *Strange Objects*, a tale of a teenager's discovery of artifacts and documents from a seventeenth century shipwreck off the Australian coast, makes archival records appear to be odd or mysterious items, more the province of antiquarians and nostalgia buffs rather than as fundamental to organizations, government, and individuals.[121] Even books about writing neglect the preservation of written materials. A book, intriguingly entitled *Writing It Down* and directed to kindergarten through third grade ages, describes the invention and nature of paper as well as writing tools such as pens, pencils, and crayons—but there is nothing mentioned about the written products.[122] Juvenile letter writing manuals share the same problem; while they provide, in one sense, a diplomatic for letters for children, they miss providing an idea of letters from an historical perspective.[123] Wouldn't it be wonderful to see some discussion of famous letters, or how historical letters are cared for and used by researchers? Wouldn't it be useful to have a book that describes electronic mail as a records process? Instead, children's books on communication or the Information Age make no references to records with continuing value or with preservation concerns. While one 1959 volume on the nature of communication starts off well, with a transition from a reliance on memory to memory devices such as the *quipu* (knotted ropes) and *tallus* (notched sticks), it skips quickly to printing and libraries with no mention of records managers or archivists.[124] While there are many fine books on the history and significance of printing, there are no counterpart volumes on writing and the record.[125] Children's books on the Information Age also lack descriptions of how records will be managed or preserved.[126]

Children's genealogy books ought to provide more about archives and records, but they do this inconsistently. One 1979 volume stresses the child examining documents kept by his family, but it never *once* mentions the existence of archives or records centers. It provides a somewhat curious lesson: "Diplomas, certificates of birth, marriage or death, and newspaper clippings are also good sources of information. . . . As you can see, the government makes out legal papers for every big event in a person's life."[127] *Where Did You Get Those Eyes?* contains a chapter on records in other locations, but (despite references to the National Archives) it mentions librarians but no archivists or records managers.[128] Another volume, with fuller descriptions of records and their repositories, still comes up short in noting that the National Archives "has all kinds of miscellaneous records," while making no statement on the role of records professionals.[129]

Some of these juvenile genealogy guides deserve more discussion. Suzanne Hilton's 1976 guide is rich in illustrations of documents and family and related photographs from the National Archives, and it does a fine job in describing archival records. However, it does not convey two essential issues records professionals should find important. Hilton reveals no distinction in significance of various "archival" records—newspapers, oral interviews, and miscellaneous documents all receive *equal* treatment with official records. Her statement that if "you are lucky if you have an attic or a cellar to raid in your search for archives materials"[130] also conveys the poor popular image of archives. Despite her heavy use of illustrations from the National Archives, the only description of the function of this institution resides in a caption under a photograph of the archives building in Washington, D.C.: "The National Archives Building houses the most important documents of the nation—including your ancestors' war records."[131] Then there is the solitary image of the archivist: "Vital records of a person who lived in a large city are often in the city archives, in the town hall or city hall. City archivists are usually very friendly and happy to lift down the books a searcher needs to look through,"[132] a statement providing new insights into the basic qualifications for archivists with little hope for a records professional engaging in important public policy issues.

Ira Wolfman's *Do People Grow on Family Trees?* reveals no significant progress in understanding archives and records. While Wolfman's book is nicely illustrated with primary documents and some efforts to convey the preservation needs of archival records,[133] there is still a lack of visibility of records and records professionals. The author explains, records can be found "by writing to, or visiting, records centers, libraries, archives, government offices, and courthouses," but the reader is hard-pressed to find many more references than this.[134] The only reference to archivists is in the following statement: "The staff of the National Archives will search for the documents for you."[135] More revealing is the caption under a photograph of the National Archives building in Washington, D.C., referring to it as " 'the Nation's Attic.' Millions of documents are preserved inside."[136] Not only does this convey a less than desirable image but also the phrase is actually used to describe the Smithsonian Institution. How do records professionals get out of the attic or basement to influence public policy?

The image of archives and records professionals seems better in children's historical research primers. Kay Cooper's *Who Put the Cannon in the Courthouse Square?* contains a good statement on the kinds of sources historians rely upon, the nature of original sources, and even the identification of historical societies and state archives as repositories of such sources.[137] There is even a statement on the significance of historical records for clarifying "conflicting facts," suggesting that the "closer you get to the original source, the more likely you are to uncover the facts that bring you nearer the truth."[138] A similar volume breaks ground in a section on "careers that use primary sources," including a definition for archivists: "These specialists collect, catalog, and restore valuable historic documents. Our National Archives in Washington, D.C. keeps important letters and papers related to our country's history. Also kept here are letters written to government officials. The original Constitution and Declaration of Independence are kept in the National Archives."[139] There is much lacking in this definition, but there is at least a recognition that records professionals *exist*.

These books are missed opportunities to explain the importance and roles of records professionals in society. There are a number of juvenile works explaining the basic documents of American history and government that make no effort to chronicle the generally fascinating stories about their maintenance and preservation. A volume on the Constitution has one photograph of the original document on display in the National Archives.[140] A volume on the "Star-Spangled Banner," the poem by Francis Scott Key that became the national anthem, includes a photograph of one of the original manuscripts with a somewhat uninspiring caption explaining its travels and housing in a historical society.[141] Here is the substance of a story about the preservation of families of their personal papers, the nature of autograph collecting and its market, and the fickle impact of fate on the survival of original manuscripts.[142]

Other works fail to provide any substantive background on the nature of records. Isabelle Brent's *The Christmas Story* mimics the art of medieval manuscript illumination, but it fails to describe this tradition or the matter of preservation.[143] Even in published collections of primary sources prepared for younger audiences, the visibility of records professionals is dim. In one volume on the American Revolution, a note about sources discusses scholars tracking down the records, but there is no effort to consider the important work of archivists. These discoveries arise from "some dusty family closet or remote local archive to illuminate a corner of the story."[144] Such volumes are the results of authors combing published records rather than through any effort to visit and examine the original records or to consult with the archivist, perhaps explaining the absence of importance of the archival program and records professionals. Even volumes of fabricated diaries and records intended to capture the sense of the importance of historical documents miss the archival dimension. The publication of a New England whaler's diary has the story begin with the author receiving the documents wrapped in oilskin and contained in a shoebox.[145]

One reference on using juvenile historical fiction for teaching history includes a research section, and historical records (limited to family papers) are discussed as artifacts and as part of "attic and community treasures."[146] Other such bibliographies, intended to assist teachers to select juvenile literature, generally ignore the topic completely, failing to include any section on source materials or historical research.[147] While these authors describe how to evaluate historical fiction for potential use in the classroom, they do not consider how to use archives or how the fiction they are evaluating might have used or not used archival sources.[148]

Is it unreasonable to expect children's books on topics like archives and records? There are fine books on museum curators, museums, librarians, and libraries.[149] Even fictionalized accounts value books, such as in Gail Haley's *The Dream Peddler*, in which books are described as "words, wisdom, ideas, and dreams."[150] Some stress the origins of libraries and provide an orientation to the beginning of archives and records management as well.[151] Beyond those volumes trying to project something about records and their maintenance, there are other volumes that either are based on or contend that they are based on archival sources. Elizabeth Noll discusses this kind of concern in American Indian children's literature, contrasting Joann Mazzio's *Leaving Eldorado* with Susan Jeffers *Brother Eagle, Sister Sky: A Message from Chief Seattle*. Mazzio's novel is carefully based on research in museums, archives, and libraries, while Jeffers' picture book is a serious distortion of archival and other historical sources.[152]

There are other examples of juvenile literature, both fiction and non-fiction, casting a pall over the importance of records. E. L. Konigsburg's *From the Mixed-Up Files of Mrs. Basil E. Frankweiler* follows two young children who run away from home, hide out in the Metropolitan Museum of Art in New York City, and become intrigued by a small sculpture attributed to Michelangelo. The children try to confirm that the sculpture is the work of the Italian Renaissance artist, and they find their way to Mrs. Frankweiler who sold the work to the museum. As it turns out, Mrs. Frankweiler possesses a document signed by the artist proving the authenticity of the statute, but she is reluctant to give it to the museum because she is offended that the museum will call in experts to authenticate the document. The author is sympathetic to Mrs. Frankweiler, and the notion of records as evidence is undermined considerably.[153]

Children's authors' self-reflections reveal other problems for the archivist and records manager. One author describes the importance of overcoming "present-day sensibilities." While mentioning such activities as a good imagination and visiting the location of her writing, there is not one mention of what could be gained by examining original records from the period in question.[154] Another article describes the need to write history and historical novels related to a "current concern," leaving "no time to think over the meaning of the events."[155] While this might explain the lack of focus by many of these writers on archives and records, it is still not satisfactory. In the news were stories of discoveries from the newly opened Eastern bloc archives, and yet there are no children's books focusing on that important topic. Another author, in writing a book on the Plymouth, Massachusetts, colonial settlement, discusses the fact that William Bradford kept a "magnificent journal" and that the "original journal survived an equally extraordinary voyage of its own and is now housed in the Massachusetts State Archives."[156] The result is still only a story of the settlers with no reference to the journal's story. Why is it that these writers cannot see the potential in these stories? Or why is it that records professionals fail to inspire interest in such stories?

Records professionals certainly have a responsibility to generate interest in the importance of records to society. Archivist Glenda Acland states, "while archivists have a duty of care to the records in their custody, there also exists a duty of care to ensure that adequate records exist and are properly maintained and managed," requiring the ability to make "ethical pronouncements" and a "flexibility in response to changing administrative patterns and requirements."[157] One of these opportunities is to reach young people about the records professions by working with educational specialists. This is part of a greater responsibility. Building a public profile requires persistence and having something to say about the relevancy of records to society. Jill Ker Conway's memoir about growing up in Australia describes her family's sheep farm as nothing less than an "act of will, a gamble on which two natural risk takers had staked everything they had."[158] Records professionals need the same will to carve out a public recognition of archives and records.

Archives are not old stuff with questionable historical value to be used by academics writing non-essential books for a few other academics. Records are not obstacles to organizational efficiency, a clog in the bureaucracy. This is a message that can be easily conveyed to children through a literature already laden with so many values for consideration. Records professionals know they cannot manage electronic records without establishing partnerships with systems designers, information policy professionals, upper level managers, and technical standards personnel. They cannot be successful in building the public recognition for their mission without influencing authors, filmmakers, journalists, and children's writers.

There are obvious choices records professionals have to make to influence the public and policy makers about the importance of archives and records. They need to get the ideas of some of their forward-looking thinkers into the public forum. Archivists and records managers need to contribute writings aimed at the educated public, a pithy article in the *Atlantic Monthly* or a compelling volume sitting alongside works by Lanham, Sanders, and Birkerts on the future of books and libraries.[159] If Donald Norman can convey in a popular and entertaining fashion the details of design,[160] then surely records professionals can find someone who can communicate the details of their work in a fashion that captures public interest.

Records professionals need to be at the meetings where decisions are made affecting legislation, funding, educational guidelines, and *any* other activity concerning the management and care of records. They must be creative, see the opportunities, and be willing to suspend other functions to take advantage of these opportunities. They need to get society worrying about the demise of the record, as it now seems to be worried about the demise of the printed book. Records professionals need to stop being afraid of being advocates for their mission. To paraphrase Bronowski, records professionals stand on the threshold of a great age of records knowledge and scholarship. They are already over the threshold, with their re-discovery of the concept of a record and its importance for corporate memory, evidence, and accountability. It is now for them to believe in their value to society and to make that future their own.

COMMUNICATING MORE THAN TWO BITS IN THE ORGANIZATION: THE START OF POLICY

Communicating the values of records has become complicated in an age where something as nebulous as information is standard currency. Records professionals can convey records' significance by getting their organizational leaders to reflect on the common, daily roles of records. Two decades ago the average American household held twenty-nine types of personal records; today the average would be higher. Many of the estimated four trillion records created annually by American institutions relate to individuals. Records, while containing information, are more than just data or aggregations of bits and bytes—and this can be seen by looking in wallets or purses for driver's licenses, credit cards, banking automated teller machine (ATM) cards, and medical or health plan cards. Students carry university identification cards, and many others possess library cards. Some people carry employee identification cards. There are numerous membership cards. People often stuff their wallets and purses with items representing the use of these various cards. Wallets and purses reflect recordkeeping regimes that have evolved over decades or even centuries. Individuals are documented by nearly every organization in society.[161]

What are the records? The automobile driver's license is the most distinct modern record, generating records for vehicle ownership, individual drivers, regulating driving schools and driving instructors, and licensing vehicle manufacturers and dealers—creating one of the largest modern government recordkeeping operations. The next most important record on one's person, at least in terms of usage, is the bank ATM card, a device changing the pattern of bank use,[162] churning out hundreds of millions of transactions each month. The combination of the ATM card, credit cards, and the checkbook all constitute a sort of financial breviary. While there is little need to maintain canceled checks, check registers, and checking statements beyond a few years, it is surprising how many people accumulate them over decades. There may be a psychological need to hang onto these things, perhaps because they have invested so much time in preparing and reconciling them or because they reflect personal and family activities. Credit cards reflect another major financial recordkeeping industry.[163] Credit cards are used in America millions of times daily, and they are one of the most noticeable forms of recordkeeping, with hundreds of billions a year in purchases using these cards and over 80 percent of American households holding at least one credit card.

Individuals carry other representations of large recordkeeping systems. The American medical system has become one of the largest of all recordkeeping operations, with the average American carrying at least one card indicating the nature of their medical insurance or health medical provider.[164] Individuals also use a variety of membership and identification cards from student photo identification cards to membership cards for entry into recreational and cultural facilities, to gain discounts at certain shops, and to acquire certain crucial services to the mighty Social Security card. Representing a system only sixty years old, the card has become a much debated and prized symbol of living in modern America. Social Security cards were issued as part of a massive plan to make sure that all Americans would have some retirement funding. The card, and its well-known number, derived from the originating legislation authorizing taxpayer identification and tax collection. There are now over 200 million accounts, with five million new accounts being added each year. This system has grown into one of the largest recordkeeping operations in the world, employing thousands of file clerks and computer operators. The Social Security number is required for paying taxes, registering to vote, applying for licenses such as fishing or hunting or driving, and registering for courses in universities and colleges.

Some of these personalized recordkeeping devices have become controversial. Library and video club cards are in the wallets or purses of the average citizen. Competing with the library card is the video rental card, the product of another technological revolution,[165] mushrooming VCRs and video stores. While the typical library creates numerous types of records, the ones relating to the library patron tend mostly to relate to borrowing from libraries and these circulation records have become contested. Some years ago a major controversy ensued when it was discovered that the FBI was trying to obtain various public and academic libraries to release information about what particular patrons had charged out.[166]

All of these cards conveniently carried about in one's pocket also contribute to what many Americans have seen as their own personal recordkeeping challenge. Self-help books for personal recordkeeping appear regularly with titles such as *Taming the Paper Tiger: Organizing the Paper in Your Life*, *Keeping Track: An Organizer for Your Legal, Business and Personal Records*, and *Conquering the Paper Pile-Up*. Such books suggest that the average citizen is "deluged with paper" or prone to turn into a "paperholic." Records remain—even in this electronic age—extremely important. Reminding the leadership of modern institutions about the importance of records in their own lives may be one way to get them thinking of the reasons why their institutional records should be better managed with realistic policies and procedures. Starting within their own organizations, records professionals must find new strategies for communicating the importance of records despite the vagaries of media attention, longstanding stereotypes of records professionals, and hyped-up interests in electronic solutions to the management of records and information. Understanding their own organizations requires archivists and other records professionals to be aware of the societal issues concerning records, their creation, maintenance, use, and disposition. At the least, the involvement by every citizen in creating records mandates that records professionals be mindful of the need to create policies protecting both the records and the individuals reflected in them.

The importance of records, their pervasiveness, and the less than adequate public recognition of their significance suggest the need for more aggressive activities by records professionals. Daily news stories (as described earlier), bestselling fiction, and major non-fiction books all underscore the importance of records for people and government, business, churches, and every other organization and place where they work, visit, or live.[167] That records professionals seem part of a *quiet* discipline is contradicted by what they encounter daily, because the records they administer are important and, at a moment's notice, can be called into courtrooms, quoted by journalists, cited in public controversies, and used by officials and scholars in public policy debates. Archivists and records managers may be records custodians, technicians, professionals, or scholars, but they must be advocates—astute in their knowledge of the public forum and legal proceedings.

The records professions can be stressful, controversial, and fraught with all sorts of personal, professional, and legal problems, dilemmas, and debates, requiring professional codes of conduct. The potential of such problems should raise many questions for records professionals about how they view ethical conduct as part of developing records policies. What is the basis of the records professionals' ethic? One effort to define "archivist" stated, in a rather straightforward manner, "as member of a profession, archivists share a set of values" and "some of these derive from ethical standards widely shared in our culture and common to other organized professions."[168] In the midst of wide professional discussion about the nature of the profession, its institutions, and the substance of archival practice, this definition was not generally accepted. Have archivists really articulated this "set" of values? The current Society of American Archivists ethics code suggests that they have not, since the code has some problems, the most important being a lack of *any* mechanism for its meaningful use.[169] Then, of course, there is the added problem of the splintering of records professionals among archivists and records managers, information resource managers and manuscript curators.

Despite ethical challenges to records management, the literature on such matters is limited.[170] These challenges run the gamut from legal and political problems to professional jealousies to debates about records users. There seems to be no place to hide in the stacks and vaults of records repositories, and there shouldn't be, for the controversies and challenges swirling about records professionals require their attention. Who controls government records? How should the records of formerly totalitarian dictatorships be managed? What should be the principles regarding scholars' access to records, security, and new laws regulating physical access to archives? Should records professionals only see news crews and the media when there is a crisis? How should these professionals relate to the media? How should records professionals approach the issues of security and access? Does the practice of many research libraries and historical societies to purchase manuscript collections only encourage problems in security? Where are archivists acquiring adequate introductions to complex legal issues and is such education and training a significant factor in their poor understanding and preparation to deal with such matters? How can records professionals re-examine every aspect of their employment and public service practices in light of such new laws as the Americans with Disabilities Act? How can records professionals deal with the complicated issues facing access to the records of recent history and a lengthy litany of accessibility controversies, ethical issues, and practical obstacles?

Records professionals are involved in controversial matters because records are often centerpieces in legal, political, and moral debates. Archivists and records managers are the caretakers of documents not just for scholarly researchers but for the essential well-being of society and society's institutions. The records they preserve and manage are the basis for the accountability of government and other institutions, as well as for understanding these institutions and the society which they inhabit. Some years ago the archivist of Canada, Wilfred Smith, mused, "only one-tenth of one percent of the population had the opportunity to have direct contacts with archival institutions." Smith added, "If the other 99.9 percent was given the opportunity to make a rewarding and exciting use of documents, the archives would be much more effective in carrying out their mandate. Their image would be greatly enhanced, and it would be easier

for them to obtain the financial resources, facilities and staff necessary to respond to ever increasing responsibilities of acquiring, conserving, and making
easily available the records of the past for the present and future generations."[171]
Getting the public and public officials and institutional administrators *into* archives and records management programs is one function of advocacy.

Records are one of the most valuable commodities produced by institutions
and individuals, more valuable than the investment made in their creation. There
are numerous instances of corporations discovering the value of older records
for administrative and public relations purposes. Records possess a variety of
important values for institutions and, indeed, all of society from *legal rights* of
the institution and individuals to the *administrative continuity* of an organization.
When the head of Wells Fargo and Company was asked why he had established
an archives, he said it was a simple decision: "He used to attend meetings and
listen to people discuss what they *thought* had happened. He wanted a place he
could call to get some facts." He had learned that "one of the facts of corporate
life is that people frequently head off in one direction—through transfers, pro-
motions, departures—and the memory and records of what happened on a project head off in another."[172]

Records professionals have only recently enunciated such values of records.
In the early 1980s the non-partisan Committee on the Records of Government,
a committee consisting of distinguished and well-known public servants and
scholars, deliberated on the problem of the management and preservation of
public records, but it ended without any substantial legislation, policy, increased
resources, or other practical benefit.[173] Archivists and records managers need to
be involved in monitoring and influencing legislation and executive policy relating to the creation, management, and use of government information and
records. The passage of the Paperwork Reduction Act of 1980, stemming from
the 1974 Commission on Federal Paperwork to "minimize the federal paperwork
burden," led in 1985 to OMB Circular A-130 establishing within the federal
government the philosophical foundation for information and records management which viewed federal information as a resource. Unfortunately, records
have not been accorded as important a place as they deserve in federal information resources management. Is this a result of a lack of effort by records
professionals or some other combination of societal and political factors?

Records professionals should be striving to alter government policy to ensure
that information contained in records is available for consultation and decision
making and that this information found in records is accessible to all citizens.
This requires that the record be defined, that archivists and records managers
have the authority to inspect records and determine their value, and that there
be reasonable mechanisms for preserving and ensuring continuing access to such
records. It also requires that records professionals make government officials
and business executives think about the utility of records as they regularly function, in the same fashion that they need to consider the ethical dimensions of
their activities. A humanities professor teaching ethics to business executives

states, "If ethics courses don't produce ethical executives then why offer courses or take seminars in business ethics? My answer is that ethics is valuable in the same way that other courses in the humanities are valuable, as a way of thinking about values. . . . Ethically defensible decisions are made by people who are morally fit, who have regularly practiced making ethically defensible decisions. When the fire starts, when the deal goes down, when pressure is on to bend the rules, nobody takes an ethics course. Executives *act*. That is why they are called *executives*. And only executives who have practiced thinking about values, who understand the full range of options, and who are driven by cultural pressures (values) of which they are unconscious will make fully informed decisions."[174] In the same fashion, records professionals should hope that government officials and corporate executives naturally think of the value of records when they work and deal with emergency situations. They will not do this unless records professionals show them the way, unless they *act* as well.

There are times when records professionals seemingly have made inroads into public policy and legislation, mostly by providing practical guides to how to manage through complicated legal and political situations. Copyright comes to mind. However, copyright issues are often resolved as case law in the courtroom, and there have been some unsettling cases in recent years for records professionals (such as the J. D. Salinger case).[175] Security, replevin, and related issues are other areas needing more policy consideration by records professionals. In the early 1960s a husband and wife team absconded with a large cache of National Archives documents, and although they were apprehended, it was obvious that professional archivists were reluctant to admit publicly the nature of the problems. By the mid-1970s security had become a more meaningful issue in professional circles, and although publicity was still a major concern for many archivists, there were new, more aggressive efforts to deal with such problems.[176] Unfortunately, archivists and other records professionals have still not learned completely how to deal effectively with such issues as security. During the 1970s and the early 1980s, other than efforts to develop networks of cooperation and communication so that manuscript thefts could be reported quickly and widely, most other attention went into legal actions to recover property rather than developing useful policies. Such efforts split records managers, archivists, and manuscript curators, alienated needlessly legitimate autograph collectors and dealers, and never really resolved the source of the problems—poor public policies, support of an autograph market by the archival community, and lax security policies at many repositories.[177] The problem was extremely complicated since many private repositories acted as surrogate public repositories before such archival programs had been formed.[178]

Records professionals have promoted legislation as a mechanism for ensuring support for their mission, and it has been met with extremely mixed success. While most of the efforts have gone into specific legislation supporting government archival and records management programs rather than ensuring that legislation about a myriad of issues is sensitive to the integrity of the record and the preservation of the documentary heritage, it is nevertheless clear that legislative solutions can be elusive. Public and organizational policies have a great potential for mixed results, primarily because policies are often developed for records objectives without consideration of funding support and because records professionals are often operating outside of policy forums with little influence on public policy and minimum means to monitor policy formulation and implementation. In 1986–1987, a brief-lived effort to establish a "documentary heritage trust of the United States" for increased financial support, especially from the private sector, never got off the ground because of lack of coordination and cooperation among the professional associations, a mixed set of objectives, and a lack of effective leadership. Several years before, state government archivists (through the National Association of Government Archives and Records Administrators [NAGARA]) published a study on the preservation needs of archival records.[179] After a brief period of discussion, mostly within the records community, the report faded in memory without sufficient attention in the public forum and, certainly, without any pledges of financial support. Why? Many explanations could be offered, but the one making the most sense is that the state government records programs had no real profile *within* their own states and certainly not in the national arena. Moreover, there was a perception that the state archives were primarily repositories of older, paper records (a perception that still remains) and such a large request for financial assistance came at a time when most states were struggling to upgrade and improve their electronic information systems.

Archivists and records managers need to come *out* of their repositories as advocates for the utility of records. There is no other way to do it. Archivists and records managers need to develop *sustained* advocacy efforts making them reputable players in public policy arenas, not only reactors to particular crises or needs. Building a case for records professionals to have a legitimate stake in information policy, helping government and institutions understand the importance of records, and making records professionals vital (to the degree that in matters of important public policy suggesting records they are called in for their advice and assistance) are things that can only occur if advocacy is sustained over time.

Advocacy and public programming intersect, support each other, and are obviously closely related. Public programming can build a level of awareness about the value of records that better targeted advocacy efforts can draw on to be successful. Some years ago, in an essay about the value of county government records, an individual observed that fires and natural disasters were often not the primary deterrent to using such records: "These records are sometimes in the keeping of suspicious clerks who size you up before granting access to their records. . . . Since we are seeking an answer to the . . . worth of county records, the answer may sometimes lie in the personality of the clerks who harbor them. If they make the records available, the most plebeian-looking title book or judge's docket may reveal a serendipitous surprise; if they inhibit use by unreasoned over protection, the record's secrets remain locked in the dusty limbo."[180] There is a valuable lesson in these words. If records professionals want to win public support and recognition to support their mission they must realize that every routine function that brings with it interaction with some element of the public can be an effort in this quest *or* a *lost* opportunity.

Records professionals should work to make government officials and business executives think naturally about the utility of records for normal functions. The confusion of records professionals, especially in many government archives, about whether they are fulfilling a cultural or service mission, must be resolved if they hope to get public officials and corporate executives to think seriously about records. When archivists and records managers can understand what their mission is, then public officials and other administrators might be able to discern the value of archives. Advocacy begins with archivists and records managers understanding their own mission as well as in communicating it and lobbying for its support.

THE GREATEST CHALLENGE: PRIVACY, ACCESS, AND HUMAN VALUES IN RECORDS POLICY

It is tempting for records professionals to reduce privacy and access issues *only* to technical concerns, by drafting policies and procedures governing who has access to what records, and when, or by literally building into records systems technological processes protecting privacy or controlling access. On a certain level there is nothing wrong with such an approach. Every records manager or archivist must be aware of the latest laws, government policies, institutional guidelines, and professional best practices relating to the use or misuse of public and private records. Even the most astute records professional could miss a critical element, however—the *social* dimensions of professional records work primarily addressed by the ethical codes of professional associations.

It is easy to lose sight of this human element because of the institutional and societal context records professionals work in. A large portion of records managers works in the for-profit sector, where approaches mostly stress the legal or economic dimensions of recordkeeping. But it is also simple for archivists, who just as often work in governmental, cultural or educational institutions, to develop a similar narrow approach to privacy and access issues by pushing aside concerns with personal privacy, for example, in order to serve the needs of their researchers.

Ethics codes promulgated by both the Society of American Archivists and the Association of Records Managers and Archivists include discussions of privacy and access. The SAA code states, "archivists discourage unreasonable restrictions on access or use, but may accept as a condition of acquisition clearly stated restrictions of limited duration and may occasionally suggest such restrictions to protect privacy." The code also indicates that "archivists respect the privacy of individuals who created, or are the subjects of, documentary materials of long-term value, especially those who had no voice in the disposition of the materials. They neither reveal nor profit from information gained through work with restricted holdings."[181] ARMA's "Code of Professional Responsibility" carries a similar statement, affirming that the "collection, maintenance, distribution, and use of information about individuals is a privilege in trust: the right to privacy of all individuals must be both promoted and upheld."[182] However, these statements are intended only to *guide* professional practice (they are *not* professional standards). While affirming important social dimensions of professional practice, they do not usually provide much detail or even definition.[183] Faced with immediate decisions in the workplace, records professionals do not always have the luxury of reflecting on their ethics statements, even if they are familiar with the general content and spirit of these documents.

The Information Age favors a technocratic perspective, tying information to a capitalistic *bottom line*. In a powerful assessment of the tensions in our era, two scholars argue that the "hallmark" of the Information Age is its "reliance on information as an item of value and economic exchange."[184] These scholars recognize the danger of a viewpoint emphasizing only economic or legal rationales. They see the need for a *sensitive* information professional: "By arguing for the indispensability of easily available information to the democratic process, and by envisioning information as a public good, librarians and information scientists have positioned themselves as the critical profession of the information society. In so doing, they have taken the position that democracy is threatened by the wholesale privatization of government information. Without their collective voice, there would be no debate."[185] Could they have included records professionals as part of the critical vocations in the information society? Examining matters such as privacy and access issues in records management reveals the need for ethics codes providing more than advice.

It should not be surprising, however, that archivists and records managers do not figure prominently in the public debates and discussions about how information is used. The focus on economic issues pushes *other* professionals to the forefront, as the matter of intellectual property suggests. Intellectual property has become for some the crucial concept in the modern Information Age. "Intellectual property is knowledge or expression that is owned by someone," Charles C. Mann writes. "It has three customary domains: copyright, patent, and trademark (a fourth form, trade secrets, is sometimes included)." "Nowadays one might best define intellectual property as anything that can be sold in the form of zeroes and ones. It is the primary product of the Information Age." This is because the Information Age has become completely wrapped up by economics. "Today the marketplace of ideas is being shaken by the competing demands of technology, finance, and law."[186] If this is an accurate assessment, it is understandable that the critical professionals seem to be lawyers, accountants, and systems designers, even though records professionals have a legitimate stake in intellectual property matters.[187] In general, however, archivists and records managers have been predisposed to stress custodial and middle management roles, *observing* rather than *participating* in the new digital marketplace.

Records factor into the emerging electronic marketplace as one of many critical information sources, representing an investment by their creators as well as a useful information resource for ongoing work. Yet, records creation is a fundamentally human impulse, involving people in a range of activities including keeping scrapbooks, taking family photographs, and maintaining old letters as keepsakes. Even in organizations, people create personal note systems and unofficial files for personal consultation. Records creation also involves people being participants in an international economy gathering information about us in virtually all of our activities. Privacy and access issues come to the fore in both the new digital economy and in modern records work, generally because the societal and organizational context for both is the same.

Adopting simplified economic and legal approaches to information and records management runs counter to the increasing voices speaking out about issues such as privacy or intellectual property or access. According to one writer concerned about the ethical consequences of such matters, we represent a society increasingly fixated on the conditions caused or exacerbated by our use of information technology: "One-third of Americans reported being concerned about invasion of privacy in 1970, at the dawn of the information age. Half of us had become concerned about privacy by 1977, and four out of five of us by 1990. This trend is understandable when you consider that personal information about each one of us is transferred from computer to computer an average of five times a day."[188] This means, of course, many people are interested in the records held by archives and records managers because of the personal data or because of the evidence about the gathering of such data.

The nature of our society's dependence on technology at first blush suggests that we act first and think latter about the consequences in matters like personal privacy. Americans go about creating trails of information and records that make it more difficult to have any privacy and that raise new challenges regarding the administration of access. One commentator ruminates, "it is virtually impossible to go anywhere or do anything without leaving a computer record. Pick up the phone—a record is made. Pass over your credit card—a record is made. Board a plane, watch a fight or a movie on pay-per-view, pay your taxes, buy a house, visit your dentist, apply for a passport, have your tires rotated. It is getting harder and harder to find occasions when there is *not* a record kept."[189] A recent report for the Brookings Institution states, "According to a 1994 estimate, U.S. computers alone hold more than five billion records, trading information on every man, woman, and child an average of five times every day" while, at the same time, we have a "patchwork of uneven, inconsistent, and often irrational privacy protection."[190] What role have archivists and records managers played in resolving such issues? Or have records professionals contributed to causing such problems?

It may be that the immense economic interests of the Information Age silence or drown out the voices of professionals such as archivists and records managers. The matter of privacy, as threatened by information technology, has been the subject of countless editorials and columns in major newspapers in recent years. Bob Herbert, in the *New York Times*, writes, "Your financial profile and buying habits have long since been catalogued and traded like baseball cards. Your medical records, supposedly secure, are not. Your boss may well be monitoring your telephone conversations and e-mail. Hidden video cameras have been installed—sometimes legally and sometimes not—in dressing rooms and public bathrooms. Thieves armed with your Social Security number can actually hijack your identity." Herbert saw "huge corporate interests and others" wanting the situation to be unchanged.[191] It may be that records professionals are little more than workers doing the bidding of those controlling the economic benefits of records and information.

Perhaps this assessment is too simplistic or harsh. It may be that the voices in our Information Age are so contradictory as to represent little more than a cacophony, merely distracting records professionals to turn their attention to matters in which there are clearer mandates and procedures. We live in a dangerous time, an era with an emphasis on information and technology that one would expect to be more hospitable for records professionals but which may provide little more than confusion. John Ralston Saul, grappling with why there is such a concentration of writing about privacy or secrecy in the last two decades, believes that secrecy results from the growing technocracy of society.[192] Records professionals need to consider such assessments and provide reasoned responses about their legitimacy in regards to records.

Others adopt a much different view. Information technology has spurred on, indeed, a new tension *between* privacy and access. Diffie and Landau see a "conflict between protecting the security of the state and the privacy of its individuals [that] is not new, but technology has given the state much more access to private information about individuals than it once had."[193] It *is*, then, a dangerous time. The *Economist*, featuring a cover story on the "end of privacy," predicts "privacy debates are likely to become ever more intense" as information technology is continually adopted, refined, and utilized.[194] Records professionals, always concerned with the technologies of records creation and maintenance, must also be aware of the degree to which the balance between privacy and access is possible.

There are closer connections between new information technologies and the creation of certain document forms. Social commentators such as Barry Sanders argue that the "more we move online the more our internal worlds shrink."[195] He is worried, interpreting reading and writing as the activities key to public discourse. Others, however, such as Alexandra Johnson, believe that the growth of interest in diary writing is perhaps a reaction to the shrinking sense of personal privacy in the Information Age.[196] There may be a renewed interest in records just when technology seems most likely to threaten records. Yet, this seems inconsistent because all records, whether the clay tablets of ancient Sumeria or the multi-media documents on the World Wide Web, are partly the result of technology. This seeming contradiction is the result of losing sight that it is humans creating and using the technology, whether in their homes or in organizations.

No issue seems to cause more consternation for the archivist and records manager than the potential conflict between providing access to records and protecting individual privacy. While the uses of electronic information technology have clearly made more complicated the possibility or choice of wider access or stronger restrictions, these complications are not merely the result of such technology. Michael Dertouzos, in his sweeping predictions about how information technology is changing society, nevertheless reined himself in when considering access and privacy by seeing it as a "nontechnical" issue, needing to be resolved by means other than that normally provided by technicians.[197] Perhaps, this is the potential and more important role for records professionals. Sociologist Amitai Etzioni looks for a "common good" setting limits on both privacy and access. For Etzioni technology is not the blame, but it is the lack of attention to matters such as the common good expressed in "our culture, policies, and doctrines" that do not defend us equally against public and private sectors.[198] Are records professionals part of the groups working for a common good or are they part of the technicians merely contributing to short-term solutions?

The recent angst by records and other information professionals about privacy and access is not surprising given the pervasive and powerful new information technologies, but that it has taken these technologies to bring renewed attention to such matters *is* surprising. After all, one recent book on privacy reminds us that the 200-year-old Fourth Amendment declares that the "right of the people to be secure in their persons, houses, papers, and effects, against unreasonable searches and seizures, shall not be violated." Then the authors comment: "When the Fourth Amendment was drafted, one's 'papers' were likely to comprise a record of one's life. They were also likely to be stored in a desk drawer, closet, or trunk—someplace in the house. Today, our papers are just as likely to comprise a record of our lives. But instead of a stack of papers on a desk, we have a paper trail that leads right out the door and into a multitude of offices and institutions. Are those papers still protected by the Fourth Amendment? For some of them, at least, the answer is no. What's more, they are not, surprisingly, even considered to be ours."[199] Others have written in a similar vein, "Our legal, governmental, and social systems are still designed for a world without computers. Our sluggish social systems, intended for the languid bygone era of only a decade ago—an era filled with filing cabinets, paper documents, and five-day mail—haven't changed to keep up. And computer technology keeps changing so fast now that perhaps they never will."[200] In such assessments we see the human dimension of records and information technology that has been lost, by society and the records and information professionals.

Records professionals must understand that matters like privacy and access are constantly shifting, not only because of technological changes but also because of other elements like the economy and social mores. Communications and other information technologies have had more than their share of influence. The home, as just one example, has been affected by waves of successive communications and technologies such as the postal system, telephone, VCR, and computer networks—moving us from realm of privacy to a different private space now openly and broadly connected.[201] The Society of American Archivists has even been willing to stretch its long-standing ethics code to accommodate such changes. In December 1998, considering grand jury records concerning the Alger Hiss case, SAA's governing body stated, "significant mitigating circumstances involved with the case justify opening customarily closed grand jury records. In reaching this decision, SAA recognized that its code of ethics calls for archivists to uphold restrictions imposed by law to protect the privacy of citizens. However, SAA also recognized that access to important records contributes to an accountable government. It was its hope that the court would recognized that, in this case, the public interest would be well served by lifting the restrictions that archivists might otherwise be forced to obey."[202]

Looking for consistency in statements by records professionals on privacy or access might be problematic because of heightened public sensitivity. What are the means records professionals need to follow in order to resolve the continuing challenges posed by the contradictory stances of full access and restrictive privacy? The first step is to realize the nature of the issues being faced by records professionals, a task they have only recently taken on. Evan Imber-Black states, "As a therapist, I'm a professional secret-keeper."[203] In a recent novel the main character, an archivist, is caught thinking, "An archivist serves the reader's desire. . . . Wasn't the writer's hunger for privacy always less compelling than the reader's appetite—voracious, insatiable—for more words?"[204] Although it is possible that archivists and records managers are privacy therapists, a popular novel's conventions seem to contrast with the reality that many records professionals have avoided assuming such a role. They often defer to others, such as corporate counsel, or hope that they will not encounter any problems of Solomon-like proportions in deciding between restricting and opening records. But, as Ann Balough suggests in a technical report on privacy and security, records professionals "need to become more accustomed to asking . . . What are we going to do with this information?"[205]

In the spirit of this book and its focus on policy, one is prone to want a policy or law to resolve *all* issues concerning privacy and access. Sissela Bok's groundbreaking study on secrecy contains this powerful statement: "With no control over secrecy and openness, human beings could not remain either sane or free."[206] Here we see the powerful connection of such issues to the essence of humanity, different from most matters handled by policies and procedures or even technical approaches. While records professionals have become more adept at issuing statements on the social and policy aspects of the use or abuse of records, they have sometimes missed broader concerns. The ending of the Cold

War brought many challenges to the opening and use of records, and in 1993 the Society of American Archivists passed a resolution on access to post–Cold War archives, encouraging "governments around the world to review their declassification policies with the purposes of pursuing policies of open access to archives." SAA leadership wanted the records opened in a "timely and equitable manner," especially in the Commonwealth of Independent States and in Eastern Europe "where archives were formerly closed to foreign researchers."[207] Such sentiments are old, based on strong notions of the good in making records available for use. Archivists, with their focus on a wide range of researchers using records for historical inquiries, hold to staunch views on the use of their records. This can be seen in various position statements, such as the older joint guidelines between the American Library Association and the Society of American Archivists, promoting "equal terms of access," making materials available "as soon as possible," informing of holdings, and not charging fees (principles now embedded in the SAA Ethics Code).

While the SAA resolution is noteworthy, and it is important that such professional associations take public stances, the statement also reveals the complexity in privacy and access. While the United States–based professional association called on governments around the world to open their records, access to government records in this country remains a mess. One author shows how a simple, unassuming sentence in the National Security Act of 1947, stating that the CIA director "shall be responsible for protecting sources and methods from unauthorized disclosure," has been used by the CIA to impose a level of secrecy never intended. From the use of secrecy contracts for federal employees to tightening restrictions over how FOIA is used, the U.S. is portrayed as a far less than open society.[208] This has continued to haunt the American people, but it should upset especially records professionals. Now the CIA is slowly, painstakingly declassifying millions of pages of records and using "retired CIA veterans" for whom the "work is an exercise in ambivalence, a daily struggle between their training never to give up secrets and a more natural human desire to want to tell their stories."[209] There has been public outrage about the CIA's actions, leading to the *New York Times* editorializing, "Unsealing archives is essential to the sound management of intelligence agencies in a free and open society. All but a handful of secrets necessitated by war, diplomacy and espionage must eventually be disclosed in a democracy, for secrecy over time breeds insularity and a lack of accountability."[210] Again, in accountability we have the essence of records and their evidence.

While the federal government has been absorbed with giving attention to the Information Age marketplace, it has become the consistent topic of scrutiny about the management of its own records and information. Another editorial about the late 1998 release of the report of the Assassination Records Review Board, reviewing records related to the John F. Kennedy assassination, accused the federal government of "needlessly and wastefully" classifying the records: "An aggressive policy is necessary to address the significant problems of lack of accountability and an uninformed citizenry that are created by the current practice of excessive classification and obstacles to releasing such information."[211] The general problem with federal government secrecy is not limited to clandestine agencies like the CIA or to events surrounding traumatic occurrences like an assassination. A 1996 law required agencies to make electronic records subject to the Freedom of Information Act, but OMB Watch, an independent watchdog group, discovered that not *one* agency compiled fully with the law.[212]

The problem is not isolated to the federal government. A series of journalistic studies about state government laws requiring open access to public records reveal how badly these laws are ignored. In Rhode Island there are "numerous complaints about possible violations of the Open Meetings Law related to public bodies that failed to disclose a reason for going into a closed or executive session or did not post proper meeting notices and agendas, thus keeping the public in the dark about the reasons for the meetings."[213] A similar series of articles about Indiana government officials found that "Those who asked for records were lied to, harassed, peppered with questions, and told subpoenas and court orders were required."[214] Both personal privacy and governmental accountability can be casualties in such widespread lack of compliance to existing records laws.

Excessive secrecy, lack of accountability, and lack of trust are all topics worthy of more attention by records professionals, but they are also matters returning us to the *human* dimensions of records systems and their management that must be embedded in records policies. Certainly records professionals need to keep speaking out about government secrecy, but they also need to understand more fully how records creating connects to basic human impulses and needs. Indeed, records professionals need to be on guard about how records are managed in the private sector, moving beyond just matters like accountability to issues of an ethical or moral nature. Novelist Joyce Carol Oates, commenting on the recent controversy about the sale of fourteen love letters by J. D. Salinger, writes that the "issue of private writing and public writing, and the distinction between them, is fundamentally an ethical one, and like most ethical issues in this Era of Law it's become a legal conundrum. Under American copyright law you own the words you've written in a personal letter, but the letter recipient owns the physical piece of paper and the symbols typed or written on it."[215] This suggests the need for more than looking only to legal solutions and guidelines.

Part of the challenge is determining what is privacy and how it affects other freedoms. Janna Malamud Smith, a social worker and the executrix of her father's (Bernard Malamud) literary estate, laments, the "Records of our bank account balances, medical prescriptions, and credit card purchases are considered saleable commodities, while we are denied our rightful ownership of this information. Yet society can only decide how to regulate these practices if we can determine what parts of privacy and private experience we wish to protect— and why."[216] This turns out to be a much more substantial challenge than it seems. In fact, her views reflect those of the protagonist in the Cooley novel

The Archivist who opts, even in his role as a university archivist, to destroy the personal papers of T. S. Eliot to fulfill what seemed to be the wishes of the author. That this seems unlikely to happen may have more to say about a lack of full recognition by records professionals of the forces propelling concerns of privacy versus those of access. Records professionals need to understand matters like privacy and access before they seek to govern or control what records are available, in what form, when, and to whom.

Some of the complexity derives from the need to discern what is a public and private record. Records professionals define these according to the standard legal and organizational attributes. There is nothing inappropriate about this. The new reliance on electronic information technologies has brought forth the notion of a recordkeeping warrant, stressing the legal, best practices, and fiscal requirements. But there are other ways to consider public and private dimensions of documents. A humanities scholar provides a different view in the tension between public and private considerations in records: "No matter how artful some private letters become, there are still important reasons, I believe, for maintaining the distinction between private and public texts. Even the artful rhetoric of a personal letter depends upon the precise relations between the writer and the recipient(s) in ways that change the meaning when others encounter the same words. When the writings that an author intended to publish are mixed together with personal letters, private journals, marginalia, or rough drafts that may not have been intended even to be read beyond the writer's own intimate circle, readers and critics are apt to misjudge the nature and quality of the writer's overall work."[217]

What is privacy? And how do we define access? Janna Smith argues, "In its most basic sense, having privacy is having control over our bodies, our possessions, our intimate environment, and the information—whether by watching, listening, touching, or reading—other people can gather about us. The wish for privacy is the wish to control what is known or revealed about ourselves and our intimate world."[218] This is a very human portrait of privacy, one that is at times ignored by records professionals defining privacy or access in terms of organizational need, part of a regulatory regime, or in light of the latest court ruling.

Even examining privacy from a societal rather than an individual perspective is fraught with problems. A Brookings Institution study notes, "Privacy is not an absolute. It is contextual and subjective. It is neither inherently beneficial nor harmful." Furthermore, as the study indicates, "There is no explicit constitutional guarantee of a right to privacy."[219] We also know that our notions of privacy and access shift over time. In describing how adoption records became more secret after the Second World War, historian E. Wayne Carp reveals the complexity of motivations for this, arguing, "those state bureaucrats and social workers who had the power to provide or deny access to adoption records acted from numerous intentions, including a desire to defend the adoptive process, protect the privacy of unwed mothers, increase their own influence and power, and bolster social work professionalism."[220] By the 1970s, more pressure had come for opening—even if to some limited degree—adoption records. Watergate increased suspicions about secrecy, and the "burden of proof shifted ever so slightly from those demanding access to adoption records to those invoking the right to conceal information."[221] The *Roots* phenomenon brought a new pressure for access to these records, and by the 1980's state laws had been adopted with more, if still limited, access.[222] Carp's study graphically highlights how personal implications for privacy mix with public policy interests and how it is difficult, if not impossible, to separate individual from societal or organizational issues. What seems to be private today may be opened tomorrow with restrictions and completely accessible the day after that. Records professionals, making appraisal and other decisions based on legal and administrative factors, may find that these factors have changed considerably, quickly, and in unforeseen ways.

Privacy is often defined as the opposite of openness or accessibility. As Charles D. Raab argues, the "claim that democracy and privacy reinforce each other means that the information-openness of democracy is not necessary achieved at the expense of privacy's information-restriction. It is not that we can have either democracy or privacy—more of one implying less of the other— or some balance between two supposedly opposing forces. The development of accountable democratic institutions and privacy-protecting processes cannot take place in separate compartments, for such is an important condition of the other."[223] While this puts the notion of privacy and access back into the broader social realm, it also reveals the difficulty of defining what must seem to be ever changing concepts or principles.

To a certain extent how we view access or privacy is dependent upon other issues, and the tendency is to define these terms in how they relate to such other societal matters. David Brin argues, the "United States has always featured a thread of cultural aversion toward official scrutiny."[224] "A generalized principle of data ownership," Brin continues, "if carried to its logical conclusions, would almost certainly produce a citizenry that spends half the next century in courtrooms, filing indignant injunctions to keep other people from sharing this or that snippet of knowledge without permission—in other words, a permanent entitlement program for lawyers."[225] Brin turns to a concept that ought to be familiar to most records professionals—accountability. Brin describes "Accountability as a tried-and-true technique for minimizing disaster in a complex society, and mutual transparency as a useful means to ensure accountability."[226] How accountability plays out against matters such as personal privacy is something that has not been fully explored.

The notion of access to records and their information seems to be a cherished principle in America. However, it is often defined in relationship to what it is not, such as being connected to concerns such as privacy. In fact, the idea of guaranteed access is not a particularly old notion in our nation. Historian Richard Brown describes that it was not until the Civil War that the idea of an informed citizenry was firmly established, even though free speech and press had long been hallmarks.[227] Others, such as Etzioni, see such ties to government or public information as far too limiting a notion. For these commentators, it is less a cherished principle and more an incomplete or flawed concept.

However, it is in the *human* dimensions of access that the real definition of access resides, especially in regards to records. Ian Buruma's comment on the girl whose story was made into the documentary *The Nasty Girl* suggests the painful memories that can be the result of access: "When, some years later, she decided to turn her findings into a book, she ran into even greater trouble. Libraries and archives shut their doors."[228] Historian Ash and his soul-searching about the Stasi File maintained about him is another indication of the challenges related to providing extremely open access to records: "What makes me decide to publish—although without naming names—is the conviction that there is also a larger purpose. Here is a chance to bring home, with the vividness that can only come from such intimate detail, how someone is drawn into a secret-police net—and to show where such collaboration will lead you."[229] Ash concludes, that in a case like the secret police files of the former East Germany, we must "Find out—record—reflect—but then move on." Here is sensitivity far beyond the mere realm of procedure or process. The opening of the Mississippi State Sovereignty Commission files in March 1998 provides a case eerily reminiscent of the Stasi files. The commission existed from 1956 to 1977 to impede the activities of civil rights workers. Originally ordered opened by U.S. District Court Judge William Barbour in 1989, nine years of appeals, especially about allowing subjects of the commission's investigations to exert their rights to keep their own files private, delayed the final opening of the records. When the state legislature abolished the commission it had voted to keep the files closed for 50 years, but the pros and cons of opening such records (taking into account the potential damage to current society and its victims) is much more complex and troubling than what it first seems.[230]

But where do we stop or start in the human dimensions affecting the parameters of privacy or access? It was recently reported that "hundreds of the Queen Mother's private papers and letters" (mostly correspondence of the previous decade) had been destroyed "in an attempt by Princess Margaret to prevent them becoming public."[231] Is this acceptable? Would it be acceptable for all public officials or figures to destroy their papers to prevent their use? What about corporations? The arrival of several thousand pages of records from Brown and Williamson Tobacco Corporation at the office of medical researcher Stanton Glantz—"internal memoranda, letters, and research reports" marked confidential—provides a glimpse into a world of accountability problems. In hindsight, it turns out that "attorney control over company research apparently was deemed necessary to assert control over evidence produced within the company so that it could not be used to prove that the company's products were dangerous, even though the evidence developed by the company specialists clearly contradicted this view."[232] In this company, the lawyers wrote up procedures for how to handle records, including destruction: "The role of lawyers in selecting research projects and methodologies and controlling the dissemination of results is, perhaps, the most important insight offered by the documents."[233] There is, of course, a substantial difference between the destruction of the personal papers of a queen and deliberate efforts to defraud the public's health, but neither pose easy questions or possess simple answers.

What about government? Is there a simple or standard mechanism for access to such records? On one end of the chronological spectrum we have the tape recordings made by the Kennedy, Nixon, and Johnson administrations of conversations *in* the Oval Office. May and Zelikow, in discussing the tapes made during the Cuban Missile Crisis, feel the "recordings subtly but significantly alter our understanding of practically every major question about U.S. policy during the crisis, sometimes by validating one interpretation over another, sometimes by spotlighting overlooked aspects of the deliberations."[234] "Perhaps, above all," they continue, "we observe in this record—more clearly than in any other documents we have ever seen—the contrary pulls of detail on the one hand and belief (or conviction or ideology) on the other. Almost from minute to minute, new information or recognition of some previously unperceived implication in information already at hand or a new argument will change in subtle or sometimes not subtle ways the form or even the character of the issue being addressed."[235] Should these recordings have been maintained and then opened? While this seems like a surprising question, it is not an unanticipated one given that the government sought to destroy the electronic mail (the precursor of the earlier Oval Office recordings?) in the late 1980s concerning the Iran-Contra Affair. Tom Blanton writes, the "authors were not writing for a public audience or even 'for the file,' the way so many government documents are created. As a result, there's an urgency, an immediacy, and a level of candor very rarely displayed in public records."[236] "Reading their e-mail puts us virtually at their desk," Blanton contends, "with a perspective no outsider has ever had before."[237] It seems logical that we would want to maintain such records.

Today, there seems to be a sentiment in government circles for greater openness. Some even contend that the entire secrecy environment stems from the project to develop and use the atomic bomb on Japan. The debate over Hiroshima demonstrates the difficulty we face as a nation and a people when dealing with the matter of access to government records. As Lifton and Mitchell demonstrate in their *Hiroshima in America*, the government and news media controlled the official view of the necessity argument for dropping the atomic bomb on Japan. The first dissent to the official view started in the mid-1960s by historians. Why so long? "Few were inclined to [challenge the official story], and those with a critical eye faced the usual problem of having to wait for personal papers and diaries to be donated to libraries, and for official records to be declassified (in the latter case, a very long wait indeed)."[238] Lifton and Mitchell also extend their concern: "What has been lost sight of is the role Hiroshima concealment has played in encouraging subsequent American cover-ups," such as Vietnam, Watergate, and Iran-Contra. "Surely Hiroshima was the mother of all cover-ups, creating tonalities, distortions, manipulative procedures, and patterns of concealment that have been applied to all of American life that followed. Secrecy has been linked with national security—and vice versa—ever since."[239] And it is likely that secrecy has affected the paranoia we have seen associated with the supposed threats of government and technology to personal privacy.

Remarkable problems remain with attitudes towards privacy and access. Look at this intriguing description in a study of the use of social history approaches in colonial Williamsburg: "While working in the archives, we [the two anthropologists conducting the study] learned of a class of documents that we thought might be useful but were not available to us without special permission. We raised the matter with the appropriate corporate vice president, who, after some consideration, denied us access on the grounds that the documents in question might refer to delicate personnel matters. When we mentioned this casually to another vice president, he immediately gave us a stack (several years' worth) of the documents in question—which, though they circulated only among administrative officers, were apparently little read by them. He would eventually, he told us, discard his copies anyway, and he let us keep them. We found that they contained few delicate personnel matters, and in any case we have not drawn on them for such material."[240] With individuals willing to hand out any records to people outside of their organization, records professionals face immense challenges in controlling legitimate privacy and access issues. As organizations become more dependent on electronic records, the possibilities for problems increase as any individual can easily transmit confidential materials to other individuals or even public discussion groups.

What records professionals are now encountering may be more a result of immense shifts in society rather than what archivists and records managers have or have not done. What records professionals have to be sensitive to is their role in developing new and effective solutions in handling access and privacy matters. The book and manuscripts thief Stanley Blumberg defended his actions by arguing that he was trying to save items that had been *forgotten* by librarians and archivists.[241] While we do not want to put much stock in the arguments of social misfits like Blumberg, it is also likely that the failure of records professionals to develop effective solutions to matters like access and privacy will result in others seeking solutions for us. Archivists and records managers administer records that may provoke controversy and reveal perspectives unknown or not wished for. As a result, they need to work through matters like privacy and access rather than merely waiting for others to resolve such issues or hoping that no problems will occur.

The tension between privacy and access is not the only conflict potentially finding its way into the work of records professionals. Archivists struggle, for example, with the contradictions of preserving records while making them available for use. Use is contradictory to preservation because it brings wear and tear to records. Records managers struggle, on the other hand, with protecting their organizations while managing records to document the activities of the same organizations. Keeping a record could open an organization to litigation; destroying the record, however, could eliminate evidence crucial to understanding what the organization is about. These tensions seem to be more difficult than the one existing between privacy and access. There is a subtlety affecting how records professionals must balance and manage privacy and access issues. Still, there are a number of practical steps records professionals can take in regards to privacy and access considerations affecting their records, and these steps should inform any policy regarding records and information. Such issues also seem to be practical for records policies in general.

Records professionals must understand that information technology has transformed the entire matter of privacy and access. While no one can assume that information technology is *the* cause for new concerns about matters such as access and privacy, records professionals need to understand that as technology changes so do the parameters of the challenges they face in managing records. One commentator argues, "Innovations in multimedia communications and computing technology increase the connections between places and the connections between people distributed in space, and as a result the intuitive sense of place and presence that governs our observable behavior can no longer be relied upon to ensure that we will not be seen, overheard, or even recorded."[242] Records professionals must be extra sensitive in advising how their organizations create and maintain records or in deciding how to appraise and acquire records from other organizations and individuals in light of such technological impacts.

Records professionals must strengthen their understanding of professional ethics in managing personal papers or public records containing personal information. One effort to develop Information Age principles notes, "We must learn to think of personal data as an extension of the self and treat it with the same respect we would a living individual. To do otherwise runs the risk of undermining the privacy that makes self-determination possible." [243] Archivists have long expressed such sentiments, while records managers have been more oriented to the concerns of the organization. Despite whatever backgrounds are involved, both archivists and records managers need to reaffirm the importance of privacy and access in a form enabling them to guide their organizations and society in the use of records. At the least, each archives or records management program must make its staff knowledgeable about the relevant ethics codes, while also applying practical illustrations of the codes use in their particular organizations. Staff should be trained in the ethical dimensions of their work. In other words, they should be made more aware of the human dimensions of records creation and maintenance.

Records professionals must understand that laws and policies are not always adequate. I have made numerous references to the problems associated with adopting a procedurally oriented solution to privacy and access matters built only or largely on laws and regulations. Colin J. Bennett laments, "The private sector is regulated through an incomplete patchwork of federal and state provisions that oblige organizations to adhere to fair information practices," while there is no oversight agency for privacy in the United States. "The approach to making privacy policy in the United States is reactive rather than anticipatory, incremental rather than comprehensive, and fragmented rather than coherent. There may be a lot of laws, but there is not much protection."[244] Records professionals need to contribute to resolving this problem, both by developing alternatives to solving privacy and access issues and by working for better and more practical laws and policies. Developing a records-centered approach in which archivists and records managers are primarily responsible for helping organizations and society comprehend how laws, regulatory regimes, and best practices affect records (the record warrant concept) would be an excellent means by which to do this.

Records professionals must understand that the commercialization of information is a potential danger in the use of their records. Simon G. Davies speculates, "The process of commodification is inimical to privacy. Every element of privacy protection is interpreted and promoted as a direct cost to the consumer. The cost factor is a powerful weapon in the armory of privacy invaders because it implies that a few 'fundamentalists' will force a rise in the production cost of an item or a service."[245] Remembering such problems is important because it is relatively easy for records professionals to be caught up in the possibility of making money from the records they manage. Generating financial resources, while attractive to records professionals working in both the private and public sectors, raises the risks in opening up records that should remain private or in closing records that should be accessible but that are expensive to maintain. Records professionals need to play a moderating role in both their organizations and society. Records managers and archivists may be called on to develop very different kinds of policy statements.

Archivists and other records professionals must realize that the matter of government and corporate secrecy is a more serious matter and work to open records. Richard Breitman bluntly writes, "Governments that withhold critical information from the historical record and the public long after the events do their countries and the world no service."[246] There is nothing more powerful than bringing to light abusive efforts to keep citizens from records created by taxpayers' funds. While Senator Moynihan urges that we need more open access to diminish conspiracy theories and paranoia, a group of essays edited by Athan Theoharis reveals we have much to be concerned about. Unlike many of the books dealing with secrecy and access, this volume focuses directly on records, revealing that there is an "antipathy toward public disclosure and accountability [that] continues to determine federal records practices."[247] These essays also point out another danger for records professionals—the price we pay for not being more vigilant. As most bluntly stated in Joan Hoff's essay on the Nixon tapes, if we do not take more aggressive stances we will be described as lacking courage and be seen as part of the problem in access to records rather than as advocates for open access, accountability, and the power of evidence found in records.[248] Resolving government secrecy matters will have a positive impact in correcting the land mines associated with personal privacy. Excessive secrecy about the activities of corporations, except for their most proprietary of information, is equally dangerous.

Records professionals need to conduct research about the effectiveness of various methods for managing privacy and access. Records professionals need to develop strategies for conducting research about privacy and access issues. Two public policy experts describe how we still lack details about actual risks or differences in attitudes, although we have much "survey research on privacy, which casts light on public attitudes toward, and knowledge of, privacy risks and privacy protection." [249] One could see research on different attitudes between archivists and records managers based on the differing clienteles they serve. Any research, at this point, would help records professionals, especially in policy formulation.

CONCLUSION, OR BITING THE BULLET

Jeffrey Archer's *Honor Among Thieves* is a fast-paced, international potboiler, revolving around the efforts of Saddam Hussein to kidnap and publicly destroy the original manuscript of the Declaration of Independence. Archives and other records seem to possess great value, as a nation risks its agents and war in order to save this document. More telling, however, is how Archer has the foreign agents infiltrate the National Archives and steal the document. His premise is based on the Archivist of the United States' frustration with his inability to get the president to visit the Archives, a fact that the foreign agents capitalize on by having an actor impersonate the president and request a visit to view the Declaration. Archer describes the premise in this fashion: "He [one of the foreign agents] drummed his fingers on the desk and gazed down with satisfaction at the file in front of him. One of the President's two schedulers had been able to supply him with the information he needed. The file revealed that the Archivist had invited each of the last three Presidents—Bush, Reagan, and Carter—to visit the National Archives, but due to 'pressing commitments' none of them had been able to find the time."[250] Only successful advocacy by archivists and records managers and their allies in building understanding about records issues and developing effective government and organization policies has a hope of making such fiction, fiction indeed.

NOTES

1. Such as "From Digits to Dust," *Business Week*, April 20, 1998, pp. 128, 130. This article stressed the loss of electronic information and records, ranging from data in space exploration to Vietnam War records to the administrative records of colleges and universities. See also Terry Cook, "It's 10 O'Clock: Do You Know Where Your Data Are?" *Technology Review* (January 1995): 48–53, one of the rare occasions when an archivist appeared in a more public forum.

2. For different views about this, refer to James Boylan, "How Archives Make News," *Midwestern Archivist* 10, no. 2 (1985): and "Of Plots, Secrets, Burrowers and Moles: Archives in Espionage Fiction," *Archivaria* 9 (Winter 1979–1980).

3. Social Research, Inc., *The Image of Archivists: Resource Allocators' Perceptions* ([Chicago]: Prepared for the Society of American Archivists Task Force on Archives and Society, December 1984).

4. And, actually, this study was to measure *what* archivists were doing; see Ann E. Pederson, "Archival Outreach: SAA's 1976 Survey," *American Archivist* 41 (April 1978): 155–162.

5. For example, Meyer Berger, *The Story of the New York Times 1851–1951* (New York: Simon and Schuster, 1951); Herman H. Dinsmore, *All the News That Fits: A Critical Analysis of the News and Editorial Contents of the New York Times* (New Rochelle, NY: Arlington House, 1969); Ruth Adler, *A Day in the Life of The New York Times* (Philadelphia: J. B. Lippincott Co., 1971); Harrison E. Salisbury, *Without Fear or Favor: The New York Times and Its Times* (New York: Times Books, 1980); and Joseph C. Goulden, *Fit to Print: A. M. Rosenthal and His Times* (Secaucus, NJ: Lyle Stuart, 1988).

6. In *Reading the News*, ed. Robert Karl Manoff and Michael Schudson (New York: Pantheon Books, 1987), p. 56.

7. Daniel C. Hallin in *Reading the News*, p. 118.

8. Herbert Gans, *Deciding What's News: A Study of CBS Evening News, NBC Nightly News, Newsweek, and Time* (New York: Vintage Books, 1980), p. 126.

9. Gans, *Deciding What's News*, p. 126.

10. Gans, *Deciding What's News*, pp. 291–292.

11. Gans, *Deciding What's News*, pp. 43–44.

12. Terry Anderson, "My Paper Prison," *New York Times Magazine*, April 4, 1993, p. 35.

13. John Noble Wilford, "In a Trove of Old Maps, a World of Communication, and of Persuasion," *New York Times*, October 9, 1992, pp. B1, B8; "Facing Up to Racial Pains of Past, Birmingham Moves On," *New York Times*, November 15, 1992, p. 12; Herbert Mitgang, "Revise, Revise: Manuscripts Tell All," *New York Times*, November 28, 1992, p. 11; "Emancipation Proclamation to Be Shown," *New York Times*, December 20, 1992, p. 11; William Grimes, "Vatican's Secular Treasures on View," *New York Times*, January 2, 1993, p. 9; Matthew Rutenberg, "Popes in Pursuit of Humanism, Up to a Point," *New York Times*, April 18, 1993, p. 31; Felicity Barringer, "Dead Sea Scrolls to Be Displayed in Washington," *New York Times* January 27, 1993, p. A12; Holland Cotter, "A Trove of Collectibles, from Bibles to Letters," *New York Times*, April 23, 1993, p. B10.

14. Vincent Canby, "Columbus as Idealist, Dreamer and Hustler," *New York Times*, October 9, 1992, p. B5; William E. Schmidt, "History or Heresy? Churchill's War Role Attacked," *New York Times*, January 9, 1993, p. 2.

15. Frank J. Prial, "A Target for the Longbows of Camelot," *New York Times*, January 27, 1993, pp. B1, B4; Herbert Mitgang, "Disney Link to the F.B.I. and Hoover Is Disclosed," *New York Times*, May 6, 1993, pp. B1, B4; John Noble Wilford, "Language of Early Americans Is Deciphered," *New York Times*, March 23, 1993, pp. B5, B9; Russell Davies, "Michael Palin's New Role: He's His Own Grandpa," *New York Times*, April 4, 1993, Section 2, pp. 24–25.

16. Jane Gross, "On Libel and the Literati: The New Yorker on Trial," *New York Times*, May 5, 1993, pp. A1, C22; Jane Gross, "In New Yorker Libel Trial the Analyst

Is Examined," *New York Times*, May 11, 1993, p. A7; Jane Gross, "Writer Defends Method in The New Yorker Trial," *New York Times*, May 14, 1993, p. A10; Jane Gross, "Writer Says Disputed Paragraph Merged Remarks," *New York Times*, May 17, 1993, p. A7; Jane Gross, "At Writer's Libel Trial, the Focus Turns to Styles of Speaking," *New York Times*, May 19, 1993, p. A8; Jane Gross, "Editor of New Yorker Article Testifies," *New York Times*, May 20, 1993, p. A8; Jane Gross, "Posthumous Testimony in Libel Trial," *New York Times*, May 21, 1993, p. A8; Jane Gross, "Articles on Analyst Hurt Their Relationship, Ex-Lover Testifies," *New York Times*, May 25, 1993, p. A8; Jane Gross, "Profile Writer Has Last Word in Defense against Libel Suit," *New York Times*, May 26, 1993, p. A7. The interest in the personalities can clearly be seen in the article by Michelle C. Quinn, "Passion Reigns in Libel Trial Gallery," *New York Times*, May 23, 1993, p. 10; Jane Gross, "Jury Hears Final Arguments in Analyst's Libel Suit," *New York Times*, May 28, 1993, p. A7; Deirdre Carmody, "Despite Malcolm Trial, Other Editors Vouch for the Accuracy of Their Work," *New York Times*, May 30, 1993, p. 14. The focus of this lawsuit was Malcolm's *In the Freud Archives* (New York: Alfred A. Knopf, 1984).

17. Neil A. Lewis, "The Tools of Remembrance," *New York Times Book Review*, May 16, 1993, p. 3.

18. Elaine Sciolino, "Justice Dept. Role Cited in Deception on Iraq Loan Data," *New York Times*, October 10, 1992, pp. 1, 4.

19. Andrew Rosenthal, "High State Dept. Official Ordered Search of Clinton's Embassy Files," *New York Times*, October 15, 1992, pp. A1, A16. Eventually, this story reappeared when the official involved was dismissed; Eric Schmitt, "Passport Search Brings Dismissal," *New York Times*, November 11, 1992, pp. A1, A7; Robert Pear, "Passport Inquiry Seeks Ties to White House or Bush Campaign," *New York Times*, November 12, 1992, p. A14; Robert Pear, "High Bush Official Is Linked to Search of File on Clinton," *New York Times*, November 14, 1992, pp. 1, 8; Robert Pear, "Top Bush Aide Denies Approving State Dept. Search of Clinton File," *New York Times*, November 15, 1992, pp. 1, 15; "Ex-Official Accuses Administration in File Search," *New York Times*, November 16, 1992, p. A9; Robert Pear, "State Dept. Official Who Searched Clinton's Passport Files Resigns," *New York Times*, November 18, 1992, p. A9; Robert Pear, "Political Motives Imputed in Search of Passport Files," *New York Times*, November 19, 1992, p. A1, A13; Robert Pear, "Many Questions Linger Following State Dept. Inquiry," *New York Times*, November 20, 1992, p. A10; "What Did the White House Know?" *New York Times*, November 20, 1992, p. A14; Robert Pear, "Evidence Prompts Further Inquiry Into Clinton Passport File Search," *New York Times*, November 25, 1992, pp. A1, A8; David Johnston, "Independent Prosecutor to Open Inquiry on Search of Clinton File," *New York Times*, December 18, 1992, p. A1; Robert Pear, "Democrats Puzzled by Naming of Prosecutor on Clinton Files," *New York Times*, December 19, 1992, p. 8; Robert Pear, "Bush Aide Accused of Lying in Inquiry on Clinton Search," *New York Times*, December 22, 1992, pp. A1, A9.

20. Robert Pear, "Bush's Lawyer Says Aides May Destroy Records," *New York Times*, November 22, 1992, p. 6; "Take the Records and Run?" *New York Times*, November 25, 1992, p. A12; Robert Pear, "Interview with Baker Sought on Clinton File," *New York Times*, December 16, 1992, p. A9.

21. Stephen Labaton, "Angry Judge Says Defiant Bush Plans to Purge Iran-Contra Data," *New York Times*, January 15, 1993, pp. A1, A9; Michael Wines, "Bush Makes Public Iran-Contra Diary," *New York Times*, January 16, 1993, pp. 1, 8; Stephen Labaton,

"Administration Is Told to Copy Computer Data," *New York Times*, January 16, 1993, p. 8.

22. "Computer Chat Private? Got a Message for You," *New York Times*, February 7, 1993, p. 15.

23. Steve Lohr, "White House: A Computer Nerdville," *New York Times*, February 20, 1993, pp. 13, 26.

24. David Johnston, "Federal Agents Investigating Loss of Iran-Contra Papers," *New York Times*, October 10, 1992, p. 6.

25. Robert Pear, "New Weinberger Notes Contradict Bush Account on Iran Arms Deal," *New York Times*, October 31, 1992, pp. 1, 9; David Johnston, "The Weinberger Notes: A Cloud Over Bush on Arms and Iran," *New York Times*, November 1, 1992, p. 22; David Johnston, "Bush Pardons 6 in Iran Affair, Aborting a Weinberger Trial; Prosecutor Assails 'Cover-up,' " *New York Times*, December 25, 1992, pp. A1, A10; David Johnston, "Sides Dispute Significance of Bush's Iran-Affair Notes," *New York Times*, December 27, 1992, p. 9; Linda Greenhouse, "Law Ill-Equipped for Politics," *New York Times*, December 28, 1992, pp. A1, C7; "The Best Case for the Pardons," *New York Times*, December 29, 1992, p. A10; Daniel Schorr, "Will Bush Pardon Himself?" *New York Times*, December 29, 1992, p. A11; Adam Clymer, "Bush Criticizes Press Treatment of the Pardons," *New York Times*, December 31, 1992, p. A8; David Johnston, "Bush Interview on Iran Deal Is Closer to Being Disclosed," *New York Times*, January 12, 1993, p. A12.

26. David Johnston, "Treasurer's Records Show Payments by Ex-Employer," *New York Times*, October 31, 1992, p. 5.

27. "Court Says Nixon Must Be Compensated for Tapes," *New York Times*, November 18, 1992, p. A10; "Richard Nixon's Unjust Reward," *New York Times*, November 19, 1992, p. A16.

28. Elaine Sciolino, "Memo from 60's May Ripple Christopher's Smooth Sailing," *New York Times*, January 12, 1993, p. A11.

29. Stephen Labaton, "Protecting History, and the Forgettable, on Disks," *New York Times*, January 8, 1993, p. B8.

30. John O'Neil, "Bush Tapes Lost, U.S. Archivists Say," *New York Times*, March 14, 1993, p. 16; Karen De Witt, "Battle to Save U.S. Files From the Delete Button," *New York Times*, April 11, 1993, p. 13.

31. Stephen Labaton, "A Judge Issues Contempt Order in Archives Case," *New York Times*, May 22, 1993, p. 6.

32. Fox Butterfield, "Secret Kennedy Tapes May Be Made Public," *New York Times*, February 5, 1993, p. A7.

33. Eric Schmitt, "C.I.A. Holds Talks on '62 Cuban Crisis," *New York Times*, October 20, 1992, p. A4.

34. David Johnston, "A Secret Memo Puts Bush Close to Hostage Deals," *New York Times*, October 23, 1992, p. A15. For related articles see Dean Baquet, "European Suppliers of Iraq Were Known to Pentagon," *New York Times*, November 2, 1992, p. A6; Elaine Sciolino, "Letter on Iraq Loans Adds New Doubts on C.I.A.," *New York Times*, November 3, 1992, p. A5.; John Markoff, "In Shift, U.S. Shrugs at Found 'Spy' Data," *New York Times*, November 28, 1992, p. 7.

35. Irvin Molotsky, "Writer Reports Contents of Secret Nixon Tapes," *New York Times*, December 7, 1992, p. A12.

36. Neil A. Lewis, "Revealed in the New Nixon Tapes: How to Handle a Vendetta," *New York Times*, May 17, 1993, p. A9.

37. Clifford Krauss, "How U.S. Actions Helped Hide Salvador Human Rights Abuses," *New York Times*, March 21, 1993, pp. 1, 8.

38. Anderson, "My Paper Prison," p. 35.

39. Krauss, "How U.S. Actions Helped Hide Salvador Human Rights Abuses," p. A1.

40. Nathaniel C. Nash, "Argentina Produces Little New Data on Nazis," *New York Times*, February 9, 1993, p. A7.

41. Nicholas D. Kristoff, "A Tale of Red Guards and Cannibals," *New York Times*, January 6, 1993, p. A6.

42. Tim Weiner, "President Moves to End Secrecy on Millions of U.S. Documents," *New York Times*, May 5, 1993, pp. A1, A10.

43. "Democracy's Obsolete Secrets," *New York Times*, May 9, 1993, p. 14.

44. John H. Cushman, Jr., "U.S. to Use Agents to Detect Mortgage Bias," *New York Times*, May 6, 1993, pp. C1, C2.

45. David Johnston, "Cable Says Bush Endorsed Secrecy for Hostage Affair," *New York Times*, October 21, 1992, p. A11.

46. Caryn James, "The Search Continues for the Real Malcolm X," *New York Times*, December 3, 1992, pp. B1, B4.

47. Tim Weiner, "The Cold War Freezer Keeps Historians Out," *New York Times*, May 23, 1993, sect. 4, p. 5.

48. James Bennet, "Who Owns Ideas and Papers Is Issue in Company Lawsuits," *New York Times*, May 30, 1993, pp. 1, 11.

49. Neil A. Lewis, "Gates Orders a Revamping of the C.I.A.'s File System," *New York Times*, January 1, 1993, p. A8.

50. Sciolino, "Justice Dept. Role Cited in Deception on Iraq Loan Data," pp. A1, A4.

51. Mary Rowland, "When a Record Is Forever," *New York Times*, April 11, 1993, p. F17.

52. Steve Lohr, "At I.B.M., the New Boss Takes to Electronic Mail," *New York Times*, April 10, 1993, pp. 13, 16.

53. Steven Prokesch, "Naturally, Less Paper Work Means Fewer Employees," *New York Times*, April 18, 1993, p. 22.

54. Glenn Rifkin, "New Momentum for Electronic Patient Records," *New York Times*, May 2, 1993, p. 8.

55. Marvina Howe, "Fighting to Become a Citizen," *New York Times*, February 8, 1993, p. A9.

56. John Markoff, "The Paperless Office Looms on the Horizon. Again," *New York Times*, May 30, 1993, p. E3.

57. Celestine Bohlen, "Russian Files Show Stalin Ordered Massacre of 20,000 Poles in 1940," *New York Times*, October 15, 1992, pp. A1, A6. On the same day another article discussed Russian President Boris Yeltsin's release of records about the 1983 shooting down of a South Korean airliner; Celestine Bohlen, "Yeltsin Turns Over Data on the KAL 0007 Disaster," *New York Times* October 15, 1992, p. A5.

58. Allan Kozinn, "Russians to Release a Million Recordings in Broadcast Archive," *New York Times*, October 19, 1992, pp. B1, B5; Barbara Basler, "Britain and China Reveal Documents," *New York Times*, October 29, 1992, p. A4; Henry Kamm, "Holo-

caust Museum Benefits from the Fall of Communism," *New York Times*, December 6, 1992, p. 14; "Arrest in Secret-Documents Case," *New York Times*, May 9, 1993, p. 11.

59. "Vietnam Gives 5,000 Photographs of Dead Servicemen to Pentagon," *New York Times*, October 21, 1992, p. A9. More information was later released identifying the American researcher; see Barbara Crossette, "American Is Key to Hanoi Photos," *New York Times*, October 25, 1992, p. 4.

60. Eric Schmitt, "U.S. Archivists to Inspect Hanoi's Files on Missing," *New York Times*, October 22, 1992, p. A7; Barbara Crossette, "Vietnamese Photos Resolve Fate of 4 Missing Americans," *New York Times*, November 1, 1992, p. 6.

61. Barbara Crossette, "Bush Says Photos Are Major Break," *New York Times*, October 23, 1992, p. A3; Crossette, "Hanoi Said to Vow to Give M.I.A. Data," *New York Times*, October 24, 1992, pp. 1–2; James Gross, "Hanoi Photos Have Families of U.S. M.I.A.'s Astir," *New York Times*, October 24, 1992, p. 2.

62. Jane Gross, "Years after a War Death, Proof Brings a New Grief," *New York Times*, November 1, 1992, pp. 1, 6.

63. Philip Shenon, "U.S. Team in Hanoi Studies Relics of the Missing," *New York Times*, November 15, 1992, pp. 1, 10; Philip Shenon, "Senators Tour Hanoi's P.O.W. Closet," November 18, 1992, p. A3; Philip Shenon, "For Vietnam, Settling the Past Could Be Good Business," *New York Times*, November 22, 1992, p. E5.

64. R. W. Apple, Jr., "U.S. to Press Hanoi to Explain '72 P.O.W Report," *New York Times*, April 13, 1993, p. A1; "Vietnam's 1972 Statement on P.O.W's Triple the Total Hanoi Acknowledged," *New York Times* April 13, 1993, p. A6; Philip Shenon, "A '72 Report on P.O.W.'s Is a Fake, Vietnam Asserts," *New York Times*, April 14, 1993, p. A7; Steven A. Holmes, "Pentagon Is Wary on P.O.W. Text; Families See Proof of Lies," *New York Times*, April 14, 1993, p. A7; Stephen Engelberg, "Old M.I.A. Theory Is Given New Life by Moscow Find," *New York Times*, April 18, 1993, p. 12; Steven A. Holmes, "Envoy Says P.O.W. Evidence Undermines Old Russian Report," *New York Times*, April 22, 1993, p. A3.

65. "New Questions on the P.O.W.'s," *New York Times*, April 14, 1993, p. A14.

66. Malcolm McConnell, with research by Theodore G. Schweitzer III, *Inside Hanoi's Secret Archives: Solving the MIA Mystery* (New York: Simon and Schuster, 1995).

67. "Senator Says Russia May Still Hold M.I.A.'s," *New York Times*, November 11, 1992, p. A3; Serge Schmemann, "Looking for Americans: Russians Move Mountain of Files," *New York Times*, November 15, 1992, Section 4, p. 5.

68. "Document Indicates Iraq Has Biological Weapons," *New York Times*, December 30, 1992, p. A4.

69. David Margolick, "After 40 Years, a Postscript on Hiss: Russian Official Calls Him Innocent," *New York Times*, October 29, 1992, p. A9; Serge Schemann, "On Hiss, Russian General Says He Was 'Not Properly Understood,' " *New York Times*, December 17, 1992, p. A9.

70. Serge Schemann, "Soviet Archives Provide Missing Pieces of History's Puzzles," *New York Times*, February 8, 1993, p. A6; Peter Steinfels, "A New Book Sheds Light on a Turning Point in American Politics and Religion," *New York Times*, October 31, 1992, p. 10; David Wise, "Was Oswald a Spy, and Other Cold War Mysteries," *New York Times Magazine*, December 6, 1992, pp. 42, 44, 46, 48. Other articles on this topic appeared from time to time, such as "Russian Papers Shed Little Light on Secrets of Hungarian Uprising," *New York Times*, March 25, 1993, p. A7.

71. John Noble Wilford, "Dead Sea Scroll Scholars End Publication Dispute," *New*

York Times, December 18, 1992, p. A10; John Noble Wilford, "New Access to Scrolls Fuels Scholars' Warfare," *New York Times*, December 22, 1992, pp. B5, B8.

72. Herbert Mitgang, "Thoreau's Last Writings on Natural History to Be Published in April," *New York Times*, February 16, 1993, p. B7.

73. William H. Honan, "On the Trail of the Many Love Letters of Hitler and Eva Braun," *New York Times*, March 13, 1993, p. 13.

74. Alan Riding, "Documents Expose French-Nazi Complicity," *New York Times*, April 7, 1993, pp. A1, A4.

75. "Museum and New Jersey at Odds Over Lindbergh Kidnapping Files," *New York Times*, April 11, 1993, p. 13.

76. In Esther B. Fein's "Book Notes" column, October 14, 1992, p. B3.

77. "Archives Yield Soviet–German Pact," *New York Times*, October 30, 1992, p. A7.

78. "KKK Auction Brings $29,000, and Anger," *New York Times*, November 2, 1992, p. C10.

79. William H. Honan, "Cole Porter Notebooks Go to Yale," *New York Times*, November 21, 1992, p. 10.

80. Allan Kozinn, "Belgian Finds a Score Berlioz Said He Burned," *New York Times*, December 2, 1992, p. B3.

81. Herbert Mitgang, "Documents Search Shows Lincoln the Railsplitter as a Polished Lawyer," *New York Times*, February 15, 1993, p. C7.

82. David Johnston, "Marshall Papers Reveal Court Behind the Scenes," *New York Times*, May 24, 1993, p. A10; Neil A. Lewis, "In Marshall Papers, Rare Glimpse at Court," *New York Times*, May 25, 1993, pp. A1, A8; Neil A. Lewis, "Chief Justice Assails Library on Release of Marshall Papers," *New York Times*, May 26, 1993, pp. A1, C19.

83. Linda Greenhouse, "Protecting Its Mystique: High Court's Anger Over Marshall Papers Is Fueled by More Than Pomp and Privacy," *New York Times*, May 27, 1993, pp. A1, C23.

84. Crystal Nix and Sheryll D. Cashin, "Library of Congress—Or School for Scandal?" *New York Times*, May 27, 1993, p. A11.

85. Neil A. Lewis, "Librarian Is Firm on Marshall Papers," *New York Times*, May 27, 1993, p. C23.

86. "Thurgood Marshall Is Heard Again," *New York Times*, May 28, 1993, p. A14.

87. Susan Diesenhouse, "Saving Books, by the Hundreds," *New York Times*, October 18, 1992, p. F9; Matt Wolf, "Britain's Film Archivists Hunt for the Missing Links," *New York Times*, January 3, 1993, Section 2, p. 18.

88. Glenn Collines, "Papp's Archives Go to New York Library," *New York Times*, May 10, 1993, pp. B1–B2.

89. "Floppy Disks Are Only Knowledge, but Manuscripts Are Wisdom," *New York Times Book Review*, March 28, 1993, p. 27.

90. William H. Honan, "New York Public Library Aids Ailing Museum," *New York Times*, November 19, 1992, p. B4.

91. William H. Honan, "Scholars Mourn and Fight Landmark Library's Closing," *New York Times*, February 9, 1993, p. B9; David W. Dunlap, "Historical Society Shuts Its Doors but Still Hopes," *New York Times*, February 20, 1993, p. 9; William H. Honan, "Historical Society Tries to Live by Subtraction," *New York Times*, March 12, 1993, p. B12; "Saving the City's 'Memory,' " *New York Times*, February 18, 1993, p. A16.

92. "Cleaning Out New York's Attic," *New York Times*, March 21, 1993, p. 16.

93. "Archivist of the U.S. Resigning Under Fire," *New York Times*, February 13, 1993, p. 6; "Archivist Resigns to Take Bush Job," *New York Times*, February 14, 1993, p. 16; Stephen Labaton, "Inquiry Is Sought into U.S. Archivist," *New York Times*, February 17, 1993, p. A8; "Archivist Tells of Bush Job Offer Before Action on Tapes," *New York Times*, March 3, 1993, p. A10.

94. "Boston University Chief Testifies about Duty to Keep King Papers," *New York Times*, May 4, 1993, p. A13.

95. Susan Spano, "Nixon Library: The Making of the Man," *New York Times*, May 30, 1993, pp. 8, 17 and Peter Applebome, "Carter Center: More Than the Past," *New York Times*, May 30, 1993, pp. 9, 18.

96. The story of the New-York Historical Society led to a case study of this institution's fiscal management, remarkable for its perceptions about the role of acquisition; see Kevin M. Guthrie, *The New-York Historical Society: Lessons from One Nonprofit's Long Struggle for Survival* (San Francisco: Jossey-Bass Publishers, 1996).

97. For more of the statistical analysis of these stories, refer to the charts accompanying my "International Perspectives on the Image of Archivists and Archives: Coverage by the *New York Times*, 1992–1993," *International Information and Library Review* 25 (1993): 195–231.

98. Michael Schudson, *Reading the News*, p. 89.

99. Sigal, *Reading the News*, p. 12.

100. U.S. Senate, Committee on Governmental Affairs, *Serious Mismanagement Problems at the National Archives and Records Administration* (Washington, DC: U.S. Government Printing Office, 1992).

101. Pear, "Many Questions," p. A10.

102. In *Reading the News*, p. 166.

103. See Steve Weinberg, *For Their Eyes Only: How Presidential Appointees Treat Public Documents as Personal Property* (Washington, DC: Center for Public Integrity, 1992) is a master statement of the problems posed by this situation.

104. See, for example, Douglas C. McGill, "Historical Society Is Planning Cuts to Meet Crisis," *New York Times*, June 28, 1988, pp. C15, C20; McGill, "Museum's Downfall: Raiding Endowment to Pay for Growth," *New York Times*, July 19, 1988, pp. C15, C18; and McGill, "Historical Society Director Quits and Trustees Dismiss His Deputy," *New York Times*, July 28, 1988, pp. A1, C24.

105. Andrew Decker, "Museums under Scrutiny: Two Institutions Face Ethical Charges," *Museum News* 67 (November–December 1988): 26–29.

106. W. Russell Neuman, Marion R. Just, and Ann N. Crigler, *Common Knowledge: News and the Construction of Political Meaning* (Chicago: University of Chicago Press, 1992), p. 4.

107. Vivienne R. Bourkoff and Julia Binder Wooldridge, "The Image of Libraries and Librarians: Is It Changing?" *Public Library Quarterly* 6 (Winter 1985–1986): 55–63; Locke J. Morrisey and Donald O. Case, "There Goes My Image: The Perception of Male Librarians by Colleague, Student, and Self," *College and Research Libraries* 49 (September 1988): 453–464; Joan R. Duffy, "Images of Librarians and Librarianship: A Study," *Journal of Youth Services in Libraries* 3 (Summer 1990): 303–308; Gaby Divay, Ada M. Ducas, and Nicole Michaud-Oystryk, "Faculty Perceptions of Librarians at the University of Manitoba," *College and Research Libraries* 48 (January 1987): 27–35; Larry R. Oberg, Mary Kay Schleiter, and Michael Van Houten, "Faculty Perceptions of Librarians at Albion College: Status, Role, Contribution, and Contacts," *College and*

Research Libraries 50 (March 1989): 215–230; Pauline Wilson, *Stereotype and Status: Librarians in the United States* (Westport, CT: Greenwood Press, 1982). Wilson's study drew numerous comments and different points of view, such as Norman D. Stevens, "Our Images in the 1980s," *Library Trends* 36 (Spring 1988): 825–851; Hans Prins and Wilco de Gier, "Image, Status and Reputation of Librarianship," *IFLA Journal* 18, no. 2 (1992): 108–119.

108. Published in J. Bronowski, *A Sense of the Future: Essays in Natural Philosophy* (Cambridge, MA: MIT Press, 1977), pp. 1–5.

109. Helen Nosworthy, "Reaching Out: A Core Program for Australian Archives," in *The Records Continuum: Ian Maclean and Australian Archives First Fifty Years*, ed. Sue McKemmish and Michael Piggott (Clayton: Ancora Press in association with Australian Archives, 1994), pp. 64–77.

110. Charlie Farrugia, "Print Media Perspectives on Recordkeeping," *Archives and Manuscripts* 21 (May 1993): 78–89. Compare his conclusions to my earlier discussion of the *New York Times*.

111. Bob Sharman, "The Hollow Crown," *Archives and Manuscripts* 21 (May 1993): 196–207.

112. Richard H. Isaacson and Gary L. Bogart, eds., *Children's Catalog*, 14th ed. (New York: H. W. Wilson Co., 1981); Carolyn W. Lima, *A to Zoo: Subject Access to Children's Picture Books* (New York: R. R. Bowker, 1982, 1986, and 1989); Virginia H. Richey and Katharyn E. Puckett, *Wordless/Almost Wordless Picture Books: A Guide* (Englewood, CO: Libraries Unlimited, 1992); James L. Thomas, *Play, Learn and Grow* (New Providence, NJ: R. R. Bowker, 1992); *Children's Books in Print 1994* (New Providence, NJ: R. R. Bowker, 1994); Lauren K. Lee, ed., *The Elementary School Library Collection*, 19th ed. (Williamsport, PA: Brodart Co., 1994).

113. The definition is as follows: "records kept in an office, library, or other place of storage; collection of such records or place where they are kept may be called an archive; most countries have a state-controlled national archive." *Children's Britannica* (Chicago: Encyclopedia Britannica, 1988), 20: 39. Other similar definitions appear in references such as *Webster's New Elementary Dictionary* (New York: G. & C. Merriam Co., 1975), p. 26 with related definitions for document, manuscript, and record (pp. 152, 305); David B. Guralnik, ed., *Webster's New World Dictionary for Young Readers* (n.p.: William Collins Publishers, 1979), pp. 37, 218, 447, 614.

114. There are no references, for example, in the following: *The Random House Children's Encyclopedia* (New York: Random House, 1991); E. L. Thorndike and Clarence L. Barnhart, *Scott, Foresman Beginning Dictionary* (Garden City, NY: Doubleday and Company, 1976), although this reference includes definitions for document, manuscript, and record (pp. 171, 356, 491).

115. Duane Champagne, ed., *The Native North American Almanac* (Detroit: Gale Research, 1994), pp. 176–181, 1197–1199.

116. Harry A. Ploski and James Williams, eds., *The Negro Almanac: A Reference Work on the African American*, 5th ed. (Detroit: Gale Research, 1989), p. 107.

117. Joy Hakim, *The First Americans, a History of US* (New York: Oxford University Press, 1993), pp. 60, 62.

118. Kathy Pelta, *Discovering Christopher Columbus: How History Is Invented* (Minneapolis: Lerner Publications Co., 1991).

119. Alice Provensen and Martin Provensen, *Shaker Lane* (New York: Puffin Books, 1987), p. 19.

120. Lynda G. Adamson, *A Reference Guide to Historical Fiction for Children and*

Young Adults (Westport, CT: Greenwood Press, 1987), p. x. Her more recent guide is *Recreating the Past: A Guide to American and World Historical Fiction for Children and Young Adults* (Westport, CT: Greenwood Press, 1994).

121. Gary Crews, *Strange Objects* (New York: Simon and Schuster, 1993).

122. Vicki Cobb (illustrations by Marilyn Hafner), *Writing It Down* (New York: J. B. Lippincott, 1989).

123. Helen Jacobson and Florence Mischel (illustrated by Laszlo Roth), *The First Book of Letter Writing* (New York: Franklin Watts, 1957), p. 5. See also, Sesyle Joslin (illustrated by Irene Haas), *Dear Dragon . . . and Other Useful Letter Forms for Young Ladies and Gentlemen Engaged in Everyday Correspondence* (New York: Harcourt, Brace and World, 1962).

124. Walter Buehr, *Sending the Word: The Story of Communication* (New York: G. P. Putnam's Sons, 1959).

125. Leonard Everett Fisher, *Colonial American Craftsmen: The Printers* (New York: Franklin Watts, 1965); Elizabeth Dean, illus. Erwin Schachner, *Printing: Tool of Freedom* (Englewood Cliffs, NJ: Prentice Hall, 1964).

126. Lynn Myring and Ian Graham, *Information Revolution* (London: Usborne Publishing, 1983).

127. Lorraine Henriod (illustrations by Janet Potter D'Amato), *Ancestor Hunting* (New York: Julian Messner, 1979), p. 32.

128. Kay Cooper (illustrations by Anthony Accardo), *Where Did You Get Those Eyes? A Guide to Discovering Your Family History* (New York: Walker and Co., 1988).

129. Henry Gilfond, *Genealogy: How to Find Your Roots* (New York: Franklin Watts, 1978), p. 62.

130. Suzanne Hilton, *Who Do You Think You Are? Digging for Your Family Roots* (Philadelphia: Westminster Press, 1976), p. 28.

131. Hilton, *Who Do You Think You Are?* p. 145.

132. Hilton, *Who Do You Think You Are?* p. 104.

133. Ira Wolfman, *Do People Grow on Family Trees? Genealogy for Kids and Other Beginners; The Official Ellis Island Handbook* (New York: Workman Publishing, 1991), pp. 77, 80, 118, 133.

134. Wolfman, *Do People Grow on Family Trees?* p. 116.

135. Wolfman, *Do People Grow on Family Trees?* p. 127.

136. Wolfman, *Do People Grow on Family Trees?* p. 143.

137. Kay Cooper (illustrated by Anthony Accardo), *Who Put the Cannon in the Courthouse Square?* A Discover It Yourself Book (New York: Avon Camelot Book, 1993), pp. 3, 13, 23, 38, 41.

138. Cooper, *Who Put the Cannon in the Courthouse Square?* p. 17.

139. Helen H. Carey and Judith E. Greenberg, *How to Use Primary Sources* (New York: Franklin Watts, 1983), pp. 71–72. One of the authors wrote a companion volume which provides considerably less detail on archives and archivists; see Helen H. Carey and Deborah R. Hanka, *How to Use Your Community as a Resource* (New York: Franklin Watts, 1983).

140. Linda Carlson Johnson, *Our Constitution* (Brookfield, CT: Millbrook Press, 1992), p. 45.

141. Peter Spier, *The Star-Spangled Banner* (New York: Doubleday and Co., 1973), p. 40.

142. For other failed opportunities, see Denis J. Hauptly, *"A Convention of Dele-*

gates": The Creation of the Constitution (New York: Atheneum, 1987); Doris Faber and Harold Faber, *We the People: The Story of the United States Constitution Since 1787* (New York: Charles Scribners, 1987). The Fabers' book includes a brief introductory mention of the fact that the original document is on display at the National Archives, but this work provides no other information.

143. Isabelle Brent, *The Christmas Story* (New York: Dial Books, 1989). There are exceptions to this problem. Deborah Nourse Lattimore's *The Sailor Who Captured the Sea: A Story of the Book of Kells* (New York: HarperCollins, 1991) also mimics the medieval illumination style, but her book concerns the making of this medieval manuscript with a brief introduction about its production and current location. Still, even this volume does not treat the issues of the book's subsequent caretakers and preservation.

144. Milton Meltzer, ed., *The American Revolutionaries: A History in Their Own Words 1750–1800* (New York: Thomas Y. Crowell, 1987), p. 201.

145. Leonard Everett Fisher, *The Death of Evening Star: The Diary of a Young New England Whaler* (New York: Doubleday and Company, 1972).

146. Maria A. Perez-Stable and Mary Hurlbut Cordier, *Understanding American History through Children's Literature: Instructional Units and Activities for Grades K–8* (Phoenix, AZ: Oryx Press, 1994), p. 126.

147. See, for example, Vandelia VanMeter, *American History for Children and Young Adults: An Annotated Bibliographic Index* (Englewood, CO: Libraries Unlimited, 1990).

148. See, for example, Evelyn B. Freeman and Linda Levstik, "Recreating the Past: Historical Fiction in the Social Studies Curriculum," *Elementary School Journal* 88 (March 1988): 329–337. Even William Bigelow, "Once Upon a Genocide: Christopher Columbus in Children's Literature," *Language Arts* 69 (February 1992): 112–120 does a comparison to children's literature with the "historical record" in which the historical record is a series of recent books on Columbus not archival sources.

149. For museums: Judith Tropea (photography by John Halpern), *A Day in the Life of a Museum Curator* (Mahwah, NJ: Troll Associates, 1991), describing the work of Niles Eldredge at the American Museum of Natural History; Lisa Weil, *Let's Go to the Museum* (New York: Holiday House, 1989); Margaret Rey and Alan J. Shalleck, eds., *Curious George and the Dinosaur* (Boston: Houghton Mifflin Co., 1989). For libraries: Anne Rockwell, *I Like the Library* (New York: E. P. Dutton, 1977); Claire McInerney, illus. Harry Pulver, *Find It: The Inside Story at Your Library* (Minneapolis: Lerner Publications Co., 1989); Barry D. Cytron, *Fire! The Library Is Burning* (Minneapolis: Lerner Publications Co., 1988), a description of the 1966 fire and subsequent recovery of the Jewish Theological Seminary in New York City; Jack Knowlton, illus. Harriett Barton, *Books and Libraries* (New York: HarperCollins, 1991); Gail Gibbons, *Check It Out! The Book About Libraries* (New York: Harcourt Brace Jovanovich, 1985); Martha Alexander, *How My Library Grew by Dinah* (New York: H. W. Wilson Co., 1983); Barbara A. Huff, illust. Iris Van Rynbach, *Once Inside the Library* (Boston: Little, Brown and Company, 1957); Deborah Hautzig, illus. Joe Mathieu, *A Visit to the Sesame Street Library* (New York: Random House/Children's Theatre Workshop, 1986).

150. Gail E. Haley, *Dream Peddler* (New York: Dutton's Children's Books, 1993), p. 7.

151. See, for example, Jack Knowlton, illus. Harriet Barton, *Books and Libraries* (New York: HarperTrophy, 1991).

152. Elizabeth Noll, "Accuracy and Authenticity in American Indian Children's Lit-

erature: The Social Responsibility of Authors and Illustrators," *New Advocate* 8 (Winter 1995): 29–43 (esp. pp. 38–39).

153. E. L. Konigsburg, *From the Mixed-Up Files of Mrs. Basil E. Frankweiler* (New York: Atheneum, 1967).

154. Eileen Van Kirk, "Imagining the Past through Historical Novels," *School Library Journal* 39 (August 1993): 50–51.

155. Dorothy and Thomas Hoobler, "Writing History for Children," *School Library Journal* 38 (January 1992): 37–38.

156. Marcia Sewall, "The Pilgrims of Plimouth," *Horn Book Magazine* 64 (January–February 1988): 33.

157. Glenda Acland, "Managing the Record Rather Than the Relic," *Archives and Manuscripts* 20 (May 1992): 59.

158. Jill Ker Conway, *The Road from Coorain* (New York: Vintage Books, 1989), p. 17.

159. I have discussed the value of such writings for education in my "Debating the Future of the Book," *American Libraries* 28 (February 1997): 52–55.

160. Donald A. Norman, *The Design of Everyday Things* (New York: Doubleday, 1988); *Turn Signals Are the Facial Expressions of Automobiles* (New York: Addison-Wesley Publishing Co., 1992); and *Things That Make Us Smart: Defending Human Attributes in the Age of the Machine* (New York: Addison-Wesley Publishing Co., 1993).

161. See, for example, James B. Rule, Douglas McAdam, Linda Stearns, and David Uglow, "Documentary Identification and Mass Surveillance in the United States," *Social Problems* 31 (December 1983): 222–234 and William H. Minor, "Identity Cards and Databases in Health Care: The Need for Federal Privacy Protections," *Columbia Journal of Law and Social Problems* 28 (Winter 1995): 253–296.

162. Ample discussion about the ATM phenomenon is in Lewis Mandell, *The Credit Card Industry: A History* (Boston: Twayne Publishers, 1990).

163. The influence of the credit card on the average American can be gained from reading Joseph Nocera's *A Piece of the Action: How the Middle Class Joined the Money Class* (New York: Simon and Schuster, 1994).

164. The problems posed by this can be seen in Thomas L. Lincoln, Daniel J. Essin, and Willis H. Ware, "The Electronic Medical Record: A Challenge for Computer Science to Develop Clinically and Socially Relevant Computer Systems to Coordinate Information for Patient Care and Analysis," *Information Society* 9, no. 2 (1993): 157–188.

165. Some understanding of the impact of the video cassette recorder can be seen in Mark R. Levy, ed., *The VCR Age: Home Video and Mass Communication* (Newbury Park, CA: Sage Publications, 1989).

166. See, Natalie Robins, *Alien Ink: The FBI's War on Freedom of Expression* (New Brunswick, NJ: Rutgers University Press, 1992).

167. Pierre Salinger, *The Dossier* (New York: New American Library, 1984); Michael Palumbo, *The Waldheim Files* (London: Faber and Faber, 1988); Steven Naifeh and Gregory White Smith, *The Mormon Murders* (New York: New American Library, 1988); Robert Harris, *Selling Hitler* (New York: Penguin Books, 1986).

168. The full statement is in "Archivist: A Definition," SAA *Newsletter*, January 1984, pp. 4–5.

169. *Code of Ethics for Archivists* (Chicago: Society of American Archivists, 1992). The code notes that "legitimate complaints about an institution or an archivist may be made through proper channels," but what are these channels? At another point, it is

stated that "Archivists avoid irresponsible criticism of other archivists or institutions and address complaints about professional or ethical conduct to the individual or institution concerned, or to a professional archival organization." It appears that the professional archival organization would be the last resort, but there is no such organization with a mechanism for effectively dealing with such complaints. The SAA Council has established a standing committee on ethics and professional conduct, but it is far too early to determine just what this committee *will* do and *how* effective it will be.

170. Karen Benedict, "Archival Ethics," in *Managing Archives and Archival Institutions*, ed. James Gregory Bradsher (Chicago: University of Chicago Press, 1989), pp. 174–184; Elena S. Danielson, "The Ethics of Access," *American Archivist* 52 (1989): 52–62; David Horn, "The Development of Ethics in Archival Practice," *American Archivist* 52 (1989): 64–71; Herman Kahn, "The Long Range Implications for Historians and Archivists of the Charges Against the Franklin D. Roosevelt Library," *American Archivist* 34 (1971): 265–275; Philip Mason, "Ethics of Collecting," *Georgia Archive* 5 (1977): 36–50; Heather MacNeil, *Without Consent: The Ethics of Disclosing Personal Information in Public Archives* (Metuchen, NJ: Scarecrow Press, 1992); Harold L. Miller, "Will Access Restrictions Hold Up in Court? The FBI's Attempt to Use the Braden Papers at the State Historical Society of Wisconsin," *American Archivist* 52 (1989): 180–190; Diane S. Nixon, "Providing Access to Controversial Public Records: The Case of the Robert F. Kennedy Assassination Investigation Files," *Public Historian* 11 (1989): 29–44; and Richard Polenberg, "The Roosevelt Library Case: A Review Article," *American Archivist* 34 (1971): 277–284 are typical of the writings that have been published in the professional literature. The other essays that could be cited are not significantly greater in number nor do they reveal a range of sufficiently broad research approaches or coverage of the potential topics.

171. "Archives and Culture: An Essay," in Peter Walne, comp., *Modern Archives Administration and Records Management: A RAMP Reader*, PGI-85/WS/32 (Paris: UNESCO, December 1985), pp. 432–433.

172. Harold P. Anderson, "Banking on the Past: Wells Fargo and Company," *Business History Bulletin* 1 (no. 1, [1988]): 12.

173. Committee on the Records of Government, *Report* (Washington, DC.: The Committee, March 1985).

174. Thomas Vargish, "The Value of Humanities in Executive Development," *Sloan Management Review* 32 (Spring 1991): 88.

175. David Margolick, "Whose Words Are They, Anyway," *New York Times Book Review*, November, 1 1987, p. 1, 44–45 describes the court decision and the various implications. See also Christopher Runkel, "Salinger v. Random House: The Case," in Mary Boccaccio, ed., *Constitutional Issues and Archives* (n.p.: Mid-Atlantic Regional Archives Conference, 1988), pp. 49–60 and Michael Les Benedict, "Salinger v. Random House: Implications for Scholars' Use," in Boccaccio, ed., *Constitutional Issues*, pp. 61–70.

176. Donald W. Jackanicz, "Theft at the National Archives: The Murphy Case, 1962–1975," *Library and Archival Security* 10, no. 2 (1990): 23–50.

177. For some of the discussion about replevin see James E. O'Neill, "Replevin: A Public Archivist's Perspective," *College and Research Libraries* 40 (January 1979): 26–30; William S. Price, Jr., "N. C. v. B. C. West, Jr.," *American Archivist* 41 (January 1978): 21–24.

178. The Society of American Archivists created an Ad Hoc Committee on Replevin

in the late 1970s to deal with the B. C. West case in North Carolina. This committee resolved the "right of public access to public records," that "archival repositories immediately cease to acquire public records if an appropriate public archival depository is available," and that "federal, state and municipal archives, within the limitation of laws governing their conduct, consider designating private and other public agencies presently holding public records 'repositories of record.' " What is *more* interesting is the apparent lack of any movement by the archival profession to lobby for stronger legislation to *protect* their archival records. The SAA response was an inward-looking action, advising archivists in their individual situations but not adopting any stronger advocacy platform other than wanting "to establish a meaningful dialogue" between various parties." See "Replevin Committee Draft Statement," *SAA Newsletter* (September 1979): 8–9.

179. [Howard Lowell], *Preservation Needs in State Archives* (Albany, NY: National Association of Government Archives and Records Administrators, February 1986).

180. Archie P. McDonald, "County Records: Are They Worth Anything?" *Texas Libraries* 38 (Spring 1976): 43–44.

181. SAA's Code of Ethics is available at http://www.archivists.org/vision/ethics.html.

182. ARMA's code is available at http://www.arma.org/codeofethics/.

183. J. Michael Pemberton and Lee O. Pendergraft, "Toward a Code of Ethics: Social Relevance and the Professionalization of Records Managers," *Records Management Quarterly* 32 (October 1998): 51–57.

184. Jorge Reina Schement and Terry Curtis, *Tendencies and Tensions of the Information Age: The Production and Distribution of Information in the United States* (New Brunswick, NJ: Transaction Publishers, 1995), p. 10.

185. Schement and Curtis, *Tendencies and Tensions of the Information Age*, p. 141.

186. Charles C. Mann, "Who Will Own Your Next Good Idea?" *Atlantic Monthly* 282 (September 1998): 57–62, 64–66, 68, 72–74, 76, 78–80, 82 (quotations pp. 57, 58, and 59).

187. See, for example, SAA's August 1997 statement on intellectual property at http://www.archivists.org/governance/resolutions/nha; pc20response.html.

188. Richard J. Severson, *The Principles of Information Ethics* (Armonk, NY: M. E. Sharpe, 1997), pp. 58–59.

189. William Wresch, *Disconnected: Haves and Have-Nots in the Information Age* (New Brunswick, NJ: Rutgers University Press, 1996), p. 159.

190. Fred H. Cate, *Privacy in the Information Age* (Washington, DC.: Brookings Institution Press, 1997), pp. 2, 80–81.

191. Bob Herbert, "What Privacy Rights?" *New York Times*, September 27, 1998, p. 15.

192. John Ralston Saul, *Voltaire's Bastards: The Dictatorship of Reason in the West* (New York: The Free Press, 1992), p. 29.

193. Whitfield Diffie and Susan Landau, *Privacy on the Line: The Politics of Wiretapping and Encryption* (Cambridge, MA: MIT Press, 1998), p. 148.

194. "The End of Privacy," *Economist*, May 1, 1999, p. 23.

195. Barry Sanders, *The Private Death of Public Discourse* (Boston: Beacon Press, 1998), p. 6.

196. Alexandra Johnson, *The Hidden Writer: Diaries and the Creative Life* (New York: Anchor Book, Doubleday, 1997), p. 18.

197. Michael L. Dertouzos, *What Will Be: How the New World of Information Will Change Our Lives* (San Francisco: HarperEdge, 1997), p. 225.

198. Amitai Etzioni, *The Limits of Privacy* (New York: Basic Books, 1999), pp. 4, 10.

199. Ellen Alderman and Caroline Kennedy. *The Right to Privacy* (New York: Vintage Books, 1997), pp. 10, 27.

200. Gregory J. E. Rawlins, *Moths to the Flame: The Seductions of Computer Technology* (Cambridge, MA: MIT Press, 1996), p. 21.

201. Stuart Shapiro, "Places and Spaces: The Historical Interaction of Technology, Home, and Privacy," *The Information Society* 14 (1998): 275–284.

202. This statement is available at http://www.archivists.org/governance/resolutions/hiss.htm.

203. Evan Imber-Black, *The Secret Life of Families: Truth-Telling, Privacy, and Reconciliation in a Tell-All Society* (New York: Bantam Books, 1998), p. 39.

204. Martha Cooley, *The Archivist: A Novel* (Boston: Little, Brown and Co., 1998), p. 322.

205. Ann Balough, "Privacy and Security in the Electronic Universe: Issues, Problems, and Opportunities," *Records and Information Management Report* 15 (June 1999): 15.

206. Sissela Bok, *Secrets: On the Ethics of Concealment and Revelation* (New York: Vintage Books, 1983), p. 24.

207. *Archival Outlook*, July 1993, p. 5.

208. Angus MacKenzie, *Secrets: The CIA's War at Home* (Berkeley: University of California Press, 1997).

209. Carla Anne Robbins, "At Secret Factory, CIA Edits Files for Public Consumption," *Wall Street Journal*, March 19, 1998. In a report of a State Department's historians committee released in the Spring 1998, there was sharp criticism of the CIA for being slow in releasing records from the 1950s and 1960s. Warren F. Kimball, chairman of the committee, stated that this is a "violation of the law and of American standards" and that "This Republic cannot survive if Government is secret and not held accountable for its actions"; Tim Weiner, "Panel Says C.I.A.'s Secrecy Threatens to Make History a Lie," *New York Times*, April 9, 1998, p. A19.

210. "The Price of History," *New York Times*, July 19, 1998, A14.

211. Tim Weiner, "A Blast at Secrecy in Kennedy Killing," *New York Times*, September 29, 1998, p. A17.

212. George Lardner, Jr., "Electronic Open Records Law Compilance 'Inadequate,' Group Says," *Washington Post*, April 26, 1998.

213. Linda Lotridge Levin, "Let the Sun Shine on Government," *Providence Journal-Bulletin*, February 26, 1998.

214. Kyle Niederpruem, "Getting Access to Public Documents in Indiana Can Be Like a Day Without 'Sunshine,' " *Indianapolis Star/News*, February 21, 1998.

215. Joyce Carol Oates, "Words of Love, Priced to Sell," *New York Times*, May 18, 1999, p. A31.

216. Janna Malamud Smith, *Private Matters: In Defense of the Personal Life* (Reading, MA: Addison-Wesley Publishing Co., 1997), pp. 11–12.

217. Donald H. Rieman, *The Study of Modern Manuscripts: Public, Confidential, and Private* (Baltimore: Johns Hopkins University Press, 1993), p. 53.

218. Smith, *Private Matters*, p. 59.

219. Cate, *Privacy in the Information Age*, pp. 31, 52.

220. E. Wayne Carp, *Family Matters: Secrecy and Disclosure in the History of Adoption* (Cambridge, MA: Harvard University Press, 1998), p. 102.

221. Carp, *Family Matters*, p. 147.

222. Carp, *Family Matters*, pp. 165–168, 188–189.

223. Brian D. Loader, ed., *The Governance of Cyberspace: Politics, Technology, and Global Restructuring* (New York: Routledge, 1997), p. 156.

224. David Brin, *The Transparent Society: Will Technology Force Us to Choose between Privacy and Freedom?* (Reading, MA: Addison-Wesley Publishing Co., 1998), p. 68.

225. Brin, *The Transparent Society*, p. 91.

226. Brin, *The Transparent Society*, p. 149.

227. Richard D. Brown, *The Strength of a People: The Idea of an Informed Citizenry in America 1650–1870* (Chapel Hill: University of North Carolina Press, 1996).

228. Ian Buruma, *The Wages of Guilt: Memories of War in Germany and Japan* (New York: Meridian, 1994), p. 264.

229. Timothy Garton Ash, *The File: A Personal History* (New York: Random House, 1997), p. 226.

230. David Oshinsky and Richard Rubin, "Should the Mississippi Files Have Been Reopened?" *New York Times Magazine*, August 30, 1998, pp. 30–37; Kevin Sack, "Mississippi Unseals Files of Agency That Fought Desegregation," *New York Times*, March 18, 1998.

231. Christopher Morgan, "Queen Mother's Papers Destroyed," London *Times*, June 21, 1998.

232. Stanton A. Glantz, John Slade, Lisa A. Bero, Peter Hanauer, and Deborah E. Barnes, *The Cigarette Papers* (Berkeley: University of California Press, 1996), p. 236.

233. Glantz et al., *The Cigarette Papers*, p. 437.

234. Ernst R. May and Philip D. Zelikow, eds., *The Kennedy Tapes: Inside the White House during the Cuban Missile Crisis* (Cambridge, MA: Belknap Press of Harvard University Press, 1997), p. 692.

235. May and Zelikow, *The Kennedy Tapes*, p. 698.

236. Tom Blanton, ed., *White House E-Mail: The Top Secret Computer Messages the Reagan/Bush White House Tried to Destroy* (New York: The New Press, 1995), p. 3.

237. Blanton, *White House E-Mail*, p. 21.

238. Robert Jay Lifton and Greg Mitchell, *Hiroshima in America: A Half Century of Denial* (New York: Avon Books, 1995), pp. 270–271.

239. Lifton and Mitchell, *Hiroshima in America*, p. 332.

240. Richard Handler and Eric Gable, *The New History in an Old Museum: Creating the Past at Colonial Williamsburg* (Durham, NC: Duke University Press, 1997), p. 22.

241. Philip Weiss, "The Book Thief: A True Tale of Bibliomania," *Harper's* 288 (January 1994): 37–56.

242. Victoria Bellotti, "Design for Privacy in Multimedia Computing and Communications Environments," in Philip E. Agre and Marc Rotenberg, eds., *Technology and Privacy: The New Landscape* (Cambridge, MA: MIT Press, 1997), pp. 63–64.

243. Severson, *The Principles of Information Ethics*, pp. 67–68.

244. Colin J. Bennett, "Convergence Revisited: Toward a Global Policy for the Protection of Personal Data?" in Agre and Marc Rotenberg, eds., *Technology and Privacy*, p. 113.

245. Simon G. Davies, "Re-Engineering the Right to Privacy: How Privacy Has Been Transformed from a Right to a Commodity," in Agre and Rotenberg, eds., *Technology and Privacy*, p. 161.

246. Richard Breitman, *Official Secrets: What the Nazis Planned, What the British and Americans Knew* (New York: Hill and Wang, 1998), p. 246.

247. Athan G. Theoharis, ed., *A Culture of Secrecy: The Government versus the People's Right to Know* (Lawrence: University Press of Kansas, 1998), p. 13.

248. Joan Hoff, "The Endless Saga of the Nixon Tapes," in Theoharis, ed., *A Culture of Secrecy*, pp. 115–139.

249. Charles D. Raab and Colin J. Bennett, "The Distribution of Privacy Risks: Who Needs Protection?" *The Information Society* 14 (1998): 264, 267.

250. Jeffrey Archer, *Honor Among Thieves* (New York: Harper Paperbacks, 1993), p. 116.

Chapter 5

Supporting Policy:
Educating Records Professionals

INTRODUCTION

Knowing that records are important to society and that records professionals face complicated and troublesome issues should say something about the nature of their education. For there to be professionals competent to develop records policies, education is a critical necessity. In this final chapter education is examined, focusing on the education of archivists for two reasons. Archival education is the older more and comprehensive of the instructional systems for records professionals, dating back sixty years and always at the graduate level. Records managers primarily continue to rely on undergraduate offerings, with less well-defined standards and reliance on an apprenticeship or career ladder system. The more important reason, however, is this author's personal conviction that graduate archival education, especially with its interdisciplinary orientation, provides the fullest platform for the education of *all* records professionals. While there are problems with this, not the least *what* this education should be called, the development of more comprehensive educational programs, a stronger professional literature, and a greater research orientation all suggest that graduate archival education programs may be evolving into the primary educational orientation to the records professions.

CONTINUING ISSUES FACING NORTH AMERICAN
ARCHIVAL EDUCATION

In 1982, before efforts to assemble comprehensive graduate programs, Richard Berner painted a gloomy portrait of archival education in the United States. The literature on the topic was "disheartening," questions about who would teach and how archival science could be taught remained, most practitioners "taught themselves while learning the job," and a "narrow mastery of mere techniques" was the norm. Berner describes the source of these problems as being the lack of formalization of archival education in the academy that would also provide teachers and graduate students who "could pursue problems that practitioners face daily but have little time to resolve with the needed care." Berner did not see, from the vantage of the early 1980s, much changing,[1] but much changed before *and* since then. A decade before Berner's assessment, the education of archivists looked worse. Robert Warner, in 1972, described archival education as being done on a shoestring with part-time faculty, modest financial resources, "programs" of one or two courses, student bodies of undetermined origins and objectives, and a weighing of teaching and course content toward the historical profession. Warner also detected a "very rapid growth" from the 1960s, but he noted some severe problems—especially the lack of "cooperation or idea sharing among instructors teaching archival courses." Warner called on the Society of American Archivists to take a more active leadership in education, ranging from a coordinating role to providing a forum.[2]

Archival education, at least in comparison with Berner's and Warner's assessments, looks better today. It is established in the academy, there is a corps of regular faculty teaching archival science, faculty and graduate students are studying archival topics, and the profession has come a long way in defining what should be taught. A decade ago Paul Conway worried about the hiring and presence of regular (full-time, tenure stream) archival educators in the academy, but this is *not* the current issue. Conway viewed the "archival education system [as] a drag on the development of the archival profession, because it [was] tied too closely to the very practitioners it serves."[3] Now there is a significant corps of educators, and some schools (like the universities of British Columbia, Maryland, Michigan, Pittsburgh, and Toronto) support two or more faculty members in this discipline. Still, some issues remain about the education of archivists.

The early development of North American archival education has been well described in articles by Frank Evans, Richard Berner, Jacqueline Goggin, and others. These essays characterize the first half century of education, from the first formal course offered by Solon Buck in 1938–1939 at Columbia University through the emergence of other individual courses, short-term institutes, the establishment of the initial multi-course specializations in library schools and history departments, to the development of the first separate degree program at the University of British Columbia in 1981.[4] The embracing, in principle at least, by the American archival profession of the concept of a separate masters' degree in archival studies and the unanticipated growth in the number of full-time archival educators teaching in North America completes the story, *except* for some recurring themes and issues that have not been resolved and require more thought, work, debate, and research. The issues discussed here—educating specialists, contending with practice and training, working with individuals established in the profession, determining the content and focus of teaching, relating archival science to other disciplines, and building the graduate education infrastructure—are representative of these issues. They reflect the "turning point" characterized by Shelley Sweeney, one of the first students in the University of British Columbia program: "From this point we can forge ahead by continuing to support advanced education for the archivist, we can dither in indecision and go nowhere, or we can languish and begin to regress by lowering our standards."[5] Equipping archivists to be able to discern and develop effective records policies is part of these concerns.

One of the unresolved issues is determining appropriate educational backgrounds for differing types of archival and records management work. In 1939 historian Samuel Flagg Bemis, in one of the pioneering American essays on archival education, argued for the concept of a first and second class of archivists. The first class would possess a doctorate and be involved in "responsible archival direction in major municipal, state, and national archives." The second class would work in "small municipal divisions, county, state and special commissions, authorities, and establishments of minor political significance, as well as archivists for business firms, corporations, banks, and other private enterprises." Not surprisingly, given Bemis's background and the time, the education for both classes would be grounded in history.[6]

While records professionals can be critical of the class structure envisioned by Bemis, he touched an issue that needed to be addressed systematically but that has been addressed by default (and *not* too successfully) via other venues. Europeans a generation later were working on this matter. English archivist Roger Ellis in 1967 describes becoming "used to seeing the archivist perform all duties, from janitor to meeting with heads of major institutions."[7] Another English archivist, Lionel Bell, provides fuller discussion of this issue, calling for understanding the differing needs for *traditional or primitive archives* ("an accumulation of records which is fairly static, generally of some antiquity, deriving from the activities of a body of limited size such as a family or long-established business house"), *pioneering archives* (a "broad subject" or "geographical or administrative area, and the archives pursues a policy of seeking out and collecting relevant material from any source"), and *establishment archives* ("archives . . . geared to servicing a single institution by regular reception of its records"). Archivists in primitive archives, according to Bell, have "only a limited need of techniques" and do not need full courses, while those in pioneering archives need exposure to the fullest range of archival techniques.[8]

The fullest articulation of targeting different archival work with a variety of educational venues comes from Michael Cook and the UNESCO harmonization program for librarians, archivists, and documentalists for developing countries. Writing in the late 1980s, Cook views paraprofessionals doing "tasks which are essentially in the professional field . . . , but which are carried out as processes, and in a setting where there is supervision by professional superiors." He adds a professional level, staffed by graduates of educational programs: "Their professional work involves the design and supervision of the professional processes, and they have to participate as active and intelligent agents in the information, administrative and research activities." Finally, there is a level doing "management and planning and [working] with external relations."[9] It is in this final, highest, level where policy resides.

North American archival education has not considered such differentiation among records professionals. There is a two-year diploma program at Algonquin College in Canada for the training of archives technicians, but this effort has occurred without consultation and coordination with the graduate programs. A more profitable route is that advocated by James O'Toole for incorporating specializations and types of repository environments into a full curriculum with an emphasis on archival knowledge,[10] but the American archival profession has yet to address such matters seriously. As a result, the Academy of Certified Archivists certification creates a separate credential having its greatest appeal to the individual who is in the profession but who lacks other professional credentials or formal work in one of the graduate archival education programs. It is a credential best suited for a lower-level technician's work.[11]

Is the North American archival profession ready or willing to make such distinctions? For a considerable time it has seemed to indicate that archivists are primarily responsible for arrangement, description and reference. Yet, there is also a need for individuals who are able to work as advocates for archival programs, work with systems designers to develop electronic recordkeeping systems, fit into the primary needs of parent organizations (to be administrators), and assist organizations to manage records for purposes of accountability, evidence, and corporate memory. Each archival educator must ask himself or herself what they think they are educating individuals for, a concern that other information professions are struggling with as well.

The relationship between practice and theory has been a major issue for every profession, including archivists and records managers. Over a half century ago Solon Buck wrote, "while experience alone cannot make one a professional archivist any more than could experience in the practice of medicine without theoretical training qualify one to be a physician, nevertheless experience coupled with extensive and intensive individual study might give one the equivalent of such training."[12] This seems still to be the prevailing sense within the archives community, although a shift has been occurring as graduate education has been established, grown, and matured. A rare survey of archival educators twenty years ago found a preoccupation with practical experience.[13] Educators associated with the masters of archival studies degree have taken a different approach. Terry Eastwood states, the "first purpose of professional education, a purpose which ought to permeate everything students are asked to do, is to inculcate a body of general principles, a theoretical framework, if you will, which supports and guides the actual practice of the profession. . . . We should not be betrayed by the practical aspects of administering archives into thinking education for archivists is primarily an osmotic process of learning how it is done."[14] Yet, many individuals enter the discipline with the barest of formal training and basic skills.

Many practicing archivists stress that all can be learned on the job, ignoring that not all jobs provide the same levels of opportunities for learning about changing professional work. Despite some excellent statements about theory as a foundation for archival knowledge,[15] educators have been lax in writing about the centrality of theory and methodology to archival work[16] and have clung too closely to the notion of practice as the preeminent aspect of archival education. If archival educators lack a firm foundation for what they teach, *what* will they teach? Research is needed to provide understanding of why records are created, how recordkeeping systems evolve, and the importance of records supported by case studies. Research supports the development of theory, and theory is merely a framework to help students understand records basics. Unfortunately, what may be taught in many programs is current technique limiting students' ability to deal effectively with many of the problems they will face on the job.

Continuing education has been a vexing concern for North American archivists. Perplexing might be a better way to characterize this issue, as the decision about what should be the nature and content of continuing education must be worked out *after* decisions have been made about the basic knowledge for archivists. American archivists have only recently agreed in principle to a full-fledged masters' degree. As long as a potpourri of graduate "programs" supposedly turning out entry-level archivists exists, ranging from a single course taught by an adjunct practitioner to multiple-course concentrations in the United States to substantial MAS degrees, consensus cannot be achieved about the purpose, content, or delivery of continuing education courses, workshops, and institutes. Nevertheless, the profession may be in better shape than it was just a decade ago because it possesses examples of comprehensive educational programs and guidelines.[17]

The concern with continuing education has been a long-term issue for the North American archival profession. Twenty years ago Frank Evans argued for an institute to be offered by the SAA to be moved geographically for reaching the profession. Evans states, "we owe it to ourselves, as well as to all of our users, to make a serious effort to have archivists train archivists in a realistic program intended to meet the needs of those without adequate training who are already in archival positions."[18] While there is evidence that short-term workshops can have a positive impact in raising the knowledge of individuals with insufficient background for archives work, this is hardly the only issue regarding continuing education archivists should be mulling over.[19] Why has the profession not focused as well on the *advanced* needs for continuing education for those with adequate educational preparation?

There are many reasons why archivists need to re-think continuing education. Electronic records management is but one example. Fred Stielow argues archivists need to develop approaches in continuing education to retain currency in electronic records management or be "relegated to antiquarian status—the medieval monks of a post-industrial society."[20] Despite the fact that archivists have had a tremendous re-birth of interest in and re-formulation of strategies for electronic records plus a careful articulation of a curriculum for educating archivists about the technology prepared by the SAA Committee on Automated Records and Techniques, only a small portion of archival programs are effectively working with electronic records.[21]

There are other issues about continuing education that are just as serious. Archivists have discussed how to build bridges to other disciplines in order to educate these individuals about the nature of archival work. Wilfred Smith, in 1969, suggested that one of the objectives be "to provide librarians with archival training suitable for their profession" and "to provide graduate students in history and related subjects with a better understanding of the role of the archivist and the use of original source materials."[22] The malformed nature of library archives is certainly a glaring problem given the growing presence of archival education in library and information science schools,[23] but similar problems in other areas such as business are also evident. Why should archivists not establish archival education programs in business, law, medical, nursing, and other professional schools? Why should archivists not develop distance education and other innovative approaches to the delivery of education and training? Despite calls of twenty and more years ago to move in this direction, North American archivists have primarily stressed more traditional workshops and institutes.[24]

The archival profession has not lacked descriptions of *what* should be taught in an archives curriculum. Ernst Posner, in 1941, stated, the "study of and instruction in the history of record making and record administration are as necessary for the archivist of our times as was diplomatics for our predecessors."[25] Roger Ellis argued in 1967 that preservation needed to be seen as the core of any curriculum.[26] English archivist Lionel Bell, in 1971, provided a description of "archival techniques" such as provenance, arrangement, records management; "auxiliary techniques" such as reading and interpretation of documents, language, and bibliographic techniques; and "subject knowledge" which is primarily historical.[27] Michael Cook, a few years later, described a core with records management and archives administration, "auxiliary sciences to history and administrative history," and subjects common with other information professions and with other disciplines.[28] Frank Evans, at about the same time, urged that the "archivist must master by study of the holdings themselves most of the administrative history and the subject content of archival holdings which are, by definition, unique. All archivists, however, need an understanding of how institutions and organizations, both public and private, originate and develop; of types and patterns of internal organization and functions; of recordkeeping and records systems past and present; and of the relationship of documentation in all of its forms to organizations and functions."[29] Then there are the SAA graduate education guidelines in 1977, 1988, and 1994 and the ACA guidelines of 1976 and 1988.

It has taken the archival profession a long time to articulate the essence of its graduate education. Twenty years ago Hugh Taylor wrote, "ironically, it is just at a time when the old fragmentation and specialization of 'jobs' is collapsing in our post-industrial society that the archivist, having remained free so long, is seeking the right of other professionals to a recognized and recognizable pigeon hole. We may be the last to do so but, for a number of reasons, it seems that, in self-defense, we must. Society deserves professional value for its money, and requires from us a recognizable badge."[30] Many archival practitioners *still* do not see the need for systematic graduate education.[31] Thirty years ago Colson argued that many think that all the archivist does are but "routine tasks" that can be best taught on job, although he thought that a "professional archivist will not have much direct contact with these chores if his institution is properly staffed and organized."[32] Professional archivists should be developing or influencing policy, after all.

Apart from the professional associations' guidelines, archivists have had few proposals for how to convey the appropriate content in the education programs. Francis Blouin, in 1978, argued that archivists should not focus on who or what they are but on how they can best prepare people to function as archivists. Blouin contended that the case method was the appropriate approach because it is useful for conveying a small number of basic principles and because it is adaptable to the great variety of venues in which archivists work. Unfortunately, as Blouin suggests, this method depends on "systematic reporting of unusual or innovative decisions" as the raw material, and records professionals still lack such reporting.[33] There are even questions about how the existing curriculum in the established graduate archival education programs hold together with separate courses on electronic records management or other media such as visual materials with little apparent "fit" with the overall curriculum. As the Information Age office continuously evolves, is it still desirable to offer separate courses on electronic records management? Won't traditional, paper-based systems need to be relegated to courses on the history of archives and recordkeeping rather than be the educational focal points? When appraisal is considered, should the examples be increasingly from electronic recordkeeping systems? When students wrestle with archival descriptive standards, should such conversations and teaching occur in the context of new recordkeeping systems?[34] How do students learn about developing records policies?

Other than the universal debate in all fields about the relationship between theory and practice, the archives discipline has been most energetic in debating its relationship to other disciplines. The history versus library science debate has been extremely acrimonious, even though the schism between archivists and records managers has been less volatile but perhaps even more damaging to both fields. Arguments about the appropriate education of archivists have always been prone to devolve rapidly into arguments about whether such education can occur in history departments or library schools. G. Philip Bauer, almost a half a century ago, suggested training in history or social science was considered as the "most germane to all work with archives."[35] Within a generation, with increasing development of graduate archival education programs in library and information science schools, there was growing reaction to the issue. John Colson believed education could be located in library schools where it "emphasizes our joint concern for the systematic organization of knowledge regardless of its origin or format."[36] In 1977 Edwin Welch provided some interesting insights on the relationship between archivists, librarianship, and history, noting that "archivists are seriously divided on what is required" in the relationship.[37] By 1986 Richard Berner saw a field torn apart by librarianship, historians, and self-taught "archival fundamentalists," but worse he concluded that "lacking intellectual foundations to distinguish the world of archives from librarianship or from history, archivists have been claimed by both librarianship and by the history profession."[38] There are more obstacles to be overcome. In the statement archivists should seriously ponder, Anita Delaries, then a recent graduate of an archives education program, laments, "we were pursuing neither careers in historical research nor careers in librarianship. We were caught in a no man's land, a void, between the two professions."[39]

There have been some moderating voices. Raymond and O'Toole urge a de-emphasis on history and an emphasis on other fields such as public administration in order to stress the utility of archives.[40] In a classic essay, Lawrence McCrank, in 1979, strongly argued for why archivists need to maintain a connection to history, noting, "as historians digest, sift, distill, describe, explain, analyze, extrapolate, generalize, and theorize . . . , they seldom reflect on the survival of their documentation and their indebtedness to record keepers. . . . The archivist's profession is therefore not on the periphery of the historical discipline, but rather at its heart."[41] For McCrank the "critical issue is balance in the interplay between the two disciplines, history and library or information science, and whether or not a true blend can be achieved if archival training is placed in one or the other, instead of both simultaneously."[42] At the time he wrote, most archivists were still educated as historians.[43]

Why all this shifting in attitudes about the primary placement of the graduate archival programs? In 1968 Schellenberg dismissed the traditional European education of the archivist because of the nature of modern records and the diversity of programs caring for these records in North America: "In brief, then, American archivists should be trained to manage recent research records, most of which are organic in character. Since they are concerned with both public and private records, they should be trained to deal with both classes. Since they are involved with current records, they should be trained in the fundamentals of records management."[44] Schellenberg saw the best training in history because it leads the archivist to understand archives as source material for research and for learning how records "came into being."[45] He also argued for the archivist to be trained in methodology and technical topics such as conservation and auxiliary fields like records management and library science. He did not think archivists should be educated in history departments because "historians, while discussing methodology, will excessively emphasize historical developments" rather than methodology and they "will excessively emphasize the historical work required in appraising, arranging, and describing documentary material."[46] Schellenberg also detected dangers in training in library schools because "librarians will mistakenly apply the techniques of their own profession to archival material" and "become so engrossed with method that they will lose sight of the scholarly aspects of archival work."[47] Library schools are the better site, argued Schellenberg, because of the emphasis on methodology and public service.

Others followed the path suggested by Schellenberg. Andrew Watson, in 1975, made reference to finding students with "suitable personalities and the right attitude to archive work," that is "that they should be primarily interested in record-keeping and making records available to other people, and that they should not be attempting to enter the profession in the belief that their time will be spent on historical research."[48] Twenty years later students show up in archives classes who think this is exactly what they will be able to do if they become archivists; this is akin to the individual wanting to be a librarian or bookstore owner so that they will have time to read books. This may be the image resulting from the endless debate about information science versus history.[49] Hopefully, as McCrank recently writes, the future may be in a more inclusive historical information science rather than archives as mere sources for history and archivists as the servants of the historical scholars.[50]

While the debate about history or information science has been noisy, the schism between archivists and records managers has been more damaging. Frank Evans, in 1970, argued for the realignment of archives and records management, drawing on Jenkinson, Schellenberg, Ian Maclean, and Posner about the increasing practical realities of modern records requiring greater use of records management techniques.[51] Numerous other essays followed, criticizing, second-guessing, and lamenting the professional split, with evidence about mutual concerns, different approaches, but also disturbing differences of opinions about matters as basic as what constitutes a record.[52] This schism weakens the records life cycle or continuum, diminishes the ability of institutional archives/records management programs to be effective advocates for the administration of records, and undercuts the knowledge base of both archives and records management. The importance has been captured well by British archivist Michael Cook in 1980, noting that previously "archivists were thought of primarily as scholars, or perhaps as academic technicians, whose main functions were in connexion with historical research. . . . Today the view most widely accepted is that archivists ought to take part in current administration, in government or business, by sharing in information management."[53] The question this implies, however, is whether archival education programs are appropriately focused on records and recordkeeping systems rather than solely on the cultural management of historical records.

From the 1930s until well into the 1980s, most of the energy expended on archival education was dissipated into debates about the placement of the graduate programs or in developing a fairly sizable continuing education system lacking a firm foundation of basic, entry education. Despite the healthy establishment of graduate archival education in the university, there are many issues remaining to be resolved about *who* teaches, *where* students are recruited from, and *how* the graduates of these programs are placed. Despite the development of workable guidelines for master's degree in both Canada and the United States, there remain questions about whether this will be the only degree acceptable for archival work, what undergraduate education is most appropriate, and whether there should also be a separate doctorate degree. Thirty years ago du Pont Breck thought archival education should not be offered at the undergraduate level because that is where archivists need the broadest and most general education. He also argued for a masters with an "emphasis in archival procedures" and a thesis. Finally, he believed there was a need for a doctorate, and while these more difficult matters were being dealt with, du Pont Breck surmised that the profession needed continuing education like summer institutes. We can see archivists have done reasonably well with continuing education, started on the right direction with the master's degree, but failed to do much more in the other areas.[54]

Another unresolved issue is *who* will constitute the archival educators of the future. Twenty-five years ago Michael Cook wrote that there was a "world shortage of academic archivists."[55] In hindsight, Cook seems extremely optimistic. While there certainly has been a shortage, there has also not been a tremendous demand, if the United States is any indication. The rapid growth in the numbers of archival educators still represents a small total, but the problem of where these new educators will come from is even greater. In the late 1960s, John Colson stated that the "professionals who engage to prepare others for the profession . . . should be more than successful practitioners; they should also be scholars in their profession and informed critics of it," and that is as good an analysis as we have of what future archival educators should look like. All records professionals obviously need to think *more* about this.[56]

Archivists also have not considered other basic issues. What about recruiting students into their graduate programs? Are archivists making efforts to attract the right kinds of students? If archivists need electronic records, it will do them little good to educate only individuals committed to managing colonial and Revolutionary War records and manuscripts. In 1984 a recent graduate of an archives education program complained that there "was no one out there promoting the archival profession and recruiting promising students into established programs."[57] Are archivists promoting any better? Students arrive by word of mouth, through the influence of a practicing archivist, or because they hear that the courses are interesting. Records are too important for this to continue.

The continuing issues facing North American archival education have not changed much in a decade. Some—regulating the quality of education programs, distinguishing educational requirements for different levels of archival specialization, building archival research and development and education, attracting qualified individuals to become archivists—continue to be unresolved. Others—the impact of individual certification, the place of the practicum, and the continuing role of the archival profession in the information society—have been largely resolved.[58] In looking back over these recurring issues, strewn over a half century of debate about the development of archival education, it is possible to see that there is an implicit assumption about a static notion of archives. From the 1930s through the 1980s archives were perceived as repositories (real places) of records (physical entities or artifacts) managed by custodians (or curators) for historical or cultural purposes. As other related professions have discovered, this conception is a time-bound artifact that is being transformed. Education will need to accommodate this transformation. In other words, the debates and the issues will change. Francis Miksa, in a 1996 conference paper, characterized the "modern" library as an "era-specific phenomenon," representing a century-old "shift" from an "essentially private space organization to a public space organization." Miksa contends the library is now moving back to a kind of private sphere where individuals can manage huge quantities of information. He argues that the education of information professionals "will have to accommodate in its teaching and research a model of the library that is not simply a social agency with large heterogeneous clienteles but rather, like the emerging library, will incorporate significant elements of the library as a personal . . . function of individual or small group needs."[59]

Archivists, archival educators, and other records professionals face the same kind of challenge described by Miksa. Organizations and individuals alike are increasingly relying on electronic technology for records creation, transmission, and maintenance with implications that archives may not continue to be physical places, archival principles based on custodianship may be revised or replaced by new principles, traditional archival functions may be reconfigured, and the archival mission focused on historical sources might give way to one stressing evidence and accountability. It is, of course, not only technology driving this but also the changing nature of organizations and society. An organization existing in a factious society marked by ethnic and cultural disharmony, political correctness, censorship, and privatization trends is one that is accountable to a much more complex set of laws, regulations, and best practices. More than sixty years ago, Prussian archivist Albert Brackmann, describing the primary educational program in his country and the various issues and concerns confronting this education, wrote, the "archivist must simply step forward of his own accord and demand a deepening of the scientific tasks which he finds in his special branch of historical knowledge."[60] The small community of archival educators can unite and work for their common cause in raising both the level of education and knowledge in their discipline. The future of effective records policies depends on it.

THE INTERDISCIPLINARY NATURE OF RECORDS KNOWLEDGE

Archivists in the United States argue about their education and knowledge, and the argument has re-heated in the past decade. In effect, there has been a *re-establishment* of graduate archival education programs, similar to Sydney Pierce's argument about the establishment of university programs being crucial to the self-image and development of disciplines and providing a needed focus for the formation of a field's intellectual content.[61] This has been, in itself, supported by a serious reconsideration of the nature of the record and the substance of the work of the archivist and the records manager driven by new electronic recordkeeping systems, leading to a stronger understanding of the interdisciplinary nature of archival knowledge and work. Bruce Dearstyne believes, "archival work is an *enterprise*—a big, bold, and sometimes difficult undertaking requiring energy and initiative. Archivists deal with history, the transmittal of knowledge, and the management of information—broad, important responsibilities requiring dedication, imagination, and adaptability. The archival profession is dynamic, adaptive, and undergoing continual change."[62] There have been similar statements for records management and various information professions. The 1983 volume *The Study of Information* included information studies from a wide range of disciplines, from the cognitive sciences to linguistics to library and information science to the social sciences—all without concluding that there is a *coherent* information discipline.[63]

The most important recent statement about the interdisciplinary aspect comes from the 1994 SAA education guidelines and the *"interdisciplinary character* of archival studies."[64] Other statements of present and future needs for the archival discipline support its interdisciplinary orientation. Consider the challenges of managing electronic records with archival value by "electronic archaelogists": "Present-day archaelogy is an interdisciplinary field. Not only does it require specialists skilled in the techniques needed methodically to uncover physical artefacts, but it relies on anthropologists, historians, linguists and sociologists to interpret the findings and construct a cohesive representation of past social, cultural and technological activities." This person then concludes, "similarly, electronic archaelogy will be an interdisciplinary activity. Engineers and physicists will use special techniques to retrieve fragments of data from a wide variety of recording media. Computer scientists with database or natural language processing skills will be needed to integrate the vast amounts of disjointed information. Linguists will be needed to translate messages written in a variety of languages or interpret colloquialisms and jargon found in informal communications. Anthropologists, sociologists, economists, historians and librarians will be required to paste together the story that is hidden in the fragments of electronic information reclaimed by the technical specialist."[65] To this could be added knowledge of archival administration.

There is a remarkable array of writing in many disciplines about records, possessing importance to archivists and records managers, and it is only in substantial graduate education programs that this research can be utilized. This may because many other fields see themselves as interdisciplinary as well. Information science, for example, possesses such a conviction, and it has been that way for well over a half century.[66] Some of this results from confusing terminologies that have information professionals thinking of books as documents and documents as entities far from what can be called records.[67] Still, many innovative studies on records and recordkeeping come from outside the records professions, implying that educators and their students need to incorporate research and perspectives from many different disciplines in creative and engaging ways. It is no longer possible to become a qualified records professional by being immersed only in the archives and records management literature, although it is important to have a firm understanding of the key writings, the historic trends, the essential principles, and the debates and discussions found there. Developing records policies requires a records professional to reach into other disciplines, from organizational management to political science.

What are the various perspectives from these disciplines? From historians, archivists have learned to support what constitutes a record and evidence found in a record, although the recent debates about evidence, the knowledge of the past, reading a text, and truth should prompt caution and concern. Literary studies have made a core contribution to archival studies, one enjoying a renaissance today. As Leonard Boyle describes, "diplomatics is simply a straightforward application of the basic principles of literary criticism to documentary sources. The critical examination of any record, whether literary or documentary, and whether in an authentic form or in a copy, or as reported, must take a full and firm account of the substance of the document and of all the circumstances surrounding the document. Only when a document has been examined with all thoroughness, externally as well as internally, can its witness be evaluated properly, circumstantantially, and fully."[68] The science or art of diplomatics arose out of the need for detecting forgeries and fakes, the production of which has plagued scholars and others for centuries.[69]

Linguistics has become a major source for understanding the nature of records and recordkeeping systems, studying the nature of language and writing systems. Scholars studying these early written languages suggest the utilitarian nature of their records. While writing enabled these ancients to develop a system of knowledge, there are few abstract terms, with a writing system based on pictography (the representation of objects by other objects).[70] Linguists have also made close studies of various kinds of government and organizational forms. Veda R. Charrow analyzed government forms generating records, with some surprising comments. He notes, for example, "one pragmatic feature of many bureaucratic documents is their lack of context," that is, that they tell the user of the form, what the document's purpose is, and the intended audience or user.[71] Archivists accept, for instance, that context is an absolutely essential element for something to be a record.

Even from the realm of art history, the records professional can find help in understanding records and recordkeeping. John Tagg's volume on photography and history, for example, reveals how photography's increasing use was tied both to the technology of photography and the changing nature of organizations, power, and representations in society during the second half of the nineteenth century. As he argues, "Its status as a technology varies with the power relations which invest it. Its nature as a practice depends on the institutions and agents which define it and set it to work. . . . It is a flickering across a field of institutional spaces."[72] While for a long time archivists and records managers struggled to manage photographic and other visual images as distinct items requiring separate treatment because of their format and potential use, Tagg's volume reminds us that most often photographs are created for specific reasons as part of larger record systems.

Sociologists have also contributed to the understanding of records and recordkeeping systems. Tora Bikson and S. A. Law examines the role of telex, facsimile, and electronic mail in United Nations organizations, concluding that the technologies continue to outstrip traditional records management and archival approaches. The study reveals, among other things, there was "a much greater awareness of records management problems stemming from the proliferation of electronic information and communication media."[73] Sociologists have also provided some of the best empirical studies of record creation. In one study of the completion of case sheets in an antenatal clinic, completing forms reflects "particular conceptions of the social world" of those completing the forms; in other words, the evidence found in these records is as much information on the organizational and individual contexts as the medical processes.[74] In fact, the study of office procedures by sociologists, anthropologists, and information scientists provide detailed glimpses into the nature of records creation, maintenance, and use, since, as one concludes, an aspect of the "material organization of personal workspace" is the manner in which records are used and maintained.[75]

Less surprising are insights made by jurists about the importance of records. One study examines a set of international conventions from 1924 to 1989 to determine "how these conventions and instruments have approached the issue of legal acceptance of electronic messaging," finding a "clear increase in the level of acceptance of electronic means over time," with the earliest language coming in the early 1970s and such language a standard by another decade. The authors conclude that this acceptance is a factor of the nature of the treaty and the increasing use of electronic information technology.[76] This suggests a use of the legal scholarship in a manner different from how archivists and records managers often approach it. Records managers have relied on the law as a guide for records retention and disposition and for insights about access issues. Archivists have used the law in this way and as part of understanding the juridical context of records creation and maintenance. As the complexities of modern recordkeeping have evolved, such views of the law and records are too limiting.

Records professionals tend to forget that other disciplines have been con-cerned with the nature and maintenance of their own records. This has been evident in the medical profession. One recent article argues that the medical establishment still has not been able to move as close as needed to an electronic medical information system that meets regulatory, social, and medical needs of patients. The now established right of patients to have their medical records available via health care providers through their lifetime, along with the richer diagnostic information, is still a difficult problem to resolve.[77] There has been a tradition of writing about records in the medical field. In a thirty-year-old essay on the use of case files at an outpatient psychiatric clinic, a medical researcher ruminates on why these records can give the appearance of being poor even though the medical personnel have been fastidious in recording in accord with their professional standards: "The troubles we speak of are those that any investigator . . . will encounter if he consults the files in order to answer questions that depart in theoretical or practical import from organizationally relevant purposes and routines under the auspices of which the contents of the files are routinely assembled in the first place."[78] The result is an excellent description of the use by external researchers of records created for purposes other than such research.

It is not surprising that students of management examine records and record-keeping systems. One study, drawing on the literary concept of genre, suggests that certain types of records as communication devices are affected by rules derived from historical, social, cultural, and technological elements. The ways certain records are created, maintained, and used derive from a complex set of conventions.[79] Records professionals have made poor use of the management scholarship. At best, they have drawn on management writing when they have addressed management issues of their own programs rather than the creation and use of records. It is probable that one reason why more disciplines have become interested in records and recordkeeping systems is because of the in-creasing dependence of organizations and individuals on electronic systems. Re-cords professionals should be alert to what they can learn from this, especially as they have to develop policies or influence existing ones.

EDUCATION AND THE INFORMATION AGE

A change of broad proportions occurred in a decade in the expectations of employers for archivists knowledgeable about automated techniques. In 1979 only four of 113 position advertisements in the Society of American Archivists' newsletter required understanding of automated techniques, and *no* advertise-ments stipulated knowledge about electronic records. In 1989, 147 archival po-sitions were advertised in the SAA newsletter, and of these 59 were very explicit in requiring knowledge of automated techniques. Of these 1989 position adver-tisements, however, only *one* made any reference to a required knowledge about electronic records (a faculty position).[80] A decade later, there was more interest in computer literacy but a complete failure to push for a knowledge of records and recordkeeping systems, a knowledge rarely described in any meaningful fashion in job advertisements—for archivists *or* records managers.[81]

The records community re-oriented itself to applying automation to the basic archival function of description, but it has not fared as well in working with electronic records. The constant reference to the U. S. MARC AMC format and now other descriptive standards (such as Encoded Archival Description) is evidence that the creation of this format in 1983 and subsequent efforts to develop related standards have had a profound effect on the conception of the work of the archivist. State government archives confirm an emphasis on very traditional aspects of archival work (such as arrangement and description) and only a minor stress on work with electronic records. State archives position descriptions stress the traditional skills and basic archival functions that the archival profession has been accustomed to for the last half century. There is a general predilection for very broad definitions of archival work, knowledge, and skills.[82]

Is there a cause and effect relationship between the archival job advertisements and position descriptions and the body of archival knowledge and its being taught in graduate and continuing archival education programs? There was little interest in automated techniques and electronic records before 1960, not surprising given the impact of information technology on institutions to that point and the relative lack of adoption of the technology by other information or historical disciplines.[83] The archival profession's concern with electronic records emerged during the next decade, but this was an issue for occasional discussion nearly exclusively by government archivists and records managers. The 1980s brought a steady stream of studies and opinions on automated techniques and electronic records, but with extremely diverse perspectives. Electronic records management reflects something completely different. In the 1970s and 1980s writing on this topic ranges from archivists contending that electronic records fundamentally transform archival work and principles to contentions that electronic records change nothing. By 1990 there was no real consensus, perhaps partly explaining the lack of position advertisements for working with electronic records, and archives lack of adequate specialization with such information systems. Over the 1990s, however, there has been rapid consensus building about the centrality of records and recordkeeping systems as a core aspect of the records professional's knowledge. While debate continues about *how* any records and records systems should be defined and managed, there are at least some models for particular organizational settings.[84]

Educators of records professionals have also only recently contended with how to educate practitioners in electronic records management or automated techniques. The guidelines for graduate archival education programs endorse the importance of automated techniques and electronic records as part of required knowledge for their students. The older ACA guidelines, for example, state, "Archivists are involved with automation in two different ways: through its application to the archival work and through the acquisition of machine-readable records. While machine-readable records should be treated in the course(s) of archival science with all other types of records, the purely technical aspects of their formation and treatment can be best analyzed in a course on automation. However, the main purpose of such a study is to provide archivists with a common grounding in the terminology, concepts and use of computer hardware and software, to enable them to understand and evaluate the professional literature dealing with automation, to use automation in their daily work, and to make judgments about the suitability of specific items of hardware or software for specific archival tasks."[85]

Despite such commitment, the slow growth of specialized courses on these subjects suggests problems. A decade ago there were only four courses on automated techniques and two on electronic records. While there has been expansion in the number of such courses, the vast majority of the courses are introductory in nature, internships, or in related fields in history, library and information science, and even museum studies. Graduate students' orientation to these topics must be largely accomplished as part of basic or introductory courses, not boding well for enabling archival institutions to hire entry-level archivists who are competent in these areas or even aware of the majority of issues that these topics have for basic archival work. While many educators integrate electronic records and automation into their introductory archives courses, the fact that only a handful of programs offer a critical mass of courses suggests that students may receive only a *general* orientation to such matters.

The archival profession compensates for deficiencies in its graduate education programs through institutes, workshops, and other forms of continuing education offerings. With automated techniques, the use of continuing education seems to have been successful, as reflected by the increasing number of advertisements requiring entry- and intermediate-level archivists to have knowledge of and experience in automated techniques and descriptive standards.[86] Something else has occurred with electronic records. Despite the fact that SAA and other professional and records management archival associations have been offering workshops in electronic records for nearly as long, the institutional response to the challenges of managing electronic records has been slower and more uneven.

There are reasons for this dichotomy of responses. Automated techniques and descriptive standards fit comfortably into what archivists have long identified their main responsibilities to be—arrangement, description, and reference. Electronic records require both more theorizing and more structured research about how to manage these records, neither activity one that the archival profession has been very successful in doing. Calls for research about basic archival reference, a function at the heart of the profession's mission as well as the mission of every archival repository, and the nexus between users and archivists in the reading rooms have met with general silence.[87] Other archivists have been extremely nervous about standards or theory in other basic archival functions because of the diversity of the archival profession.[88] This is graphically portrayed in the series of articles following Frank Burke's 1981 essay on archival theory.

The articles split off in two distinct directions: one group makes an effort to refine the notion of archival theory, while the other group poses arguments about a lack of knowledge and theoretical substance in the profession.[89] Allan Pratt, in an analysis of information science, notes "a message must have some recognizable connection with a part of one's image [meaning their own personal background, cognitive abilities, and other similar aspects], beyond being in a known language, before it can be understood."[90] The same has occurred within archival education.

Records professionals must re-think how they are educated to work with modern records and recordkeeping systems. Expanding graduate programs make the archival profession more visible in the university, more capable of attracting quality students, and better equipped for securing resources needed for acquiring technology for instruction about automated techniques and electronic records, building multiple-faculty programs, and making ties to other professional schools. Archival knowledge's interdisciplinary nature is especially important for working with electronic information systems, responsibilities that challenge archivists to be aware of technical, market, and related issues and able to work as part of interdisciplinary teams for research and product development. Librarians and other information professionals, such as Jesse Shera[91] and William Paisley,[92] have known this for decades. Despite similar epistemological interests and purposes, archivists have not pursued the interdisciplinary aspect of their education as fully as other related disciplines, preferring to debate *where* they should be educated. Change is in order.

A better structure is needed for research leading both to improved archival applications and a stronger theoretical foundation for practice. The North American archival profession has over-emphasized skills, placing an undue burden on continuing education and in-service training. Graduate archival education should encompass research and systematic theory, providing the basis for more satisfactory work with automated techniques and electronic records. The relationship between archival education and the employers of archivists has never been particularly good, and the research and theory requirements are a definite strain. There has been little in the way of coherent statements from archival institutions about what they require from graduate programs and archival employers have given the impression of taking what they can get by hiring anyone and giving them in-house training in basic archival principles, practices, and theories. The American archival profession has failed to attract undergraduate and graduate students to their archival education programs and employing institutions, and students continue to stumble into these programs in all manner of ways. Library educators have sometimes bemoaned the lack of suitable undergraduate programs allowing one-year master's programs to be functional.[93] Archivists, on the other hand, lack *both* a sufficient number of undergraduate and comprehensive programs and the mechanism for effective recruiting; while we now have some comprehensive programs, the records professions still lack a structure for recruiting people.

It is no wonder that problems with automated techniques and electronic records remain difficult to resolve. Graduate archival educators need to undertake a variety of research about employers' needs that they can use to develop a suitable curriculum providing students the best possible education and training. The profession needs to consider whether there is any need for more than a half-dozen or so comprehensive graduate education programs in the United States and the few master's level archival degrees in Canada to meet employment requirements. The graduate educators have to join forces to determine various specialized areas that the programs might stress (perhaps only a few graduate level programs need to develop full educational offerings in modern automated information technology) and how to best market their schools to attract the right students. Is continuing education useful for recruiting into the graduate programs?

CONTINUING EDUCATION AND RECORDS PROFESSIONALS

Continuing education remains an important mechanism for maintaining archivists' skills, improving their knowledge, and re-tooling when necessary. It is clear that continuing education has played an important, if not essential, role in spreading the use of automated techniques and descriptive standards. However, the greatest success of continuing education will be in providing educational offerings that build on the strongest possible graduate archival education curriculum, addressing topics like developing records policies. As Timothy Ericson states well, archivists in the United States have tended to be workshop, seminar, and institute happy, paying "too much attention to the *form* of archival education, and not enough to its *content*."[94] Indeed, so much energy has been expended in developing basic or remedial workshops and institutes, that there is little time and resources to offer more advanced continuing education.

Despite the fact that continuing education has become a staple in the education and training of records professionals, there has been very little critical assessment of its effectiveness. Paul Conway, examining continuing education in archives, states, that the "existing literature on continuing education in the archival context is extraordinarily weak, given the proliferation of course offerings."[95] Most evaluation is anecdotal, suggesting that such professionals rely on sustained enrollment for continuing venues or adequate attendance for one-time offerings. Is this satisfactory? What is really understood about the nature of continuing education?

There has been no development of continuing education "models" for records professionals, even though there are models for other information disciplines. These models range from registry systems for tracking individual involvement in continuing education programs to statewide efforts to provide comprehensive continuing education, usually focused on a clearinghouse or local groups coordinating such training.[96] Occasional surveys of continuing education needs, while not providing more formal models, help to provide some understanding for identifying the parameters of such a model.[97] There may be good reasons for this lack of development for records professionals. A definition of library continuing education is "all education which librarians acquire from library schools after they have received the Master's degree in librarianship."[98] Records managers and archivists have a wide range of degrees, from history, American Studies, literature, anthropology, business, and public administration to library and information science, archival studies, and records and information resources management. Continuing education is also seen as essential to rectify deficiencies in initial graduate education, develop competencies, control entry into professional disciplines, maintain professional boundaries, and maintain a certain professional image.[99] Conway, drawing on educational literature, notes that the goals of continuing education may include "broad participation," "personal growth," "acquisition of knowledge, skills, or aptitudes," "performance improvement," and/or "organizational development."[100]

Formal professional education is essential to the effectiveness of both the entry-level professional and the experienced practitioner. One educator describes the situation as follows: "Professional education is responsible for preparing aspiring professionals for a lifetime of practice, commonly without further formal academic training. Professional education must therefore develop students' understanding of, and mechanisms for, self-directed, life-long learning."[101] Perhaps the best explanation as to why so little work has been accomplished on continuing education programs for records professionals is that assessing the nature and effectiveness of such education is a difficult tasks. The same educator notes that learning takes place through formal education, continuing education, reading, collegial contacts, and experience. At the same time, focused on continuing education, it can be discerned that individuals follow continuing education activities in a self-directed fashion and that the responses to and effectiveness of continuing education are based on complicated notions of "performance" and a perspective gained from practical experience.[102]

Although there is a lack of work on continuing education, its importance cannot be ignored or a determination made about the most effective means by which continuing education can be offered. Despite the popular perception of the placid professional lives of archivists or the clerk-like roles of other records professionals, it is clear that they work in an array of disciplines undergoing immense change and facing complex problems. These professionals need to develop a synergetic relationship between formal education and the practitioners, utilizing continuing education as a connecting rod between the two in order to develop timely responses to specific problems and to influence what the academic educators actually do in their classrooms. Robert Rippey, examining models of corporate education programs, states, "As new challenges or technologies arise, the response time of traditional professional education is too long. By the time the research is done, the texts written, the faculty trained, and the curriculum change approved, a problem may reach epidemic proportions."[103]

There are alternative means by which to obtain education and training in records work. Records professionals go to annual national and international conferences, read professional publications, use standards and guidelines, drop in on regional and local conferences, *and* take formal workshops on many different topics. Do these provide a *sufficient* continuing education for records managers and archivists? It is impossible to determine the impact and influence of these activities for these professionals, and there needs to be a more systematic effort in this direction. Do all these venues provide adequate continuing education? Are there gaps? Are there aspects that are over-emphasized? Does the current state of continuing education work given the nature of graduate education such professionals usually possess?

A few efforts have been made to evaluate continuing education for records professionals. While these efforts provide no conclusive findings or even approaches, they are suggestive of the work needed by a discipline relying on continuing education. The main point is that with the reliance on continuing education, it is expected one would have seen more analysis of the impact and value of these educational and training venues on the archival community. Such analysis has not materialized, most of the writings being either position statements for some aspect of archival education or personal reflections on what occurs in archival education programs. There is even less analysis in the records management field.

The reliance of the American archival community on continuing education does not mean that there is a coherent sense of what this education constitutes or that it has been evaluated in any meaningful way. Research on such professional issues is rare in the archival profession, as is even straightforward reporting on workshops and institutes. One continuing education program in the archival field, which has been evaluated, is a two-year project (1987–1989)—the Religious Archives Technical Assistance Project (RATAP) run by the Archives of Religious Institutions (ARI)—a New York metropolitan based organization—with funding by the National Historical Publications and Records Commission.[104] This project was intended to accomplish three objectives: "break down the professional isolation often characterizing small archival programs"; develop a more "integrated program" for continuing education, "linking basic workshops with concentrated planning efforts, on-site consultation visits and reports by a trained archivist, cooperative interinstitutional programs, and various forms of technical assistance"; and, finally, help small programs deal with some specific persistent problems—"rapid personnel turnover, minimal commitment by parent organizations, limited funding, and lack of internal visibility." The results were uneven. It proved difficult to encourage cooperation, convince individuals to undertake individual internships, or to get programs to share archival resources and facilities. The project also found it difficult to stimulate more use of the repositories' holdings, generate preservation efforts, and encourage greater participation in professional associations. The greatest success occurred in enabling these small archival programs "to articulate and define

basic administrative elements" (such as mission statements and collection policies) and to gain ground in arranging and describing their archival holdings.
Such evaluation is crucial because it reflects needs in the archival community
that can only be addressed through careful targeted educational efforts and deliberate monitoring of the results.

The most comprehensive analysis of continuing education in the archival field
was the study by Paul Conway on a group of 320 archival repositories sending
staff to participate in one of the Society of American Archivists Basic Conservation Workshops offered from 1981 to 1987.[105] As he states, his "central thesis
postulates that meaningful patterns exist between the level of ongoing preservation activities in archival repositories and the perceptions by those who manage them that information and advice about preservation are available and
useful."[106] To gather data for his study, Conway used an eight-page questionnaire to collect information about preservation program activity, the nature of
the administrative structure and placement of the organization, and sources of
information utilized by the institutions.

Conway brings several strengths to a superb study all records professionals
need to read. First, Conway has an excellent grasp of the relationship of preservation to broader archival functions. His review of the literature and his chapter on definitions and the research problem provide the clearest descriptions of
this relationship. Second, Conway develops a number of original indexes to
measure such things as "intensity of care," "prevention planning," "prevention
implementing," renewal planning," "renewal implementing," and the uses of a
variety of potential information sources. These measures enable him to deal
effectively with his thesis. Third, Conway brings a strong knowledge of archival
institutions and experience in conducting research about them to this study,
primarily as the architect of the 1985 Society of American Archivists Census
of Archival Institutions and as the leading advocate for archival user studies.
The utility of his measures certainly derives from this previous work.

Conway's study provides excellent descriptions of how and when archivists
acquire and use information. The main point of his study is the correlation (using
his indexes and standard correlation coefficients) between preservation practice
and the use of information sources (including continuing education programs).
Conway concludes that archivists put a greater emphasis on "personal networking, both face-to-face and in writing," and that "those archivists who connect
directly to the larger world of professional advice appear to be more able to
marshal the intellectual and physical resources necessary for constructive action."[107] The implications for formal continuing education are indeed profound,
suggesting either that formal educational ventures should be reconsidered or that
they should be utilized mainly as mechanisms to establish the networks.

There have been only a few efforts to evaluate the effectiveness of major
institutes in archival administration. Starting with the Modern Archives Institute
in the late 1930s, there developed a series of multi-week institutes by the early
1970s essentially providing an alternative to more formal graduate courses—of

which there were few in this period. As Linda Matthews describes, the Georgia Archives Institute originated in the late 1960s because the Georgia Department of Archives and History was having a difficult time finding qualified archivists given the dearth of graduate programs and short-term institutes.[108] At their peak, there were major institutes at the National Archives (the Modern Archives Institute) and in Colorado, Georgia, Ohio, and California. Their basic mission was to provide an intensive orientation to the basics of archival work, usually in a two-week framework, sometimes with a single major faculty member but more often with a number of guest lecturers drawn from archival programs in the immediate geographic area.

Despite the importance of these institutes, their assessments have been very rudimentary. Matthews' evaluation of the Georgia version was more a descriptive history. She only notes the nature of students who attended this institute over the years, concluding that a major portion consisted of individuals already employed as archivists, usually newly entering professionals, and half were employed by small archival programs such as local historical societies or church archives. Most, (60 percent) were Georgia-based professionals, although the remainder came from a wide geographic area. Linda Matthews's analysis is most helpful for its insight into how such institutes have been transformed, mainly as other educational venues have developed and matured. She notes that the "institute's role as a vehicle for socialization into the profession, as basic training for beginning staff, and as a framework and network of support for small institutions and organizations whose archives staff will continue to be part-time or voluntary remains a major contribution. Its future will depend, as in the past, on the available resources for support of its programs and a continuing assessment of its place in the changing professional environment."[109]

Matthews's analysis can be compared to a recent study of the students attending the Modern Archives Institute, a continuing education venue in existence since 1945,[110] serving as the "model" for continuing education in this field. Several interesting facts stand out about the participants: they attend because of a lack of other opportunities to acquire basic archival training, they are mostly practicing archivists not by conscious career choice but by other circumstances, most are not members of professional archival associations, and the majority are in search of practical information rather than theoretical discussions. Is it likely that either these individuals or these training venues will equip individuals to tackle critical policy matters?

Unfortunately, there have been few *general* descriptions of continuing education in this field, although some articles reveal important clues about how such evaluation should be done. James Fogerty's description of a series of basic archival workshops offered by the Minnesota Historical Society notes, the "participants completed a four-page questionnaire, giving information about their backgrounds, experiences, and the facilities and manuscript holdings in their institutions," enabling a profile of institutions and participants. Fogerty also notes that the ten workshops offered in this series "provided an excellent opportunity for experimentation" with instructors attending each other's sessions and some of the sessions being revised considerably. Finally, he notes that the success of the workshops can be "measured" through documented increased usage of acid-free storage materials, an increase in information requests from local repositories, and an increased sophistication in the nature of these requests. "A tangible measure of the success of the project is that a basic level of knowledge has been absorbed, and it can be built upon with further training and experience."[111]

It seems that the best that can be said about the archival community's continuing education efforts is they have served as a form of *remedial* training for those without sufficient pre-appointment education and as a form of socialization. The problems with viewing continuing education in this manner can be seen by considering one of the greatest challenges to the profession, the rising dependence on electronic information technology. While there has been a long-term commitment by the Society of American Archivists to offer continuing education in electronic records management, there has been a very slow development of programs to manage such records. The reasons seem clear. Basic archival education (meaning an understanding of basic archival concepts and principles) has been insufficient to support continuing education efforts. Moreover, the growing consensus of electronic records archivists about how to manage such records seems only recently to have grown beyond a small group of professionals. The effort by the Society of American Archivists' Committee on Automated Records and Techniques to develop a curriculum for electronic records archivists both admits the previous failures *and* adopts as a principle that an electronic records archivist can only be good if this person is *first* a good archivist; this principle reflects that for continuing education to succeed it must take into account the knowledge that is commonly held by the particular program's participants.

There needs to be more evaluation of continuing education in the records professions. All varieties of methodologies are possible, and virtually any kind of evaluation would be better than what is now possessed. Questionnaires of records professionals about their interests in and priorities for continuing education, surveys gathering information on various factors (such as geographic and subject areas, gender, age, employer support and interest) affecting the attendance at continuing education workshops, longitudinal studies on the long-term impact of continuing education on careers, and follow-up assessments of particular continuing education courses to determine their impact and effectiveness would all be a good place to start. Conway demonstrates at least *one* reason why records professionals have conducted little evaluation, arguing that the nature of the evaluation needs to suit the purpose of the continuing education venture. Does anyone completely understand what it is that they are trying to accomplish in continuing education in the records professions? Conway notes that there is a "standard notion of professional education" extending from the entry-level degree to in-service training to specialized continuing education, but archivists (and others) have not followed such a linear line: "People who consider themselves a part of the archival profession and who are sufficiently committed to join the profession's only national association simply start working in an archival repository and increase the full variety of their educational experiences as they work their way up the ranks of the organization or gain additional years of experience."[112]

If an evaluation in continuing education in archives and records management is to be done, where should the evaluation begin? Chobot suggests continuing education can be considered from four perspectives, from basic planning and definition to design, then delivery, and, finally, evaluation procedures.[113] There is a need to re-consider what all this continuing education activity means. Even with the diversity, it cannot really be assumed that sufficient strengths or important gaps have been identified or what overall purposes are being met. Are these programs to help advanced professionals? Are they intended to provide training for those working with records that for one reason or another have not acquired a sufficient pre-appointment education? There has not been a systematic effort to develop comprehensive continuing education opportunities in the records professions. At the moment, workshops and institutes come and go, but based on what—*perceived* needs or *personal* interests? There is also little connection with graduate programs, perhaps because they are only now beginning to develop fuller educational offerings. If continuing education could build off of graduate programs—at least for the education of full-fledged professionals or for certain specialists—this would go a long way towards providing a framework for making sense out of continuing education.

Why not bring together individuals who have been offering continuing education programs to discuss the overall need of records professionals? Let them share whatever form of internal evaluation they conduct, and, more importantly, let them rate their sense of the effectiveness of continuing education offerings in records work. Why not encourage a study that does an evaluation by participants in some of our major continuing education venues? How has their attendance assisted their work and their careers? What do they need? Why not bring together graduate educators and leaders in the fields to discuss their needs and what the relationship between graduate education and continuing education ought to be? The Society of American Archivists has tried to do this in the past, holding a major education conference in 1987 in Savannah that brought together educators, practitioners, and the leaders of national and regional professional associations. But even with this, SAA has never sustained such cooperation or, at its minimum, a simple exchange of information. Why not try to bring together employers and educators to discuss the educational needs for records professionals? While there will be major differences in their perspectives, it is hard to imagine that this would not provide some additional information that could strengthen the effectiveness and relevance of continuing education. The lack of such leadership by professional associations puts the burden on the backs of educators and, given their increasing number and mission that may be exactly where it belongs anyway.[114]

There probably is a fairly coherent set of continuing education needs among those working with records, ranging from technical matters such as digitizing holdings for preservation and access to more mundane but important matters such as security, communication networks, and facilities management and evaluation. Issues such as cost, location of educational offerings, frequency of offerings, financial support for professionals' attendance, and other related matters also need to be considered for future planning. Without some effort to assess and build consensus about these needs, however, it remains difficult to determine the types of workshops and institutes that should be offered or how new venues such as distance education and Internet courses can be utilized.

There is another set of issues that can be addressed by evaluating continuing education. By knowing more about present activities and current perceptions of continuing education needs, a benchmark can be created for subsequent analysis. For example, is it correct to assume individuals being attracted to archives and records management positions will continue to bring the same educational backgrounds, skills, interests, and attitudes as now exist? In the archives profession, the past decade has brought the establishment of more comprehensive and intensive graduate education programs, meaning that many individuals entering the field are better educated than they were twenty years ago. Attitudes about and expectations for continuing education have probably significantly changed in a relatively short time, while what constitutes continuing education has remained relatively static.[115]

David Damrosch, looking at specialization in higher education, chronicles the threats of specialization to the quality of education offered by the university, wondering if we should "ask how, if at all, something resembling the ideal of general education can be restored."[116] These comments seem particularly relevant in considering continuing education in records work, where continuing education exists with few guiding principles or coherence. What is needed is to get to the heart of what records managers and archivists should know and then determine if there are sufficient opportunities for them to gain such education and training. The field can inform both the academy and the various professional associations about the nature and substance of continuing education in a way that is now left to chance or the initiatives of a few individuals and institutions.

ADVOCACY IN THE GRADUATE ARCHIVES CURRICULUM

Nearly every archival or records management topic taught relates to the records professional being an advocate, suggesting why education is even more important. The archivist or records manager is not cloistered but is involved with making the public, policy makers, and associated colleagues understand the vital importance of records to society and all its institutions. The traditional focus of education for records professionals has always been basic skills, with the closest to a concern about education being the belief that those who entered the archival profession should have a firm knowledge in history.

What was lost? Everything was related to basic archival arrangement and description, reference and use. There was little emphasis on an archival body of knowledge, little concern for research, and only a modest interest in such essential matters as archival appraisal or archival advocacy and public programs. There are still the lingering remnants of this concentration of resources on only part of what it means to be an archivist. For many archivists, a basic reference or two, such as the Society of American Archivists Archival Fundamental Series, will suffice to guide them in their work. They do not seem to see the subtleties or nuances in their practice or the need for questioning and re-thinking much of what constitutes practice. This is the impoverishment of the profession, an intellectual poverty far more dangerous than the financial and human resources matters that most archivists are prone to lament. Everything is reduced to practice, nothing else is important. It is precisely what leads to archivists' failing to rally behind national or international concerns, to articulate what is important to their employers, and to help society understand the importance of archives.

Education incorporates practice, but it implies understanding. Derek Bok, the former president of Harvard, provides a glimpse into professional schools where future records professionals will be educated: "Most educators are convinced that professional schools can reach a high level of quality only when practical teaching and applied research are combined with basic inquiry and instruction of a kind that can only exist within a university setting."[117] The key words are teaching, research, and inquiry. To teach even the most basic applied activity requires pulling it apart, examining it from a variety of perspectives, and explaining it in different ways. This is what is also meant by inquiry, and inquiry means curiosity. Inquiry means critically examining an archival finding aid or records inventory or records schedule, trying to understand what led to it, and comprehending whether it is still relevant. Inquiry, of course, is fundamental to applied research. As a profession, archivists and records managers possess so little research about their basic practices, principles, and assumptions that they really do not know if much of what they do really works as it should or could. The long-term separation of the education of archivists (meaning the reliance on brief workshops and institutes or adjuncts with little influence in the university) from the university model of education is at the heart of the problem with the modern American archival community. Jaroslav Pelikan argues that the "four legs" of the university are the "advancement of knowledge through research, the transmission of knowledge through teaching, the preservation of knowledge in scholarly collections, and the diffusion of knowledge through publishing"[118]— and this captures what has been missing in the education of records professionals.

Archivists and records managers need to become *scholars* of recordkeeping, meaning they need to understand what a record is, what makes a record an archival record, the history of recordkeeping systems, the organizational context of such systems, and the social, cultural, and other importance of such records. Records professionals must become activists within their own organizations and within the broader society. Derek Bok, in his other book on higher education, provides an insight into this when he states, "another phenomenon that makes the world seem more complicated is the rapid increase in the sheer amount of information to be learned. Knowing that this growth will surely continue, we can no longer be content with teaching students to remember a fixed body of knowledge; instead, we must help them to master techniques of problem-solving and habits of continuous learning."[119] It is this notion of problem-solving and continuous learning that makes advocacy so crucial to the education of records professionals.

Archival education programs, in particular, should be less concerned with sending out graduates to work in archival establishments and more directed to getting them into *other* positions concerned with records and information in government, corporations, professional associations, and cultural institutions. In North America, archivists and other records professionals have not done as good a job as is needed in building public support for the importance of records. They have also not done well in being effective advocates for the preservation and management of archival records. If they placed individuals with a knowledge of archives and records in crucial positions they might stand a far better chance of rectifying glaring weaknesses in certain areas, such as the management of electronic records with archival value and the establishment of viable and comprehensive archives programs in corporations.

Tackling this latter strategy suggests re-evaluating what has been taught in graduate archives programs. The stress has been on arrangement and description, especially now with the advent of increasingly detailed descriptive standards supporting networked bibliographic utilities. Much of the time spent in the classroom is devoted to this archival function, and in the United States the continuing use of the practicum or internship as a major component of archival education provides an even greater emphasis on archival arrangement and description responsibilities. How does such a concentration enable archivists to operate in modern organizations? Will this practical training enable archivists to be effective advocates for the basic mission of preserving archival records? Does this practical training assist archivists to perceive that arrangement and description may be a time-consuming and costly endeavor best carried out by technicians under the supervision of the professional archivist? A better emphasis for the professional archivist might be to stress enabling records creators, resource allocators, policy makers, users and potential users of archival records, and the public to understand what archives are and why they need to be preserved and managed (as well as the more general importance of records).

There is not a single records issue, function, or activity that can be taught without understanding how the archivist or records manager may have to be a publicist, lobbyist, or advocate or, at the least, be aware of potential political, social, economic, and other dimensions of supporting their work. It gets us to a simple truth that Jacques Barzun states, "when all is said and done, one does not teach a subject, one teaches a student how to learn it."[120] Advocacy or public programming is simply knowing the context of recordkeeping systems enabling prospective records professionals to be able to operate with the organizational and societal environments that create and sustain recordkeeping regimes.

Advocacy is as crucial a subject for the prospective archivist as any other knowledge or skill area and, in many cases, it is impossible to teach without including advocacy issues or concerns. Appraisal is the most basic of all archival functions, but it is one of the most difficult areas because it forces archivists to grapple with how they document or what of the documentary heritage they preserve in a society beset by multiculturalism, political correctness, and numerous other divisive issues. David Gracy got to the heart of the connection between appraisal and public understanding of archives in his homily on the use of the terms "active" versus "inactive" records, suggesting that using "inactive" doomed archivists to being irrelevant in their own organizations and society.[121] Archivists also know that the acquisition of certain archival records, such as those emanating from existing organizations, requires the negotiation of responsibilities by archivists with those organizations, their administrators, and their records and information resources managers.[122] Sincere efforts to document elaborate aspects of modern society are almost indistinct from efforts to influence the organizational creators of such records.[123] Archivists and other records professionals acknowledge that the technical natures of organizational recordkeeping systems are dictating an entirely new thinking about appraisal, leading from traditional, centralized repositories to decentralized programs.[124]

There are other issues affecting appraisal. The recent writings on archival appraisal stress the problems of dealing with the complexities of modern society, and these writings have nudged archivists into the realization that appraisal is hardly to be separated from contemporary issues, ideologies, controversies, and social and political agendas.[125] The origins of these writings were, to a certain extent, the products of a generation of archivists trained as social historians with a particular orientation to the relevance of history to contemporary society.[126] The connection of appraisal to advocacy can be discerned in many ways. Archivists, while becoming more systematic in appraisal practice, still need to be aware of and sensitive to the particular needs of certain groups in society.[127] There are arguments about how certain records can only be effectively appraised by archivists becoming more involved in the creation of recordkeeping systems.[128] Some honest assessors of appraisal have factored in the political aspects of appraisal decisions, although even these could not be objectively measured.[129] Archivists must also acknowledge that many of the records finding their way into their repositories are the result of legal cases, administrative needs, and less than scientific or objective criteria.[130] The challenge in education may not be to shun such obvious influences on appraisal but to use them to create dialogues for students, demonstrating to them the impact of such influences.[131] And with an increasing number of fine studies on such aspects as memory, meaning, objectivity, and truth, there is much to stimulate archival students to consider the many issues they will encounter.[132]

Preservation is a form of appraisal and, as a result, faces all the challenges and issues just described. While there has been a shift from an item-level conservation treatment mentality to the larger concerns of preservation management, preservation is often taught more as craft than as something using the best skills of the archivist as appraiser, administrator, and advocate. Preservation is costly. It is often the last thing that records professionals want to sink financial resources into, often because they do not have those resources. Preservation requires that archivists be more assured of their appraisal decisions, and it takes skillful negotiation with those who control the financial resources and with whom they must contract for services (since so few archival programs possess in-house, comprehensive conservation and preservation laboratories and staff).

Teaching preservation within an archival education program requires as much advocacy consideration as imparting the basic principles supporting what preservation represents. There is the matter of winning support for costly preservation programs. In North America, especially the United States, the archival community seems committed to encouraging institutions of even the most modest resources to maintain valuable archival records, but how do archivists equip them to become better advocates and fund-raisers to build viable preservation programs? How can archivists equip an archival program, with no substantial financial resources and often poorly educated and trained staff, to do the right thing in regards to something requiring sophisticated thinking and hard decisions? How can archivists convince institutional archives, often coupled with economy- and efficiency-obsessed records management programs, to invest in what must look like a bottomless pit of expenditures? Then, there is the matter of electronic records and recordkeeping systems, which seem to curtail appeal to the symbolism of archives and their preservation, in favor of software engineering requiring new partnerships and new technical and communications skills?[133] Even something as basic as making a decision about the reformatting of a record for preservation purposes is burdened by numerous issues about the integrity of the record, the notion of its evidence versus its information, and other concerns that are as much advocacy matters as anything else. All of these can make for invigorating, fun, and frustrating classroom encounters, although intimidating to the student who wants to know *little* more than to know *how* to do something.

Arrangement and description, especially with the addition of automation and its consequent focus on descriptive standards, seems to be a natural for thinking about advocacy because of its close connection to user needs and the reference function. Historians of archival arrangement and description theory and practice demonstrate how the evolution of this function was a mixture of results dependent on personalities, historical events, organizational vagaries, and, conceptualization based on practice.[134] There are other important dimensions as well. Archivists have been influenced, and supported, by the library profession's development of bibliographic standards and networks. Here is a two-edged sword. There is little question that the archival profession, because of its size, could have developed such standards (at least in a marketable sense, securing vendors' support) on its own. Besides, librarians have been more effective advocates for their own professional needs. This needs to be taught in the classroom, both to understand the importance of advocacy and to help prospective archivists see how advocacy has helped even in the most basic of archival functions.

By archivists becoming involved in such descriptive work they enter the world of standards and standardization, a world dominated by technical knowledge and political skills.[135] The question profitably asked is if archivists' move to standards in description has not made it that much more difficult to communicate with one another, with their constituencies, and with colleagues in related professions. Have archivists created a nightmare for fostering the understanding of archives and records?[136] All of the recent activity in descriptive standards should be doubly of concern to educators because, for better or worse, they are influencing the requirements for employment as well as what is passing for their curriculum.[137]

Reference and access is a natural meeting place for archival education and advocacy. Reference and advocacy are as closely related as any two functions could be. The reference room is where archival public relations and advocacy commence. The literature on reference certainly confirms this equation. From descriptions of the interaction between the reference archivist and the researcher[138] to proposals about how to study research use,[139] even to studies about the use of historical and archival records,[140] all contain interesting, controversial, and complex issues prospective archivists need to grapple with as they prepare for their careers. In some cases, what they must be prepared for is to reflect on how they might consider changing some accepted aspects of archival practice in order to provide better service as well as to provoke more public discussion about the value of records, archives and the documentary heritage.

There is probably no other topic, more than access, opening itself up to discussion about the archivist as advocate. Securing access to certain important records, such as the Robert F. Kennedy assassination investigation records or the tape recordings done by Richard M. Nixon while in the White House, requires archivists to be astute legal experts, political lobbyists, and skillful negotiators.[141] To this can be added numerous discussions by different groups, all with competing interests and agendas, about what kinds of services they expect from archivists.[142] Privacy, freedom of information, intellectual property ownership and copyright are all-important issues given short shrift in the profession and in the classroom (and perhaps the classroom is the source or origins of the larger professional problems).[143]

As managers, archivists need to understand that organizations creating records establish an environment in which the records professional must be visible for participating in decision making and goal setting. Records and information are at the heart of all organizations, representing a function essential to their financial health, competitiveness, and overall viability. Prospective archivists can learn about this in several ways. They can be introduced to the history of re-cordkeeping, revealing how and why records and archives are so intimately connected to the administration of institutions.[144] The irony of this connection between records and their organizational creators is that the American archival profession has not done well in establishing and nurturing institutional ar-chives,[145] and that is, of course, precisely where advocacy should play a role. As a profession archivists have tended to operate a sort of collecting triage, and while negotiating for donations of records to historical records repositories re-quires public relations and other such skills, they are probably of a lesser type than what is needed for convincing organizations to establish their own viable archives programs.[146]

The reasons for such failures? Archivists have not been technically proficient and relevant to the modern Information Age organization.[147] They have allowed records management and archival administration to become two separate disci-plines, weakening both in the process.[148] The splintering of these professions has also pulled apart what is generally considered to be the key elements of a record—its structure, content, and context, and the life cycle of the records and recordkeeping systems.[149] The end result of this is a severe weakening of the ability of archivists or records managers to act as advocates for their own mis-sion and to have a more prominent role in society for accountability and other purposes for which records are essential.[150]

Since modern organizations are continually evolving, and information (and records) is crucial to the rate and result of this evolution,[151] archivists need to be in the position of constantly negotiating for their mission and, using some of the current management language, they need to be re-engineering and re-inventing their own programs.[152] They also need to be constantly following the market for new software products with implications for recordkeeping that might be adopted by their organizations. Better yet, they should work to put themselves in the position of being able to influence the organization about what sorts of software should be acquired and how it should be refined.[153] Educators, then, need to help their students to understand not just basic archival principles, meth-odology, or practice but also to see how these principles operate in their organ-izational and societal environments.

All of this means archival educators need to re-examine their education. A. Bartlett Giamatti wrote, the "humanists knew better than anyone that the word education is derived from the Latin educere, 'to lead out'; it was the leading out of private wisdom for the greater public good that was the constant end of humanistic study."[154] Archival educators need to educate their students in that fashion as well, leading them out into the world that creates records and that will ultimately decide whether they will preserve those that have archival value. And it is in keeping with the very notion of profession, which is religious in its origins and reflecting a commitment to a calling.[155] This is the key to archival advocacy, and it is the key to archival education. It is, finally, the *key* to all records work—the place where I started this book and where it now ends.

NOTES

1. Richard C. Berner, "Toward National Archival Priorities: A Suggested Basis for Discussion," *American Archivist* 45 (Spring 1982): 171–173.

2. Robert M. Warner, "Archival Training in the United States and Canada," *American Archivist* 35 (July–October 1972): 347–358.

3. Paul Conway, "Archival Education and the Need for Full-Time Faculty," *American Archivist* 51 (Summer 1988): 254–265 (quotation p. 255).

4. These essays are Frank B. Evans, "Educational Needs for Work in Archival and Manuscript Depositories," *Indian Archives* 21 (July–December 1972): 13–30; Evans, "Postappointment Archival Training: A Proposed Solution for a Basic Problem," *American Archivist* 40 (January 1977): 57–74; Evans, "UNESCO and Archives Development," *UJISLAA* 4 (July–September 1982): 159–176; Evans, "The Organization and Status of Archival Training: An Historical Perspective," *Archivum* 34 (1988): 75–91; Richard C. Berner, "Archival Education and Training in the United States, 1937 to Present," *Journal of Education for Librarianship* 22 (Summer–Fall 1981): 3–19; Jacqueline Goggin, " 'That We Shall Truly Deserve the Title of Profession': The Training and Education of Archivists, 1930–1960," *American Archivist* 47 (Summer 1984): 243–254; Karl L. Trever, "The Organization and Status of Archival Training in the United States," *American Archivist* 11 (April 1948): 154–163.

5. Shelley Sweeney, "A Guinea Pig's Perspective on the UBC Master of Archival Studies Programme," *Archivaria* 18 (Summer 1984): 263.

6. Samuel Flagg Bemis, "The Training of Archivists in the United States," *American Archivist* 2 (July 1939): 158–159.

7. Roger H. Ellis, "The British Archivist and His Training," *Journal of the Society of Archivists* 3 (1967): 265–271.

8. Lionel Bell, "The Professional Training of Archives," *UNESCO Bulletin of Librarianship* 25 (July–August 1971): 191–197.

9. Michael Cook, "An International Standard for the Training of Archivists and Records Managers," *UNESCO Journal of Information Science, Librarianship and Archives Administration* 4, no. 2 (1988): 116.

10. James M. O'Toole, "Curriculum Developments in Archival Education: A Proposal," *American Archivist* 53 (Summer 1990): 460–466.

11. My views about certification are expressed in a position paper available on my homepage on the World Wide Web. See my page at the following: http://www.lis.pitt.edu/~rjc. I was originally a strong advocate for the concept of certification, as is evident from my writings in the 1980s; see my *American Archival Analysis: The Recent Development of the Archival Profession in the United States* (Metuchen, NJ: Scarecrow Press, 1990).

12. Solon J. Buck, "The Training of American Archivists," *American Archivist* 4 (April 1941): 86.

13. Ames Sheldon Bower, "Whence and Whither: A Survey of Archival Education," *Georgia Archive* 5 (Summer 1977): 44–61.

14. Terry Eastwood, "The Origins and Aims of the Master of Archival Studies Pro-

gramme at the University of British Columbia," *Archivaria* 16 (Summer 1983): 40. In an even grander and more persuasive fashion, Eastwood returned to this theme in his "Nurturing Archival Education in the University," *American Archivist* 51 (Summer 1988): 228–251.

15. A good starting point would be Terry Eastwood's "Nurturing Archival Education in the University."

16. Despite Frank Burke's 1981 argument that a corps of archival educators would provide what was missing in the development of archival theory; see Burke, "The Future Course of Archival Theory," *American Archivist* 44 (Winter 1981): 40–46. In looking at the number of educators who have published in the *American Archivist* or who have published books on archival topics, the results are not particularly impressive.

17. For an example of how rudderless continuing education appeared a decade ago, read Timothy L. Ericson, "Professional Associations and Archival Education: A Different Role, or a Different Theater?" *American Archivist* 51 (Summer 1988): 298–311.

18. Evans, "Postappointment Archival Training," p. 74.

19. See, for example, James E. Fogerty, "The Minnesota Basic Workshops Project," *American Archivist* 44 (Summer 1981): 237–240.

20. Frederick J. Stielow, "Continuing Education and Information Management: Or, The Monk's Dilemma," *Provenance* 3 (Spring 1985): 13.

21. The SAA Committee on Automated Records and Techniques published its curriculum, with many supporting papers, as a special issue of the *American Archivist* 56 (Summer 1993).

22. Wilfred I. Smith, "Archival Training in Canada," *Canadian Archivist* 1, no. 7 (1969): 39.

23. Richard J. Cox, "Library History and Library Archives," *Libraries and Culture* 26 (Fall 1991): 569–593.

24. Edwin Welch, for example, mentions archivists had not considered new techniques such as production of audiovisual materials; see his "Continuing Education for Archivists," *Canadian Archivist* 2, no. 5 (1975): 41–46.

25. Ernst Posner, "European Experiences in Training Archivists," *American Archivist* 4 (January 1941): 37.

26. Ellis, "The British Archivist and His Training."

27. Bell, "The Professional Training of Archives."

28. Michael Cook, *Archives Administration Today: The Background to Professional Training* (Lectures delivered at the Department of Library Science, University of Istanbul, and at the Departments of Library Science of Ankara University and Hecettepe under the auspices of the British Council, April–May 1982).

29. Evans, "Postappointment Archival Training," pp. 72–73.

30. Hugh A. Taylor, "The Discipline of History and the Education of the Archivist," *American Archivist* 40 (October 1977): 395–402.

31. Victoria Irons Walch, in her report on state government records programs, commented on the low average entry-level salary for professionals working in these programs by posing questions: "more than half of the state archives report that they require neither a masters degree nor specific archival training as a prerequisite for an entry-level position. Does this reflect the history of the development of this sector of the profession, the slowness or resistance of government personnel systems to revise requirements, the lack of new hires, a lack of acceptance of graduate education or specialized training as useful preparation for work in a government archives, or a non-competitive salary structure?"

Maintaining State Records in an Era of Change: A National Challenge; A Report on State Archives and Records Management Programs (St. Paul: Council of State Historical Records Coordinators by the Minnesota Historical Society, April 1996), p. 28.

32. John Colson, "On the Education of Archivists and Librarians," *American Archivist* 31 (April 1968): 173. See also his "Archivists and Education: Modifying Library School Curricula," *RQ* 12 (Spring 1973): 267–272.

33. Francis X. Blouin, Jr., "The Relevance of the Case Method to Archival Education and Training," *American Archivist* 41 (January 1978): 37–44 (quotation p. 43). The SAA has published a brief series of case studies, but it is unclear whether there is a commitment to continue these.

34. I thought about such questions when examining the revision of the University of British Columbia Master of Archival Studies curriculum. UBC has courses on the nature of archival materials, the juridical context of Canadian archives, office systems records, courses on all the basic archival functions such as appraisal and arrangement and description, *and* the management of electronic records as an elective. Can any of the other courses be taught without full or at least serious consideration of electronic recordkeeping systems? For the revised curriculum, see Terry Eastwood, "Revised MAS Curriculum at UBC," Association of Canadian Archivists *Bulletin* 18 (May 1994): 14–16.

35. G. Philip Bauer, "Recruitment, Training, and Promotion in the National Archives," *American Archivist* 18 (October 1955): 293.

36. Colson, "On the Education of Archivists and Librarians," p. 171.

37. Edwin Welch, "Archival Education," *Archivaria* 4 (1977): 51–52.

38. Richard C. Berner, "Archival Management and Librarianship: An Exploration of Prospects for Their Integration," in *Advances in Librarianship*, ed. Wesley Simonton (Orlando, FL: Academic Press, 1986), vol. 14, pp. 256–257.

39. Virginia Cain, ed., "Archives by Degree: Personal Perspectives on Academic Preparation for the Archival Profession," *Provenance* 2 (Fall 1984): 47.

40. Andrew Raymond and James M. O'Toole, "Up from the Basement: Archives, History, and Public Administration," *Georgia Archive* 6 (Fall 1978): 18–31.

41. Lawrence J. McCrank, "Present Developments in Archival Education: The Future Care of the Past," in Janet Fyfe and Clifford Collier, eds., *Symposium on Archival Education* (London, Ont.: School of Library and Information Science, 1980), p. 13.

42. McCrank, "Present Developments in Archival Education," p. 14.

43. A survey of archivists in the South suggested that education tended to be historical with one or two courses in archival administration and with a view to library science only as a "useful adjunct"; George W. Whitbeck, "The Education of Archivists: Needs as Perceived by Sampling of the Profession in the South," *Southern Quarterly* 13 (January 1975): 143.

44. T. R. Schellenberg, "Archival Training in Library Schools," *American Archivist* 31 (April 1968): 157.

45. Schellenberg, "Archival Training in Library Schools," p. 158.

46. Schellenberg, "Archival Training in Library Schools," pp. 161–162.

47. Schellenberg, "Archival Training in Library Schools," p. 162.

48. Andrew G. Watson, "The Training of Archivists in Great Britain," *Archives et Bibliotheque des Belgigue* 46 (1975): 223.

49. There is a continuing backlash to the shift to archival education in library and information science schools from those who view archives from the perspective of a

public history or historical vocation; for a testy example of this, with plenty of argument with my writings (for those wanting to see this), see Vernon R. Smith, "Pedagogy and Professionalism: An Evaluation of Trends and Choices Confronting Educators in the Archival Community," *Public Historian* 16 (Summer 1994): 23–43.

50. See Lawrence J. McCrank, "History, Archives and Information Science," *Annual Review of Information Science and Technology* 30 (1995): 281–352. The domain of "historical information science" "lies at the intersection of such methodology with modern information technology applied to historical sources, information systems and processes, and communications" (p. 285).

51. Frank B. Evans, "Modern Concepts of Archives Administration and Records Management," *UNESCO Bulletin of Librarianship* 24 (September–October 1970): 242–247.

52. See, for example, Robert L. Sanders, "Archivists and Records Managers: Another Marriage in Trouble?" *Records Management Quarterly* 23 (April 1989): 12–18, 20.

53. Cook, *Archives Administration Today*, pp. 8–9.

54. Allen du Pont Breck, "New Dimensions in the Education of American Archivists," *American Archivist* 29 (April 1966): 173–186 (quotation p. 181).

55. Michael Cook, "The Planning of an Archives School: Some Comments on the Proposed Regional Institute of Archives Science for South-East Asia," *Journal of Society of Archivists* 5 (October 1975): 243.

56. Colson, "On the Education of Archivists and Librarians," p. 173.

57. Cain, ed., "Archives by Degree," p. 44.

58. Richard J. Cox, "Educating Archivists: Speculations on the Past, Present, and Future," *Journal of the American Society for Information Science* 39 (September 1988): 340–343.

59. Francis Miksa, "The Cultural Legacy of the 'Modern Library' for the Future," paper delivered at the Association for Library and Information Science, San Antonio, TX, January 17, 1996; available at http://www.sils.umich.edu/ALISE/.

60. Albert Brackmann, *Archival Training in Prussia*, Staff Information Paper 1 (Washington, DC: National Archives and Records Service, 1975 reprint), p. 5.

61. Sydney Pierce, "Subject Areas, Disciplines, and the Concept of Authority," *Library and Information Science Research* 13 (January–March 1991): 21–35.

62. Bruce Dearstyne, *The Archival Enterprise: Modern Archival Principles, Practices, and Management Techniques* (Chicago: American Library Association, 1993), p. ix.

63. Fritz Machlup and Una Mansfield, eds., *The Study of Information: Interdisciplinary Messages* (New York: John Wiley and Sons, 1983); for a lengthy review of this work, refer to E. Glynn Harmon, "The Interdisciplinary Study of Information: A Review Essay," *Journal of Library History* 22 (Spring 1987): 206–227.

64. "Society of American Archivists' Guidelines for the Development of a Curriculum for a Masters of Archival Studies," at http://www.archivists.org.

65. Sylvan Katz, "A Cache of Ancient Floppy Discs," *New Scientist* 19 (December 26, 1992): 70–71.

66. J. Michael Pemberton and Ann E. Prentice, eds., *Information Science: The Interdisciplinary Context* (New York: Neal-Schuman Publishers, 1990).

67. For such problems, see Linda Schamber, "What Is a Document? Rethinking the Concept in Uneasy Times," *Journal of the American Society for Information Science* 47 (September 1996): 669–671.

68. Leonard Boyle, "Diplomatics," in James M. Powell, ed., *Medieval Studies: An Introduction*, 2nd ed. (Syracuse, NY: Syracuse University Press, 1992), p. 89.

69. For a broader view of the nature of forgeries and fakes, refer to Gilbert Bagnani, "On Fakes and Forgeries," *The Phoenix* 14 (Winter 1960): 228–244.

70. For descriptions of Mesopotamian writing and archives, see Jean Bottero, *Mesopotamia: Writing, Reasoning, and the Gods*, trans. Zainab Bahrani and Marc Van De Mieroop (Chicago: University of Chicago Press, 1992).

71. Veda R. Charrow, "Language in the Bureaucracy," in Robert J. Di Pietro, ed., *Linguistics and the Professions: Proceedings of the Second Annual Delaware Symposium on Language Studies* (Norwood, NJ: Ablex Publishing Corporation, 1980), pp. 173–188 (quotation p. 174).

72. John Tagg, *The Burden of Representation: Essays on Photographies and Histories* (Minneapolis: University of Minnesota Press, 1993), p. 63.

73. T. K. Bikson and S. A. Law, "Electronic Information Media and Records Management Methods: A Survey of Practices in UN Organizations," *Information Society* 9, no. 2 (1993): 125–44 (quotations pp. 141–142).

74. Sally Macintyre, "Some Notes on Record Taking and Making in an Antenatal Clinic," *Sociological Review* 26 (August 1978): 595–611.

75. Lucy Suchman and Eleanor Wynn, "Procedures and Problems in the Office," *Office: Technology and People* 2 (January 1984): 133–154 (quotation p. 149).

76. Judith Y. Gliniecki and Ceda G. Ogada, "The Legal Acceptance of Electronic Documents, Writings, Signatures, and Notices in International Transportation: A Challenge in the Age of Global Electronic Commerce," *Northwestern Journal of International Law and Business* 13 (June 1992): 117–158 (quotations pp. 122, 126).

77. Thomas L. Lincoln, Daniel J. Essin, and Willis H. Ware. "The Electronic Medical Record: A Challenge for Computer Science to Develop Clincially and Socially Relevant Computer Systems to Coordinate Information for Patient Care and Analysis," *Information Society* 9, no. 2 (1993): 157–188.

78. Harold Garfinkel, *Studies in Ethnomethodology* (Englewood Cliffs, NJ: Prentice Hall, 1967), p. 191.

79. JoAnne Yates and Wanda J. Orlikowski, "Genres of Organizational Communication: A Structurational Approach to Studying Communication and Media," *Academy of Management Review* 17, no. 2 (1992): 299–326.

80. SAA *Newsletter*, November 1989, p. 30.

81. See my "Employing Records Professionals in the Information Age," *Information Management Journal* 34 (January 2000): 18–20, 22–23, 26–28, 30, 32–33.

82. See, for example, David J. Murrah, "Employer Expectations for Archivists: A Review of a 'Hybrid Profession,' " *Journal of Library Administration* 11, nos. 3 and 4 (1990): 165–174.

83. W. Boyd Rayward, "Library and Information Science: An Historical Perspective," *Journal of Library History* 20 (Spring 1985): 120–136.

84. Paul Marsden, "When Is the Future? Comparative Notes on the Electronic Record-Keeping Projects of the University of Pittsburgh and the University of British Columbia," *Archivaria* 43 (Spring 1997): 158–173 and Margaret Hedstrom, "Building Record-Keeping Systems: Archivists Are Not Alone on the Wild Frontier," *Archivaria* 44 (Fall 1997): 44–71 provide views on the chase for a better definition of records and recordkeeping systems.

85. "Guidelines for the Development of a Two-Year Curriculum for a Master of Archival Studies," *ACA Bulletin* 13 (March 1989): 16.

86. See Lisa B. Weber, "Educating Archivists for Automation," *Library Trends* 36 (Winter 1988): 501–518.

87. The calls for more research have been Paul Conway, "Facts and Frameworks: An Approach to Studying the Users of Archives," *American Archivist* 49 (Fall 1986): 393–407 and Lawrence Dowler, "The Role of Use in Defining Archival Practice and Principles: A Research Agenda for the Availability and Use of Records," *American Archivist* 51 (Winter–Spring 1988): 74–86.

88. Such as Max Evans, "The Visible Hand: Creating a Practical Mechanism for Cooperative Appraisal," *Midwestern Archivist* 11, no. 1 (1986): 8.

89. Frank G. Burke, "The Future Course of Archival Theory in the United States." The responses to Burke were Lester J. Cappon, "What, Then, Is There to Theorize About?" *American Archivist* 45 (Winter 1982): 19–25; Michael A. Lutzker, "Max Weber and the Analysis of Modern Bureaucratic Organization: Notes toward a Theory of Appraisal," ibid. 45 (Spring 1982): 119–130; Gregg D. Kimball, "The Burke-Cappon Debate: Some Further Criticisms and Considerations for Archival Theory," ibid. 48 (Fall 1985): 369–376; and John W. Roberts, "Archival Theory: Much Ado about Shelving," ibid. 50 (Winter 1987): 66–74.

90. Allan Pratt, *The Information of the Image* (Norwood, NJ: Ablex Publishing Corporation, 1982), p. 9.

91. Jesse Shera, *The Foundations of Education for Librarianship* (New York: Becker and Hayes, 1972), p. 132.

92. William Paisley "Information Science as a Multidiscipline," in *Information Science: The Interdisciplinarity Context*, ed. J. Michael Pemberton and Ann E. Prentice (New York: Neal-Schuman Publishers, 1990), p. 6.

93. Edward G. Holley, "Current Developments in Education for Librarianship and Information Science," in *Changing Technology and Education for Librarianship and Information Science, Foundations in Library and Information Science*, vol. 20, ed. Basil Stuart-Stubbs (Greenwich, CT: JAI Press, 1985), pp. 55–75.

94. Ericson, "Professional Associations and Archival Education," p. 299.

95. Paul Conway, "Effective Continuing Education for Training the Archivist," *Journal of Education for Library and Information Science* 34 (Winter 1993): 40.

96. See Ethel Auster and Laurent-G. Denis, "Striving Toward Excellence: Continuing Education for Library Personnel," *Canadian Library Journal* 43 (April 1986): 81–89 as an example of such efforts.

97. Sandy Donnelly, "Professional Development Survey," *College and Research Libraries News* 48 (April 1987): 199–200 as an example.

98. John A. McCrossan, "Beyond the Master's Program: Library Schools and Continuing Education of Library, Media, and Information Professionals," *Advances in Librarianship*, vol. 12, ed. Wesley Simonton (New York: Academic Press, 1982), p. 279.

99. Norman Roberts and Tania Kohn, "Continuing Education and Training for Academic Library Staff," *Journal of Librarianship* 21 (April 1989): 110–111.

100. Conway, "Effective Continuing Education," pp. 40–42.

101. Sally Hixon Cavanaugh, "Connecting Education and Practice," in Lynn Curry, Jon F. Wergin, and associates, *Educating Professionals: Responding to New Expectations for Competence and Accountability* (San Francisco: Jossey-Bass Publishers, 1993), pp. 114–115.

102. See, for example, Nancy L. Bennett and Robert D. Fox, "Challenges for Continuing Professional Education," in Lynn Curry, Jon F. Wergin, and associates, *Educating Professionals: Responding to New Expectations for Competence and Accountability*, pp. 262–278.

103. Robert Rippey, "Learning from Corporate Education Programs," in Curry, Wergin, and associates, *Educating Professionals: Responding to New Expectations for Competence and Accountability*, p. 216.

104. See Peter J. Wosh and Elizabeth Yakel, "Smaller Archives and Professional Development: Some New York Stories," *American Archivist* 55 (Summer 1992): 474–482.

105. Paul Conway, "Archival Preservation in the United States and the Role of Information Sources," Ph.D. dissertation, University of Michigan, 1991.

106. Conway, "Archival Preservation," p. 2.

107. Conway, "Archival Preservation," p. 207.

108. Linda M. Matthews, "The Georgia Archives Institute and the Training of Archivists, 1967–1989," in *Society of Georgia Archivists: 20 Years in Celebration 1969–1989* (n.p.: [Society of Georgia Archivists, c. 1990]), pp. 48–50.

109. Matthews, "Georgia Archives Institute," p. 59.

110. Bruce Ambacher, "The Modern Archives Institute: A Profile of Recent Students," *Archival Issues* 18, no. 2 (1993): 109–119.

111. James Fogerty, "The Minnesota Basic Workshops Project," *American Archivist* 44 (Summer 1981): 237–240 (quotation p. 239).

112. Conway, "Effective Continuing Education," p. 39.

113. Mary C. Chobot, "Improving the Quality of Continuing Education," *IFLA Journal* 15, no. 3 (1989): 213.

114. With the increasing number of major graduate archives programs with an interest in attracting the best students for the best education in order to obtain the best professional positions, it is obvious that there is a severe clash of missions, if not professional cultures, between educators and the associations. Professional associations have a mission to attract a wide array of professionals, while education programs have a much more restricted function, what some might term an "elitist" one. It is possible that the current National Forum on Archival Continuing Education might provide some leadership: "The National Forum on Archival Continuing Education (NFACE) is a project developed by the Council of State Historical Records Coordinators (COSHRC) in partnership with the American Association for State and Local History (AASLH). It is being funded through a grant from the National Historical Publications and Records Commission"; see the Web site at http://www.coshrc.org/nface/index.html.

115. Some of these changes can be reflected in the most recent SAA guidelines, "Guidelines for the Development of Post-Appointment and Continuing Education and Training (PACE) Programs," adopted in 1997 and available at http://www.archivists.org. For example, these guidelines distinguish between "introductory," "advanced," and "ancillary" audiences, an indication that this professional association is recognizing the changing needs of the records professionals. A major additional step would be for the society to give up its emphasis on basic training and invest its resources in advanced education and in reaching policy makers and resource allocators about the importance of archives and records management. Such a move would strengthen graduate education, basic professional criteria defining archivists, and the ability of individual archivists to work in increasingly more complex technological and administrative environments.

116. David Damrosch, *We Scholars: Changing the Culture of the University* (Cambridge, MA: Harvard University Press, 1995), pp. 23, 122.

117. Derek Bok, *Beyond the Ivory Tower: Social Responsibilities of the Modern University* (Cambridge, MA: Harvard University Press, 1982), p. 72.

118. Jaroslav Pelikan, *The Idea of the University: A Reexamination* (New Haven, CT: Yale University Press, 1992), pp. 16–17.

119. Derek Bok, *Higher Learning* (Cambridge, MA: Harvard University Press, 1986), p. 5.

120. Jacques Barzun, *Begin Here: The Forgotten Conditions of Teaching and Learning* (Chicago: University of Chicago Press, 1991), p. 35.

121. David B. Gracy, "Archivists, You Are What People Think You Keep," *American Archivist* 52 (Winter 1989): 72–78.

122. David J. Klaassen, "The Archival Intersection: Cooperation Between Collecting Repositories and Nonprofit Organizations," *Midwestern Archivist* 15, no. 1 (1990): 25–38.

123. This is especially seen in the efforts to document modern, post–World War II science and technology. See, for some stimulating reading, Philip Alexander and Helen W. Samuels, "The Roots of 128: A Hypothetical Documentation Strategy," *American Archivist* 50 (Fall 1987): 518–531; Bruce H. Bruemmer and Sheldon Hochheiser, *The High-Technology Company: A Historical Research and Archival Guide* (Minneapolis: Charles Babbage Institute, Center for the History of Information Processing, University of Minnesota, 1989); Joan D. Krizack, ed., *Documentation Planning for the U.S. Health Care System* (Baltimore: Johns Hopkins University Press, 1994); Nancy McCall and Lisa A. Mix, eds., *Designing Archival Programs to Advance Knowledge in the Health Fields* (Baltimore: Johns Hopkins University Press, 1994); Clark A. Elliott, ed., *Understanding Progress as Process: Documentation of the History of Post-War Science and Technology in the United States; Final Report of the Joint Committee on Archives of Science and Technology* (Chicago: Distributed by the Society of American Archivists, 1983); Bruce V. Lewenstein, "Preserving Data about the Knowledge Creation Process: Developing an Archive on the Cold Fusion Controversy," *Knowledge: Creation, Diffusion, Utilization* 13 (September 1991): 79–86.

124. Compare Margaret Hedstrom, *Archives and Manuscripts: Machine-Readable Records* (Chicago: Society of American Archivists, 1984) and Harold Naugler, *The Archival Appraisal of Machine-Readable Records: A RAMP Study With Guidelines* (Paris: UNESCO, 1984) with David Bearman, *Electronic Evidence* (Pittsburgh: Archives and Museum Informatics, 1994).

125. Hans Booms, "Society and the Formation of a Documentary Heritage," *Archivaria* 24 (Summer 1987): 69–107; Hans Booms, "Uberlieferungsbildung: Keeping Archives as a Social and Political Activity," *Archivaria* 33 (Winter 1991–1992): 25–33; D. Laberge, "Information, Knowledge, and Rights: The Preservation of Archives as a Political and Social Issue," *Archivaria* 25 (Winter 1987–1988): 44–49.

126. The foremost example of this are the three seminal writings of F. Gerald Ham: "The Archival Edge," *American Archivist* 38 (January 1975): 5–13; "Archival Strategies for the Post-Custodial Era," *American Archivist* 44 (Summer 1981): 207–216; and "Archival Choices: Managing the Historical Record in an Age of Abundance," in *Archival Choices: Managing the Historical Record in an Age of Abundance*, ed. Nancy E. Peace (Lexington, MA: D.C. Heath, 1984), pp. 11–22. The innovative and original perspective of Ham has been weakened in his *Selecting and Appraising Archives and Manuscripts*

(Chicago: Society of American Archivists, 1992). For an even more blatant statement of this, refer to Andrea Hinding, "Toward Documentation: New Collecting Strategies in the 1980s," in *Options for the 80s: Proceedings of the Second National Conference of the Association of College and Research Libraries*, ed. Michael D. Kathman and Virgil F. Massman (Greenwich, CT: JAI Press, 1981), pp. 531–538. In this regard, we would also do well to read from other disciplines; for some examples of interesting readings, see John D. Dorst, *The Written Suburb: An American Site, An Ethnographic Dilemma* (Philadelphia: University of Pennsylvania Press, 1989); Kevin Lynch, *What Time Is This Place?* (Cambridge, MA: MIT Press, 1972); Susan M. Pearce, *Museums, Objects, and Collections: A Cultural Study* (Washington, DC: Smithsonian Press, 1993); Harry Rubenstein, "Collecting for Tomorrow: Sweden's Contemporary Documentation Program," *Museum News* 63 (August 1985): 55–60; and Thomas J. Schlereth, "Contemporary Collecting for Future Recollecting," *Museum Studies Journal* 113 (Spring 1984): 23–30. I have tried to deal with this complex issue in my "Archival Anchorites: Building Public Memory in the Era of the Culture Wars," *Multicultural Review* 7 (June 1998): 52–60.

127. Terry Cook, "Many Are Called but Few Are Chosen: Appraisal Guidelines for Sampling and Selecting Case Files," *Archivaria* 32 (Summer 1991): 25–50.

128. Lauren R. Brown, "Present at the Tenth Hour: Appraising and Accessioning the Papers of Congresswoman Marjorie S. Holt," *Rare Books and Manuscripts Librarianship* (1988): 95–102.

129. Frank Boles and Julia Marks Young, "Exploring the Black Box: The Appraisal of University Administrative Records," *American Archivist* 48 (Spring 1985): 121–140; Frank Boles, *Archival Appraisal* (New York: Neal-Schuman Publishers, 1991).

130. See, for example, Susan D. Steinwall, "Appraisal and the FBI Files Case: For Whom Do Archivists Retain Records?" *American Archivist* 49 (Winter 1986): 52–63; Elizabeth Lockwood, " 'Imponderable Matters': The Influence of New Trends in History on Appraisal at the National Archives," *American Archivist* 53 (Summer 1990): 394–405.

131. Perhaps what I have in mind here is the notion of "dialogue" going back to the ancient Greeks. As used by Jane Jacobs, it is a "form—disagreements, speculations, second thoughts, questions, answers, amended answers— . . . suited to the problematic subject matter." See her *Systems of Survival: A Dialogue on the Moral Foundations of Commerce and Politics* (New York: Vintage Books, 1992), p. 20.

132. Some examples of such books are Peter N. Stearns, *Meaning Over Memory: Recasting the Teaching of Culture and History* (Chapel Hill: University of North Carolina Press, 1993); Joyce Appleby, Lynn Hunt, and Margaret Jacob, *Telling the Truth About History* (New York: W. W. Norton and Company, 1994).

133. If you have not read anything about electronic records management, then David Bearman and Margaret Hedstrom, "Reinventing Archives for Electronic Records: Alternative Service Delivery Options," in *Electronic Records Management Program Strategies*, ed. Margaret Hedstrom (Pittsburgh: Archives and Museum Informatics, 1993), pp. 82–98 is the place to start. They argue that archivists must start by re-examining their "program structures and methodologies" (p. 82). Bearman and Hedstrom first discuss why current approaches fail with electronic records. They then consider alternative models, which they characterize as "steering rather than rowing," "empowering others rather than serving," "enterprising," "customer-driven," and "decentralized."

134. Robert F. Reynolds, "The Incunabula of Archival Theory and Practice in the United States: J. C. Fitzpatrick's *Notes on the Care, Cataloguing, Calendaring and Ar-

ranging of Manuscripts and the Public Archives Commission's Uncompleted 'Primer of Archival Economy,' " *American Archivist* 54 (Fall 1991): 466–482. There are even elements of political and other attitudes reflected in some of the results of research (rare as it is) on basic archival arrangement and description; see, for example, Avra Michelson, "Description and Reference in the Age of Automation," *American Archivist* 50 (Spring 1987): 192–208.

135. Archivists have created standards, appropriated standards, and tried to keep pace with standards. For suggestive sources on this, refer to Victoria Irons Walch, *Standards for Archival Description: A Handbook* (Chicago: Society of American Archivists, 1994); Richard J. Cox, "The Archival Profession and Information Technology Standards," *Journal of the American Society for Information Science* 43 (September 1992): 571–575; Steven L. Hensen, *Archives, Personal Papers, and Manuscripts: A Cataloging Manual for Archival Repositories, Historical Societies, and Manuscript Libraries*, 2nd ed. (Chicago: Society of American Archivists, 1989).

136. For some suggestive readings, see Robert P. Spindler and Richard Pearce-Moses, "Does AMC Mean 'Archives Made Confusing'? Patron Understanding of USMARC AMC Catalog Records," *American Archivist* 56 (Spring 1993): 330–341; International Council on Archives, "Statement of Principles Regarding Archival Description," *Archivaria* 34 (Summer 1992): 8–16; International Council on Archives, "ISAD(G): General International Standard Archival Description," *Archivaria* 34 (Summer 1992): 17–32; David Bearman, "Documenting Documentation," *Archivaria* 34 (Summer 1992): 33–49; Michael Cook, "Description Standards: The Struggle Towards the Light," *Archivaria* 34 (Summer 1992): 50–57; Kent Haworth, "The Development of Descriptive Standards in Canada: A Progress Report," *Archivaria* 34 (Summer 1992): 75–90; Hugo Stibbe, "Implementing the Concept of Fonds: Primary Access Point, Multilevel Description and Authority Control," *Archivaria* 34 (Summer 1992): 109–137; Steven L. Hensen, "Standards for the Exchange of Descriptive Information on Archival and Manuscript Material in the United States," *Archivaria* 34 (Summer 1992): 272–278.

137. Donald DeWitt, "The Impact of the MARC AMC Format on Archival Education and Employment during the 1980s," *Midwestern Archivist* 16, no. 2 (1991): 73–85.

138. Mary Jo Pugh, "The Illusion of Omniscience: Subject Access and the Reference Archivist," *American Archivist* 45 (Winter 1982): 33–44.

139. Paul Conway, "Facts and Frameworks," and his *Partners in Research; Improving Access to the Nation's Archives* (Pittsburgh: Archives and Museum Informatics, 1994).

140. Ann D. Gordon, *Using the Nation's Documentary Heritage* (Washington, DC: Historical Documents Study, 1992).

141. Diane S. Nixon, "Providing Access to Controversial Public Records: The Case of the Robert F. Kennedy Assassination Investigation Files," *Public Historian* 11 (Summer 1989): 29–44; Seymour M. Hersh, "Nixon's Last Cover-Up: The Tapes He Wants the Archives to Suppress," *New Yorker*, December 14, 1992, pp. 76–82, 84–88, 90–95. See also Heather MacNeil, *Without Consent: The Ethics of Disclosing Personal Information in Public Archives* (Metuchen, NJ: Scarecrow Press, 1992).

142. For some readings on this, from a wide range of perspectives, see Bruce W. Dearstyne, "What Is the *Use* of Archives? A Challenge for the Profession," *American Archivist* 50 (Winter 1987): 76–87; Elsie T. Freeman, "In the Eye of the Beholder: Archives Administration from the User's Point of View," *American Archivist* 47 (Spring 1984): 111–123; Page Putnam Miller, *Developing a Premier National Institution: A Report from the User Community to the National Archives* ([Washington, DC]: National

Coordinating Committee for the Promotion of History, 1989); Mary N. Speakman, "The User Talks Back," *American Archivist* 47 (Spring 1984): 164–171; Barbara C. Orbach, "The View From the Researcher's Desk: Historians' Perceptions of Research and Repositories," *American Archivist* 54 (Winter 1991): 28–43.

143. Janet Malcolm, *In the Freud Archives* (New York: Alfred A. Knopf, 1984) is a perfect example of this, focusing on personal and professional aspects of this particular case with no real testing of why the Library of Congress had agreed to have the Freud records with such tight family and professional control of access to the records. For a rebuttal of sorts, see Jeffrey Moussaieff Masson, *Final Analysis: The Making and Unmaking of a Psychoanalyst* (New York: HarperPerennial, 1991).

144. This historical relationship is well-documented by a variety of writings, such as: Jack Goody, *The Logic of Writing and the Organization of Society* (London: Cambridge University Press, 1986); Rosalind Thomas, *Literacy and Orality in Ancient Greece* (Cambridge: Cambridge University Press, 1992); M. T. Clanchy, *From Memory to Written Record: England, 1066–1307* (Cambridge, MA: Harvard University Press, 1979); Lawrence J. McCrank, "Documenting Reconquest and Reform: The Growth of Archives in the Medieval Crown of Aragon," *American Archivist* 56 (Spring 1993): 256–318; Denise Schmandt-Besserat, "The Earliest Precursor of Writing," in William S-Y. Wang, ed., *The Emergence of Language: Development and Evolution* (New York: W. H. Freeman and Co., 1991), pp. 31–45; David Cressy, " 'A Constant Intercourse of Letters': The Transatlantic Flow of Information," in *Coming Over: Migration and Communication Between England and New England in the Seventeenth Century* (Cambridge: Cambridge University Press, 1987), pp. 213–234; James H. Cassedy, *Demography in Early America: Beginnings of the Statistical Mind, 1600–1800* (Cambridge, MA: Harvard University Press, 1969); Patricia Cline Cohen, *A Calculating People: The Spread of Numeracy in Early America* (Chicago: University of Chicago Press, 1982); JoAnne Yates, *Control through Communication: The Rise of System in American Management* (Baltimore: Johns Hopkins University Press, 1989); Margarey W. Davies, *Woman's Place Is at the Typewriter: Office Work and Office Workers 1870–1930* (Philadelphia: Temple University Press, 1982); Margo J. Anderson, *The American Census: A Social History* (New Haven, CT: Yale University Press, 1988); Barbara L. Craig, "The Introduction of Copying Devices into the British Civil Service, 1877–1889," in Craig, ed., *The Archival Imagination: Essays in Honour of Hugh A. Taylor* (Ottawa: Association of Canadian Archivists, 1992); Alan Delgado, *The Enormous File: A Social History of the Office* (London: John Murray, 1979); James R. Beniger, *The Control Revolution: Technological and Economic Origins of the Information Society* (Cambridge, MA: Harvard University Press, 1986); Graham S. Lowe, " 'The Enormous File': The Evolution of the Modern Office in Early Twentieth-Century Canada," *Archivaria* 19 (Winter 1984–1985): 137–151.

145. I tried to consider this in my *Managing Institutional Archives: Foundational Principles and Practices* (Westport, CT: Greenwood Press, 1992).

146. And, we probably need to begin to understand something more about the psychology and ethics of collecting that influences our own professional agendas. Again, there are many fine readings that can get students to reflect on such matters, such as Werner Muensterberger, *Collecting: An Unruly Passion; Psychological Perspective* (Princeton, NJ: Princeton University Press, 1994) and Phyllis Mauch Messenger, ed., *The Ethics of Collecting Cultural Property: Whose Culture? Whose Property?* (Albuquerque: University of New Mexico Press, 1989). I have discussed these and other related works

in my "The Archivist and Collecting: A Review Essay," *American Archivist* 59 (Fall 1996): 496–512.

147. See my *The First Generation of Electronic Records Archivists in the United States: A Study in Professionalization* (Binghamton, NY: Haworth Press, 1994) and the following writings: Charles M. Dollar, *Archival Theory and Information Technologies: The Impact of Information Technologies on Archival Principles and Methods* (Macerata, Italy: University of Macerata Press, 1992); Terry Cook, "Easy to Byte, Harder to Chew: The Second Generation of Electronic Records Archives," *Archivaria* 33 (Winter 1991–1992): 202–216; Terry Cook, "Electronic Records, Paper Minds: The Revolution in Information Management and Archives in the Post-Custodial and Post-Modernist Era," *Archives and Manuscripts* 22 (November 1994): 300–328. Margaret Hedstrom, "Understanding Electronic Incunabula: A Framework for Research on Electronic Records," *American Archivist* 54 (Summer 1991): 334–355.

148. There is a long, very repetitive literature on this topic, but the following provide a fairly good sense of the issues involved and causes of the professional schism: Robert L. Sanders, "Archivists and Records Managers: Another Marriage in Trouble?" *Records Management Quarterly* 23 (April 1989): 12–14, 16–18, 20; Frank B. Evans, "Archivists and Records Managers: Variations on a Theme," *American Archivist* 30 (January 1967): 45–58; Frank G. Burke, "Chaos through Communications: Archivists, Records Managers and the Communications Phenomenon," in Barbara Craig, ed., *The Archival Imagination*, pp. 154–177; Tyler O. Walters, "Rediscovering the Theoretical Base of Records Management and Its Implications for Graduate Education: Searching for the New School of Information Studies," *Journal of Education for Library and Information Science* 36 (Spring 1995): 139–154.

149. See, for example, David Roberts, "Defining Electronic Records, Documents and Data," *Archives and Manuscripts* 22 (May 1994): 14–26; Jay Atherton, "From Life Cycle to Continuum: Some Thoughts on the Records Management–Archives Relationship," *Archivaria* 21 (Winter 1985–1986): 43–51.

150. Marion Renehan, "Unassailable Evidence: The Nexus Between Recordkeeping and Public Sector Accountability," *Archives and Manuscripts* 21 (May 1993) 62–76 and Eldon Frost, "A Weak Link in the Chain: Records Scheduling as a Source of Archival Acquisition," *Archivaria* 33 (Winter 1991–1992): 78–86 provide an important contrast in purpose and result. And this is a role all archivists, especially those in government and public organizations, should possess and which Margaret Cross Norton wrote so eloquently about half a century ago; see Thornton W. Mitchell, ed., *Norton on Archives: The Writings of Margaret Cross Norton on Archival and Records Management* (Evanston: Southern Illinois University Press, 1975). Contrast Norton's objectives with the critical assessment of the National Archives in U.S. House Committee on Government Operations, *Taking a Byte Out of History: The Archival Preservation of Federal Computer Records* (Washington, DC: U.S. Government Printing Office, 1990).

151. My current favorites are David Osborne and Ted Gaebler, *Reinventing Government: How the Entrepreneurial Spirit Is Transforming the Public Sector* (New York: Penguin, 1993) and Michael Hammer and James Champy, *Reengineering the Corporation: A Manifesto for Business Revolution* (New York: HarperBusiness, 1993).

152. David Bearman and Margaret Hedstrom, "Reinventing Archives for Electronic Records: Alternative Service Delivery Options," in *Electronic Records Management Program Strategies*, ed. Margaret Hedstrom (Pittsburgh: Archives and Museum Informatics, 1993), pp. 82–98.

153. Mark Brogan, "Regulation and the Market: A Micro-Economic Analysis of Strategies for Electronic Archives Management," *Archives and Manuscripts* 22 (November 1994): 384–394. And this also takes us back to such issues as participation in the standards-setting industry; see Carl Cargill, *Information Technology Standardization: Theory, Process and Organizations* (Bedford, MA: Digital Press, 1989).

154. A. Bartlett Giamatti, *A Free and Ordered Space: The Real World of the University* (New York: W. W. Norton, 1990), p. 134.

155. I highly recommend William M. Sullivan, *Work and Integrity: The Crisis and Promise of Professionalism in America* (New York: HarperBusiness, 1995) for an explication of this dimension of professionalism.

Index

Abbott, Andrew, 68
Academy of Certified Archivists, 192.
  See also Certification of archivists
Access, to records, 51, 73–77, 79, 152,
  156–171, 219
Accountability, and records, 5, 17, 25, 31–
  32, 34, 50, 54, 55, 64, 78, 90, 102,
  119, 132, 149, 152, 162, 163, 165,
  166, 170, 192
Acland, Glenda, 148
Adams, Scott, 87, 89
Adamson, Lynda, 144
Administrative value, and records, 17–18,
  31. *See also* Records' values
Adoption records, 164–165
Advocacy, and records, 152–156, 171,
  214–221
African Americans, 144
Alderman, Ellen, 76
Algonquin College, 192
American Association for State and Local
  History, 227 n.114
American Library Association, 162
Americans with Disabilities Act, 152
Anderson, Terry, 133, 135–136
Anthropologists, 200, 202
Appraisal, of records, 7, 13, 21, 27–30,
  33, 46, 87–120, 215, 217–218. *See*

also Collecting; Documentation strat-
  egy; Functional analysis; Macro-
  appraisal; Records' values
Archaeology, 115
Archer, Jeffrey, 171
Archival mission, 29, 30
Archival science, 33
Archives, as a term, 7–19
Archives of Religious Institutions, 209
Archivist of the United States, 51. *See
  also* United States National Archives
Archivists. *See* Records managers and ar-
  chivists
Argentina, 136
Arrangement and description, of archival
  records, 218–219. *See also* Descriptive
  standards
Art history, 202
Ash, Timothy Garten, 166
Assassination Records Review Board,
  162
Association of Canadian Archivists, 90,
  194, 204–205
Association of Records Managers and
  Administrators, 69, 79, 157
Atherton, Jay, 17–18
Atlanta, 132, 140
Atlantic Monthly, 54

Atlas, James, 29
Attinger, Monique, 19, 20
Australia, 143, 144, 148
Australian records approaches, 4, 24, 28, 34–35, 49–50, 61, 62, 70, 88
Authenticity, of records, 48–49
Automated teller machine (ATM) cards, 149, 150

Balough, Ann, 161
Barbour, William, 166
Barzun, Jacques, 217
Bauer, G. Philip, 195
Bearman, David, 62, 117
Belgium, 139
Bell, Lionel, 191, 194
Bemis, Samuel Flagg, 191
Bennett, Colin J., 169–170
Berlioz, Hector, 139
Berner, Richard, 24, 189–190, 196
Berry, Wendell, 58
Bikson, Tora, 202
Birkerts, Sven, 149
Birmingham Civil Rights Institute, 133
Blanton, Tom, 72–73, 76, 167
Blouin, Francis, 195
Blumberg, Stanley, 168
Bok, Derek, 215, 216
Bok, Sissela, 161
Boorstin, Daniel, 110, 111, 112
Bower, Tom, 70
Boyle, Leonard, 201
Brackmann, Albert, 199
Bradford, William, 148
Branscomb, Anne Wells, 50
Braun, Eva, 138
Breitman, Richard, 170
Brent, Isabelle, 147
Brichford, Maynard, 110, 112, 113
Brin, David, 165
British royal family, 166
Brogan, Mark, 27
Bronowski, Jacob, 142–143, 149
Brookings Institution, 158, 164
Brown, Richard, 165
Brown and Williamson Tobacco Corporation, 70, 166
Buck, Solon, 190, 192

Buckland, Michael, 26–27, 109
Burke, Frank, 205–206
Burnum, John, 63
Buruma, Ian, 166
Bush, George, 134, 140; administration, 135
Business archives. See Institutional archives

Calculators, 99
California, 211
Canada, 24, 28, 30, 152, 192, 198, 207. See also Association of Canadian Archivists
Cappon, Lester, 30
Carey, James W., 141
Carp, E. Wayne, 164–165
Carter, Jimmy, 140
Censorship, 53. See also Secrecy
Central Intelligence Agency, 135, 137, 162, 163
Cerf, Vincent, 58
Certification, of archivists, 192, 199
Charrow, Veda R., 201
Checkbooks, 150
Chicago, 132
Children's literature, and records, 142–149
China, 136, 137
Chobot, Mary C., 213
Christopher, Warren M., 133
Churchill, Winston, 133
City of Bits, 97–98
Civil War, 165
Clanchy, M. T., 55
Clay tablets, 159
Clinton, Bill, 52, 134, 136, 141; Clinton–Al Gore administration, 70, 135
Cognitive scientists, 200
Cold War, 136, 161–162
Collecting, 28–29, 96–97, 116, 139, 146, 154, 231 n.146
Collecting policy, 115
Collection analysis, 115, 128 n.127
Colorado, 211
Colson, John, 195, 196, 198
Columbia University, 93, 190
Columbus, Christopher, 133, 144

Combest, Larry, 74
Commerzbank AG, 14
Commission on Federal Paperwork, 153
Commission on Protecting and Reducing
  Government Secrecy, 73–77
Committee on the Records of Govern-
  ment, 153
Commonwealth of Independent States,
  162
Computer literacy and records profession-
  als, 56–65, 78, 203–204
Computer networks, 161
Computers, and their evolution, 98–99
Constitution, 146
Context, of records, 114–115, 201, 217
Continuing education: and preservation,
  93–94; and records professionals, 193–
  197, 207–214. See also Education of
  records professionals
Convergence of technologies, 65–77
Conway, Jill Ker, 148
Conway, Paul, 190, 207, 208, 210, 212–
  213
Cook, Michael, 191–192, 194, 197, 198
Cook, Terry, 26, 47, 117, 118
Cooley, Martha, 163–164
Copyright, 51, 154, 219. See also Intel-
  lectual property
Corporate archives. See Institutional
  archives
Corporate memory. See Organizational
  memory
Coulson, Jim, 62–63
Council of State Historical Records Coor-
  dinators, 227 n.114
County government records, 155
Credit cards, 149, 150
Crew, Gary, 144
Crews, Frederick, 63
Cuban missile crisis, 135, 167
Cunningham, Adrian, 23–24, 28
Custody of records, 24, 32, 49, 56, 91–
  92, 95, 106, 199

D'Amato, Alfonse, 70
Damrosch, David, 68, 69, 214
Davies, Simon G., 170
Davis, Shelley, 71–72

Data processing, 8–9, 21, 22, 99
Daynard, Jodi, 140
Dead Sea Scrolls, 133, 138, 141
Dearstyne, Bruce, 88, 200
Declaration of Independence, 146, 171
Declassification of records, 135. See also
  Secrecy
Delaries, Anita, 196
Dertouzos, Michael, 160
Descriptive standards, 30, 33, 195, 204,
  216, 219. See also Encoded Archival
  Description
Devlin, Keith, 63
Diaries, 147, 159
Diffie, Whitfield, 159
"Dilbert," 87
Diplomatics, 2–3, 30, 33, 48, 64, 111,
  145, 194, 201
Disaster-preparedness plans, 91
Disney, Walt, 133–134
Distance education, 194, 214
Documentation strategy, 30, 108, 118,
  119. See also Appraisal of records
Document management systems, 100
Dollar, Charles, 3
Dowlin, Kenneth, 110–111
Driver's licenses, 149, 150
Drucker, Peter, 60–61, 90, 113
du Pont Breck, Allen, 198
Duranti, Luciana, 30, 53, 110, 112

Eastern Europe, 137, 162
East Germany, 166. See also Germany
Eastwood, Terry, 61, 192
Economist, 159
Economists, 200
Education of records professionals, 20,
  189–221. See also Continuing educa-
  tion; Library and history as educational
  venue for records professionals
Eichmann, Adolf, 136
Electronic mail, 5, 11, 13, 121 n.18, 134,
  145, 167, 202. See also PROFS case
Electronic records management: issues, 1–
  4, 193, 195, 203–207, 212; and per-
  sonal papers, 22–31; and preservation,
  91–96; research about, 47–50. See also
  PROFS case

Eliot, T. S., 164
Ellis, Roger, 191, 194
El Salvador, 135, 136
Emancipation Proclamation, 133
Encoded Archival Description, 204. *See also* Descriptive standards
Endelman, Judith, 115
England, 6
Enola Gay exhibition controversy, 53
Ericson, Tim, 96, 207
Erlandsson, Alf, 106
Ethical issues, 93, 100, 108, 151–152, 153–154, 156–157, 158, 161, 163, 169
Evans, Frank, 190, 193, 194, 197
Evidence, and records, 4–7, 16, 17, 23, 25, 26, 27, 28, 31, 32, 33–34, 46, 55, 64, 96, 101, 102, 104–105, 109, 132, 148, 149, 170, 192, 201, 218
Etzioni, Amitai, 160, 166

Facsimile, 202
Farrugia, Charlie, 143
Federal Bureau of Investigation, 133–134, 136, 151
Federal Records Act of 1950, 5, 134, 135
Film, 140
Floyd, Candace, 14
Fogerty, James, 211–212
Forgery, 201
Fourth Amendment, 76, 160
France, 5, 139
Freedom of Information Act, 74, 133, 136, 162, 163
Freud, Sigmund, 134, 142
Functional analysis for appraisal, 118, 129 n.129. *See also* Appraisal of records
Functional requirements for recordkeeping, 31–34, 48, 50, 54–55, 92–93

Galvin, Thomas J., 67
Gans, Herbert J., 132–133
Genealogy, 145–146
General Accounting Office, 71
General Records Schedule 20, 104, 106
Genres, of records, 203
George Washington University, 72
Georgia Archives Institute, 211

Georgia Department of Archives and History, 211
Germany, 53, 71, 139. *See also* East Germany
Gerstner, Louis V., 137
Giamatti, A. Bartlett, 220
Glantz, Stanton, 166
Goggin, Jacqueline, 190
Goody, Jack, 46
Government records, 29
Gracy, David, 19, 24–25, 217
Great Britain, 137
Greene, Mark, 62

Haley, Gail, 147
Ham, F. Gerald, 110, 111, 118, 128 n.128
Harvard Business Review, 15–16
Harvard University, 215
Hedstrom, Margaret, 47
Heim, Michael, 45
Herbert, Bob, 159
Hersh, Seymour, 75, 135
Hilton, Suzanne, 145
Hinding, Andrea, 115
Hiroshima, 167
Hiss, Alger, 138, 161
Historians, 200
Historic preservation, 115
Historical societies, 116, 123 n.51
History Associates, Inc., 14
History Factory, 14
Hitler, Adolf, 138–139
Hives, Christopher, 96
Hoff, Joan, 170
Holocaust, 53, 69–71, 120
Hollerith, Herman, 63, 79
Hong Kong, 137
Hoover, J. Edgar, 134
Horton, Forest Woody, 4
Howard, Philip K., 74–75, 103
Hussein, Saddam, 171

IBM, 63, 137
Illinois, 139
Imber-Black, Evan, 161
Imperial War Museum, 107
Indiana, 163

Indiana University, 49
Information resources management, 18, 20
Information science, 201, 202
Institutional archives, 9–19, 112, 220; in corporations, 96–102
Intellectual property, 101, 157–158, 219. *See also* Copyright
Interdisciplinarity, 68, 94
Interdisciplinary characteristics of records knowledge, 200–203
Internal Revenue Service, 70, 71–72
Internet and records, 12–13, 79, 121 n.17, 160
Intrinsic value, of records, 113–114
Iran-Contra affair, 5, 46, 51, 70, 72–73, 75, 76, 104, 120, 134, 135, 137, 167
Iraq, 138
Israel, 70

Jackall, Robert, 100
Jagmetti, Carlo, 70
Jameson, J. Franklin, 105
Japan, 53, 71, 167
Jeffers, Susan, 147
Jenkinson, Hilary, 5, 6, 25–26, 35, 110, 111, 112, 115, 197
Johnson, Alexandra, 159
Johnson, Lyndon B., administration, 167
Jones, H. G., 105
Joyce, James, 139
Jurists, 202

Kansas City, 132
Kanter, Jerry, 59
Kennebunk, Maine, 139
Kennedy, Caroline, 76
Kennedy, John F., 133, 138, 162; administration, 135, 167
Kennedy, Robert F., 219
Kensington Stone, 144
Kesner, Richard, 20, 53–54
Key, Francis Scott, 146
King, Martin Luther, Jr., 142
Knoke, William, 65
Knoppers, Jake, 21
Konigsburg, E. L., 147–148
Korean War, 138

Kozol, Jonathan, 57–58
Ku Klux Klan, 139

Laberge, Danielle, 117
Landau, Susan, 159
Landauer, Thomas, 56, 57, 61, 68, 69
Lanham, Richard A.,149
Law, S. A., 202
Lebanon, 135
Legal requirements for recordkeeping, 31, 93, 108. *See also* Records' warrant
Letter writing, 107, 145, 158
Librarians, 142, 147, 200, 219
Librarians' image, 67
Libraries, 123 n.51, 143, 147, 199
Library archives, 194
Library cards, 150
Library and history as educational venue for records professionals, 195–197. *See also* Education of records professionals
Library of Congress, 133, 134, 139–140, 231 n.143
Life cycle of records concept, 6, 12, 17–18, 32, 109, 117, 119, 197, 220
Lifton, Robert Jay, 167
Lincoln Legal Papers, 139
Lindbergh, Charles, 139
Linguists, 200, 201
Literary manuscripts, 140
Los Angeles, 132
Lowenthal, David, 116
Lutzker, Michael, 114

McClure, Charles, 113
McCrank, Lawrence, 196, 197
McGovern, George, 135
McKemmish, Sue, 34–35
Maclean, Ian, 197
Macro-appraisal, 27, 102, 103, 118, 120. *See also* Appraisal of records
Madison, James, 50
Maier, N.R.F., 113
Maine, 139
Malamud, Bernard, 163
Malcolm, Janet, 134, 142
Malcolm X, 136
Mann, Charles C., 157
Maps, 114

Marchand, Roland, 12
Marsh, George, 60
Marshall, Thurgood, 139–140, 142
Martin Luther King, Jr. Center for Nonviolent Social Change, 140
Massachusetts Institute of Technology, 97
Masson, Jeffrey M., 134
Material culture studies, 115
Matthews, Linda, 211
May, Ernst, 73, 167
Mazzio, Joann, 147
Media coverage of records, 51–53
Medical records, 4, 11, 52, 63, 103, 137, 149, 150, 202, 203
Medieval recordkeeping, 55
Menne-Haritz, Angelika, 3
Metadata, 30, 41 n.111, 49
Metropolitan Museum of Art, 147
Metzenbaum, Howard M., 136
Michelangelo, 147
Michigan, 139
Miksa, Francis, 199
Miller, Page Putnam, 104–105
Minnesota Historical Society, 211–212
Mission, of records professionals, 156
Mississippi State Sovereignty Commission, 166
Mitchell, Greg, 167
Mitchell, William J., 97–98
Mitgang, Herbert, 133
Modern Archives Institute, 210, 211
Moody, Fred, 44, 57
Mormon murders case, 52–53
Moynihan, Daniel Patrick, 73, 170
Muller, S., J. A. Feith, and R. Fruin, 114
Multiculturalism, 217
Murphy, Cullen, 90
Museums, 116, 123 n.51, 143, 147

National Archives of Canada, 64–65
National Association of Government Archives and Records Administrators, 155
National Coordinating Committee for the Promotion of History, 104
National Forum on Archival Continuing Education, 227 n.114. See also Continuing education of records professionals

National Historical Publications and Records Commission, 31, 47, 209, 227 n.114
National Security Act of 1947, 162
National Security Archive, 72, 73
National Security Council, 46, 72, 75, 135
Native Americans, 144
Naval Research Laboratory, 107
Nazi gold, 69–71
Netherlands, 5
Networks, 77–79, 98–99
Neustadt, Richard, 73
New England, 147
New York, 132, 209
New Yorker, 135, 142
New-York Historical Society, 140, 141, 142
New York Public Library, 133, 140
New York Shakespeare Festival, 140
New York State Archives and Records Administration, 49, 51–52
New York Times, 19, 51–52, 132–142, 162
Nichols, George, 61
Nixon, Richard M., 75, 134, 136, 141; administration, 167; tape recordings, 170, 219
Noll, Elizabeth, 147
North, Ollie, 46, 72
Norton, Margaret Cross, 5, 110, 111, 116
Novick, Peter, 116

Oates, Joyce Carol, 163
Objectivity, and appraisal, 115–116. See also Appraisal of records
O'Brien, Conor Cruise, 29
Office equipment, 99
Ohio, 211
Ohio Historical Society, 107
OMB Circular A-130, 153
OMB Watch, 163
Organizational memory, 16, 18, 25, 32, 34, 54, 64, 78, 103, 119, 132, 149, 192
O'Toole, James, 192, 196

Pacey, Arnold, 68
Paisley, William, 206

Paleontology, 115
Palin, Michael, 134
Paper: and corporate records, 97, 98, 99–
    100, 137; and preservation, 92
Paperwork Reduction Act of 1980, 153
Papp, Joseph, 140
Peale, Norman Vincent, 138
Pelikan, Jaroslav, 215
Penn, Ira, 119
Personal papers and archives, 22–31, 32,
    149–151
Peterson, Trudy, 136
Philadelphia Electronic Records Project,
    49
Philippines, 137
Phillips, Faye, 115
Photographic records, 11, 64, 158, 202
Pictographic systems, 201
Pierce, Sydney, 200
Piermont Morgan Library, 133
Pikhoya, Rudolf, 137
Planning, for archives, 115
Plymouth, Massachusetts, 148
Poindexter, John, 46, 72, 136
Poland, 137
Policy and records, 34, 49, 55, 56, 57, 77–
    79, 93, 94, 95, 98, 102, 111, 112, 113,
    114, 120
Political correctness, 217
Porter, Cole, 139
Position descriptions, 203–207
Posner, Ernst, 194, 197
Postal system, 161
Practicum, 199
Pratt, Allan, 110, 206
Preservation, 91–96, 123 n.51, 140, 155,
    168, 194, 210, 218
Presidential libraries, 141
Presidential Records Act of 1974, 5
Privacy, 51, 55, 79, 101, 156–171, 219
PROFS case, 5, 46, 51, 105–106, 134.
    See also Iran-Contra affair
Provensen, Alice and Martin, 144
Prudential Insurance Company, 14
Prussia, 5
Public history and historians, 11–12, 14
Public memory scholarship, 70–71

Public programs and records administra-
    tion, 132, 143, 155–156, 215
Punch cards, 63, 98

Queensland, Australia, 70
Quipu, 145

Raab, Charles D., 165
Rapport, Leonard, 118
Raymond, Andrew, 196
Rayward, Boyd, 26
Reagan, Ronald–George Bush administra-
    tion, 70, 135
Reappraisal, 115, 118. See also Appraisal
    of records
Records, and their importance, 43–47, 50–
    51, 53–56, 131, 151–152
Records, definitions, 1–35, 36 nn.10, 18,
    45–46, 54, 55, 92–93, 220. See also
    Accountability; Evidence; Functional
    requirements for recordkeeping
Records as artifacts, 26, 45–46, 56
Records continuum, 28, 109, 119, 197
Records' life cycle. See Life cycle of re-
    cords concept
Records management: origins, 5, 6; text-
    books, 88–89
Records managers, and archivists, 16–19,
    21, 87–91, 197, 220
Records policy, 169
Records professionals' image, 19, 132–
    149
Records retrieval, 99–100
Records structure, content, and context,
    26
Records' values, 11–12, 13, 14, 15, 17–
    18, 104–105, 119–120. See also Ad-
    ministrative value and records; Ap-
    praisal of records
Records' warrant, 16–17, 26, 31–34, 44,
    48, 50, 103, 112, 119–120, 164, 170
Reference, 219. See also Access
Reformatting, 91, 94–95
Rehnquist, William, 139
Reliability of records, 48–49
Religious Archives Technical Assistance
    Project, 209
Replevin, 158, 183 n.178

Research about records, 215
Rheingold, Howard, 50
Rhode Island, 163
Richardson, Margaret Milner, 71
Richey, Charles R., 135
Rippey, Robert, 208
Risk management, 54–55, 94
Roberts, David, 27
Romano, Carlin, 132
Roots, 165
Rosenberg, Duska, 63
Russia, 137, 138
Rybczynski, Witold, 21–22

Safdie, Elias, 65, 66
Salinger, J. D., 154, 163
Sampling, of records, 115
Samuels, Helen, 114
Sanders, Barry, 149, 159
Sanders, Robert, 21, 87–88
Saul, John Ralston, 159
Savannah, Georgia, 213
Scheduling records, 7, 21, 87–120
Schellenberg, T. R., 5, 24, 30, 35, 108,
    111, 114, 196–197
Schiller, Herbert, 69
Schlereth, Thomas, 111, 116
Schudson, Michael, 141
Schultz, George, 134
Schuurman, Egbert, 60
Schwartz, Joan, 64
Scientific American, 54
Scrapbooks, 158
Second World War, 53, 107, 136, 137,
    164
Secrecy, 73–77, 135–136, 136–137, 139,
    161–163, 168
Security, 153, 154
Sharman, Bob, 143
Shera, Jesse, 206
Shore, John, 56
"Shreddergate," 70
Sigal, Leon V., 141
Skupsky, David, 16
Smith, Anthony, 77
Smith, George David, 15
Smith, H. Jeff, 101
Smith, Janna Malamud, 163, 164

Smith, Vernon, 62
Smith, Wilfred, 152, 194
Smithsonian Institution, 53, 146
Slouka, Mark, 56
Social history, 117
Social science data archives, 32
Social Security cards, 150
Society of American Archivists, 61–62,
    64, 69, 79, 118, 132, 152, 156–157,
    161, 162, 190, 193, 194, 203, 205,
    210, 212, 213, 215, 227 n.115
Sociologists, 200, 202
Soviet Union, 137, 138, 139
Southern, Edwin, 3
Stalin, Josef, 137
Standards and recordkeeping, 33, 48, 60,
    93, 95, 219
Stanford University, 134
"Star-Spangled Banner," 146
Stasi records, 166
State Department, 134
State government archives and records
    management, 49, 51–52, 204, 222 n.31
Steadman, Laurence E., 15
Stephens, David, 106
Stielow, Fred, 193–194
Stoll, Clifford, 65
Sumeria, 159–160
Supreme Court, 139
Sweeney, Shelley, 191
Switzerland, 69–71, 120
Symbolic value of records, 23, 26, 29, 34

Tagg, John, 202
Tallus, 145
Taylor, Hugh, 111, 195
Tax Analysts, 71
Tax records, 137
Technological determinism, 69
Telephone, 161
Telex, 202
Tenner, Edward, 62
Texaco, 13–14, 19
Theoharis, Althan, 170
Theory and practice, 23, 33, 36 n.8, 67,
    108–109, 124 n.62, 125 n.65, 129
    n.130, 192–193, 195, 205–206
Thinking in Time, 73

Thoreau, Henry, 138
Tobacco litigation case, 52, 70, 120
"Total archives," 24
Turkle, Sherry, 77
Typewriters, 99

United Nations, 135, 202
United States Advisory Council on the
    National Information Infrastructure,
    101
United States Holocaust Museum, 137
United States National Archives, 5, 23,
    70, 71, 72, 74, 75, 76, 77, 104, 105,
    106, 107, 121 n.18, 134, 135, 136,
    137, 141, 143, 145, 146, 154, 171, 211
University of British Columbia School of
    Library, Archival, and Information
    Studies, 48, 49, 190, 191, 223 n.34
University of Maryland, 190
University of Michigan School of Infor-
    mation, 48, 190
University of Pittsburgh School of Infor-
    mation Sciences, 31, 48, 49, 190
University of Texas at Austin, 93
University of Toronto, 190
Upward, Frank, 6
U.S. Census Bureau, 63
U. S. MARC AMC format, 204. See also
    Descriptive standards
U.S. Treasury Department, 72

Values of records, 88–89, 108–109, 113,
    153, 154
Vatican Library, 133
VCR, 161

Vera Cruz, 134
Video membership cards, 150
Vietnam, 137–138, 167
Vineland Map, 144
Voice mail, 13
Von Ranke, Leopold, 116

Waegemann, Peter, 9, 19
Wallace, Mike, 71
Warner, Robert, 190
Warrant for recordkeeping. See Records'
    warrant
Watergate, 165, 167
Watson, Andrew, 197
Weinberger, Caspar, 134
Weisner, Mark, 58
Welch, Edwin, 196
Wells Fargo and Company, 153
Western New York, 118
White House, 46, 52, 72, 137
White House E-Mail, 72–73
Wilford, John Noble, 133
Wilson, Don, 51, 135
Winner, Langdon, 47
Wired, 99
Wolfman, Ira, 146
World War II. *See* Second World War
World Wide Web. *See* Internet and re-
    cords
Wright, Robin, 43–44
Writing, 3

Yates, JoAnn, 112, 114

Zelikow, Philip D., 167
Zuboff, Soshana, 77

About the Author

RICHARD J. COX is Professor at the University of Pittsburgh's School of Information Sciences. He is the author of *Closing an Era: Historical Perspectives on Modern Archives and Records Management* (Greenwood Press, 2000).